The Formation of the Nazi Constituency 1919–1933

Edited by
THOMAS CHILDERS

BARNES & NOBLE BOOKS
Totowa, New Jersey

© 1986 Thomas Childers
First published in the USA 1986 by
Barnes & Noble Books
81 Adams Drive
Totowa, New Jersey, 07512
Printed in Great Britain

Library of Congress Cataloging-in-Publication Data

The Formation of the Nazi constituency, 1919-1933.

   1. Germany — Politics and government — 1918-1933.
2. Nationalsozialistische Deutsche Arbeiter-Partei —
History. 3. Nationalsozialistische Deutsche Arbeiter-
Partei — Party work. I. Childers, Thomas, 1946-
DD256.5.F67 1987   943.085   86-22217
ISBN 0-389-20680-6

CONTENTS

CONTRIBUTORS

Richard Bessel is Lecturer in History at the Open University and the author of *Political Violence and the Rise of Nazism*. At present he is completing a work on German demobilisation at the end of the First World War.

Jane Caplan is Assistant Professor of History at Bryn Mawr College. She has written numerous articles and reviews on modern German history and is preparing a study of the civil service in Nazi Germany.

Thomas Childers is Professor of History at the University of Pennsylvania and the author of *The Nazi Voter*. He is currently at work on a history of Nazi propaganda before 1933.

Jürgen W. Falter is Professor of History at the Freie Universität in West Berlin. He is the author of works on political sociology and electoral behaviour and is at present director of a major research project on National Socialist voting in Germany and Austria.

Michael H. Kater is Professor of History at York University in Canada. He has written extensively on Weimar and Nazi Germany. His most recent book is *The Nazi Party*, and he is currently working on a study of the medical profession under National Socialism.

Rudy Koshar is Associate Professor of History at the University of Southern California and the author of many essays and reviews in the field of modern German history. His most recent book is *Social Life, Local Politics, and Nazism* (1986).

Detlef Mühlberger teaches history at Oxford Polytechnic and is the author of a dissertation on National Socialism in Westphalia as well as articles on the social composition of the pre-1933 NSDAP.

Michaela W. Richter is Assistant Professor of Political Science at the University of Pennsylvania. At present she is completing an analysis of the relationship between European protest movements and political parties in both contemporary and historical contexts.

Zdenek Zofka is an historian based in Munich. He was a participant in the important 'Bayern in der NS Zeit' project, and is the author of *Die Ausbreitung des Nationalsozialismus auf dem Lande*.

ABBREVIATIONS

Parties and Organisations

DDP/DSP	Deutsche Demokratische Partei/Deutsche Staatspartei
DNVP	Deutschnationale Volkspartei
DVP	Deutsche Volkspartei
KPD	Kommunistische Partei Deutschlands
NSÄB	Nationalsozialistisher Ärtzebund
NSDAP	Nationalsozialistische Deutsche Arbeiterpartei
NSDStB	Nationalsozialistischer Deutscher Studentenbund
RL	Reichsleitung (der NSDAP)
RPL	Reichspropaganda Leitung (der NSDAP)
SPD	Sozialdemokratische Partei Deutschlands
VB	Völkischer Block
Z	Zentrum

Publications

DHS	Deutsche Hochschulstatistik
DSt	Deutsche Studentenschaft
HJLG	Hessisches Jahrbuch für Landesgeschichte
HLZ	Hessische Landeszeitung
HMB/Mfr.	Halbmonatsberichte/Mittelfranken
HMB/Ofr.	Halbmonatsberichte/Oberfranken
HT	Hessisches Tageblatt
HV	Hessische Volkswacht
NSBZ	Nationalsozialistische Beamtenzeitung
OZ	Oberhessische Zeitung
SJDS	Statistisches Jahrbuch deutscher Städte
StDr	Statistik des Deutschen Reichs
SVB	Schwäbisches Volksblatt
VB	Völkischer Beobachter

Archives

AUWAR	Archiv der Universität Würzburg. Archiv der ehemaligen Reichsstudentenführung und des NSDStB
BA	Bundesarchiv (Koblenz)
BDC	Berlin Documents Center
BHSA	Bayerisches Hauptstaatsarchiv (Munich)
GSAMA	Geheimes Staatsarchiv München
GStA	Geheimes Staatsarchiv Preussischer Kulturbesitz (Dahlem)
HA	NSDAP Hauptarchiv (Microfilm)
HHSAW	Hessisches Hauptstaatsarchiv Wiesbaden
HSAM	Hessisches Staatsarchiv Marburg
MINN	Akten des Staatsministerium des Innern
NSAH	Niedersächsiches Staatsarchiv Hanover
SAG	Staatliches Archivlager Göttingen
StAD	Staatsarchiv Detmold
StAM	Staatsarchiv Münster
UK	York University Archives

1 INTRODUCTION

Thomas Childers

On 31 July 1932 almost 14 million Germans went to the polls to cast ballots for Adolf Hitler's National Socialist German Workers' Party (NSDAP). With 37 per cent of the vote, the Nazis had succeeded in mobilising the largest electoral constituency in German history. It was a remarkable political achievement. Only four years before, in the spring of 1928, the National Socialists had failed to draw even 3 per cent of the vote, and the party seemed destined to languish in obscurity on the lunatic fringes of German politics. Thus, as the NSDAP's dramatic ascent gathered momentum, a number of inter-related sociopolitical questions were posed with increasing urgency. Who were these millions of supporters who flocked to the party between 1928 and 1932, and how had the Nazis mobilised them? How was National Socialist propaganda, the scope and sophistication of which impressed virtually all observers, formulated, organised and conducted? What was the relationship between the party's propaganda strategy and immediate economic developments, social structures and political traditions? These are questions that contemporary commentators raised repeatedly in the last traumatic years of the Weimar Republic, as the Nazis marched relentlessly from one electoral triumph to another, and historians, sociologists, political scientists and psychologists have been grappling with them ever since.[1]

It is to this set of important issues that the essays assembled in this volume are addressed. Each of these essays is new, written specifically for this collection, and each is substantive in nature, presenting the results of original archival research or statistical analysis. They do not represent a 'new school' of thought on these issues, but they do reflect a number of important new assumptions concerning the political sociology of National Socialism derived from recent works on the NSDAP and its following. Although differing in methodology and theoretical orientation, these works are in basic agreement that the social foundations of Nazi success before 1933 were far broader and more diverse than the traditional literature

1

assumed, extending far beyond the party's lower-middle-class base to encompass elements of both the affluent and educated upper bourgeoisie and the blue-collar working class. By 1932 the NSDAP had mobilised an extraordinarily heterogeneous social coalition, becoming a remarkably successful catch-all party of protest. Yet that coalition was extremely volatile, and support for the NSDAP varied in both depth and duration from group to group and from period to period. Motivational impulses behind party membership or electoral support for the NSDAP were, therefore, far more varied and the interaction between Nazi propaganda and social structures more complex than traditionally believed.

The essays that follow reflect that heightened sense of complexity. The research of the past decade or so has made it increasingly inadequate to describe National Socialism merely as a 'revolt of the lower middle class'[2] or explain Nazi successes after 1928 simply as a reflection of the genius and tenacity of the Nazi propaganda apparatus.[3] Thus the essays presented here are sharply focused on different aspects of Nazi mobilisation in the Weimar era, examining, among other things, the social language of political recruitment, the informal channels of political communication in rural communities and small towns where the Nazis were so successful, the political traditions of ostensibly 'apolitical' bourgeois associational life, the role of violence in National Socialist appeal, and the relationship of local Nazi agitational activities to the NSDAP's national propaganda strategies. With their different methodological approaches and thematic concerns, these essays provide a representative cross-section of the new research on the formation of the National Socialist constituency, offering a useful guide to the methodological innovations of the past decade and presenting important findings of the most recent scholarship on the social bases of Nazism during its rise to power.

Within the volume, the essays fall into three distinct but overlapping groups that reflect the basic analytic approaches adopted in the vast historical scholarship devoted to National Socialist propaganda and mobilisation. Among them, the regional or local study has been by far the most prevalent, and that pre-eminent position is clearly reflected in this collection. Although Rudolf Heberle's classic case study of Schleswig-Holstein appeared in 1945, it was the publication of William S. Allen's pathbreaking analysis of Northeim 20 years later that inspired the massive wave of case study literature that has been rising ever since. These valuable

studies have focused on the rise of the NSDAP in specific locales —
either in small towns, cities, rural counties, or entire regions — and
possess the great virtue of being able to examine at close range the
interactions between Nazi propaganda operations and social groups
in a tangible context of local personalities, institutions and traditions. Indeed, it is from this considerable corpus of case study literature that most of our knowledge of Nazi propaganda tactics and
public responses to them has been drawn.[4]

Five of the following nine chapters are firmly grounded in this
case study tradition, and each in its own way reflects the central
thematic concerns and analytic departures of the past decade. Rudy
Koshar's investigation of *Vereineswesen* in the university town of
Marburg suggests that middle-class attitudes and traditions, deeply
entrenched in local politics and organisations, were as critical for
the success of National Socialist mobilisation as the techniques and
strategies of Nazi propaganda. In a remarkable dissection of
middle-class organisational life, Koshar outlines the development
of a tradition of what he calls bourgeois 'apoliticism' that dominated
local politics and social life from the Empire into the National
Socialist period. That tradition, as he demonstrates, was anything
but apolitical, possessing instead an implicit ideological content that
ultimately facilitated the acceptance and growth of National
Socialism. Thus Koshar stresses the need for closer examination of
Nazism's 'prehistory', especially a growing 'bourgeois asymmetry
between social life and [political] power' that developed during the
imperial period, was aggravated by World War I, and reached crisis
proportions in the last turbulent years of the Weimar Republic.
Finally, by examining patterns of local political and social affiliation, as well as the NSDAP's informal methods of disseminating its
message, Koshar is able to chart the actual spread of National
Socialist sympathies throughout the middle-class population.

Zdenek Zofka's discussion of the Nazi movement in the heavily
Catholic district of Günzburg in Bavaria also emphasises the importance of local political developments and traditions in explaining the
appeal of the NSDAP. In his examination of the spread of National
Socialism among the rural population, Zofka stresses the critical
role of informal channels of political communication, local social
organisations, and the role of local opinion leaders. He argues
persuasively that the NSDAP's ability to attract respected local
notables was a crucial factor in the party's mobilisation of support in
the rural electorate. Indeed, Zofka contends that it was not simply

what the Nazis said but *who* said it that is of critical importance in explaining Nazi success in rural communities and small towns.

While the contributions of Koshar and Zofka approach Nazi mobilisation by focusing on local social structure, political traditions and personalities, the essays of Detlaf Mühlberger, Michaela Richter and Richard Bessel are more immediately concerned with National Socialist strategy and tactics. Mühlberger's essay addresses itself to a key issue in the analysis of Nazi mobilisation — the question of central versus local control over National Socialist propaganda. Since the great majority of studies that deal with Nazi propaganda focus on grassroots operations, they tend to conclude that the party's propaganda was largely the product of local initiative and design. Yet little research has actually been undertaken to determine the extent to which Goebbels and his staff in the Reich Propaganda Leadership (RPL) were able to determine the content and conduct of Nazi propaganda. Mühlberger approaches this critical issue by following the campaign directives of the RPL for the presidential elections of 1932 through the *Gau* to the grassroots level in Westphalia. Although it would certainly be an error, he concludes, to view Nazi propaganda as a centrally controlled monolith, he discovers that in Westphalia, *Gau* and local Nazi propaganda operatives did follow the guidelines and directives dispatched by the RPL. Local variations were allowed, even encouraged, by the RPL, but Mühlberger's findings suggest that the degree of centralised direction over Nazi propaganda may have been greater than often assumed in much of the case study literature.

In her analysis of National Socialist propaganda tactics in Franconia, Michaela Richter employs 'resource mobilisation theory' developed by social scientists in recent studies of collective violence and current forms of mass protest. She examines Nazi electoral strategy from 1924 to 1932 within the framework of the structural opportunities and constraints presented by the Weimar party system and more broadly by German political culture. Using Franconia as the geographic basis for her analysis, she demonstrates how the NSDAP was able to convince middle-class Protestant voters that it alone protected them from the dangers of socialism, that it alone represented their specific economic and social interests, and at the same time that it alone could transcend the traditional narrowness of German *Interessenpolitik* to stand for the common good. At the same time, she emphasises the importance of the NSDAP's ability to mobilise its own internal resources for propaganda operations, effectively deploying the revolutionary SA in the party's electoral campaigns and recruitment offensives.

The role of the SA — and especially SA violence — in Nazi propaganda stands at the centre of Richard Bessel's essay. Drawing on local sources from the eastern provinces of Prussia, Bessel examines the Nazi use of violence to create a powerful image of a dynamic and aggressive party that was 'prepared to take its message on to the streets'. Nazi violence after 1923, however, was not intended to overthrow the Weimar state but was viewed as an important weapon in the party's propaganda arsenal, especially when directed against the Left. The NSDAP, Bessel argues, trod a very fine line between 'roughness and respectability' in cultivating its public image, determined on the one hand to create 'an impression of toughness and manliness' but careful to stop well short of a frontal assault on state power. Although Nazi violence did alienate some voters, especially in late 1932, it remained, Bessel argues, an essential component of Nazi appeal in a male-dominated political culture.

A second major research strategy employed to probe the political sociology of Nazism has been to examine the NSDAP's efforts to mobilise support in a particular social or demographic group. The works of Heinrich August Winkler on artisans and shopkeepers, Jürgen Kocka on white-collar employees, and Hans-Jürgen Puhle on peasants, to name just a few, have analysed not only National Socialist appeals to these important groups but have also sought to evaluate the affinities and responses of these *Berufsgruppen* to National Socialism.[5] For the most part, these studies have concentrated on elements of the German middle class, especially the *Kleinbürgertum*, where support for the NSDAP was particularly well developed. More recently, however, this mode of analysis has been extended to examine other groups — workers, civil servants, professionals[6] and women. Since the Nazi rise to power took place before the advent of survey research, these studies have provided important insights into the social values, political attitudes and economic concerns of major elements of the German population and Nazi efforts to manipulate and mobilise them.

Two of the essays presented here adopt this group-specific approach. Michael Kater, whose seminal quantitative work on the National Socialist membership has made a major contribution to the analysis of the social bases of the NSDAP,[7] turns his attention here to a group that until recently has been largely ignored in the scholarship on Nazism. One of the major organisational devices employed by the NSDAP to recruit support in specific target groups was the establishment of National Socialist auxiliary associations such as the party's lawyers' union or student league. In his contribution, Kater traces the development of one such organisation, the Nazi Physicians League, from its inception in 1929 to the party's assumption of power. He examines economic and career pressures within the medical profession in the late Weimar era and analyses the NSDAP's appeal to physicians, medical students and other health professionals, groups that were hardly undereducated or lower middle class. Indeed, Kater's analysis reveals how such Nazi professional organisations were used by the party to act 'as a catalyst in the ongoing process of social and organisational bonding between the Nazi party and the upper bourgeoisie'. The ability of the NSDAP to cultivate significant support among elements of the established or upper middle class has, in fact, become one of the major themes of new literature on National Socialism.

In her essay Jane Caplan also discusses the efforts of the NSDAP to mobilise support within a segment of German society often treated as an integral component of the traditional elite — the civil service. Caplan has written widely on the *Beamtentum* in the Weimar and National Socialist periods,[8] and here she turns her attention to an important and largely unexplored aspect of German political culture — the social language of politics. Using the texts of Nazi campaign leaflets addressed to civil servants, Caplan analyses the party's appeal to *Beamten*, focusing on the NSDAP's careful policy of 'tightrope walking between the vocabularies of revolution and restoration'. She finds that even when appeals were couched in terms appealing to professional pride and solidarity, terms that might suggest the lingering of a *ständisch* mentality among civil servants, their content was increasingly 'pragmatic and practical', dealing with immediate economic concerns. Caplan's analysis implies that while notions of estate or *Stand* had not disappeared from German political culture, they had certainly been transformed and filled with a new content that revealed a growing awareness of class distinctions and divisions.

Along with case and group-specific studies, a growing number of statistical analyses of both the National Socialist membership and electorate have appeared over the past few years that have identified the social loci of Nazi support with far greater precision than previously possible. Using a variety of advanced statistical techniques and large national samples, these studies have established nationwide patterns or trends in Nazi support, providing an essential national framework for the case study and group-specific analyses described above. Although sometimes differing on specific points of interpretation or methodology, these statistical works are in broad agreement that the NSDAP was able to mobilise support from a significantly wider range of social and demographic groups than previously believed.[9]

In his contribution to this volume, Jürgen W. Falter employs a battery of sophisticated statistical procedures to examine one of the major unresolved issues of the NSDAP's massive surge of electoral support between 1928 and 1933. That surge coincided with a vast increase in voter turnout, and contemporary observers and many subsequent analysts attributed the Nazis' dramatic gains to the party's putative ability to mobilise previous non-voters, especially the young. Using a large national sample and a number of different statistical techniques, Falter tests this hypothesis. He measures the influence of turnout rates, crossovers and, in so far as is possible, newly eligible voters on the Nazi electoral performance, concluding that in the critical campaigns of 1930 and 1932 crossovers from the bourgeois parties played a more important role in the NSDAP's rising political fortunes than new voters. His results do indicate that the party enjoyed considerable support among young voters, but at the same time his computations reinforce recent findings that suggest that the NSDAP was also surprisingly successful in mobilising older voters as well.[10]

The final essay of the collection — my own — does not fit easily into any of the analytic categories defined above. Although many of its broader conclusions on the limits of Nazi mobilisation are based on my previous statistical work, the essay is focused more directly on a top secret internal Nazi assessment of its potentially disastrous electoral 'defeat' in November 1932, when the party lost two million votes and was hurled into the throes of a serious internal crisis. In the aftermath of that election, Goebbels' Reich Propaganda Leadership conducted an extensive post mortem on the campaign, drawing on detailed reports from local and regional party functionaries to evaluate the reasons for the party's failure and to assess its future electoral prospects. That investigation revealed that the NSDAP had reached the limits of its electoral potential, that continuation of its revolutionary catch-all strategy was at best problematic and most ominously for Nazi strategists, that the socially heterogeneous electoral constituency that the NSDAP had mobilised between 1928 and 1932 was suddenly but unmistakably fragmenting. Only a Nazi seizure of power, they believed, could halt the party's slide.

Although many of the essays presented in this collection emphasise long-term developments or structural factors in explaining the NSDAP's remarkable ability to mobilise mass support, none suggests that the triumph of National Socialism was an inevitability, an inescapable product of a tragic German *Sonderweg*. Nor are they content to ascribe the NSDAP's stunning success to the manipulative tactics of the party's admittedly effective propaganda machine. Instead, they shift the focus of our analysis to the complex social mechanisms of political mobilisation, dissecting the multifaceted appeal of National Socialism to its socially diverse constituency in a wide variety of contexts from the grassroots to the national level. In the process, they locate the sources of National Socialist success in the layered interactions between the party's propaganda, in all its profuse forms, and political traditions, social structures and networks of sociopolitical communication in a period of profound economic crisis.

With its limitations of space, this volume cannot hope to provide a comprehensive analysis of this complex set of interactions, but it does, we believe, offer the reader a valuable cross-section of the most recent research on the formation of the Nazi constituency. In so doing, it raises and re-examines from a variety of new perspectives a crucial complex of questions — Who were the millions of Nazi followers? What was the nature of National Socialism's appeal? How did the NSDAP mobilise the masses? They are questions that remain today no less central to the understanding of modern German, indeed, Western history than they did to those who posed them so urgently over 50 years ago.

Notes

1. In spite of the intense interest devoted to Nazi propaganda in general, or to specific aspects of the party's agitational activities in specific locales, no comprehensive analysis of the organisation, strategy or content of National Socialist propaganda in the Weimar period exists. Z.E.B. Zeman's frequently cited *Nazi Propaganda* (Oxford, 1964), and E.K. Bramsted's *Goebbels and National Socialist Propaganda* (Michigan, 1965), deal almost exclusively with the period after 1933. H. Balle's 'Die propagandistische Auseinandersetzung des Nationalsozialismus mit der

Weimarer Republik und ihre Bedeutung für den Aufstieg des Nationalsozialismus',
Ph.D. Dissertation, Erlangen, 1963, is an attempt to provide something of an
overview but suffers from a number of important methodological and substantive
shortcomings. The most useful examination of the Nazi propaganda apparatus and
its activities on a national level is Thomas W. Arafe, Jr., 'The Development and
Character of the Nazi Political Machine, 1928–1930, and the NSDAP Electoral
Breakthrough', Ph.D. Dissertation, Louisiana State University, 1976.

2. The adequacy of the almost exclusive emphasis on the lower middle class in the
traditional analyses of Nazi support has been challenged by a growing number of
studies of both the party's membership and electoral constituency. On the
heterogeneous social composition of the NSDAP membership, see the works of
Michael H. Kater, especially 'Sozialer Wandel in der NSDAP im Zuge der national-
sozialistischen Machtergreifung', in Wolfgang Schieder (ed.), _Faschismus als soziale
Bewegung_ (Hamburg, 1976), pp. 25–67; and _The Nazi Party. A Social Profile of
Members and Leaders, 1919–1945_ (Cambridge, Mass., 1983). See also James P.
Madden, 'The Social Composition of the Nazi Party, 1919–1930', Ph.D. Disserta-
tion, University of Oklahoma, 1976. On the Nazi electoral constituency, see Thomas
Childers, 'The Social Bases of the National Socialist Vote', _Journal of Contemporary
History_, 11, 1976, pp. 17–42; _The Nazi Voter. The Social Foundations of Fascism in
Germany, 1919–1933_ (Chapel Hill and London, 1983); and Richard F. Hamilton,
Who Voted for Hitler? (Princeton, 1982), who argues, rather problematically, that
the lower-middle-class emphasis is not simply inadequate but entirely misplaced. See
also the recent work of Jürgen W. Falter, 'Die Wähler der NSDAP 1928–1933:
Sozialstruktur und parteipolitische Herkunft', in Wolfgang Michalka (ed.), _Die
nationalsozialistische Machtergreifung_ (Paderborn, 1984), pp. 47–59.

3. See the essays of Ian Kershaw, 'Ideology, Propaganda, and the Rise of the Nazi
Party', in Peter D. Stachura (ed.), _The Nazi Machtergreifung_ (London, 1983), pp.
162–81; and Richard Bessel, 'The Rise of the NSDAP and the Myth of Nazi
Propaganda', _Wiener Library Bulletin_, 13, 1980, pp. 20–29.

4. The case study literature on National Socialism before 1933 is truly vast.
Among the most useful in analysing Nazi propaganda and mobilisation are: Rudolf
Heberle, _From Democracy to Nazism_ (Baton Rouge, 1945), expanded as
Landbevölkerung und Nationalsozialismus (Stuttgart, 1962); William S. Allen, _The
Nazi Seizure of Power_ (New York 1965), revised edition 1983; Jeremy Noakes, _The
Nazi Party in Lower Saxony 1921–1933_ (Oxford, 1971); Detlaf Mühlberger, 'The
Rise of National Socialism in Westphalia 1920–1933', Ph.D. Dissertation, University
of London, 1975; Jutta Ciolek-Kumper, _Wahlkampf in Lippe: Die Wahlkampf-
propaganda der NSDAP zur Landtagswahl am 15. Januar 1933_ (Munich, 1977);
Zdenek Zofka, _Die Ausbreitung des Nationalsozialismus auf dem Lande_ (Munich,
1979); Michaela W. Richter, 'The National Socialist Electoral Breakthrough.
Opportunities and Constraints in the Weimar Party System', Ph.D. Dissertation,
City University of New York, 1982; Johnpeter Horst Grill, _The Nazi Movement in
Baden, 1920–1945_ (Chapel Hill, 1983); and Rudy Koshar, _Social Life, Local Politics,
and Nazism: the Bürgertum of Marburg/Lahn, 1880–1935_ (Chapel Hill and London,
1986). Also of great value for this period is Lawrence D. Stokes (ed.), _Kleinstadt und
Nationalsozialismus: Ausgewählte Dokumente zur Geschichte von Eutin 1918–1945_
(Neumunster, 1984).

5. See Heinrich August Winkler, _Mittelstand, Demokratie und National-
sozialismus: Die politische Entwicklung von Handwerk und Kleinhandel in der
Weimarer Republik_ (Cologne, 1972); Jürgen Kocka, _Angestellte zwischen
Faschismus und Demokratie. Zur politischen Sozialgeschichte der Angestellten: USA
1890–1940 im internationalen Vergleich_ (Göttingen, 1977); and Hans-Jürgen Puhle,
_Politische Agrarbewegungen in kapitalistischen Industriegesellschaften: Deutschland,
USA und Frankreich im 20. Jahrhundert (Göttingen, 1975)._

6. See Timothy W. Mason, *Sozialpolitik im Dritten Reich. Arbeiterklasse und Volksgemeinschaft* (Opladen, 1977); Peter D. Stachura, 'The NSDAP and the German Working Class, 1925–1933', in Isidor Walliman and Michael Dobkowski (eds.), *Towards the Holocaust. Fascism and Anti-Semitism in Weimar Germany* (New York, 1982); Hans Mommsen, *Beamtentum im Dritten Reich* (Stuttgart, 1966); Jane Caplan, 'Civil Service Support for National Socialism: An Evaluation', in Gerhard Hirschfeld (ed.), *Der 'Führerstaat': Mythos und Realität* (Stuttgart, 1981); Michael H. Kater, *Studentenschaft und Rechtsradikalismus in Deutschland 1918–1933* (Hamburg, 1975); Michael S. Steinberg, *Sabers and Brownshirts: The German Students' Path to National Socialism, 1918–1935* (Chicago, 1977); Michael H. Kater, 'Professionalization and Socialization of Physicians in Wilhelmine and Weimar Germany', *Journal of Contemporary History*, 20, 1985, and his contribution to this volume; Lawrence D. Stokes, 'Professionals and National Socialism: The Case Histories of a Small-Town Lawyer and Physician, 1918–1945', *German Studies Review*, 8, 1985, pp. 449–80; Claudia Koonz, 'Nazi Women before 1933: Rebels against Emancipation', *Social Science Quarterly*, 1976, pp. 553–63; Richard J. Evans, 'German Women and the Triumph of Hitler', *Journal of Modern History*, xlviii, 1976, demand supplement; and Jill Stephenson, *The Nazi Organization of Women* (London, 1981).

7. See note 2.

8. Caplan, 'Civil Service Support for National Socialism: An Evaluation'; 'The Imaginary Universality of Particular Interests: "The Tradition" of the Civil Service in Germany History', *Social History* 4, 1979, pp. 299–317; and 'The Politics of Administration: The Reich Interior Ministry and the German Civil Service, 1933–1943', *Historical Journal*, 20, 1977, pp. 707–36.

9. These works are cited in note 2.

10. On the role of youth in the rise of the NSDAP see Michael H. Kater, 'Generationskonflikt als Entwicklungsfaktor in der NS-Bewegung vor 1933', *Geschichte und Gesellschaft*, 11, 1985, pp. 217–43. Nazis' efforts to mobilise support among older voters and their apparent success in doing so are examined in Childers, *The Nazi Voter*, pp. 80–87, 159–66, 224–8.

2 CONTENTIOUS CITADEL: BOURGEOIS CRISIS AND NAZISM IN MARBURG/LAHN, 1880–1933

Rudy Koshar

Nowhere is history writing more open to debate than in the study of German politics from 1870 to 1945. Haunted by overpowering moral questions, shaped by competing methodologies and paradigms, the field has entered an axial period that has produced much valuable work but also heated scholarly exchanges, new research problems and a lot of unfinished business.[1] Though debate over continuity between the Imperial period and Weimar has been extremely fruitful, it has so far produced no satisfying empirical and theoretical syntheses of German politics from Bismarck to Hitler.[2] Similarly, historians of Nazism refer to the pre-1914 roots of that movement, but their research continues to focus mainly on World War I and the Weimar Republic.[3] The excellent sociographical research of the last two decades has meanwhile concentrated on the occupational background of NSDAP voters, members and leaders.[4] However, it has given us too little information about the Nazi movement in two other crucial spheres of social interaction, namely the family and organisational life. And finally, there has been too little cross-fertilisation between such endeavours, as scholarship in each area becomes increasingly self-contained due to growing academic specialisation and the proliferation of documentation on twentieth-century German history.

This essay can hardly claim to address each issue. But by discussing the organisational fabric of political conflict in one community from roughly 1880 to the Nazi seizure of power, it can suggest new perspectives for the study of Nazism and the social history of modern German politics.[5] The following embeds the rise of Nazism in a general sociopolitical history of the bourgeoisie (*Bürgertum*) in a single German city from Bismarck to Hitler. The goal is to evoke rather than to discuss fully a mounting political crisis of the bourgeoisie — an inability of bourgeois groups to match their tremendous social power with political unity at the level of the national state — and to view this crisis in relation to the rise of an unprecedentedly popular social movement, that of German

11

fascism. Emphasis will be placed on the role of ostensibly unpolitical social organisations in bourgeois political practice. Moreover, we take particular note of the NSDAP's reliance on many organisational cross-affiliations and word of mouth propaganda, two unmapped dimensions of the rise of National Socialism that deserve as much scholarly attention as Hitler's charisma or formal party agitation.

The location is the Hessian university and service city Marburg an der Lahn, an overwhelmingly Protestant town that showed early and extensive electoral support for National Socialism. It is well known that few cities, save for the Swabian university town Tübingen, matched Marburg's occupational, political and cultural peculiarities.[6] Economically dependent on the university, without substantial large-scale industry, Marburg featured smaller proportions of workers and manufacturers and larger shares of service employees, self-employed artisans and retailers, retirees and students in its population than did cities of comparable size or the nation. In addition, the city was the scene of extraordinarily contentious party political conflict and an unusually rich organisational life. All this made of the city a singular community, characterised by some critics as a conservative 'citadel of reaction', and by others as the Nazified home of a 'fascist university'.[7] Marburg was a citadel — a medieval fortress city that political groups from both right and left tried to storm once the age of popular politics began in the 1880s. But it was not an island. Certain tendencies — especially bourgeois political disunity — were exaggerated in the Hessian town, but Marburgers experienced social and political tensions that affected all Germans. Like a good microscope, Marburg enlarged the texture and detail of a wider political crisis that produced Nazism.

In a valuable critique of key assumptions of modern German historiography, David Blackbourn and Geoff Eley have argued that the German bourgeoisie gained significant economic and social unity in the nineteenth century, but that it was thwarted when it attempted to transfer this unity to the national polity and state.[8] In short, the German bourgeoisie faltered when it tried to constitute itself as a national political class. The reasons were many and complex: rhythm and shape of German capitalism; specific content of the continued power of a landholding elite in the state; structure and ideology of liberal and conservative political parties; tremendous social diversity of the bourgeoisie itself; bourgeois social and economic successes, which often lessened the desirability of and need for political power in the national state; the Bismarckian constitutional system; rapid mobilisation of a socialist working-class movement that rejected bourgeois patronage; and confessional conflicts that hampered the rise of a reformist coalition in Reich politics. The consequences of this shortcoming remained unclear to most contemporaries before World War I. But in the interwar period, when a violent recasting of state authority and the class alliances on which it was based occurred in Germany,[9] the political costs of bourgeois disunity at the national level became obvious. New formulas were needed for integrating popular forces in the state and for reshaping internal power alignments between elite and non-elite classes and strata that made up the German bourgeoisie.

Prior to and during the Weimar Republic, the bourgeoisie relied on grassroots power bases — *Land* and city parliaments, local branches of the liberal and conservative parties, universities and churches, regional chambers of trade and commerce, and local and regional voluntary associations — to counterbalance its national political disunity and 'disengage' itself from rancorous class and party strife in the Reich.[10] Central to this disengagement was a distrust for mass politics. Bourgeois critics viewed the latter as an immoral battle for electoral power in a political marketplace increasingly dominated by organised sectional interests and shaped by large, bureaucratic groups such as the Social Democratic and Catholic parties. Multiform and changeable, this 'apoliticism' was hardly a retreat from thinking about power relationships.[11] Anti-party sentiment was a functional response to a national polity in which bourgeois disunity prevailed. Thus the institutional and organisational fabric of city and region provided refuge or alternatives to national political conflict.

Product of a non-industrial town, the Marburg bourgeoisie (*Bürgertum*) consisted mainly (though not exclusively) of groups that in the nation would be referred to as 'middle strata' or 'lower middle and middle classes'. It was thus a broader grouping than the classic bourgeoisie, the owners of the means of production and their agents. Moreover, living in a community in which more than 80 per cent of the inhabitants were Protestant, the Marburg *Bürgertum* was far more coherent from a confessional standpoint than its counterpart in the Reich. Like the latter, however, the town *Bürgertum* was an ideological notion rather than a socioeconomic category.[12] It comprised groups — city officials, other service employees, small-scale manufacturers, free professionals, university professors, self-employed artisans and retailers, apprentices, retirees, university students, and non-socialist workers — that were tenuously united by an antipathy for the Social Democratic movement. In addition, various Marburg *bürgerlich* groups believed in economic thrift, loyalty to community organisations, a strong family life, and the need for regulation of large-scale industrial capitalism. These were linked with a moralistic distrust of mass politics and opposition to the language of class. Not all bourgeois groups subscribed to these varied ideological elements at all times. And shared values and practices did not result in loyalty to a single political party or movement. Therein originated some of the political tensions of local bourgeois life.

Judging from the importance of the local polity in bourgeois political practice, one should have expected the Marburg *Bürgertum* to have achieved relative political harmony at home in contrast to the cacophony of the national arena. But Marburg was different. The university provided a link between national events and local power conflicts, increasing the critical mass of local people who possessed the time and willingness to be active politically. University professors were especially prominent in Reichstag and Landtag politics. Partly because of the resources contained in the university, partly because of the small size of the town (23,299 in 1925), political candidates came to see Marburg as a manageable laboratory for campaigns that had little chance of success elsewhere. This experimentation increased the unpredictability of political conflict in the Hessian community.

Not socialist challenge, but party fragmentation of the town *Bürgertum* itself proved to be most disruptive in local political life. The Social Democratic Party (Sozialdemokratische Partei Deutschlands, SPD) was established in Marburg in 1869, five years before the founding of a Liberal Association.[13] But lack of large-scale industry narrowed the social field in which the SPD could operate and lessened the perceived urgency for bourgeois unity against the Left locally. In contrast, numerous non-socialist competitors battled for the Marburg Reichstag seat. The opening shot was fired in 1887, when the Marburg librarian and former university student Otto Böckel became the first political anti-Semite and youngest man ever to gain a seat in the national parliament. Böckel's initial success and subsequent conflicts with enemies and allies created tensions not only in the Marburg Reichstag district but in the national anti-Semitic movement as well. Hellmut von Gerlach, erstwhile Stöcker devotee, became the first challenger to unseat Böckel and the only member of Friedrich Naumann's left liberal National Social party to gain a Reichstag seat in 1903. Von Gerlach was followed in 1907 and 1912 by socially conservative anti-Semitic candidates supported by National Liberal and conservative groups, the latter having become mere adjuncts in wider right-wing coalitions. Significantly, at no time after Böckel's victory did a member of the local liberal or conservative parties place a representative in the German Reichstag.[14] Thus, whereas bourgeois political fragmentation nationally could be counterbalanced with coherent regional alternatives, the Marburg *Bürgertum* found itself increasingly divided and uncertain in Reichstag politics.

The structure of the Bismarckian constitutional system, lack of full parliamentary sovereignty in the Second Empire, internal weaknesses of liberal and conservative parties, and bourgeois disengagement from the national party universe, allowed economic pressure groups, nationalist associations and other organisations to gain extraordinary influence in mobilising political opinion and shaping party loyalties. The activities of social organisations, a term I use to refer to all non-party voluntary groups, reflected an asymmetry between bourgeois political parties and their constituencies. Unlike the youth groups or trade unions of Social Democratic and Catholic movements, bourgeois social organisations were never effectively embraced by liberal and conservative parties, never controlled from a political and ideological centre.[15] At the local level, many different organisations gave bourgeois groups an alternative focus for political activity. Including not only economic associations, which often stressed sociability more than agitation, but also social clubs, sports societies and song clubs, these ostensibly unpolitical associations gave Germans an opportunity to talk about politics, to make contacts, and to educate themselves in parliamentary procedure. Depending on local circumstances, grassroots organisational life compensated for bourgeois party disengagement or enlarged already substantial bourgeois power in the electoral sphere.[16]

Not unlike many German municipalities, elite social clubs, influential *Stammtische*, church associations and other groups virtually substituted for political parties in Marburg city politics, where restrictive suffrage arrangements limited popular involvement until the Weimar Republic. In contrast with other cities, however, comparatively greater political conflict in Marburg increased the political role of non-party associations there. Social organisations, many championing their own versions of apoliticism, tried to blunt and muffle the effects of rancorous party politics. To take but one example, Martin Wenck, who had taken over the editorship of the left liberal *Hessische Landeszeitung* in Marburg in 1901, noted the 'class spirit and party narrowness' of the Hessian town's social life. When Wenck applied for membership in the elite social club Museum, dominated by National Liberals and conservatives, he ran into difficulties. In contrast, his counterpart at the conservative *Oberhessische Zeitung* gained immediate entrance to the club. Acceptance came only after Wenck reminded Museum officials of his university education and prior status as a Protestant pastor.[17] The disgruntled Wenck saw only petty political jealousies in this experience. But he failed to realise that education and profession, badges of the educated upper middle classes (*Bildungsbürgertum*), not only allowed entrance into an elite club but overrode party division; in this corner of local public life there existed mechanisms to balance and absorb — however belatedly — political contention.

Social diversity within organisations could have similar ideological effects in the Second Empire. Associations less privileged than the Museum provided a social location in which the local upper middle classes came into contact with the lower middle classes, as occurred in the Marburg Sharpshooting Association, a prominent club with relatively high dues that nevertheless included numerous modest shopkeepers. Voluntary groups such as the large Gymnastics Club 1860 facilitated social interaction between petty bourgeois groups and 'better' workers who rejected the Social Democratic Party. Pointing to their diverse memberships as proof that the *Bürgertum* could overcome class and party divisions, numerous club spokesmen used ritualistic nationalism to champion a notionally higher interest that was morally superior to the sectional conflicts of party politics. They argued that party loyalties found little sympathy in the ranks of local *Vereine*. Even Marburg student duelling fraternities and alumni associations, self-contained entities increasingly isolated from other students or alumni and from the town population, emphasise the muffling function of non-party groups.[18] These traditions and practices decreased the authority of parliamentary life, lessened the ability of liberal and conservative parties to gain full dominance over their constituencies, and made of the local *Verein* a supposed counterbalance to the perceived immorality of fractious party politics in town, region and nation. All this strengthened the moral authority and power of local bourgeois elites, who enjoyed continued social hegemony in an age of heightened political dissension.

Whereas local social organisations argued convincingly that they repressed party divisions in the town bourgeoisie in the Imperial period, they faced a more troubled political sphere in World War I and the Republic. This was an era of unprecedented conflict shaped locally by: dissatisfaction with city economic policy in the war; the decision of the socially conservative anti-Semitic district Reichstag representative to support a Deutsche Fraktion vote for the peace resolution in 1917; the founding of the Fatherland Party, the 'party of those without parties' and champion of national goals supposedly unsullied by partisanship and material interest; the organisation of a People's League for Freedom and Fatherland, which mobilised liberal elites locally against the much larger Fatherland Party; the virtual dissolution of liberal and conservative parties, whose constituencies were now more disengaged than ever before from the Reich party system.[19]

In the Republic, bourgeois groups witnessed the evolution of a qualitatively new polity marred by unprecedented violence and inscribed by a popular politics that had originated in the Second Empire. At first the town bourgeoisie successfully limited the influence of the new politics, continuing to use social organisations in muffling party strife. When the Workers' and Soldiers' Council was established in the Hessian town, for instance, its work as 'controlling instance of the Revolution' was made superfluous by the actions of city government, the university, economic associations, civic groups and student fraternities, which took command of virtually all public functions save for those that the Council undertook to ease demobilisation.[20] But these successes were short-lived. Paralysed by its own power limitations, the new German state relied on a growing tangle of temporary volunteer military formations, civil guards and *Freikorps* units to establish the social conditions of parliamentarism.[21] In Marburg, this effort brought local fraternity students into the political fray. Members of local fraternities were mobilised for temporary military action after the abortive Kapp Putsch of March 1920, sent off to Thuringia to calm fighting that broke out after the *coup* attempt, and charged with the responsibility of transporting suspected agitators from the village of

Thal. They killed 15 prisoners near Mechterstädt. Evidence suggested an execution, but civil and military courts exonerated 14 fraternity students who had been brought to trial. Supported by many local university professors who wanted to maintain local power arrangements and shield the university from political strife, the fraternity students' actions poisoned class relations in both the Hessian town and the nation.[22]

Matters worsened for the town bourgeoisie thereafter. So often dominating scholarship of the interwar period, economic crisis was only part of the problem. This requires some explanation. Because of the bitter hardships they caused, the hyperinflation of 1922–3 and the Depression of 1929 appear at first glance to have been virtually inexplicable events, like twin outbreaks of Camus' plague in an unsuspecting population. Dramatic though these developments were, they took place in the context of a larger universe of tensions — growing political conflict in the last decade before World War I, the tragic losses of the pointless global conflagration, the violence and instability of the first years of the Republic. The inflation and Depression worsened certain longstanding economic problems locally, but they did not devastate or uniformly make 'previously comfortable people into beggars', as one town historian insisted.[23] Indeed, as that same historian admitted in the early 1930s, 'things were more bearable in Marburg than in pure industrial communities' because 'the relative lack of industry . . . hindered a deeper decline'.[24]

The political economy of the Hessian town determined how economic crisis affected the local population. Saddled with geographical limits on industry and city officials' project to keep the community free of the social ills of heavy manufacturing, Marburg possessed an inadequate tax base, a chronically unemployed and underemployed working class and artisanry, an inordinate number of retirees dependent on fixed incomes, and a business community that rose and fell with university enrolments and service employment. World War I increased Marburg's problems, as the national state's demands forced the municipal government to create jobs, print money, mobilise the population for the military effort, and regulate an industry-poor economy that gained little advantage from national policies for manufacturing the weapons of war.[25] Marburg was thus vulnerable to economic crisis, but the effects of the hyperinflation were notoriously uneven, and townspeople were affected so variously that no single characterisation suffices to describe who lost and who gained. Subsequently, in the early 1930s, townsfolk possessed a built-in resilience to sweeping economic crisis, because the lack of big industry kept unemployment in check. And university enrolments increased until 1932, keeping up a modest stream of students into local shops, theatres and bars.[26] 'The great mass of civil servants, officials' widows, and pensioners were no doubt weakened by emergency decrees and cuts in income', Walther Kürschner said of Marburgers in the Depression, 'but they nevertheless always helped to keep up the buying power of townspeople.'[27]

Winners could think of themselves as losers,[28] certainly, but it is important to emphasise that even losers needed organisational resources to voice their grievances. In Marburg, the hyperinflation and Depression made people angry and bitter, but they hardly devastated the town or reduced the long-term capacity of the population to act politically. Not economic panic, but the continued social resilience of a large part of the town *Bürgertum* was the most noteworthy aspect of bourgeois daily life in the Republic. This was of tremendous political importance, because the *Bürgertum*'s resilience would leave it disgruntled but organised, bitter but capable of mounting effective political action against the local working class, city government and the state. The economic difficulties of Weimar were so harsh that they hindered the building of bourgeois loyalty to the new state, but they were not serious enough to undercut anti-system opposition.

Having survived the political violence and economic hardships of 1918–23, local *bürgerlich* groups experienced mounting political fragmentation in the notionally calm middle years of the Republic from 1924 to September 1930. As Thomas Childers has convincingly argued, political and economic stabilisation was as damaging to liberal and conservative parties nationally as the hyperinflation itself.[29] In Marburg, decades of bourgeois party fragmentation now culminated in the uneven but unmistakable splintering of the polity.

In Reichstag politics, the DDP (Deutsche Demokratische Partei) was the strongest local party in 1919, having gained 31.2 per cent of the vote in the city. But its electoral influence quickly fell, and by 1928 only 8.7 per cent of city voters supported the Democratic Party. The fortunes of the right-wing liberal German People's Party (DVP, or Deutsche Volkspartei) and conservative German National People's Party (DNVP, or Deutschnationale Volkspartei) fluctuated in the middle Republic and plummeted in the fateful 1930

Reichstag elections. More revealingly, splinter groups such as the Economic Party (Wirtschaftspartei), which garnered more than 7 per cent of the vote in 1928, gained increasing support from local voters. In municipal politics, self-proclaimed unpolitical electoral alliances gained more than one-half of all eligible votes in 1924 city elections. This was an unprecedented showing that was sustained in 1929 elections, when more than four of every ten voters for municipal parliament seats cast ballots for non-party alliances including representatives from business, civil service, renters' and retirees' associations. Considering the volatility of the local party scene and the disengagement of Marburg voters from bourgeois parties in both Reich and locale, the intrusion in local Reichstag politics of the Nazi-conservative coalition Völkisch-Soziale Block (VSB), which gained more than 17 per cent of the city vote in May 1924, and of the NSDAP in September 1930 and July 1932, when the party received 28.8 and 53.3 per cent, was less than surprising.[30] Local electoral patterns indicated that before the onset of the worst part of the Depression, the town bourgeoisie was politically more homeless than ever before and willing to support challengers to the liberal and conservative parties.

Local bourgeois groups said they had found a refuge from fractious Reich politics in the supposedly unpolitical and patriotic realm of organised social activity, which continued in the Weimar era despite the after-effects of war, revolution and hyperinflation. But Weimar was not the *Kaiserreich*. Bourgeois social organisations had co-operated to calm local politics in the early revolution; student fraternities had killed workers in Thuringia; political divisiveness disrupted the internal life of many clubs and associations that previously appeared immune to party rancour;[31] and special-interest organisations rather than formal political parties had mobilised more than one-half of all voters in 1924 municipal elections. Political activity by ostensibly unpolitical associations tested the capacity of organisational life to 'absorb' contentiousness.

One response was a more intense championing of organised social activity as such, an attempt to cushion political debate in the routine of *Verein* and *Stammtisch*. A large and unusually organised *Stammtisch*, the prestigious Käsebrod, announced in 1927 that, in contrast to the prewar period, 'political gossip' was displaced by a 'relaxed social tone' among the club's more than one hundred members.[32] More wish than reality, this statement reflected bourgeois elites' desire to immunise social organisations from political conflict. Many other club spokesmen had similar aims, demanding inattention to party loyalties during *Verein* activities. This was an understandable tack for social clubs with members who belonged to competing parties. In the respected Sharpshooting Association, for instance, 28 members had 39 party affiliations between 1918 and 1933, including 15 to various special-interest coalitions, 14 to the NSDAP, 3 apiece to the DNVP and DVP, 2 to the DDP, and 1 to the Economic Party.[33] These *Vereine* were not burying their political heads in the social sand, but continuing prewar practices of using apoliticism — manifested here in attempts to muffle debate over party loyalties — as a functional solution to political divisiveness.

But intensification of traditional responses to party politics led to a novel heightening of apoliticism. Rejecting parties as vehicles of an immoral interest group politics, some spokesmen of local clubs claimed that non-party associations did more than absorb conflict. Social clubs would provide an alternative to power struggles, thereby overcoming 'party political viewpoints', and achieving the 'victory of morality over the crass materialism of the present', as the chair of the County Veterans' Association said in 1928.[34] It was hardly coincidental that this sentiment was voiced at the founding celebration of the second Reich, held annually in January and organised in separate university and town festivals, the latter led by local veterans' clubs in co-operation with song clubs, gymnastics societies and youth groups.[35] Patriotic festivals assumed a new significance for leaders who wanted visible forums for demonstrating the notionally classless harmony of the town *Bürgertum*. But it was not only social clubs that filled the local polity with unprecedentedly strong moralistic condemnations of Weimar politics. Supposedly narrow special-interest groups such as the Landlords' Association, a mouthpiece of *petit bourgeois* property owners in Marburg, also made use of such propaganda, stressing that in contrast to most Weimar social groups 'the *Mittelstand* doesn't fight for reasons of naked egoism, but rather for culture and morality'.[36] Threatened by a system that seemed to reduce all political questions to interest-group bargaining, disdainful of liberal and conservative parties unable to harness popular energies, and distrustful of a state that seemed weak and directionless, the town bourgeoisie endorsed moralistic apoliticism more passionately than ever before.

The town *Bürgertum* faced two sets of limits in this mobilisation against the German state. First, though the Social Democratic Party had been pushed to the margins of the local public sphere, it could make a show of support for the Republic when it gained help from powerful groups outside the Hessian city. Local workers had gained such support in March 1920 when they protested the actions of local duelling fraternities during the Kapp Putsch and Thuringian killings. In September 1929, Hessian locals of the district Reichsbanner demonstrated in Marburg against the anti-Young Plan referendum drive. Hardly a strong challenge to the dominance of bourgeois groups, such actions nevertheless had the effect of making 'one finally admit [that] . . . Marburgers also live in a Republic', in the words of the left liberal daily, the *Hessisches Tageblatt*.[37]

More serious, however, was a limit imposed by apoliticism itself. Disengagement from the party system and distrust of mass politics could be effective only when they presented a real alternative to the Weimar polity. Traditional methods of burying party conflict in *Verein* custom or emotional condemnations of interest politics were not enough if a notionally superior moral politics was to displace the Weimar state. In short, apoliticism could be successful only when it was organised politically, only when it generated a party. It did not suffice to lead a referendum against the Young Plan, a project that gained support in Marburg from the DNVP, a number of artisans' associations, fraternity-dominated student government and other organisations.[38] Important as substructures of political mobilisation, social organisations could not provide the political direction offered by a central party apparatus. And the liberal and conservative parties were too weak, too unwilling to go beyond limited reforms they had undertaken since the Second Empire, and too fearful of the consequences of leading a truly popular revolt against the hated Weimar Republic. Only a disciplined political movement could transform the moral power of apoliticism into real material strength. What organisation would provide this political anchor?

The NSDAP faced seemingly few obstacles in its attempts to exploit *bürgerlich* political conflicts in Marburg. The city had been a haven of political experimentation since the Second Empire, and Marburg had acquired a reputation as a citadel of anti-Republic activity soon after Weimar's inception. But the local Nazi party was unable to make use of these advantages in the early Republic. Formed in spring 1923, the Marburg NSDAP first drew on members of the city's Young German Order, temporary volunteer military units, the anti-Semitic Deutschvölkischer Schutz- und Trutzbund, and other organisations. Its members embraced the symbolism of postwar military activity, and built strong interpersonal ties through a variety of social activities. But the group was a militarised social club rather than a political party, a racist *Stammtisch* rather than an electoral machine. Its adherence spent more time in marching than in thinking about politics or organising electoral campaigns.[39] Though claiming to represent the new Germany, the NSDAP reinforced its members' stated antipathies to party politics, bureaucratic organisation and interest-group negotiation. In short, by rejecting the political marketplace of the Republic, the NSDAP relegated itself to the margins of the Weimar polity.

This apoliticism was never completely eradicated from Nazi ideology but would be transformed and adapted to the require-ments of political action in postwar Germany. A first sign of this was the Nazi-conservative coalition in spring 1924, the VSB. The VSB introduced the swastika to townspeople by running flashy campaign advertisements in the *Oberhessische Zeitung*, the city's most widely circulated daily newspaper. Appealing to sympathisers of both Hitler and Ludendorff, the VSB made a surprisingly good electoral showing in May 1924, when it gained 17.7 per cent of the local vote, well above the coalition's national or Bavarian average.[40] A beneficiary of protest voting against harsh stabilisation of German economic life after 1923, the VSB also exploited Hessian anti-Semitism, anti-party sentiment and other prewar traditions of the regional political culture. The VSB gained support ultimately because it represented an important ideological bridge in local politics, one that uneasily spanned a gap between the *völkisch* elitism of Ludendorff and the plebeian racism of Hitler. But the bridge would soon fall; many local coalition members were distrustful of one another, wary of party discipline, and convinced that 'organisation is the deathly enemy of almost every movement'.[41] Such disagreements hardly facilitated lasting political power, but they did reflect a contentious debate over adaptation to the rules of the political game.

In spite of Nazi rhetoric against party politics — an exaggeration and deepening of a widely shared apoliticism — the NSDAP worked to become an accepted part of the society it so bitterly attacked between 1924 and the national electoral breakthrough of September 1930. Some observers have seen in this a Machiavellian strategy designed to destroy the Republic. Whereas the duplicity of

Hitler's politics can hardly be overlooked, one must also recognise that grassroots Nazism was sustained in this period by individuals who saw in the movement a sphere of legitimate social activity that dovetailed with local traditions and practices. This was evidenced in the history of Nazi 'joiners', individuals who belonged to both the NSDAP and non-Nazi voluntary associations. Coming from the ranks of almost all local strata from skilled workers to local notables, joiners possessed contacts and influence in town social life, and were therefore instrumental in folding the Nazi project into grassroots political networks. In the Hessian town before September 1930 there existed at least 46 Nazi party members with 73 cross-affiliations. For the period before 30 January 1933 overall, there were at least 84 Nazi students and 116 non-student party adherents with 375 cross-affiliations to occupational associations, sports clubs, non-party municipal electoral slates, civic associations, student fraternities and other local voluntary groups. Joiners were not driven solely by a conspiratorial design for diffusing Nazism in all areas of local life, though such motivations were certainly present. They often acted without specific party direction, relying on their own influence and abilities as opinion brokers. Rooted in local traditions, they sought to make of Nazism an acceptable political alternative to the established bourgeois parties, to elite politics, and to the supposedly immoral dance of interest group conflict at the national level.[42]

Like its counterparts elsewhere, the Marburg NSDAP sunk into electoral oblivion in local politics after the 1924 Reichstag elections. The party garnered only 6.2 per cent of the vote in December 1924 Reichstag elections, just 5.5 per cent in national elections in 1928, and only 480 votes, or 5.3 per cent of the total, in municipal elections on 17 November 1929.

Fanatical zeal for the Nazi cause and Hitler's charisma hardly serve to explain why the NSDAP survived these lean years. More important was the social diffusion of the party, the uneven and gradual interpenetration of party and voluntary group membership. This gave the NSDAP an important social foundation that counterbalanced political impotence and served as a springboard for party successes after September 1930, when the Nazis exploited a large protest vote against the worsening economic crisis and the state's inability to deal with social and political conflict. There is a very concrete way of putting this. Imagine that all of the 46 pre-1930 Nazi joiners mentioned above used their more than 70 cross-affiliations to talk about Nazism at voluntary groups meetings, at churches, in *Stammtische*, at home, and in the workplace. Imagine, moreover, that after 1930 opportunities for such face-to-face contact between Nazi supporters and the wider town population were multiplied tremendously. Obviously, we do not know if particular joiners shouted loudly for the Nazi cause, acted as quiet examples to their friends in local associations by simply wearing a party or student league (Nationalsozialistischer Deutscher Studentenbund, or NSDStB) lapel pin, or remained silent about their involvement in the Hitler movement. Moreover, it is important to remember that the NSDAP was a volatile organisation subject to considerable membership and electoral fluctuation; party members with cross-affiliations probably slipped in and out of the NSDAP just as frequently as did other less well-connected National Socialists. Nonetheless, already before the 1930 gains, there existed numerous opportunities for promoting the Nazi critique of Weimar politics through word of mouth propaganda that was independent of Hitler's demagogy and official party pronouncements. Indeed, word of mouth propaganda was probably more important than the unsteady party line because the former came from presumably trusted individuals in familiar settings of home, workplace, tavern and *Verein*.[43]

Joiners' activity was a necessary but hardly sufficient element in Nazism's later success. Other features, namely stable organisation and activist leadership, had to be added to transform the NSDAP's disparate social ties into electoral power and to exploit Weimar political and economic crises. Though not without dedicated rabble-rousers, the Marburg NSDAP lacked disciplined leadership and bureaucratic organisation until Hans Krawielitzki became city group leader (*Ortsgruppenleiter*) in late 1927 and district (*Bezirk*) party chief in 1928.[44] Like so many Nazi Party activists, Krawielitzki fell 'between the classes'[45] of Weimar Germany. He was a member of the town's educated upper middle class, having been the son of a Protestant pastor who moved his family to Marburg before World War I, but he was unable to gain a doctorate after failing university examinations. He believed that 'propaganda . . . is the decisive thing' in the political arena,[46] but he possessed little of the personal dynamism that would have made him an effective speaker. He possessed energy, astuteness in financial matters and bureaucratic skills. He was attracted to National Socialism because it offered him an outlet for his talents and leadership ambitions, but above all because it gave political meaning to the uncertainty of his social existence.

Word of mouth propaganda depended on shifting social interaction in voluntary associations and friendship or kinship networks. But the work of dedicated agitators such as Krawielitzki depended on a handful of people with the time and resources to devote themselves fully to the party. Local university students — unidentified with previous party lineages, capable of spending large amounts of time on party work, and socially acceptable to townspeople who saw in students not only potential elites but indispensable economic resources — dominated the ranks of local activists.[47] They laboured tirelessly to make the party organisation more efficient than before; to stabilise party finances; to make of the NSDAP the most vocal political organisation in city and hinterland; and to spread the Nazi message. What was this message?

We know that Nazi propaganda was unusually malleable and syncretic, a result of lack of party centralisation and the extreme social and geographical diversity of the movement.[48] In Marburg, where traditions of political anti-Semitism were strong, the party line consisted of large doses of racism, expressed in attacks on 'Jewish finance capital' before audiences of farmers and rural artisans, or in quasi-intellectual warnings against 'inferior peoples' before an assembly of fraternity students and the *Bildungsbürgertum*. It hinged on direct appeals to the economic interests of specific groups, but it nested these appeals in a wider attack on parliamentarism, the Weimar polity and interest group politics as such. Therein lay a significant element of the Nazi project, namely, the attempt to appeal to sectional concerns while championing a completely new state in which 'the common good goes before individual interest'.[49] This was hardly a paradox in the eyes of party activists or their audiences. It was an attempt to avoid notionally immoral liberalism and socialism, which allegedly reduced public life to a tangle of material interests. In addition, it was an attack on traditional town elites, who allegedly possessed neither ability nor willingness to harness popular energies unleashed before World War I and now fully mobilised in the Weimar system. The Nazi claim of being a new alternative to these traditions meshed with the moralistic impulse of apoliticism, which likewise condemned party politics of both the left and the right. In this regard, Nazi propaganda steered between the pillars of materialism and elitism, between 'new' interest group politics and 'old' notables' politics

(*Honoratiorenpolitik*). Though replete with the radical potential of a new *völkisch* state based on race rather than class, Nazi propaganda appeared to blend with local traditions while avoiding identification with the radical or moderate left on one side or the conservative and nationalist right on the other.

We must be careful not to endow Nazi propagandists with too much perspicacity. Ultimately, 'ecological' factors were most important to Nazi success. This is obvious in the case of local bourgeois organisational life, where traditions of anti-party sentiment nurtured a congenial atmosphere for Nazi attacks on the Weimar state despite important contradictions between *Verein* narrowness and Nazi activism.[50] But other factors also played a role in easing the entry of National Socialism into the local polity. For instance, the lord mayor Müller and successive university chancellors indirectly facilitated Nazism. In spring 1930 Müller said he wanted to avoid making 'unnecessary martyrs' of Nazi activists and thus counselled less repressive measures against the NSDAP than those desired by county or provincial officials.[51] University administrators wanted calm in an era in which higher education became increasingly fragmented along political, economic and social lines. This goal made them wary of challenging the Nazi Student League at the university, especially once the latter became more than a loud and contentious voice on the margins of student life.[52] Though designed to limit the terrain on which NSDAP agitators could manoeuvre, both strategies ultimately shielded the NSDAP from more vigorous attacks by already weakened Social Democratic and trade union opponents, and allowed Nazism to persist and expand despite its initial disorganisation and impotence.

In 1930–31 the Marburg NSDAP gained substantial electoral successes, receiving 28.8 per cent of the city vote in Reichstag elections in 1930 and close to one-half of the vote in student elections in summer 1931. It received the support of some new voters, but, judging from a rather modest increase in voting participation in Marburg compared to the previous Reichstag election,[53] it appears that defectors from other bourgeois parties and splinter groups made up the bulk of Nazi voters. The world economic crisis surely played a role in facilitating such gains. However, the worst effects of the Depression still awaited townspeople, who experienced the most serious downturns in the tourist trade and most substantial increases in unemployment in 1932.[54] Moreover, in 1931 the NSDStB devoted little direct propaganda to the Depression or economic matters, demanding a 'secure future' for students but spending more time on issues such as 'the exclusion of foreign races from German universities . . . the intellectual and material strengthening of German capabilities for military defence . . . [and] the awakening of German folk consciousness.'[55] More important than economic crisis *per se* was the fact that the NSDAP seemed to be a familiar commodity in a time of upheaval. The Marburg polity had given rise to many alternatives to liberal and conservative parties since the Second Empire — the Böckel movement, the National Social Party represented locally by von Gerlach, right-wing anti-Semitic coalitions that attracted National Liberal and conservative support in 1907 and 1912, the VSB in 1924, and municipal non-party and anti-party coalitions in three city elections from 1919 to 1929. The Nazi Party was yet another group that tried to storm the Hessian citadel.

Although many townspeople saw in the NSDAP a familiar outgrowth of local traditions of political protest, the party had to distinguish itself from all other local groups in order to gain support. Nazi dynamism played a significant role in this project. The NSDAP and NSDStB became the most active and vocal of all political organisations in town and university, railing against the ineffectual liberal and conservative parties in the former arena and against the 'philistinised' fraternities in the latter.[56] Part of this criticism resulted from Nazism's swallowing of local traditions of apoliticism, which spread distrust of all political contenders associated with the Weimar state. But part of it was a matter of necessity. Chronically underfinanced, subject to constant membership fluctuations, still uncertain of its place in the local political map, the Nazi Party used constant activity and sweeping criticism of all parties to set itself apart from other contenders. It was less important to identify one's aims than to ensure — however clumsily — that townspeople perceived the Nazi party in a different light than other groups. In this sense, dynamism was a matter of survival, a product of the need to overcome the movement's political backwardness, rather than a result of keen insight.

Electoral success brought new opportunities to advance the Nazi project with 'informal' agitation. Between the September break-through and Hitler's gaining of the chancellorship, word of mouth propaganda surely helped to enhance the social reach and moral authority of the National Socialist movement. By January 1933 there had been at least one Nazi Party member in 104 local associations, or about one-quarter of all voluntary groups in the city. Opportunities for promoting the Nazi message were far more numerous in this 'underground' interpenetration of the Nazi Party and organisational life than in big demonstrations or protest marches. But one cannot gainsay the significance of the latter after the party gained electoral prominence, that is, after the NSDAP was carried to many townspeople through networks of quotidian sociability. The NSDAP and NSDStB became highly visible agents of a *völkisch* polity, one that represented an alternative to seemingly lifeless bourgeois parties and the 'materialistic' Weimar state. Large, emotional assemblies laced with ringing attacks on the political system and a good deal of popular entertainment seemed to be perfect collective actions for bringing more attention to this polity. Thus when Hitler spoke in Marburg in April 1932,[57] many of the 20,000 people in the audience were undoubtedly not only curious about the *Führer* but aware of the unique political alternative represented by the NSDAP. Hitler's much-emphasised personal appeal must not be abstracted from this historical context.[58] Hitler was popular because the party was; and the latter was appealing because of its positive image, ratified in large public assemblies but built on social exchange in local living rooms, fraternity houses, university classrooms, club meeting halls and soccer fields.

Having gained cross-affiliations, electoral success and high public visibility, the local NSDAP also achieved a wide membership drawn from the town bourgeoisie. This is not the place for a lengthy discussion of the social composition of the Marburg party, but one can note that before 1933 university students, white-collar employees, formerly non-socialist craft and skilled workers, other non-students without professions (*Berufslosen*), and women were overrepresented in the NSDAP compared to other local bourgeois parties or non-party electoral coalitions.[59] Nonetheless, the party attracted a following drawn from all points of the social spectrum, from university students and town elites to self-employed artisans, storeowners and officials. Whereas the party was a product of the town *Bürgertum*, the tremendous social differentiation of the latter made of Nazism a people's movement that encompassed elite and non-elite, men and women, student and non-student. Accustomed to its often castelike social life and numerous political divisions, Marburg now witnessed the growth of a party that attracted an unprecedentedly wide field of local groups.

In the summer of 1932 the Marburg NSDAP gained 53.3 per cent of the local vote in Reichstag elections and 63.2 per cent in student government. Striking though these proportions were, they suggest that there were also important limitations to Nazi popularity. In February 1931, well before these successes, the party experienced an embarrassing defeat in its efforts to win a propaganda victory in Marburg's working-class suburb of Ockershausen, having to rely on local police for protection from a rock-throwing crowd of neighbourhood dwellers, Reichsbanner members, and leftist party supporters. The liberal daily *Hessisches Tageblatt* castigated the Nazis for their part in the 'bloody brawl' and criticised Nazism on numerous occasions in the twilight of the Republic.[60] In summer 1931 NSDStB attempts to take over the theology department student council misfired completely, as Nazi students gained only 18 of 268 votes.[61] Party electoral fortunes dipped in November 1932 Reichstag elections in Marburg just as they did in the Reich, as the local NSDAP fell below the 50 per cent mark. Bourgeois voluntary groups persisted in their daily rounds of sociability, suggesting they could not be politicised completely and that they would slow Nazi plans for swallowing all public organisations in a total state after Hitler achieved power. And finally, the NSDAP found it difficult to gain a stable hold over a rapidly growing but fluctuating party membership and electorate.[62] By the eve of Hitler's escort into the halls of power, grassroots Nazism had achieved startling gains but also faced an uncertain future.

This overview necessarily telescopes many issues—the interwar crisis of the German state; changing relationships between city and national state; precise contours of local elite politics and bourgeois party dissolution; specific mechanisms whereby social organisations 'absorbed' conflict; the social location and multitude of forms of apoliticism; aims and interests of local parties; unevenness of economic hardship in the city; the role of local newspapers; concrete actions of Nazi Party activists; the scope and diversity of Nazi Party members' cross-affiliations; 'resolution' of prior social and political conflicts during the Nazi dictatorship. A full treatment of these problems would take us far beyond the present article and at some point overload the analytical capabilities of a local study.

Yet enumerating them does more than provide a disclaimer. It suggests that one cannot discuss grassroots Nazism without discussing a more general phenomenon, namely the sociopolitical history of the bourgeoisie in the widest sense of the term. More than an element of Nazism's 'prehistory', bourgeois inability to translate social power into united political action at the level of the national state opened the way for numerous political alternatives, the most vocal and aggressive of which was the NSDAP. Bourgeois asymmetry between social life and power crystallised in the late nineteenth century,[63] heightened in World War I, arguably lessened during Germany's faltering steps toward a parliamentary republic right after the war, and reached crisis proportions in the middle and last stages of Weimar. To understand the tensions and unpredictability of this asymmetry, we need to rethink the chronology of German history, extending discussion into the *Kaiserreich* without falling prey to teleological interpretations of the German past.

Similarly, we need to rethink periodisation of the study of Nazism, making of the pre-World War I era an integral chapter rather than preface of the story. The NSDAP's appeal was based on a promise to protect any social group prepared to accept race as the organising principle of the polity, and to remake the German state according to *völkisch* principles. The latter rejected an allegedly immoral interest group politics that began in the Empire and gained unparalleled prominence in the Republic. Nazism was not a simple extension of prewar traditions, but it was not the first party in German history to attack interest group politics and 'the parliamentary Babel'[64] either. If we are to understand Nazism's brutal originality as Germany's first non-socialist and non-Catholic people's movement, then we have to locate it in a longer chronological field contested by many previous groups. The point is not to see Nazism as an inevitable outcome of German history, but to formulate an open-ended conceptual map made up of pre-World War I political features that underwent profound transformations in the Weimar Republic and that were later manipulated by gambling and uncertain Nazi agitators. The unpredictable asymmetry of bourgeois power — sharpened by the violent interwar crisis of German state authority — is one of these features.

All this demands the study of local society, where Nazism gained its popular following and where bourgeois groups formulated their most original responses to class and political strife in town, province and nation. The point may seem unoriginal in the light of current work, but there are many uses to which grassroots history can be put. For me the aim of local research is not to explore a hitherto unexplored region, or to add nuance to a national picture allegedly more 'representative' of the culture than case studies — though these are useful applications of such scholarship. Local history should try to integrate the study of everyday life into the disputatious mainstream of history writing on German politics. In the case of Nazism, we know that Hitler gained support partly because of skilful propaganda and charismatic leadership. But something we know much less about — informal word-of-mouth communication in families, voluntary associations, classrooms and other places — carried the Nazi message deep into German society. What precisely was the significance of these institutions of local life in bourgeois political culture? What were the important continuities and discontinuities of the local polity — in contrast to and in relation with those of the national polity and state — from Empire to Republic? How and why did grassroots Nazism gain a more favourable hearing in social settings outside the workplace than other political groups did? We have had general arguments on these issues for some time. But historians of Germany have just begun to go to the province, and the time and ink spent on this research may contribute to a real questioning of previous perspectives.

Notes

1. For debates of the last two decades, see Konrad Jarausch, 'Illiberalism and Beyond: German History in Search of a Paradigm', *Journal of Modern History*, 55, 2, June 1983, pp. 268–84.

2. For an overview, see the opening remarks in Richard J. Evans, 'The Myth of Germany's Missing Revolution', *New Left Review*, 149, February 1985, pp. 67–94.

3. This will change. Historians of Weimar Germany have begun to think more systematically than before about the pre-1914 roots of post-World War I politics, as is evidenced in Richard Bessel, 'Introduction: Themes in the History of Weimar Germany', in R. Bessel and E.J. Feuchtwanger (eds.), *Social Change and Political Development in Weimar Germany* (London, 1981), pp. 11–20. This will undoubtedly have an effect on the study of Nazism. Additionally, see the introductory chapter on long-term cleavages in German electoral behaviour in Thomas Childers, *The Nazi Voter. The Social Foundations of Fascism in Germany 1919–1933* (Chapel Hill and London, 1983).

4. Richard Bessel, *Political Violence and the Rise of Nazism. The Stormtroopers in Eastern Germany 1925–34* (New Haven, 1984), pp. 33–45; Childers, *The Nazi Voter*; Jürgen Falter, 'Wer verhalf der NSDAP zum Zieg?', *Aus Politik und Zeitgeschichte*, B28–29, 14 July 1979, pp. 3–21; Conan Fischer, *Stormtroopers. A Social, Economic, and Ideological Analysis 1929–35* (Winchester, Mass., 1983); Richard Hamilton, *Who Voted for Hitler?* (Princeton, 1982); Mathilde Jamin, *Zwischen den Klassen. Zur Sozialstruktur der SA-Führerschaft* (Wuppertal, 1984); Michael Kater, *The Nazi Party. A Social Profile of Members and Leaders 1919–1945* (Cambridge, Mass., 1983); Peter Merkl, *The Making of a Stormtrooper* (Princeton, NJ, 1980); Merkl, *Political Violence under the Swastika. 581 Early Nazis* (Princeton, NJ, 1975); Detlef Mühlberger, 'The Occupational and Social Structure of the NSDAP in the Border

Province Posen-West Prussia in the early 1930s', *European History Quarterly*, 15, 3, July 1985, pp. 281–311; Lawrence D. Stokes, 'The Social Composition of the Nazi Party in Eutin, 1925–32', *International Review of Social History*, 23, 1978, pt.1, pp. 1–32.

5. For more discussion and data, see Koshar, *Social Life, Local Politics, and Nazism: Bourgeois Marburg, 1880–1935* (Chapel Hill and London, forthcoming).

6. Koshar, 'Two "Nazisms": the Social Context of Nazi Mobilization in Marburg and Tubingen', *Social History*, 7, 1, January 1982, pp. 27–42.

7. *Hessische Volkswacht* (hereafter HV), 4/5 July 1931; *Volksstimme* (Frankfurt-Main), 25 October 1929.

8. D. Blackbourn and G. Eley, *The Peculiarities of German History: Bourgeois Society and Politics in Nineteenth-Century Germany* (Oxford, New York, 1984).

9. Charles S. Maier, *Recasting Bourgeois Europe. Stabilization in France, Germany, and Italy in the Decade After World War I* (Princeton, NJ, 1975). See also the opening remarks in Michael Geyer, 'The State in National Socialist Germany', in Charles Bright and Susan Harding (eds.), *Statemaking and Social Movements: Essays in History and Theory* (Ann Arbor, Mich., 1984), pp. 193–232. For a quite different approach that nevertheless also stresses political crisis, see Geoff Eley, 'What Produces Fascism: Preindustrial Traditions or a Crisis of a Capitalist State', *Politics and Society*, 12, 1, 1983, pp. 53–82.

10. James J. Sheehan, *German Liberalism in the Nineteenth Century* (Chicago, 1978), pp. 237–8; Dan S. White, *The Splintered Party. National Liberalism in Hessen and the Reich, 1867–1918* (Cambridge, Mass., 1976), pp. 159–98.

11. The term is adopted from Antonio Gramsci, 'The Modern Prince', *Selections from the Prison Notebooks of Antonio Gramsci*, ed. and trans. by Quinton Hoare and Geoffrey Nowell Smith (NY, 1971), p. 147. Gramsci's necessarily undeveloped discussion of 'apoliticism' dealt with sociocultural obstacles to building a united popular movement, but I employ the word in reference to a bourgeois aversion to mass politics. The term is more accurate than 'unpolitical politics', which I used in earlier writing, and which suggests a disinterest in rather than aversion to mass parties. Finally, 'apoliticism' has the virtue of being more economical than the earlier phrase.

12. On the grassroots *Bürgertum*, see Hansjoachim Henning, *Das westdeutsche Bürgertum in der Epoche der Hochindustrialisierung 1860–1914*. Teil I: *Das Bildungsbürgertum in den westdeutschen Provinzen* (Wiesbaden, 1972); Robert Hopwood, 'The Bavarian *Kommerzienräte*: Small Town Economic Elites and the Vertical Lines of Authority and Power', in Michael B. Barrett (ed.), *Proceedings of the Citadel Symposium on the National Socialist Era* (Charleston, SC, 1982), pp. 131–7; Hopwood, 'Paladins of the *Bürgertum*: Cultural Clubs and Politics in Small German Towns 1918–25', *Historical Papers* (1974), pp. 213–35; Gerd Zang (ed.), *Provinzialisierung einer Region. Zur Entstehen der bürgerlichen Gesellschaft in der Provinz* (Frankfurt-Main, 1978).

13. Bernhard vom Brocke, 'Marburg im Kaiserreich 1866–1918', in Erhart Dettmering and Rudolf Grenz (eds.), *Marburger Geschichte. Rückblick auf die Stadtgeschichte in Einzelbeiträge* (Marburg, 1980), pp. 459–61, 494–504.

14. Ibid., pp. 474–95; Richard Levy, *The Downfall of the Anti-Semitic Political Parties in Imperial Germany* (New Haven and London, 1975); Dieter Düding, *Der Nationalsoziale Verein 1896–1903. Der gescheiterte Versuch einer parteipolitischer Synthese von Nationalismus, Sozialismus, und Liberalismus* (München, Wien, 1972), p. 177; Hellmut von Gerlach, *Von Rechts nach Links* (Hildesheim, 1978), pp. 170–74.

15. On extraparliamentary groups and liberal and conservative politics, see Roger Chickering, *We Men Who Feel Most German. A Cultural Study of the Pan-German League 1886–1914* (Boston, 1984); Geoff Eley, *Reshaping the German Right*.

Radical Nationalism and Political Change after Bismarck (New Haven and London, 1980); Sheehan, *German Liberalism*; Dirk Stegmann, *Die Erben Bismarcks. Parteien und Verbände in der Spätphase des Wilhelminischen Deutschlands* (Köln, Berlin, 1970).

16. Historians of bourgeois town life after roughly 1860 would do well to match the finely textured research on Social Democratic Vereine and local politics contained in Klaus Tenfelde, *Proletarische Provinz. Radikalisierung und Widerstand in Penzberg/Oberbayern 1900–1945* (München, Wien, 1982), pp. 68–85, 154–60, 215–16.

17. For the quote, details and acceptance of Wenck's perspective on this issue, see vom Brocke, 'Marburg im Kaiserreich', p. 527.

18. Schützenverein Marburg, *Festschrift zum 50 jährigen Bestehen des Schützenvereins Marburg* (Marburg, 1912), pp. 38, 43–46; Verein für Leibesübungen, *Festschrift 1860–1950* (Marburg, 1950), pp. 17–21; Turnverein board of directors, 2 April 1894, 15 September 1894, 28 October 1897, 25 September 1903, 25 October 1906, all in Hessisches Staatsarchiv Marburg (hereafter, HSAM) 180, Landratsamt Marburg, 760; 'Verzeichnis der Marburger Vereine', *Adreßbuch der Stadt Marburg 1913* (Marburg, 1913), pp. 43–47; *Lieder für die Feier des 50. Stiftungsfestes des Turn-Vereins Marburg am 6.7. and 8. August 1910* (Marburg, 1910); interview with Karl Wilser, former Kriegerkameradschaft official, Marburg, 29 July 1976; interviews with Hermann Bauer, former publisher of *Hessisches Tageblatt* (hereafter, HT), 1 April 1977 and 5 March 1980; Wilhelm Fischdick, 'Der Marburger Studenten-Ausschuß', *Wingolfsblätter*, 45, 12 (16 March 1916), cols. 332–35; Georg Heer, *Marburger Studentenleben 1527–1927* (Marburg, 1927), pp. 157–75.

19. Hermann Neuschaefer, 'Kriegs-Chronik der Stadt Marburg (Lahn)', typescript, HSAM 330, Marburg A, II, 51; *Oberhessische Zeitung* (hereafter, OZ), 24 August 1917, 27 August 1917, 26 September 1917, 6 October 1917, 17 October 1917, 19 December 1917, 9 March 1918; *Hessische Landeszeitung* (hereafter, HLZ), 15 June 1918; 'Übersicht über die in den Monaten Februar bis Juni 1918 veranstalteten und verbotenen Versammlungen', Landrat, HSAM 180, Landratsamt Marburg, 897, Bd. 2.

20. HLZ, 13 November 1918, 21 November 1918, 16 December 1918; Gunther Mai, 'Der Marburger Arbeiter- und Soldatenrat und die Militärpolitik im Bereich des XI. Armeekorps (Kassel) 1918–19', in Dettmering and Grenz, *Marburger Geschichte*, pp. 541–57; Mai, 'Der Marburger Arbeiter und Soldatenrat 1918/20', *Hessisches Jahrbuch für Landesgeschichte* (hereafter, HJLG), 26, 1976, pp. 149–99.

21. James M. Diehl, *Paramilitary Politics in Weimar Germany* (Bloomington and London, 1977), pp. 23–46.

22. James Weingartner, 'Massacre at Mechterstädt. The Case of the Marburg Studentenkorps', *Historian*, 37, 1975, pp. 598–618; Hellmut Seier, 'Marburg in der Weimarer Republik 1918–1933', in Dettmering and Grenz, *Marburger Geschichte*, pp. 572–73. For university officials' responses to the Mechterstädt incident, see Rektor to Kurator, 31 March 1920; Rektor and Depuation to Konrad Haenisch, Culture Minister, 17 July 1920; Rektor to Kurator, 28 September 1920; declaration of Rektor and Deputation, 27 December 1920; all in HSAM 310, Acc. 1975/42, 2190.

23. Walther Kürschner, *Geschichte der Stadt Marburg* (Marburg, 1934), p. 299.

24. Ibid.

25. Vom Brocke, 'Marburg im Kaiserreich', pp. 428–50. For World War I: Regierungspräsident (Cassel) to Landräte, 25 August 1914, HSAM 180, Landratsamt Marbug, 892; Neuschaefer, 'Kriegs-Chronik', HSAM 330, Marburg A, II, 51.

26. On various groups during the inflation: OZ, 11 February 1922, 13 March 1922, 1 May 1922, 30 June 1922, 11 August 1923, 7 November 1923. On students' conditions: *Deutsche Studentenschaft* (hereafter DSt) announcement, summer 1921,

HSAM 305a, Acc. 1950/9, 635; DSt questionnaire, winter 1924/25, Archiv der Universität Würzburg. Archiv der ehemaligen Reichsstudentenführung und des NSDStB (hereafter AUWAR), I*6, phi 564; and Georg Heer, *Die Marburger Burschenschaft Arminia* (Marburg, 1951), pp. 124–5. For unemployment: 'Arbeitslose und Arbeitslosenhilfe 1930 und 1931', *Statistisches Jahrbuch deutscher Städte* (hereafter SJDS), 27, 1932, pp. 310–20; 'Arbeitslose und Arbetislosenhilfe 1932', SJDS, 28, 1933, pp. 543–49. For enrolments, *Deutsche Hochschulstatistik* (hereafter, DHS), 4, 1930, p. viii; 10, 1932/33, p. 11; and 12, 1933/34, p. 20.

27. Kürschner, *Geschichte*, p. 299.

28. Robert G. Moeller, 'Winners as Losers in the German Inflation: Peasant Protest over the Controlled Economy 1920–23', in Gerald Feldman, Carl-Ludwig Holtfrerich, Gerhard A. Ritter and Peter-Christian Witt (eds.), *Die Deutsche Inflation. Eine Zwischenbilanz* (Berlin, New York, 1982), pp. 255–88.

29. Thomas Childers, 'Interest and Ideology: Anti-System Politics in the Era of Stabilization 1924–1928', in Gerald Feldman (ed.), *Die Nachwirkungen der Inflation auf die deutsche Geschichte, 1924–1933* (München, 1985), pp. 1–20.

30. These and all subsequent computations for Marburg electoral politics are based on data derived from: Rosemarie Mann, 'Entstehen und Entwicklung der NSDAP in Marburg bis 1933', HJLG, 22, 1972, pp. 336–40; 'Ergebnis der Gemeindewahlen 1933 in Preußen', SJDS, 28, 1933, pp. 550–62; Ermenhild Neusüß-Hunkel, *Parteien und Wahlen in Marburg nach 1945* (Meisenheim am Glan, 1973), pp. 35, 42; OZ, 3 March 1919, May 1924, 18 November 1929, 13 March 1933.

31. For examples: OZ, 2 August 1924; *Burschenschaftliche Blätter*, 40, 1, October 1925, p. 19; Heer, *Burschenschaft Arminia*, p. 138; Marburger Hausfrauenverband, Protokollbuch, II, pp. 174–82 (my thanks to the Hausfrauenverband for the opportunity to photocopy parts of this unpublished source); Hessischer Bauernverein, entry of 23 March 1929, Amtsgericht Kreis Marburg, Vereinsregister (hereafter AKMVR), 61.

32. Käsebrod, *Servus* (Marburg, ca. 1927), pp. 15–19, HSAM 325g, Acc. 10/1947, Paket 1.

33. Computations based on Schützenverein membership list, ca. 1930 HSAM 165, Regierungsbezirk Kassel, 1061; and numerous additional sources for local organisations cited throughout Koshar, *Social Life, Local Politics, and Nazism*.

34. OZ, 24 January 1928.

35. For examples: OZ, 19 January 1927, 20 January 1930.

36. See Marburg Landlords' Association report of a Wiesbaden rally in OZ, 28 November 1926.

37. For 1920: Kreisrat's report, 9 April 1920, HSAM 165, Regierungsbezirk Kassel, Abt. I, 1230, Bd. 1. For 1929: HT, 30 September 1929.

38. HT, 30 September 1929; OZ, 2 October 1929; Mann, 'Entstehen und Entwicklung', pp. 303–7.

39. For details and self-serving recollections: NSDAP Marburg, *Festschrift zum 10(12) jährigen Bestehen der NSDAP in Marburg* (Marburg, 1935), pp. 15–20.

40. OZ, 3 May 1924; *Hessischer Beobachter* (hereafter HB), 12 April 1924, 19 April 1924; Eberhart Schön, *Die Entstehung des Nationalsozialismus in Hessen* (Meisenheim am Glan, 1972), pp. 56–63. For the Bavarian VSB, see Peter D. Stachura, *Gregor Strasser and the Rise of Nazism* (London, 1983), p. 32.

41. Quoted from 'Aus der völkischen Bewegung', HB, 10 May 1924.

42. The basic source for Marburg NSDAP membership is Namenszverzeichnis von Mitgliedern der NSDAP (n.d.), HSAM 327/1, 5488, which has been compared with numerous other associational membership rosters, address book listings, newspaper articles, police reports, and *Vereinsregister* entries to generate data for Nazi cross-affiliations. For sources, examples of individual joiners' actions, and methodology, see Koshar, *Social Life, Local Politics, and Nazism*.

43. Without offering the necessary evidence on cross-affiliations and other social ties, Zdenek Zofka has made similar observations on word-of-mouth propaganda in *Die Ausbreitung des Nationalsozialismus auf dem Lande* (München, 1979), pp. 37, 81, 92, 103, 139–40.

44. Hans Krawielitzki, 'Lebenslauf (handschriftlich)', n.d., NS Reichsleiter. Personalakte d. Obersten Parteigerichtes, Berlin Document Center; NSDAP Marburg, *Festschrift*, pp. 25–6.

45. Jamin, *Zwischen den Klassen*.

46. Quoted from interview with Hans Krawielitzki, Marburg, 20 March 1980.

47. See Mann, 'Entstehen und Entwicklung', pp. 280–97.

48. For recent discussion, see David Welch (ed.), *Nazi Propaganda. The Power and Limitations* (London, 1983).

49. Landjägerpost Wetter II to Landrat, 27 February 1929, HSAM 165, Regierungsbezirk Kassel I, 3866; Kuno von Eltz-Rübenach, Marburg NSDStB leader, to Reich NSDStB, 15 January 1928, AUWAR, II/A, 10; Mann, 'Entstehen und Entwicklung', p. 283.

50. I have tried to deal with this issue in Koshar, 'From *Stammtisch* to Party: Nazi Joiners and the Contradictions of Grass Roots Fascism in Weimar Germany', *Journal of Modern History*, forthcoming, 1986.

51. Quoted from typed minutes of 26 March 1930 meeting in Kassel, HSAM 165, Regierungsbezirk Kassel I, 3815.

52. Seier, 'Marburg in der Weimarer Republik', pp. 584–91.

53. Voting participation in national elections in Marburg, in percent of all eligible voters: 1919: 76.4; 1920: 75.3; 1924 (I): 75.4; 1924 (II): 80.0; 1928: 69.0; 1930: 73.0; 1932 (I): 88.0; 1932 (II): 84.0; 1933: 90.0. Source: Neusüß-Hunkel, *Parteien und Wahlen*, p. 35. Mann, 'Entstehen und Entwicklung', pp. 336–40, is incomplete with regard to electoral data, and I have therefore relied on Neusüß-Hunkel.

54. For tourism, see OZ, 4 January 1929, 12 December 1929, 30 December 1932. For unemployment, see the relevant citations in note 26 above.

55. HV 4/5, July 1931.

56. Ernst Schwarz, Marburg NSDStB leader in summer 1928, to Reich NSDStB, 31 July 1928, AUWAR, II/0A, 10; Mann, 'Entstehen und Entwicklung', pp. 280–334.

57. OZ, 19 April 1932, 21 April 1932, HT, 21 April 1932.

58. For a compatible argument, see Zofka, *Ausbreitung*, p. 84.

59. Using the addresses of party members listed in the membership list cited in note 42 above, I determined the occupational makeup of the Marburg NSDAP by referring to 'Straßenverzeichnis', *Marburger Einwohnerbuch* (Marburg, 1930/31), pp. 107–83. The membership data in NSDAP Marburg, *Festschrift*, pp. 32–33, are based on the entire district and are therefore completely unusable for the city. For data and comparisons with other Marburg parties, see Koshar, *Social Life, Local Politics, and Nazism*, chapter 6.

60. Polizeiverwaltung Marburg, reports of 24 and 25 February 1931, HSAM 165, Regierungsbezirk Kassel I, 7015; HT, 24 February 1931; interviews with Hermann Bauer, former HT publishers, 1 April 1977 and 5 March 1980.

61. Marburg NSDAP, *Festschrift*, p. 49.

62. For membership growth in 1931–2, refer to ibid., pp. 60–61.

63. David Blackbourn, *Class, Religion, and Local Politics in Wilhelmine Germany. The Centre Party in Württemberg before 1914* (New Haven, London, 1980); Eley, *Reshaping the German Right*; Richard J. Evans (ed.), *Society and Politics in Wilhelmine Germany* (London, 1978).

64. Denis Donoghue uses the phrase in a discussion of Kenneth Burke's writing on Hitler's *Mein Kampf* in 'American Sage', *The New York Review of Books*, 32, 14, 26 September 1985, p. 40.

3 BETWEEN BAUERNBUND AND NATIONAL SOCIALISM. THE POLITICAL REORIENTATION OF THE PEASANTS IN THE FINAL PHASE OF THE WEIMAR REPUBLIC

Zdenek Zofka
Translated by Thomas Childers

Introduction

Why did so many Germans vote for Hitler? This pressing question still occupies centre stage when one attempts to understand or explain the phenomenon of the Nazi dictatorship in Germany. Today the question of who voted for Hitler or among which social groups or strata the NSDAP found support seems to be largely settled. Basically we know that it was not the workers or unemployed who gave Hitler their votes but the middle classes — white-collar employees, artisans, shopkeepers and peasants whose economic and social existence seemed threatened.

Although the rise of the NSDAP was a general nationwide phenomenon, the degree of its success varied from region to region. If one wishes to determine the causes for the spread of National Socialism, these regional differences cannot be ignored but must be incorporated into the explanation. Indeed, the purpose in undertaking regional case studies on this theme is to examine the processes of political reorientation at the grassroots and to explain the varying degrees of electoral support for the National Socialist movement by examining the role of regional preconditions.

This essay is extracted from a regional case study of the spread of National Socialism in the countryside using the *Landkreis* of Günzburg, a rural Catholic region in Bavarian Swabia, as an example.[1] In that study the attempt was made to use both quantitative and qualitative methods to examine the process of 'Nazification' within the rural population and to explain gross differences in Nazi electoral success by analysing the different structural preconditions in a number of communities.

Since peasants made up the bulk of the National Socialist

37

electorate in Günzburg, this essay will concentrate on the political behaviour of this element of the population. The fact that a large proportion of the peasantry gave their vote to the NSDAP is actually a phenomenon that is difficult to grasp. The Bavarian Peasants' League (Bauernbund), to which most peasants of the region felt attached, was undoubtedly a party that somehow corresponded to the mentality and character of the Swabian peasantry. In contrast, the NSDAP didn't fit in the political landscape of middle Swabia, where a strong consciousness of estate (*Standesbewusstsein*) and distinct interest orientation among the peasantry dominated the political culture of the region. Even its name — National *Socialist Workers' Party* — seemed out of place. What then had happened? Had the mentality of the Swabian peasantry changed to such an extent in the radicalised phase of the Weimar Republic, in that period of severe economic distress, or had the NSDAP adapted itself to the dominant mentality of the region, or both? In order to be able to answer these questions, we must first subject the basic preconditions — the economic structure and political culture of Günzburg — which confronted the Nazis in the region to much closer examination.

The Preconditions: Economic Structure and Political Traditions in the Region

As an overwhelmingly agrarian region, 90 per cent of whose 38,412 inhabitants were Catholic, the Günzburg district represented a 'normal' rather than exceptional example of the Bavarian provinces. In the 1930s the county was divided almost equally between forests, meadows and cultivated land. Natural conditions favoured a mixed agricultural economy with such crops as wheat and potatoes and cattle raising. Cultivation of speciality crops such as hops or grapes did not exist in the area. With over 50 per cent of its population engaged in agriculture and forestry, the Günzburg district approximated the average for Bavarian *Landkreise* (rural counties), and the same could be said of the income levels and social stratification of the district's peasant inhabitants. Yet, while good soil conditions provided a relatively good potential for agriculture in the district, the subdivision and splintering of holdings meant that most peasants could maintain only a meagre existence. In the majority of communities, small farms, many of which held less than five usable hectares, predominated. The owners of these small farms usually owned three or four cows and a similar number of pigs and chickens. Only in a few communities did a larger group of middle-sized farms exist, but in almost every community several big farms with 50 hectares or more were present, including, in a few cases, a noble estate (*Grossgrundbesitz*) with a suitable number of farm workers.

Most of the agrarian population lived in small villages. Of the 67 communities in the district, 31 had fewer than 300 inhabitants, 15 between 300 and 500, and another 15 between 500 and 1,000. Aside from Günzburg, the county seat, with approximately 6,500 inhabitants, there were two small towns, Ichenhausen (2,500 inhabitants) and Burgau (2,300 inhabitants), as well as three small market towns (*Marktflecken*) with about 1,500 inhabitants each (Leipheim, Offinge and Jettingen). These six small towns, all of which were situated on the Günzburg-Krumbach branch of the Munich-Stuttgart rail line, constituted the centres of the industrial and artisanal working class, which comprised 25.5 per cent of the population and as such made up a rather larger proportion than in the neighbouring districts with poorer transportation links.

Only at the turn of the century had industry established itself in the district. Several small and medium-sized industrial enterprises, mostly branches of larger concerns, were founded, most belonging to branches of the textile and food industries. Here and there old, established artisanal enterprises also evolved into industrial concerns, the most prominent being a large farm machinery factory in Günzburg that employed several hundred people and was the largest firm in the district.

The industrial workers lived mostly in the small towns or in workers' communities in their immediate vicinity. In the communities along the rail line, the number of commuters grew, while many of the small peasants were forced to rely on a second job in industry or construction. Aside from a few tile making firms, however, few non-agricultural opportunities existed in the countryside since the rural artisan establishments were almost exclusively family enterprises.

With the exception of a small minority of Protestant workers, civil servants and shopkeepers who had moved to the area, 64 of the 67 communities in the district were almost exclusively Catholic. The small town of Leipheim as well as Riedheim in the extreme northwest of the district and Burtenbach in the extreme southeast were unique in being almost completely Protestant, a consequence of dynastic history. While the rest of the district formed the nucleus of the former Catholic *Markgrafschaft* Burgau that belonged to Austria, Leipheim and Riedheim belonged to the territory of the Protestant Free City of Ulm and Burtenbach was in the possession of an imperial knight who converted to Protestantism in the sixteenth century.

These three Protestant communities and Ichenhausen, a small town with an unusually large Jewish minority (more than 300 people), notwithstanding, Catholicism set the social and cultural tone and to a considerable extent shaped the political environment in the Günzburg district. As in other Catholic areas in Bavaria and Swabia, the brief supremacy of political liberalism during the 1870s — a supremacy carried more by the state bureaucracy than the weak middle class — was supplanted by political Catholicism. Under the impact of the *Kulturkampf* and as a sign of peasant/lower-middle-class protest against the liberalisation of the economy and the pro-Prussian *Kleindeutsch* orientation of the liberals, the great majority of rural voters turned to the Patriots' Party, a party led by the lower clergy, and then after 1881 to the Bavarian Zentrum. Between 1880 and 1914 a stable pattern of electoral behaviour was established and a clearly delineated 'political landscape' emerged. More than 60 per cent of the population voted for the Zentrum. Only the Protestant and a few Catholic communities — mostly in the western and central portions of the district where a strong peasant consciousness was linked to a basic anti-clerical attitude — remained strongholds of liberalism or, since the 1890s, the Bavarian Bauernbund.

Alongside the liberal or Bauernbund vote that averaged between 25 and 35 per cent, the SPD, which also surfaced at the outset of the 1890s, was able to attract about 10 per cent of vote, beginning in the years just before the outbreak of World War I. The Social Democrats found their support almost exclusively among the workers in the small towns and neighbouring workers' communities. Indeed, it was typical that the former liberal electoral support among the peasantry had already shifted almost entirely to the Bauernbund, an 'interest party', by the 1890s. Thereafter, the contours of the district's political landscape remained completely the same, except that the former liberal strongholds in the countryside became bastions of the Bauernbund. Liberalism could really count only on the Protestant portion of the 'bourgeois' elements in the small towns, where, however, it had been outflanked by Social Democracy, even before 1914.

World War I and the revolution brought a substantial change in this stable political landscape. The elections for the national assembly in 1919 revealed that the Zentrum, and its successor the BVP, had lost its absolute majority in the district. Then in the following years a further splintering of the BVP's electorate occurred, a splintering that redounded to the benefit of the Bauernbund. In 1928 the Bauernbund collected 36.5 per cent of the district's vote, while the BVP fell to 26.2 per cent. The socialist parties, on the other hand, consistently received between 15 and 20 per cent after 1919. In the political landscape of the 1920s, only a few stable 'black' communities (communities with substantial BVP majorities) remained. The Bauernbund had won numerous new strongholds, most of them in the immediate vicinity of its already existing *Hochburgen*. In the other communities, the Bauernbund and BVP competed for the peasant vote, and shifting majorities were frequently recorded. In the small towns dominated by the well-to-do *Mittelstand*, the lower-middle class and workers, the BVP and SPD were the chief competitors.

The political division of the Catholic peasantry into BVP and Bauernbund supporters had come about not least because during the 1920s the Bauernbund had managed to overcome its anti-clerical image in the district. It also succeeded in winning a Catholic priest for the party, who was presented as its local spokesman. By gaining a prominent position in peasant associations and agricultural interest organisations, it created a stable organisational 'infrastructure'. The party also succeeded in placing sympathetic notables in leading positions in village associational life (*Vereins-wesen*), especially in the fire departments and veterans' associations.

The growing popularity of the Bauernbund down to 1928 was based on its clear interest-oriented political stance and its embodiment of peasant *Standesbewusstsein*, its sense of peasant solidarity. In its propaganda the Bauernbund articulated above all a protest against the ostensible economic and tax discrimination against peasants and the feeling that all other social groups had turned their backs on the peasantry. It is, therefore, perhaps not surprising that the Bauernbund was able to reach the apex of its electoral success in the district during 1928 when the agricultural crisis had already begun while the prosperity of the previous years continued to hold for business.

By its own definition, the Bauernbund was a peasant organisation
for the purpose of political self-help, for the political organisation,
formulation and assertion of agricultural interests. Its posture *vis-à-
vis* other parties was distinctly reserved. Despite all its interest-
based opposition to Social Democracy, especially on the issue of
agricultural import tariffs, the propaganda of the Bauernbund was
largely free of hatred and defamation. Indeed, the organisation of
workers in the SPD was not infrequently held up as a model for
farmers. The Bauernbund was attacked by the BVP above all with
the argument that peasants were numerically much too weak to be
able to build a majority party. This charge touched a sore spot in the
politics of the Bauernbund, which responded in 1922 by renaming
itself the Bavarian Peasants' and *Mittelstand*'s Party. Still, its
success in attracting votes from the small town *Mittelstand* was
modest. The gap between peasants and the *Mittlestand* was too
great to overcome for a party which had traditionally appealed to
only one of these two groups.

Between Protest and Expectation — The Electoral Successes of the NSDAP

The origins of the NSDAP in the district go back to the years 1922–
3, when the first *völkisch*-National Socialist local branches
(*Ortsgruppen*) were formed in the small towns. The National
Socialist movement developed out of the bourgeois defence organisations (*Bürgerwehrvereinigungen*), originating primarily as an
anti-socialist, counter-revolutionary movement. It was viewed as a
response by the small town *Mittelstand* to the 'Geiselhart dictatorship', named for the leader of the Social Democratic workers'
movement, which had temporarily gained ascendance in the
Günzburg region during the revolutionary years 1918–19. Yet, after
the ban on the NSDAP in 1923, the National Socialist organisations
— even the party's disguised successor formations — disappeared
very quickly from the scene.

The electoral successes of the '*Völkischer Block*', or NSDAP, in
the Reichstag campaign of May 1924, thus remained an episode.
The party was able to draw 10 per cent of the vote and, significantly,
it had notable success not only in the small towns but also in several
rural communities. Its greatest successes were registered in a
number of Bauernbund strongholds, above all in Riedheim and

Burtenbach, the two Protestant rural communities. This election was, however, a typical protest election in which peasants and *Kleinstädtler* wanted to express their dissatisfaction without breaking their already established partisan loyalties, a tendency vividly reflected in the plummeting Nazi vote in new Reichstag elections just six months later. In the Reichstag election of 1928, the National Socialists drew only 3.6 per cent of the vote in the district and did very badly in the rural communities. Only a quarter of the National Socialist votes were cast in the villages, although the rural population made up more than 60 per cent of the total population of the district.

Less than a year later, however, a reorganisation of the party in the district began. In Günzburg a National Socialist *Ortsgruppe* was re-established in 1929, while in two rural communities the NSDAP founded branches in the same year — one in Röfingen, a Catholic community with a mixed population of peasants and workers near the small town of Burgau and one in Burtenbach, one of the two Protestant rural communities in the district. In the same year the Nazis organised the referendum against the Young Plan and won roughly 5 per cent of the district's eligible voters for this NSDAP-DNVP sponsored project.

Although the first propaganda operations of the NSDAP in 1929 were carried out largely by the party's regional organisation, the Günzburg branch increasingly seized the initiative. In the communal elections at the close of 1929 the Nazis achieved notable success only in Günzburg, where a four-man National Socialist delegation moved into the city council and became an important factor in the political life of the district. Reports on the sessions of the city council occupied considerable space in the local press, and the small National Socialist delegation proposed many initiatives and frequently thrust itself into the centre of public attention. Above all, the Günzburg *Ortsgruppe* sought confrontation with the Social Democrats, whom they attacked in countless newspaper articles, public notices and letters to the editor. Indeed, the propaganda offensives of the *Ortsgruppe* focused almost exclusively on the Social Democrats. Attacks on the bourgeois parties or the Bauernbund were omitted, as were tirades against Jews or anti-clerical allusions. This pronounced anti-socialist thrust in Nazi propaganda clearly represented a direct link with the local party's past during 1922–3.

At the outset of 1930 the National Socialists launched a drive in the countryside. In a well-planned, spectacular propaganda campaign, announced as a 'National Socialist Action', over 30 events were held in rural communities. For the most part party speakers from outside the area spoke on the theme 'Fight the Organised Swindle of the *Volk*', though some party activists from Günzburg sometimes appeared as speakers as well. In terms of the Action's geographic scope, a broad cross-section of communities in the district were included, with only the smallest hamlets being bypassed. At the same time, however, a certain concentration on the Bauernbund strongholds and a neglect of the BVP communities can be discerned. The 'National Socialist Action' also sought to extend the party's organisation in the countryside. In this regard, however, it was a complete failure. Not a single new branch or 'strongpoint' (*Stützpunkt*) could be founded.

Propaganda activities were also continued in the small towns — especially in Günzburg — with a series of rallies boasting prominent National Socialists, including Streicher and Gregor Strasser, as speakers. These activities reached their apex with an appearance by Hitler shortly before the start of the 1930 Reichstag campaign. The highly touted visit by the party leader was accorded great attention, but it was not yet a great sensation. Even the impression made by Hitler was hardly overpowering. His aggressive, polemical speech, in which he sharply criticised the government, found a mixed reception. In a second rally on the same day, the '*Diplomlandwirt*' Heinrich Himmler spoke on the theme 'National Socialism and Agriculture', but Hitler's unexpected failure to appear at this event provoked considerable exasperation among the largely peasant audience. The explanation — the *Führer* was too exhausted after the first rally — evoked little sympathy. Yet, aside from this embarrassment, the day did provide the regional NSDAP with the opportunity to make the kind of militant public appearance that was the hallmark of the party. For the first time in Günzburg the NSDAP staged a great march, which, however, had to be carried out in white shirts due to the ban on uniforms.

In the ensuing Reichstag campaign, relatively few events were staged, a result, no doubt, of the season which found the peasants in the midst of the harvest. The party's campaign platform can be characterised very concisely: total obstructionism expressed in general attacks against all 'old' parties, which were characterised as weak and incompetent and were held responsible for all the abuses suffered by the masses of the population. The slogan of the campaign was: '14 September is judgement day for the nation — Voters, declare your rejection of the old parties by voting for us . . .' In its platform the party still did not raise any claim to power but 'sold' itself exclusively as a party of protest.

There were certainly ample reasons for a mood of protest, especially in the economic realm. The agricultural crisis of 1928 had now expanded to become a general worldwide depression, the effects of which were, of course, felt directly in the Günzburg region. The crisis of the agricultural market was now further exacerbated, since the growing army of the unemployed was forced to reduce its consumption of foodstuffs. As a result, the agricultural credit crisis intensified, and the auctioning of bankrupt farms became a common occurrence in the Günzburg district. The results of the Reichstag election revealed the mood of protest among the agrarian population only too clearly: the National Socialist vote had swollen to almost 18 per cent. The 'spatial pattern' of the election results was to a great extent consistent with that of the protest election of May 1924. In general the Nazis again won their votes in the same Bauernbund strongholds, only this time to a greater extent. The Nazis registered their best results in both Protestant communities: 68 per cent in Burtenbach and almost 61 per cent in Riedheim. In 14 Catholic rural communities they won over 20 per cent of the vote, completely at the expense of the Bauernbund. The Bauernbund was not, however, entirely devastated. With about 20 per cent of the vote in the district, the Bauernbund still averaged a few points higher than the NSDAP. Moreover, the NSDAP was not the sole beneficiary of Bauernbund defections. In a few Catholic communities the BVP was able to profit from the gradual decline of the Bauernbund.

This first great electoral triumph spurred the NSDAP to intensify its efforts to win new supporters. The propaganda activities of the party continued almost without pause and increasingly shifted to the countryside. In 1931 alone, a year without elections, the party staged 24 events in the rural communities and 13, by contrast, in the small towns. In the rural communities especially, only speakers from the region were used, among whom were the county leader of the NSDAP, himself an agricultural official in Günzburg who was well acquainted with farm issues, and his deputy, a farmer who had left the Bauernbund for the NSDAP in 1930.

The NSDAP's electoral showing in 1930 had created an entirely new situation for the party. A seizure of power no longer seemed an

utter illusion, and one could talk about it without provoking
ridicule. The propaganda of the party's regional organisation
gradually adjusted itself to this new situation. The theme of one
Günzburg speaker at a rally held in May of 1932 — 'Is National
Socialism only an opponent?' — was indicative of the party's shift
from sheer obstructionism and negativism. One of the party's
campaign speakers expressed it in the following way: 'If earlier it
was the duty of the NSDAP . . . to point out to the masses the
mistakes of German domestic, economic and foreign policy, today
it is obligated to show them how the German state under the
leadership of Adolf Hitler will appear.'[2]

From the middle of 1931 onward, the NSDAP increasingly made
direct appeals to specific target groups, a tactic that inevitably
necessitated a turn to stronger programmatic declarations. Almost
all of the rallies held in the rural communities during the fall and
winter of 1931 had as their theme 'National Socialism and Agriculture'. These public meetings dealt with aspects of economic policy
and were directed by local speakers, most of whom were themselves
farmers.

Along with this transition to more positive programmatic statements, the NSDAP's propaganda events held between the 1930
Reichstag campaign and the 1932 presidential elections also
exhibited a completely different trait: they tried to generate an
almost mystic, apocalyptic mood of ruin, revolutionary change and
catastrophe. 'What awaits us? This can't go on!' was the theme of
many rallies, or 'The German People at the Crossroads —
Bolshevism or Hitler?', with Bolshevism equated, of course, with
ruin and catastrophe. The Nazis certainly understood how to exploit
the advantage they had gained from their electoral success, coining
the slogan: 'Now it comes down to Bolshevism or National
Socialism. Now only major parties can help.' Thus the recently
achieved size of the party was made into a major factor in the party's
popularity.

As the party's popularity grew, not only voters but also several
influential figures of the Bauernbund turned to the NSDAP. The
support of several respected 'peasant leaders' for the NSDAP
strengthened the credibility of the party's self-portrait as a
champion of peasant interests. The mayors of both Protestant rural
communities, Johann Deininger of Burtenbach and Christoph
Honold of Riedheim, were the most important of these leaders.
Honold had been among the most prominent leaders of the

Bauernbund in the district, but in 1930 he resigned and participated in many National Socialist campaign events, without, however, actually becoming a member of the party. Deininger had formally been a member of the DNVP but had not been active for the party for some time. Both men were members of the district *Bauernkammer* and both enjoyed great reputations as recognised advocates of peasant interests not only in their communities but in the whole district. Their public stand for the NSDAP, therefore, had not only local but regional impact.

Mayor Deininger became the county advisor for agricultural affairs in 1931, and his involvement in the party helped establish the image of the NSDAP as a party in which agrarian interests were very important. Especially a man like Deininger, who was nominated as a National Socialist Reichstag candidate in 1932, was seen as a guarantee that the influence of peasants on the party was secured. This was a decisive precondition for winning a certain trust in the broad rural population. Pro-peasant slogans alone would no doubt have faded without much notice had they not come from the mouths of trusted and confidence-inspiring persons.

The effectiveness of the newly won peasant representatives of the party was clearly revealed during the presidential campaigns in the spring of 1932. The fact that Hitler's opponent in these campaigns was named Hindenburg posed a ticklish problem for the Nazis, which they nonetheless solved with an astonishing instinct for and psychological sensitivity to the mentality of their potential voters. They knew only too well how many admirers Hindenburg had in this region, having themselves almost to a man voted for the Field Marshal in 1925. Thus any sort of attack on Hindenburg personally was avoided at all costs. Only in his function as the candidate of the 'bankrupt system parties' was he attacked. These parties, the Nazis implied, had 'appropriated' this honourable personality, because otherwise they had no one to put up. In addition, Hindenburg's advanced age was also brought into play in a very smooth way. An appeal in the regional press signed by Mayor Deininger noted that it was hardly a shame when the old peasant passed his farm on to the young. That was language the peasants understood.

The results of the presidential elections in the district as well as the returns from the Reichstag elections later in the same year demonstrated the effects of the NSDAP's ability to present itself as a 'pro-peasant' party. The Bauernbund again lost more than half of its votes, dropping from 20.7 (1930) to 8.2 per cent, while the

NSDAP, with almost 35 per cent of the vote in each of these elections, became the strongest party in the district. The number of elections in 1932 (two rounds of the presidential elections, one Landtag campaign and two Reichstag elections) also revealed that the transformation of the district's electoral behaviour had now stabilised and that a new, stable political landscape had emerged. The basic regional pattern remained in tact, only now the strongholds of the Bauernbund were almost completely occupied by the NSDAP. The bastions of the BVP, on the other hand, proved essentially stable, while the working-class communities remained the domain of the socialist parties.

The NSDAP was increasingly becoming a party of peasants and country dwellers. In 1930 the small towns and rural communities had each contributed approximately half of the party's votes, but in 1932 the latter accounted for over 63 per cent. As expected, the Nazis achieved their best results in the two Protestant villages, Riedheim and Burtenbach (over 90 per cent), but in five Catholic villages, all of which had been strongholds of the Bauernbund, the party gained an absolute majority. In 27 communities they attracted between 25 and 50 per cent, and in 33 communities the Nazi vote fell below 25 per cent. In 1930 there had been at least one community in which the NSDAP failed to win a single vote, but in 1932 the lowest Nazi vote reached almost 10 per cent. All the communities were infected with the Nazi virus, though to varying degrees. Indeed, the Nazi vote ranged between 10 and 90 per cent.

The stabilisation of these new electoral patterns, of this new political landscape, cannot be attributed to the spread of the NSDAP's organisation, for it remained extraordinarily underdeveloped in the countryside. During 1930 not a single new branch was established, and only six came into being in the rural communities in 1932. Membership figures were also quite low in these *Landgemeinden*. The degree of organisation, measured by local membership expressed as a percentage of the local Nazi vote, lay only between 5 and 7 per cent in the small towns and at a mere 3 per cent in the rural communities. The image of a 'radical party', which the NSDAP was not completely able to shake despite its efforts at social recognition, may well have been the reason for this reserve among peasant notables.

Those communal leaders who had set off this electoral transformation were certainly sympathisers but only rarely members of the NSDAP. In communities with only an average Nazi vote it was exceptional to find well-known and respected local notables who were openly committed to the NSDAP. By contrast, all the community councillors of Protestant Burtenbach and Riedheim were seen as enthusiastic National Socialists, though that didn't necessarily mean that they were actually party members. While Mayor Deininger of Burtenbach was involved in the party as a county agricultural advisor and Reichstag candidate, Mayor Honold confined himself to endorsements at campaign rallies without himself actually joining the party. In Burtenbach, the pastor also openly endorsed the NSDAP, and the leadership of the NSDAP's local branch was in the hands of a forestry official, who as chairman of the veterans' association also belonged to the circle of local notables.

A definite 'infrastructure' of pro-Nazi opinion leaders can also be located in the Catholic strongholds of the NSDAP, but the relationships are somewhat more complicated and murkier than in the clearly Nazi-oriented Protestant *Landgemeinden*. In the Nazi Catholic communities, a number of respected local notables could be found who acted on behalf of the NSDAP and thus set the tone for the views of the majority of local voters. In general, however, the notables tended to refrain from joining the party. If an *Ortsgruppe* or 'strongpoint' was present in a community, its leadership was usually composed of people who did not enjoy any special standing in the community and did not belong to the circle of peasant notables.

A few examples will illustrate the relationships in pro-Nazi Catholic communities. In Deffingen, the entire community council was viewed as National Socialist, the sole exception being the pro-BVP mayor. The most active party members, however, were two young peasants — two friends, both very much involved in the local agricultural associations. Both sprang from respected families. Their fathers were local notables (chairman of the veterans' association, for example) who were certainly pro-Nazi but did not actively participate in the party. Similarly, in Limbach the majority of the community councillors sympathised with the NSDAP, but the local branch leader was a younger peasant who had not played any significant role in the life of the community. A similar constellation existed in the National Socialist stronghold of Landensberg. In Autenried, on the other hand, the community council remained divided between Bauernbund supporters and advocates of National Socialism. Again, however, the leading party activist and branch leader was the village school teacher. This constellation was also quite common. Although young peasants were numerically dominant in the NSDAP's rural elite, civil servants, especially teachers and forestry officials, were strikingly overrepresented, constituting a high proportion of the rural party leadership.

One segment of the party's activists in the rural communities were former members of the Bauernbund, another segment young peasants who had not been previously active politically. The rest, especially the civil servants and teachers, were Nazis who had long stood close to the party. While teachers and civil servants became involved in the NSDAP for ideological reasons, the young peasants brought thoroughly economic hopes to their participation in the party. The leader of the NSDAP's *Stützpunkt* in Landensberg, described his political path in the following way:

I was born on 12 June 1901 as the thirteenth child of a farm family . . . After attending primary and secondary school, I learned farming from my father . . . During the World War six of my brothers were in the field, three of whom died a hero's death while two others came back severely disabled.

In 1926 I married and took over the farm. Since I had three children from this marriage, I began the hard struggle for a living. The farm consisted of nothing but old buildings and only . . . about seven hectares. At that time I had four cows, two oxen and a few calves in the barn. In addition, I incurred about RM5000 in debts . . . Years of hard work followed for my wife and me, for we couldn't afford any help on the farm. Then came the time of economic collapse. The price of milk sank and the price of cows fell more and more. Occasional accidents in the barn increased our woes. Soon I couldn't see my way out, for in spite of our great thrift and effort, the money just wouldn't go around any more.

During these years a good friend helped me sometimes during the harvest. He worked as an apprentice for my brother and already belonged to the NSDAP. We sometimes talked about current political issues, about the general economic situation, and he used these opportunities to familiarise me with the party's basic points. He knew how to convince me salvation and help could be expected only from this party. I finally gave in to his pressure and 1 May 1930 became a member of the Nazi Party. I didn't stand alone as a member of this party, for the majority of the peasants were already Hitler supporters and voters . . . Until

31 December 1931 I was, however, the only member of the party in the village. At this time the branch leader of Röfingen held a recruitment meeting in nearby Glöttweng with the Günzburg county leader as speaker. The latter recruited twelve new members, who then elected me as *Stützpunktleiter* on the following Sunday.[3]

The NSDAP was certainly no longer merely a protest party presenting itself to the public as a political vehicle for the expression of disaffection and dissatisfaction. For peasants it had become a party that awakened positive expectations and on which they placed their hopes. Like the leader of the Landensberg 'strongpoint', many peasants believed that 'salvation and help' could only be expected from the Nazis.

Continuity of Interest or a Shift in Consciousness? Causes and Motives for Political Reorientation

In the Günzburg district the NSDAP emerged as the successor of the Bauernbund not only in the political landscape but in the expectations of the voters as well. Yet, how could the party cut a profile of itself as a quasi agrarian interest party? In its electoral campaigns, the NSDAP appealed more directly and frequently to farmers than to any other occupational group. In each campaign of 1932 a major peasants' rally was held, and the theme 'National Socialism and Agriculture' had dominated Nazi propaganda events in the rural communities since 1931. At these rallies, the peasants actually heard almost nothing concrete about the causes of the current agricultural situation or about the measures for improvement proposed by the Nazis. Campaign speeches in the rural communities — as elsewhere — were largely devoted to descriptions of the general economic and foreign policy situation, attacks against the government and the 'Bolshevist threat'. Romantic themes, glorifying work and sometimes 'Blood and Soil', were also frequently sounded.

Participants in such events actually found out very little about the NSDAP's agricultural programme. The slogan — 'Break Interest Slavery!' — was still the party's most concrete statement. Frequently listeners had to be satisfied with the general declaration that Hitler, the saviour, would lead Germany and the *Bauernstand* out of misery 'with a strong hand'. Just how the planned 'total solution', the creation of work and bread for the entire *Volk*, and mysterious job creation programme would look, one simply had to infer from suggestions and hints.

Attuned to the practices of the Bauernbund, the peasants were accustomed to hearing specific measures discussed in detail during such meetings. Thus in National Socialist gatherings, specific questions about, for example, blocking the importation of refrigerated meat, raising butter tariffs, or introducing a beer tax were repeatedly raised, but such queries remained almost completely unanswered.

The success of the NSDAP among the agrarian electorate simply cannot be explained by National Socialist electoral propaganda. Indeed, the formal campaign had only a limited function and was supplemented by 'unofficial' or informal word-of-mouth agitation. Even though only indirect indications of the content of this underground propaganda can be found, these examples are certainly sufficient to illustrate the differences between the sober propaganda of the Bauernbund and National Socialist *Interessenpolitik*. In a truly unscrupulous and demagogic way, the Nazis appealed to very specific economic interests, promising solutions to agrarian problems that defied all sense of political responsibility. When, for example, shortly after the Nazi seizure of power, many peasants began to pay their help below the established wage scale, it was because the disappearance of such 'Marxist achievements' had been promised or at least intimated by the Nazis. Without doubt the slogan 'Break Interest Slavery!' was translated into everyday speech in such a way that many peasants hoped for a quick cancellation of all debts. From the reports of the regional administration it is clear that many peasants who could not pay their taxes were encouraged to go on a tax strike 'since soon everything will be different'.

This revolutionary mood encouraged by the Nazis represented a last hope of somehow coming out of economic chaos for many financially strapped peasants, since many peasants saw certain bankruptcy in the preservation of orderly conditions and a strict observance of the laws of the state. If, for example, a peasant, in his despair, simply slaughtered a not yet paid for pig immediately after delivery, the sheriff would mercilessly intervene on behalf of the livestock dealer. Given this oppression by the severity of the state and the law, symbolised and personified by the 'tax collector' (finance officials), the sheriff, mayor,[4] and police, something like an 'anarchistic', anti-state attitude arose within broad segments of the peasantry. In their campaign speeches, the Nazis, who otherwise boasted so often about law and order, didn't hesitate to exploit this basic attitude for their own purposes. The deterioration of the economic situation brought peasants increasingly into conflict with virtually every group with which they came into economic contact. In this desperate situation, one had to fight for every penny in order to keep prices as high and costs as low as possible. This, of course, led to countless conflicts with all purveyors of agricultural supplies, cattle dealers, suppliers of fertiliser, artisans who repaired farm machines (buying new equipment was out of the question), as well as with farm hands — indeed, with all sources of external costs, including agricultural co-operatives and occupational organisations, insurance companies and, naturally, with the state in its function as 'tax collector'.

Peasant demands for more 'forcefulness' and militancy were particularly vocal in the conflict over the price of electricity. In dealing with this issue, there was a strong need, many felt, 'to talk to the gentlemen with a different vocabulary'. The way in which the peasant chamber of the district — elected by majority vote — approached this problem was criticised with disdain, although the chamber was naturally compelled to proceed via the protracted legal path of negotiations. The Bauernbund tried to meet this palpable desire for a strong stance by changing its campaign style, appearing as the 'Green Front' and allowing its youth division to march with flag waving. Compared to the NSDAP, however, these efforts were too little too late.

Still, it is hard to understand why so many Bauernbund voters and their opinion leaders turned to a party that presented itself not as a *Standespartei* but as a party of the *Volksgemeinschaft*, a party that aside from almost mystical incantations about 'salvation' remained exceedingly vague in its programmatic statements on peasant interests. One major factor was undoubtedly the realisation that the Bauernbund was much too small and weak to be able to assert peasant interests effectively. It had always been the great flaw in the otherwise thoroughly expedient argumentation of the Bauernbund, which soberly and objectively analysed the situation of agriculture, endorsed certain relief measures and yet couldn't produce the necessary political clout to push through the agreed upon solution.

Even in the early years of the Weimar Republic, the question of whether a *Standespartei* or a *Volkspartei* was better suited to assert peasant interests had played a major role in the competition for rural voters between the BVP and Bauernbund. The Bauernbund argued that the division of the peasantry into two parties was the principal reason for its limited ability to realise its objectives. Only a great 'unification of peasants' and their integration into a single *Standespartei* could improve the situation of the peasantry. The BVP countered this almost mystical demand for a *Bauernverein-igung* with the sober argument that even in the event of complete peasant unity, the *Bauernstand* was simply too weak numerically to attain a majority in parliament.[5]

At the outset of the deepening economic crisis, the idea of peasant unity acquired new life. In early 1929, on the initiative of the Günzburg *Bauernkammer* and with the participation of both the Bauernbund and BVP, a large peasant assembly was held, which, at least at the district level, sealed the long sought peasant union. It was decided to halt hostilities between the parties representing peasant interests, to recognise the necessity of common efforts to press for agreed upon measures (particularly tariff legislation) and to set a good example for the parties by unifying the peasantry on a regional level. Behind this action stood the unspoken admission by the Bauernbund that it alone was too small and weak to advance the interests of the *Bauernstand*.

As the depression deepened, the 'failure' of the peasant *Standes-partei* became increasingly evident. The Nazi slogan 'Only big parties can help now' seemed to indicate the only solution. In addition, the character and extent of the economic crisis made it increasingly clear that in this situation, a policy oriented exclusively toward *Standesinteressen* could not produce a solution, especially for agriculture. The general economic crisis could be mastered only by a general solution, by a political and economic 'total solution'. Only in a prosperous economy could the peasantry thrive once again. Only in such an economy could agriculture count on adequate markets for its products.

Nazi propaganda, of course, left no doubt that the total solution sought by the NSDAP would naturally be favourable to peasants and that the NSDAP felt itself particularly bound to the *Bauernstand*. The ideology of *Volksgemeinschaft* propagated by the Nazis was not directed against the interests of the peasants but against the class interests of the workers who were politically respresented by the SPD. The NSDAP also benefited from the fact that anti-labour, anti-socialist resentment of the peasants was given new impetus by the economic crisis.

The conflict of interest between workers and peasants originated in the last years of the nineteenth century and centred in general on the question of tariffs. While the peasants desired high tariffs on agricultural products to protect price levels, the Social Democrats sought low tariffs to secure lower prices for food and thus a higher standard of living for the working class. Yet this rather abstract battle, fought out in parliament, hardly encroached directly on relations between the Bauernbund and working-class organisations at the regional level. The conflict was viewed as unavoidable. 'The opposition between producers and consumers is just a fact of life. The producer demands a fair price for his work, while the consumer wants his food at prices he can afford.'[6] The Bauernbund's campaign speakers naturally treated the Social Democrats as political opponents but as worthy opponents. The SPD was a 'legitimate German party'.[7] Indeed, the Social Democrats could serve as a model for peasants, since they had succeeded in organising the workers and thus effectively asserting their interests politically.

During the revolution of 1918–19, however, sharp conflicts and direct clashes took place between working class and *Bauernstand* at the regional level. The source of this conflict centred on the controls over food supplies and agricultural products introduced by the workers' councils, which were violently rejected by the peasants' councils. The peasants' councils threatened a 'meat strike', refusing to meet the prescribed quotas, and the workers' councils responded with open or veiled threats of a civil war.[8]

At the height of the depression a new and fierce conflict between representatives of peasant and working-class interests erupted at the grassroots level. Since contemplating strikes or wage hikes was impossible with six million unemployed, the unions concentrated their energies on prices. The first 'pro-consumer action' was initiated by the Günzburg Labour Cartel in response to an effort by the district *Bauernkammer* to prop up the price of milk. In order to do something about the catastrophic situation in the milk sector, farmers, acting together, were to withhold a portion of their milk and thus stabilise milk prices. The Social Democrats and unions threatened an organised boycott. With this conflict directly touching the lives of its combatants, this 'milk war' was not fought with the necessary coolness and sobriety but with open hostility and hate.

The anti-socialist resentment of the peasants was not, however, based exclusively on the 'pro-consumer' posture of the working-class organisations but was also directed against the sociopolitical successes of the workers' movement, against 'excessive social legislation', especially the binding wage scale with its 'levelling' tendencies that 'alienated worker from employer'. The fact that flight from the land could not be braked, not to mention reversed, in spite of high unemployment in industry must have seemed strange to peasants. The unemployed obviously preferred to live off their paltry relief than to take jobs available to them in agriculture. In the eyes of many peasants, this merely confirmed the 'perversity' of the 'excessive social legislation'.

While the intensification of this anti-socialist resentment clearly redounded to the benefit of the National Socialist movement, anti-communist, 'anti-Bolshevist' sentiment probably played a much less significant role in the political orientation of peasants toward the NSDAP than it might superficially appear. To be sure, the mounting threat of Bolshevism was stressed in Nazi electoral propaganda, and yet the fear of a Bolshevist takeover cannot have played a central role as a motive, as an impetus for turning to National Socialism. No such fear existed in a practical sense, because the spectre of Bolshevism, in spite of the six million KPD votes, was simply too unrealistic. While one can easily ascertain signs of a growing anti-socialist sentiment in the everyday life of the region, similar indications of a serious, realistic fear of a communist takeover cannot be found.

On the other hand, the suggestive and autosuggestive fear of Bolshevism did play an important psychological role. It justified the call for a large party and created an artificial polarisation, an apparent *Zwangssituation*, in which one could convince oneself that no other course was possible except to support the only large party that could ward off this 'menace'. This may have helped many 'apostate' Bauernbund supporters overcome their cognitive dissonances, their internal contradictions and scruples in turning to National Socialism. Indeed, it may have helped justify their 'betrayal of the Bauernbund' to themselves and others.

What role did nationalism play in the political reorientation of the peasantry, in the shift from the Bauernbund to National Socialism? Does the rush to the NSDAP reflect a surge of nationalist sentiment? Before we can ask whether, and, if yes, why a rise in nationalism occurred at this time, we must first come to grips with peasant attitudes at the outset of the period. What were the national sentiments of the peasants in general? According to the reports on public opinion sent by the district commissioner to the regional governor, peasant national consciousness was very weakly developed. He frequently complained about the peasants' strong economic or materialist orientation, maintaining that their indifference to national questions had reached 'a lamentable degree . . . of unreliability'. This orientation was particularly obvious in the reaction to the Franco-Belgian invasion of the Ruhr. Although a certain upsurge of patriotic feeling could be initially observed in the countryside, interest in these events quickly faded. In the city of Günzburg protest demonstrations were held, but 'despite the efforts of the district commissioner', none took place in the countryside.[9] It would, however, certainly be wrong to conclude from the statements of the ardently nationalistic district commissioner that the peasants lacked any national consciousness. Indeed, nationalist sentiment occupied a firm place in the culture of rural everyday life, in associational life, especially in the veterans' associations, and on certain occasions, especially during the 1925 presidential elections, it came very clearly to the surface.

A rise of nationalist feeling during the Depression cannot, however, be seen. Even if one can assume that economic misery might have led to a search for a 'new scapegoat' and that the Versailles treaty might be viewed as the cause of all Germany's troubles, there is simply no evidence to support such a supposition. If this sort of resentment had played a central role in the attitudes of the rural population it would most certainly have been exploited by Nazi propaganda. Yet the Nazis rarely dealt with the Versailles treaty in their agitation. Instead, it was the ineffectual German parties — 'quacks trying to heal the German people' — that were singled out as being responsible for Germany's agony.

Nationalism may, on the other hand, have played a psychological role similar to fear of Bolshevism in the political reorientation of the peasantry — not as a motive, a driving force, but as an integrating factor for the heterogeneous National Socialist movement. Nazi opinion leaders in the countryside represented more than interest-oriented options; they also embodied a living nationalism in the culture of the region's everyday life.

Anti-Semitism also probably played a minor role in the turn to National Socialism. The Nazi campaigns were not messianic crusades for *völkisch*, anti-Semitic ideas. Indeed, anti-Semitic themes were clearly underplayed — and not just in this region.[10] There was, to be sure, a clearly discernible anti-Semitic sentiment among the peasants that was primarily economic in origin (many cattle dealers in the district were Jews). This sentiment was, however, accompanied by a certain respect for the accomplishments of Jewish dealers, a respect which found expression in the district with the common saying: 'If no Jew is at the market, there will be no trade.'[11] It is certainly conceivable that for some peasants mounting conflicts with cattle dealers during the difficult economic situation increased this anti-Semitic attitude, but for the peasantry as a whole, anti-Semitism probably did not possess the necessary attraction for it to constitute important political capital.

At any rate, the Nazi peasant leaders of the region did not personify the radical anti-Semitism that was so typical of the old guard of the National Socialist movement. When trade with Jews was forbidden after Hitler's assumption of power, police investigations revealed that many Nazi Party members and functionaries were among the peasants still secretly doing business with Jews. The attitude of the National Socialist peasant leaders is strikingly illustrated by a case involving Christoph Honold, the mayor of Riedheim. Honold was considered one of the strongest early supporters of the NSDAP in the district, a man who had actively campaigned for the party without, however, officially joining before 1933. Since he was widely recognised as an energetic advocate of peasant interests and was a member of the district *Bauernkammer*, his influence extended far beyond his own community.

When in 1935 a Jewish cattle dealer was forbidden to conduct his business in the district by the Nazi *Kreisleitung*, the Nazi authorities promised him that if he could produce written confirmation from ten communities that he had always behaved properly, they would grant him a permit. Of course, they were confident that no mayor would dare extend any support to him. Yet, when the cattle dealer tried, he discovered that several mayors were willing to help him but didn't want to be the first to sign on. Honold, however, agreed to sign, and when he did, all the other mayors followed his example. When Honold was subsequently interrogated by outraged Nazi officials, he refused to buckle, stating that he was 'bound by [his] oath of office to aid in establishing the truth in all matters regardless of the individuals involved'.[12]

This example of unusually courageous behaviour should make it clear that anti-Semitism was certainly not the decisive factor that drove peasant opinion leaders into the arms of the National Socialists. On the other hand, the radical anti-Semitism of the party, even if it was temporarily downplayed, cannot have been hidden from these men, whose moral guilt lies in the fact that they basically ignored such 'ugly side-effects' of the NSDAP. Without the support of peasant opinion leaders like Mayor Honold, who clearly and not entirely unjustly enjoyed the trust of their communities and who placed their own personal reputations in the service of this criminal movement, the NSDAP would hardly have been able to win the peasant electorate to the extent that it did.

Conclusion

The growth of the National Socialist electorate within the peasantry proceeded in two distinct phases. The first phase from 1928 to 1930 can be characterised as the phase of the protest movement. The party's electoral propaganda in the 1930 Reichstag campaign was completely obstructionist without offering a political alternative or ideological self-portrait. The NSDAP presented itself as a political vehicle for expressing protest and dissatisfaction, as the embodiment of 'a great reckoning' with the old 'ineffectual' parties which were made responsible for all that had gone wrong. That election constituted a more pronounced, more radical version of the other protest election of May 1924. In both 1924 and 1930 what might be termed the 'radicalisation effect' was in operation, an effect anchored in Weimar political culture and reflected in the tendency to vote for a radical party during periods of economic crisis without, however, breaking completely with one's traditional partisan allegiances.

The results of the 1930 Reichstag election created an entirely new situation for the party. The prospect of actually attaining power was now no longer completely unrealistic, and the party was, therefore, compelled to indicate what it would do with that power, to make, in other words, programmatic statements. The second phase in the rise of the NSDAP can, therefore, be viewed as the phase of the pseudo-programme party. People expected answers from the party, and Nazi campaign leaders, especially at the grassroots, played heavily on these expectations. Defaming the government and the old parties, of course, remained a major component of the party's campaign appeals but slipped increasingly into the background. More and more the NSDAP sought to present National Socialist solutions, to offer a National Socialist alternative. Despite the utterly vague and unreflective 'programmatic' pronouncements — hence pseudo-programme party — the NSDAP succeeded in developing the image of a 'constructive' party. As an exclusively destructive protest party it would not have been able to maintain and expand its constituency over time.

Had the party relied exclusively on its inadequate electoral propaganda, the NSDAP would never have succeeded in portraying itself as a constructive party of regeneration. Nor would it have been able to win the trust needed by a programme party to mould a durable partisan affiliation — something lacking in protest movements which are tied to swings of the public mood. Nor was the written programme of the NSDAP — the Twenty-Five Points and the agricultural programme — decisive for the success of the party. The written or spoken word alone cannot manufacture trust. Far more decisive is *who* says something, who represents the party and presents its programme.

During 1931–2 the NSDAP developed very rapidly in the region. The 'movement' attracted a great number of sympathisers, local opinion leaders and agitators. As difficult as it was for the party, with its still troublesome radical image, to win the broad circle of rural notables, much less induce them to join the party, the NSDAP did succeed in attracting a whole set of important grassroots opinion leaders, especially in the agricultural occupational associations. These people — not campaign pronouncements — personified the programme of the NSDAP for the voters, providing the ostensible guarantee of a 'pro-peasant' Nazi policy. This process of winning opinion leaders with established interest-political credentials cannot, as is so often done, be subsumed under the concept of Nazi 'infiltration' or 'occupation' of peasant interest organisations. It was not penetration of these organisations from without but the conversion of important opinion leaders within them that created the foundations on which the NSDAP could build the trust of the peasant electorate.

One of the major preconditions for the conversion of opinion leaders and voters to National Socialism was the decay and decomposition of traditional partisan loyalties. Growing doubts about the ability of the Bauernbund to represent and assert the interests of agriculture finally led to the search for a new, effective interest organisation. The new party had to guarantee both a continuity of interest representation and a greater capacity to assert those interests. Both seemed assured by the NSDAP. Its militant anti-socialist, anti-union orientation, its agricultural programme and its internal organisation of agricultural interests (the agrarpolitischer Apparat, with its agricultural advisors at all levels) seemed to guarantee the continuity of peasant interest representation. Similarly, the size of the NSDAP after its electoral victory as a protest party in 1930 became one of the most important sources of its attraction. This provided the basis for peasant expectations of great effectiveness in attaining political goals. Equally important in this regard was the convincingly militant posture of the NSDAP, its demonstration of energy and activity. The militance and radicalism of the party spoke to the needs of broad electoral strata in this situation and eliminated from the field the BVP, which was also competing for Bauernbund voters.

The move to National Socialism was, therefore, based on the continuity of basic interest-political positions, though in the new form of internal party representation. The principle of internal representation and organisation within a party was nothing really new for the political culture of the region. The competition between the Bauernbund and the BVP for the rural electorate was charac-terised by a conflict between the principles of representation in one's own *Standespartei* or internal representation within a broader *Volkspartei*. The movement for unity between the BVP and Bauernbund and the electoral shift from the Bauernbund to the BVP and ultimately to the *Sammlungsbewegung*, the people's party NSDAP, signalled the growing desire during the Depression for unity, for concentration in a large and powerful party.

With its salient posture as a party that transcended *Stand*, the NSDAP would, however, never have succeeded in becoming so attractive to former Bauernbund supporters if they had not become convinced that a comprehensive solution to the economic crisis — one that went beyond *Standesinteressen* — was necessary. The Social Democrats had formulated this most succinctly: without an increase in the purchasing power of the workers, there can be no recovery for agriculture. It was the Nazis, however, who profited from this insight.

The NSDAP's concrete statements about the much-sought-after 'comprehensive solution' were nonetheless exceedingly thin. In this regard, the party tried to generate a completely irrational trust in

'Hitler, the saviour'. Sober opinion leaders and voters apparently believed they had no other choice than to play the unknown Hitler card. Only the panic engendered by the Depression and the lower expectations of this situation can explain how so many peasant opinion leaders could fall victim to the seductive power of this blind faith in recovery.[13]

Thus, for these men, turning to National Socialism represented a decision that was in its essence sheer expedience. It was an expedient search for a new, more effective representation of their interests. Basic National Socialist affinities and anxiety over the Bolshevist threat certainly had psychologically important 'catalysing functions' in overcoming cognative dissonances in this political reorientation. But this core of expedience, of myopic pseudo-rationality, which was reflective of a willingness to renounce political control in exchange for ostensible protection of peasant *Standesinteressen*, was an important precondition for the NSDAP's successful campaign to win peasant voters and their opinion leaders.

Notes

1. Zdenek Zofka, *Die Ausbreitung des Nationalsozialismus auf dem Lande. Eine regionale Fallstudie zur politischen Einstellung der Landbevölkerung in der Zeit des Aufstiegs und der Machtergreifung der NSDAP 1928–1936* (Munich, 1979). The notes in this revised excerpt are based throughout on the original. References to secondary literature and other sources, which are provided in detail there, have, therefore, been omitted here.

2. NSDAP speaker Otto Herrmann/Mindelheim in a campaign rally during 1932. See the *Schwäbisches Volksblatt* (*SVB*), 8 March 1932.

3. Spruchkammer Günzburg, File Georg Rössle.

4. The mayors also complained about persecutions. See, for example, the letter to the editor, *SVB*, 27 February 1932.

5. First uttered by the 'peasant doctor' Georg Heim, chairman of the Bavarian Christian Peasants' Association, a peasant organisation linked to the BVP. See *Günz-und Mindelbote*, 22 May 1920.

6. The leader of the Swabian Peasants' League Theodor Dirr/Anhofen at a Bauernbund rally 1918. *SVB*, 30 December 1918.

7. As late as the Landtag elections in April 1932 the Bauernbund defended the SPD, condemning Nazi attacks against this 'legitimate German party'. See *SVB*, 23 April 1932.

8. See Zdenek Zofka, *Streiflichter zur Geschichte der Arbeiterbewegung im Landkreis Günzburg* (Günzburg, 1979), p. 26.

9. Reports to the Regierungspräsident, 31 January and 15 February 1923, Staatsarchiv Neuburg/Danube, Fasc. 4100.

10. See Martin Broszat, *Der Staat Hitlers* (Munich, 1969), p. 45.

11. Report of the Gendarmeriestation Ichenhausen, 30 January 1934, Staats-

archiv Neuburg/Danube, Fasc. 4424. The report describes the difficulties of teaching the population the 'correct' anti-Semitic consciousness.

12. Police transcript of the interrogation of Honold on 5 December 1935. Staatsarchiv Neuburg/Danube, Fasc. 6864.

13. See Karl Dietrich Bracher, *Die deutsche Diktatur. Entstehung, Struktur, Folgen des Nationalsozialismus* (Frankfurt, 1979), p. 169; Broszat, *Der Staat Hitlers*, p. 62; and Zofka, *Die Ausbreitung des Nationalsozialismus auf dem Lande*, p. 344f.

4 CENTRAL CONTROL VERSUS REGIONAL AUTONOMY: A CASE STUDY OF NAZI PROPAGANDA IN WESTPHALIA, 1925–1932

Detlef Mühlberger

The idea that propaganda played a crucial role in the growth and success of Nazism has been firmly established by historians of quite diverse persuasions. The view is now quite commonplace in numerous accounts dealing with the rise of Nazism that it was primarily the formidable and increasingly sophisticated propaganda machine developed by the Nazis which contributed so much to the transformation of the NSDAP from peripheral political sect, on the fringes of German politics in the 1920s, to its dominant position in Weimar politics by the early 1930s.[1] This current orthodoxy, despite one recent attempt at revision, generally still holds.[2]

Given the centrality of the importance attached to propaganda in the explanations advanced by historians to account for the growing Nazi success in the increasingly violent political contests which punctuated the final years of the Weimar Republic, it is surprising how variable in scope and quality our knowledge is of diverse aspects of Nazi propaganda. Specialist works dealing specifically with Nazi propaganda concentrate primarily on the Third Reich and give limited space to developments before 1933.[3] Although the general structure of the Nazi Party and its organisational development before 1933 has been subjected to detailed analysis, there is comparatively little information on the formation and history of the *Reichspropaganda Leitung* (RPL) of the NSDAP as such.[4] This manifests itself in the continued confusion among historians as to who headed the apparatus and when.[5] To date, the best insight into the RPL's development is a by-product of a biography of Gregor Strasser.[6] It is only recently that Thomas Childers has closed a major information gap by providing a comprehensive content analysis of the propaganda material furnished to the party by the RPL from the mid-1920s, the volume of which increased into a veritable flood by the time of the 1932 elections.[7]

It is at the regional and local level that Nazi propaganda activity has been most closely investigated.[8] Although the studies available collectively provide a penetrating and fascinating insight into various facets of Nazi propaganda, they generally give little information on the question of the relationship between the RPL and *Gau* propaganda organisations.[9] The one study in which this relationship is clearly portrayed is J. Ciolek-Kümper's work on the Lippe *Landtag* election of 15 January 1933.[10] In this election the RPL stepped in and assumed total control over a regional electoral campaign which had initially been planned, and controlled, by the *Gauleitung* of Westphalia-North.[11] But the Lippe campaign, conducted at a particularly critical stage in the seemingly flagging fortunes of the NSDAP, was extraordinary even by Nazi standards, bringing virtually the whole hierarchy of the party to the villages and small towns of this rural backwater.[12] Given the special circumstances surrounding the election, the conduct of the Lippe campaign does not provide meaningful answers to the issue of central versus regional control of propaganda, nor to such questions as to the degree to which, and the effectiveness with which, regional and local propaganda units transmitted ideas formulated by the RPL. In the Lippe case, the RPL determined tactics and policy from quite early on in the campaign, and completely subordinated the regional propaganda machine to its control, pushing regional issues aside in the process.[13]

The need for specific studies which focus on the as yet unclear relationship between the RPL and the local and regional propaganda apparatus of the Nazi Party, is generally recognised by historians and social scientists working on the problem of the formulation and dissemination of Nazi propaganda. One can but agree with Richard Hamilton that there are a number of problems which need examination, for

> We have an unresolved question with regard to the competing central-control versus local-autonomy hypotheses. The party sent out directives or guidelines for the conduct of campaigns. The question is the degree to which local units adhered to those directives or, alternatively, the degree to which they exercised (or were allowed) local autonomy, following their sense of issue viability.[14]

It is to this set of questions that this case study of the NSDAP's propaganda activities in Westphalia addresses itself.

I

Following the re-formation of the NSDAP by Hitler on 27 February 1925, the prime concern of the rudimentary *Reichsleitung* (RL) which emerged in Munich in 1925, was to create a basic national organisational framework for the NSDAP. This structure was to provide the instrument through which Hitler and the RL were to establish effective organisational and financial control over the party at all levels. It was the energetic party secretary Bouhler, and the efforts of the party treasurer Schwarz, who determined the relationship which developed between the RL and the *Gauleitungen* and *Ortsgruppenleitungen* from 1925 onwards.[15] In contrast to the bureaucratic dynamism of Bouhler and, to a lesser degree, that of Schwarz, the organisational activity of the first head of the RPL, Hermann Esser, appears to have been very limited. It was Bouhler, not Esser, who signed a secret *Rundschreiben* dated 20 March 1926, which was sent to Nazi *Ortsgruppen*, in which the development of a vertical organisational structure for the RPL was initiated.[16] The *Rundschreiben* made clear the considerations which moved Bouhler and the RL in their efforts to create an effective propaganda system. Beyond the simple fact that the NSDAP lacked a centralised, co-ordinated propaganda arm, which was perceived by Bouhler as a major handicap in Nazi efforts to enlighten 'the masses enthusiastic for our idea', Bouhler pointed out that the creation of such a national propaganda framework, linking party headquarters and the localities, was essential if *Ortsgruppen* were to be made aware of the attitude of the RL on policy issues. The desire to project a more uniform propaganda is implicit in the *Rundschreiben*. It suggested that the first task of the propaganda framework was to co-ordinate a nationwide campaign against the ban imposed on Hitler from speaking at public meetings in virtually the whole of Germany. The argument was also put forward in the *Rundschreiben* that a co-ordinated propaganda organisation would place the NSDAP in a stronger position when combating its political opponents, especially the Marxist parties. It was indeed the propaganda apparatus of the latter which served as a model for the Nazis. The *Rundschreiben*, to which an organisational plan was attached, called for the creation of propaganda cells, which were to be established by the *Ortsgruppen* by 26 March. These were to report directly to the propaganda section attached to the *Völkischer Beobachter* in Munich.

The response to the *Rundschreiben* in Westphalia appears to have been somewhat limited as far as generating organisational activity.[17] Even in the efficiently run Bochum district, well administered by Josef Wagner, only the large Bochum *Ortsgruppe* had a propaganda organisation in 1925. The development of a more extensive and effective propaganda network in the Bochum area did not take place until late 1926.[18] It was to be a considerable time before the Westphalian Nazi Party was to possess an adequate propaganda arm. This was due not to any resistance on the part of the local leaders to the ideas contained in Bouhler's *Rundschreiben*, but to the fact that the construction of a propaganda cell was simply beyond the organisational and financial resources of the great majority of Nazi *Ortsgruppen* in Westphalia, many of which were very small. Of the 52 *Ortsgruppen* active in Westphalia by May 1926, 28 had fewer than ten members, of which 13 had a membership of five or less.[19] Most *Ortsgruppen* were hardly in a position to fulfil Bouhler's bureaucratic dreams. The evidence suggests that many struggled to create even a rudimentary party organisation by 1926, never mind propaganda cells.[20] Nor were the organisational demands eased over time, for following the relatively expansionist phase of 1925 and 1926, the Westphalian Nazi movement began to suffer from stagnation. In the course of 1927 and 1928 some *Ortsgruppen* actually lost a significant proportion of their membership.[21] Lacking members, cash and a supply of able organisers, many *Ortsgruppen* lived a shadowy existence until the late 1920s. It was not until the rapid growth of the Westphalian NSDAP in 1929 and 1930 that the Nazis were in a position to overcome these handicaps. It was then that the regional and local party administrations enjoyed rapid growth, funded by a mushrooming membership.[22] In these more favourable circumstances the basic propaganda network, painstakingly developed in the *Gau* by 1928, expanded more rapidly.

In 1926 the desire of the RL to secure greater control over the party's propaganda activity was but one aspect of a determined effort by Hitler, working through the RL, to enforce the *Führerprinzip* on to the party.[23] Bouhler and Schwarz were the instruments used in concretising the concept, and their bureaucratic activism was gradually to enforce the RL's control over the party at the regional and local level. That these centralising efforts created friction and conflict is well known.[24] It took some considerable time before the Westphalian *Gauleiter* Pfeffer was prepared to accept the necessity of administrative centralisation, and the need for the RL's control over such matters as the issue of membership cards.[25] Like so many of his fellow *Gauleiter*, Pfeffer had carved out his *Hausmacht* in the course of 1924. He was used to autonomy, content to rule his *Gau* in his own authoritarian fashion, and resented Munich's insistence on full control, and the restraints on his authority and independence which this implied.[26]

Although Pfeffer had declared for Hitler in the spring of 1925, he did not adopt an attitude of subservience to him.[27] Both in his capacity as *Gauleiter* of Westphalia, and then as part of the tripartite *Gauleitung* of the Ruhr, created in March 1926 through the fusion of *Gaue* Westphalia and Rhineland-North, Pfeffer was not much inclined automatically to accept all of the RL's administrative objectives and ideological pronouncements. Before Hitler called on Pfeffer to head the party's *Sturmabteilung* (SA) in the summer of 1926, Pfeffer was out of step with the RL on a number of issues. As is true even more of Goebbels and Kaufmann, his two colleagues in *Gauleitung* Ruhr, Pfeffer was interested in a more pronounced socialist slant to Nazi propaganda, an approach dictated, in his case, primarily by the socioeconomic structure of the region. This manifested itself in Pfeffer's interest in the formation of a Nazi trades union movement in 1925, an idea which found a negative response from Hitler and the RL.[28] On economic questions in general, and on the issue of the expropriation of the German royal houses in particular, Pfeffer also took a different line from Munich.[29]

How far Pfeffer's ideas and attitudes influenced the propaganda content of the Westphalian NSDAP is difficult to determine. His chief strength was his organisational flair, though as one of the regionally important speakers of the Nazi Party, Pfeffer was in regular contact with the *Bezirksleiter* and the bulk of the *Ortsgruppenleiter*, who were undoubtedly aware of his views. The limited evidence available for 1925 and 1926 suggests that local leaders, beyond the odd general directive which came from the *Gauleitung* occasionally, carried out their propaganda activities as they saw fit, and as local circumstances dictated. *Ortsgruppen* were free to decide on their own priorities in the mid-1920s. For example, in the Bielefeld region *Bezirksleiter* Homann generally determined his propaganda to suit his audiences, and at times even suggested the content and approach to be used by visiting speakers, as is clear from Homann's correspondence with important regional speakers such as Goebbels, who spoke quite frequently in the Bielefeld area from 1925.[30] In the Bochum area, Wagner also allowed the three-man committee in charge of propaganda in his area the freedom to decide on their own priorities. Whereas one argued that the Communist Party (KPD) should be the sole target of attack, the second committee member took the line that all the socialist parties, as well as the parties of the Right, should be fought vigorously. The third member thought it might be useful to co-ordinate and centralise propaganda actions.[31]

There was no uniformity of propaganda content in Rhineland-Westphalia in the mid-1920s, and flexibility of approach characterised the regional propaganda effort. This situation was accepted, indeed encouraged, by Goebbels when he took charge of propaganda following the formation of *Gau* Ruhr.[32] In his speech at the Bochum district conference in October 1926, just before he left the Ruhr to take up his position as *Gauleiter* of Berlin, Goebbels argued that a uniform approach to propaganda was not feasible since the differing political situations in various parts of the *Gaue* had always to be taken into consideration in the framing of propaganda. Goebbels went on to say that the experience he had gathered on his many speaking tours for the party had taught him that propaganda designed to appeal to specific economic interests and the various social groups had to be shaped accordingly.[33]

Given the degree of autonomy enjoyed by the *Ortsgruppenleiter* in Westphalia in the mid-1920s, direct *Gau* control over propaganda content, never mind RPL control, was negligible. There is, however, one significant exception to this situation, provided by the participation of the Westphalian Nazi party in the protest campaign organised by the RL against the ban which prohibited Hitler from speaking at public meetings. The protest campaign was initiated by the RL in the shape of Bouhler's *Rundschreiben* of March 1926, which was followed up by further information and instructions in the *Völkischer Beobachter*.[34] It is clear that *Gauleitung* Ruhr responded to the Munich exhortations and specifically instructed *Bezirksleiter* on 6 April 1926 to agitate against the ban in their areas.[35] Wagner certainly responded to the *Gau Rundschreiben*, and switched his propaganda activity to focus on the ban throughout the Bochum region, and demanded that *Ortsgruppen* under his control do likewise.[36] His instructions were complied with, for a series of Nazi meetings held in Recklinghausen, Buer, Bottrop and Osterfeld in April and May were devoted exclusively to the theme 'Why is Hitler not allowed to speak?' At each meeting members of the audience were encouraged to sign petitions protesting against the ban.[37] Public meetings on similar lines were also organised by Homann in the Bielefeld area.[38]

In the latter half of 1926 changes in personnel took place in the leadership positions of both *Gau* Ruhr and of the RPL. *Gauleitung* Ruhr collapsed in the summer of 1926 due to increasing tensions and differences between the three *Gauleiter*.[39] The problems of the *Gau* were only temporarily solved through the election of Kaufmann as sole *Gauleiter* in June 1926. Following Pfeffer's transfer to Munich to head the SA, and the appointment of Goebbels as *Gauleiter* of Berlin, Kaufmann was soon embroiled in a succession of conflicts with ambitious elements active in various parts of *Gau* Ruhr, a situation which undermined the efficiency of the *Gauleitung* and diminished Kaufmann's authority in 1927 and 1928.[40] At the national level Gregor Strasser took over from Esser as *Reichspropagandaleiter* in September 1926, an appointment which also brought Himmler into the RPL in his capacity as Strasser's deputy. Under the new leadership the RPL began to be more efficient and effective, especially in such matters as the use of propaganda leaflets, posters and the press, and the deployment of party speakers.[41]

These changes in personnel did not affect the conduct of propaganda in *Gau* Ruhr in any significant way. After the campaign against the Hitler ban had dissipated itself in the summer of 1926, the direct connection between regional and local propaganda actions and the RPL was very limited. In one area the forging of a more permanent link between the RPL and the *Gau* can be detected. From 1926 the *Gau* propaganda department began to rely more noticeably on material produced by the RPL. Pamphlets, leaflets and placards printed in Munich, but considered suitable for the region, began to be used in *Gau* propaganda. The use of such RPL material became more evident by the time of the Reichstag election campaign in May 1928.[42] For the most part, however, the period to 1928 was one in which the autonomy of the *Gau* to determine and develop its own propaganda continued. What influenced the content of propaganda was not the RPL, but the outlook of the regional party functionaries, and the influence exerted by the social and religious structure of the Westphalian population. The main propagandists active in Rhineland-Westphalia from 1925, important speakers such as Goebbels, Kaufmann and Wagner, and external speakers who were popular in the area, primarily Gregor

Strasser, generally expressed anti-capitalist and pro-labour sentiments, and attempted to convince the public that the Nazi Party was
a working-class, socialist movement.[43] The dominance of the
working class in the social structure of Westphalia made it impera-
tive, if the NSDAP was to be of any significance, that Nazis
operating in the region projected a leftist orientation and
emphasised those parts of the Nazi programme which had a socialist
flavour. In the Ruhr towns the Nazi speakers generally stressed
their proletarian background, while some occasionally went so far
as to assert that the programmes of the NSDAP and of the KPD
'were almost the same'. The nationalisation plans of the party,
especially of the banks and other financial institutions, were also
frequently stated.[44] These Nazi overtures had some success in
attracting working-class members to the party in *Gau* Ruhr from the
mid-1920s.[45] Beyond these consistent attempts to create a left-wing
image, much of the Nazi propaganda in Westphalia involved the
clarification of what National Socialism stood for. The most
common titles of speeches in the years from 1925 to 1928 were 'The
Aims of the NSDAP', 'What does Adolf Hitler want?', and 'The
Goals of National Socialism'. Anti-Semitism also figured prominently in many of the speeches, while the condemnation of the
Republic, of democracy, of parliament, of the Dawes Plan, and of
the 'System' in general, were also standard features.[46]

The major propaganda activity of the Nazi movement in *Gau*
Ruhr to 1928 was concentrated almost entirely on the urban
centres.[47] This is not surprising given that the NSDAP had first
taken root in the cities and towns of the region in the early 1920s.
The limited organisational base which the NSDAP had acquired by
1925 was concentrated in the towns, where the bulk of its
membership also resided. This is not to ignore the significant rural
propaganda campaigns carried out by Homann in north-east
Westphalia, or by Teipel in the Sauerland.[48] But it was in the towns
that the Nazis were able to develop quite sizeable *Ortsgruppen* by
1928, which could boast a much more developed organisational
structure than had been the case in the mid-1920s. Despite the
generally slow growth of the Nazi Party in Westphalia, the bureaucratisation tendency within the party at the regional and local levels
after 1925 was inevitable, given the increasing administrative
demands made, and financial controls introduced, by the RL.[49] The
'one-man-band' type of *Ortsgruppenleitung*, quite typical in 1925,
was no longer feasible in later years as the size of *Ortsgruppen*

increased, and as the tasks allotted to *Ortsgruppenleiter* by both the *Gauleitung* and the RL became more onerous, and more difficult to avoid.[50] The propaganda arm of the Westphalian Nazi Party benefited to some extent from the bureaucratisation of the party. By 1928 propaganda sections were the norm in the larger *Ortsgruppen*, and the nucleus of a corps of able speakers had emerged at the *Gau* and at the *Ortsgruppen* level.[51] Even though propaganda specialists were still few in number, those who had survived their apprenticeship in the rough and tumble of local agitation were generally experienced speakers committed to the rag-bag of ideas which National Socialism represented.[52] The Reichstag election of May 1928 was to provide the party and its propaganda section, both at the national and regional level, with its first major test since the re-formation of the NSDAP in 1925.

II

At the national level the party had been preparing itself for an election for some considerable time. As early as September 1927 the RL had warned the *Gaue* and *Ortsgruppen* to prepare themselves financially for the 'coming election campaign'.[53] By the end of the year the RL announced the details of its planning and control procedures, which would allow the pursuit of a more centralised, co-ordinated election campaign.[54] At the beginning of 1928, on 2 January, important personnel changes took place in the RL and RPL, when Strasser took over the office of *Reichsorganisationsleiter* from the ineffective Heinemann, while Hitler, at least nominally, became head of the RPL. For the RPL the change meant little in terms of the administration of RPL affairs, which Himmler continued to control, as he had done under Strasser.[55]

It is probable that the RL's increasing concern about the possibility of coming elections also began to exercise Kaufmann's mind, for in the spring of 1928 he urged *Ortsgruppen* to establish reserve funds so that they would not be surprised by a snap election.[56] When that possibility became reality, Kaufmann made it crystal clear that neither the RL nor the *Gauleitung* could provide any financial help to the *Ortsgruppen* during the election, and that credit would not be extended for the purchase of election material required by the *Ortsgruppen*. The latter were to receive only such pamphlets and posters for which they had paid in advance. Moreover, those

Ortsgruppen still in arrears with the payment of membership dues were threatened that they would not receive either speakers or election material unless the arrears were settled.[57]

In the run-up to the polling day of 10 May, which involved *Gauleitung* Ruhr in conducting a Reichstag and a Prussian *Landtag* campaign simultaneously, both the RL and the *Gauleitung* had plenty of advice to offer the *Ortsgruppen* as to how they should conduct their campaign. The general guidelines for the election were sent out to the *Gaue* and the independent *Ortsgruppen* in a *Rundschreiben* by the RL in early May. This emphasised in particular that 'polemics against *Wehrverbände* such as the *Stahlhelm*' were to be avoided, and that critical remarks concerning the monarchy and the ex-Kaiser should not be made, since such criticism, it was argued, could alienate potential right-wing voters from the NSDAP. The authority of Hitler was invoked towards the end of the *Rundschreiben* to underline the need for the movement to observe the policy lines as laid down in the *Völkischer Beobachter* when preparing speeches, or in the drafting of articles in the party press.[58] More detailed instructions on specific aspects of campaign activity were pumped out through the *Völkischer Beobachter*, perhaps the only instant channel of communication between the RL and the Nazi movement at large at that time.[59]

The overall guidelines sent out by the RL on 8 May do not appear to have been passed on to the *Ortsgruppen* by Kaufmann, at least not in written form. The last of Kaufmann's set of campaign instructions had probably been sent to the *Ortsgruppen* before the RL's *Rundschreiben* of 8 May reached him.[60] Overall, Kaufmann's *Rundschreiben* dealt almost exclusively with organisational aspects of the electoral campaign, and did not give any specific instructions as to which issues were to be projected in campaign propaganda. Kaufmann did, however, recommend a number of posters which he deemed effective, one of which was locally produced by the Düsseldorf *Ortsgruppe*, while three others which he thought useful were available through the Streiter Verlag of Zwickau. For house-to-house canvassing the *Ortsgruppen* were advised to use Goebbels' *Das kleine ABC,* Jung's *Nationaler oder internationaler Sozialismus*, and past numbers of the *NS-Briefe*, the latter available at a cheap rate of 150 for 8 Marks. The nearest Kaufmann came to determining the content of local propaganda was in the provision of a number of texts for leaflets, which *Ortsgruppen* were encouraged to use.[61] It was made clear to the *Ortsgruppen* that the acquisition of material provided by the RPL was up to them. It was the responsibility of the *Ortsgruppen* to order, and pay for, such literature as they required.[62] All the *Ortsgruppen*, and especially those with limited finance, were instructed to use the texts appearing in the *Völkischer Beobachter*, since these could be cheaply reproduced locally.

It was in the techniques of the art of grassroots campaigning that Kaufmann's *Rundschreiben* were most precise and detailed. Here one can see a centralising attempt by the *Gauleiter*, who tried to influence the propaganda methods employed in the campaign. The suggested strategy to be adopted by the *Bezirke* and *Ortsgruppen* involved specific activity in two distinct phases. In phase one, in the month before polling day, *Ortsgruppen* were instructed to put their major emphasis on the distribution of leaflets through intensive house-to-house canvassing, the suggested ideal time for this to be done being a fortnight before polling day. Particular attention was to be given in phase one to those areas of the *Gau* in which the party had neither *Ortsgruppen* nor members. In phase two, the last few days before the election, *Bezirksleiter* and *Ortsgruppenleiter* were exhorted 'to mobilise all their human and material resources' to maximise impact. This was the time, as far as Kaufmann was concerned, when posters, placards and general street propaganda were most productive and effective.

These various instructions emanating from the *Gauleitung* reflect a quite sophisticated approach to campaigning, at least by the standards of the 1920s. The projected 'ideal-type' campaign did not, however, materialise at the local level to any extent, for few of the *Ortsgruppen* in *Gau* Ruhr had the necessary resources to finance an effective campaign in 1928. Probably only the very large Nazi *Ortsgruppen*, those of Hattingen and Bochum in the case of Westphalia, had the manpower and finance to conduct a vigorous and enterprising election.[63] In much of *Gau* Ruhr Nazi activity was severely restricted by lack of cash, paucity of able speakers, limited membership, and the often poor response made to the few public meetings the party was able to organise.[64] With polling day but 12 days away, Kaufmann was in despair and bemoaned the very limited effort that was being made by the bulk of the *Ortsgruppen*. As he lamented in his last *Rundschreiben* before the election, few *Ortsgruppen* had ordered even the cheapest propaganda material, such as placards and posters, from the *Gau* propaganda centre.[65] The type of campaigning actually carried out on a shoe-string budget, which many *Ortsgruppen* were forced to do by necessity, is typified by the Bielefeld *Ortsgruppe*, which lacked even the cash to buy sufficient posters to make its presence felt in the town, and resorted to daubing slogans on houses and on public buildings.[66] The RL's and *Gauleitung*'s theory of how an election campaign should be conducted, and the way in which it was actually carried out at the local level, were hardly identical.[67]

That the outcome of the election, which brought the NSDAP a mere 2.6 per cent of the national vote, was a disappointment for the leadership of the party, is an understatement.[68] The only ray of light discerned by the RL in its analysis of the national poll were the good results achieved by the party in a number of predominantly agrarian areas.[69] In Westphalia the Nazis performed well below the national average. In Westphalia-South (electoral district 18) the party secured only 1.6 per cent, marginally better than the 1.1 per cent polled by the NSDAP in Westphalia-North (electoral district 17).[70] In *Gau* Ruhr, Kaufmann's analysis of the party's performance noted that while the urban returns were 'satisfactory', the results achieved by the party in rural areas, such as the Arnsberg, Siergerland and Bielefeld regions, were 'astonishing'.[71] In the Protestant Siegerland the party did indeed secure some very good returns in small communities such as Niederschelden (23 per cent) and Buschhütten (14.5 per cent), with an overall poll share of 6.4 per cent for *Kreis* Siegen as a whole. Why Kaufmann picked out the Arnsberg and Bielefeld areas for specific mention is more difficult to understand. In the predominantly Catholic *Kreis* Arnsberg the party did not do all that well, securing only 1.4 per cent of the vote, though in *Stadtkreis* Arnsberg a creditable 5.3 per cent was achieved. Overall the returns in both Catholic and Protestant rural areas were pretty poor. In 11 solidly Catholic *Kreise* in Westphalia, the NSDAP secured less than 0.5 per cent of the vote. The percentage polled in the predominantly Protestant rural *Kreise* was better, but also not impressive, since the Nazis secured less than 2 per cent in all but two *Kreise*, those of Altena (2.07 per cent) and of Hattingen (6.3 per cent), the latter percentage being primarily the consequence of the high vote secured in Hattingen itself (15.6 per cent). By far the worst performance of the NSDAP came in the Protestant *Kreis* Hörde, in which the party scraped together a mere 0.004 per cent of the vote.

In Westphalia the returns achieved in the 1928 Reichstag election confirmed the NSDAP as essentially an urban phenomenon. It secured the bulk of its support in small- and medium-sized towns, and did not do all that well in rural communities (see Table 4.1). What probably impressed Kaufmann in his reflections on the election was the greater return for less effort achieved by the party in those rural areas where it had been active since the mid-1920s. On the basis of the equation 'low input = high output', Kaufmann concluded that the party had 'to follow up the successes', and called for the expansion of the party in those areas which had demonstrated receptivity to Nazism.[72] But the implementation of the plan to develop the presence of the party in rural areas was not to be realised by Kaufmann. In the summer of 1928 renewed internal regional disputes led to a fundamental reorganisation of the Rhenish-Westphalian NSDAP, initiated by the transfer of Kaufmann to *Gau* Hamburg, and the dissolution of the large *Gau* Ruhr.[73]

Table 4.1: Share of the vote by the NSDAP in Westphalia according to community size in the 1928 Reichstag election

Community size	share of poll (%)
over 100,000	18.6
10,000 to 99,999	27.3
2,000 to 9,999	36.5
under 2,000	17.6

III

The new *Gauleiter* of the reconstituted *Gau* Westphalia, the *Bezirksleiter* of Bochum, Josef Wagner, officially took up his post on 1 October 1928. From July to October, following Kaufmann's enforced 'vacation' in July, Wagner provisionally headed *Gau* Ruhr. He set about ending the organisational laxity which had characterised *Gau* Ruhr for much of 1928. Wagner's *Rundschreiben* to the *Bezirksleiter* and *Ortsgruppenleiter* left no doubt as to his leadership style. His instructions were peremptory in tone, and left no room for argument.[74] Wagner was just the type of dedicated, ruthless individual to put momentum into the Westphalian Nazi movement. A good bureaucrat and effective speaker, he had served a long apprenticeship in the heart of the Ruhr, and was beginning to receive some reward for his commitment and efforts in 1928.[75] Although the party which he took over in Westphalia was in a poor financial and organisational state, Wagner rapidly knocked it into shape in the autumn of 1928 through a series of meetings and *Rundschreiben*, which started even before he officially became *Gauleiter*.[76]

Wagner took over the Westphalian NSDAP at a time when the party was on the threshold of its meteoric rise, which was to transform it from an insignificant splinter group on the extreme right of the political spectrum into a party in the forefront of Weimar affairs. In Westphalia the rise of the Nazi party, both in terms of its membership support and electoral performance, was not as dramatic as in many other parts of Germany, but impressive nevertheless. From 1928 Nazism was to thrive due to the combination of agrarian and industrial crises, which manifested themselves most brutally in Westphalia, as elsewhere in Germany.[77] The resultant social crisis, and the increasing political uncertainty which the crises engendered, could be ruthlessly exploited by a force which viewed the democratic framework of the Weimar state with intense hostility. The Nazis flourished in the gloom of the late 1920s and early 1930s. Aided by an activism which was unmatched by any other political movement at that time, the NSDAP expanded in all directions, developed an increasingly refined vertical and horizontal organisational structure, created efficient lines of communications between all levels of the party, secured growing electoral support, increased its membership, and transformed itself into a major party by the end of 1930.[78]

Reports by the authorities on the Westphalian Nazi movement begin to record the surge towards the party from the spring of 1929, especially in the urban centres, in which the party had stagnated for much of 1927 and 1928.[79] In the *Ortsgruppen* situated in the Dortmund area, for example, the Nazis recorded membership increases ranging between 150 to 400 per cent.[80] As the agrarian crisis deepened, and as the Nazis began to give the rural population more of its attention, the Westphalian NSDAP started to obtain widespread support in the predominantly Protestant rural areas in southern and north-eastern parts of the province. The acute agrarian crisis moved even the dour Westphalian farmers to respond to Nazi overtures.[81] The respectability acquired by the party through its very active participation in the anti-Young Plan campaign in 1929, further enhanced its acceptability and reputation. Wagner exploited the campaign quite cynically to increase the membership of the party.[82]

The rapid increase in party membership in 1929 and 1930 soon necessitated, and resulted in, a significant expansion of the network of *Ortsgruppen* in Westphalia.[83] Alone between April and September 1930 the number of *Ortsgruppen* in the province almost doubled, from 118 to around the 200 mark.[84] Parallel to the organisational penetration of the movement into all parts of Westphalia, including the predominantly Catholic *Kreise*, came a rapid expansion of its auxiliary organisations, especially of the SA. The growth of the SA facilitated the propaganda drive of the party in the urban centres, in which both Communists and Socialists often took the motto 'Slay the fascist where you find him' quite literally.[85] Without the protection afforded by the SA, and indeed even with it, propaganda activities by the Nazis in many of the urban strongholds of the KPD and SPD were always problematical.

The expansion of the Nazi membership in Westphalia was in part due to 'environmental' factors, namely the push-factor in the form of the general economic crisis. It was also the consequence of the pull-factor in the shape of the skilful projection of Nazi propaganda, characterised by a mixture of opportunism and conviction. With the general growth of the party, and the resultant expansion of its bureaucracy, the propaganda arm of the movement also improved.[86] By 1930 the party was in a position in Westphalia to realise the construction of the propaganda cell network first suggested by the RL back in 1926. By mid-1930 large *Ortsgruppen*, as is clear in the case of Dortmund, possessed a quite sophisticated, well-oiled propaganda machine, with an established chain of communications upwards to the *Gauleitung*, and downwards to the *Sektion* level. The specific propaganda duties of the *Ortsgruppenleiter* and *Sektionsleiter*, and their relationship to one another and to their superiors, as well as their respective rights and limitations, had all been clearly laid down. To ensure the efficient transmission of propaganda instructions to the grassroots level, *Sektionsleiter* were instructed, by the time of the September Reichstag election, to be in daily contact with the *Ortsgruppenpropagandaleiter*.[87]

The propaganda pursued by the Nazis in 1929 and 1930 continued to be strongly fashioned by the social realities which faced them in Westphalia. A reorientation away from the working class, a switch of tactics suggested by some leading Nazis in the RL after the Reichstag election of 1928, was not an option open to the Westphalian *Gauleitung*.[88] Socialism, as interpreted by the party, continued to be the dominant theme in urban propaganda. The success of the pro-labour propaganda, centred essentially on the concept of social justice, though not dramatic, invited its continuation.[89] Moreover Wagner thought that the 'bourgeois-orientated forces' affected by the economic crisis, would turn to the NSDAP in any case, without much effort by the party to attract their support.[90] In their attempts to attract support from the working class, and in their pursuit of the working-class voter, the rhetoric used by the Nazis in the region was so radical in tone as to be almost indistinguishable, at least in its anti-capitalist sentiments, from that of the Left.[91] The projection of the idea of 'the destruction of interest slavery', attacks on the 'parasitic exploitation' of the *Volk* by trusts and syndicates, and constant reference to the *Volksgemeinschaft* concept, were standard ingredients of Nazi appeals in Westphalia.[92] In the cities and towns of the Ruhr the predominantly working-class audiences attracted to Nazi meetings were promised that the seizure of power by the NSDAP would be accompanied by 'an end to the exploitation of the workers by capital', and that the Nazis would 'effect a reorganisation of the existing economic system responsible for the rising unemployment'. Nazi propaganda emphasised that the choice facing the working class was a clear-cut one of either a continuation of 'capitalist servitude' under the existing system, or of 'freedom under National Socialism'. Part and parcel of the vague socialist content of the Nazi message were bitter attacks on both the SPD and KPD, with the former as the primary target. Popular themes were also attacks on the 'system', and a general condemnation of parliamentary government and of democracy along the lines developed in the mid-1920s. The whole propaganda effort was laced with anti-Semitism, a standard feature of the Nazi package, irrespective of which social group was being appealed to, and irrespective of whether the propaganda was framed to suit urban or rural audiences. In the eyes of the Westphalian Nazis the 'exploitation of the worker', and 'excesses of capitalism', the 'high unemployment' of the time, the 'distress of the artisans' and of the middle class in general, were 'all attributable to the Jew'.

From 1929 Nazi propaganda also latched on to, and systematically exploited, the growing economic crisis. Emphasis on the misery and distress generated by the agrarian and industrial crises became a common feature of numerous public meetings, with such titles as 'People in Need, who will save you?', 'Our Fight for Freedom and Bread', 'Who will Save Germany?', and 'The Struggle of the German Farmer (or worker or women, as it suited the occasion) for Freedom and Bread' being particularly frequent. The disaster prophesies these speeches were framed around undoubtedly had the effect of heightening the general uncertainty of the population. This demonstrated itself in most acute forms at times. Thus a series of Nazi meetings in *Kreis* Halle in 1930, at which two Bielefeld Nazis launched forth on the theme 'Germany is facing State Bankruptcy', led to a minor run on the Versmold Savings Bank.[93] Though the speeches underlined what everyone knew already, the predictions of doom and disaster, and the remedies on offer by 'the only party which could save the nation', were hammered home relentlessly. The exploitation of fear and anxiety was also at the heart of the rural propaganda campaign which gathered pace in the province in 1929.[94] Since the party as a whole did not have any specific agrarian programme until 1930, Westphalian Nazis agitating in rural areas in 1929 concentrated primarily on heightening the existing fears of the rural communities. 'Farmer, Your Farm is in Danger', 'Why is the German Farmer facing Extinction?', and 'The Difficulties of Agriculture' were all popular themes at meetings. From the spring of 1930 the Westphalian NSDAP began to project the agrarian policies formulated by the RL, which were sent to the *Gauleitung* in February.[95] A more positive aspect is noticeable from that time in the speeches directed at rural audiences, with greater attention being given to the measures the Nazis would introduce to protect agrarian interests in the event of their acquisition of power. In the run-up to the September Reichstag election one particular point made in the RL's February *Rundschreiben*, which stated that the right to inherit property was a central pillar of National Socialist policy, was especially underlined in the rural campaign.[96]

From 1929 the authorities gave much greater attention to the NSDAP as it grew in significance. The volume of information gathered by the police, and their ability to secure the often confidential *Rundschreiben* from the RL and the RPL to the *Gauleitung* of Westphalia, and their talent in laying hands on copies of even the most secret memoranda submitted by Wagner to the RL or RPL, suggests an extensive police infiltration into the Nazi apparatus at regional level. Police reports on Nazi internal correspondence, and copies of many of the Nazi *Rundschreiben* and memoranda, as well as the extensive monitoring by the police and civil authorities in the province of many Nazi meetings, including verbatim accounts of many Nazi speeches, allow one a useful insight into the content of

Nazi propaganda, as well as into the relationship between the various levels of Nazi party administration. The picture which emerges from these sources is one of a party increasingly centralised at the national level, and a *Gau* apparatus which became more and more responsive to the wishes of the RL and the RPL, even though some vestiges of independence can still be detected, both in organisational and propaganda aspects. For example, the decision by the RL, with Hitler's backing, to further the organisational development of the *NS-Schülerbund* at the outset of 1930, was initially ignored by the *Gauleitung*, which decided 'not to further its formation (in Westphalia) at present'.[97] At the *Gau* level, although the *Gauleitung* exercised broad control over propaganda and organisational activities of the *Bezirksleitungen* and *Ortsgruppenleitungen*, it still allowed them considerable freedom to determine their own issue priorities and select the target groups for special attention as they saw fit.[98]

Though the content of Nazi propaganda in Westphalia had a more pronounced 'socialist' emphasis than that of the RPL material, the propaganda output in the region was increasingly in tune with the wishes of the RL and RPL. From 1930 *Gau* propaganda was beginning to be adjusted to the twists and turns of the RL with considerable alacrity. This can be seen in the acceptance at *Gau* level of the hostile attitude adopted by the RL in the spring of 1930 towards the NSDAP's former campaign partners in the anti-Young Plan referendum, a change of attitude which was faithfully reflected in the activities of the Westphalian Nazi movement.[99] The attacks on the German National Peoples' Party (DNVP) and on the *Landbund*, and the hostility directed towards the *Stahlhelm* and its leadership, especially Seldte, which were initiated by a *Rundschreiben* of the RL, also became a prominent feature of the Westphalian Nazi Party's propaganda repertoire in the course of 1930. The *Gauleitung* also closely followed the RL's instructions which exploited the political developments of the time. The assaults on Brüning's internal and external policies, which were determined by the RL, were taken up in Westphalia at the regional and local level.[100]

The evidence available suggests that the autonomy of the Westphalian NSDAP was beginning to be reduced by the RL and by the RPL in the course of 1930, and that the *Gauleitung* became increasingly responsive to central directives in both organisational and propaganda matters. However, the extent of the control and co-

ordination of regional propaganda by the RPL must not be exaggerated, for it still fell far short of the kind of close control it exercised
by the time of the major election campaigns which took place in
1932. Although the regional and local propaganda output was
broadly conditioned by the ideas and instructions flowing from the
RL, the freedom of the *Gauleitung* and its propaganda department
to determine and control propaganda issues was not seriously
curtailed as yet. The ambitions of Goebbels, appointed to head the
RPL's *Abteilung* I in April 1930, to centralise and control the
propaganda output of the Nazi movement through the RPL, was
only gradually achieved in the course of 1931–2, and then only
within his sphere of operations.[101] In the run-up to the September
election, much of the work of the RPL continued to be handled by
Himmler, who signed, at least until September 1930, all the correspondence of RPL *Abteilung* I, after which time Goebbels' deputy
Franke began to take over. Goebbels' appointment came at a tricky
moment for him, since it fell in the middle of the Otto Strasser crisis,
which kept Goebbels occupied in Berlin for much of the time until
the end of July, so that many of the campaign decisions for the
September election had already been made before he could intervene.[102] Although Goebbels may well have achieved a highly
centralised, controlled propaganda output in his own *Gau* Berlin,
the efforts of the RPL to translate Goebbels' proclaimed ambition,
to give maximum uniformity to the entire national campaign, was
only partially achieved.[103] In comparison with the 1928 election, the
Westphalian *Gau* propaganda machine undoubtedly did rely more
heavily on the texts produced by the RPL in the conduct of its
electioneering, but it did not concentrate on the 'For or against
Young' theme around which Goebbels tried to shape the 'entire
electoral propaganda'.[104] In Westphalia the dominant themes of
Nazi meetings, in both urban and rural areas, focused on economic
aspects and explanations as to what National Socialism meant, and
what it had to offer. In the towns emphasis was again placed, as in
1928, on attacking the Left, while anti-Semitism was an integral part
of the whole of the campaign. In general, the propaganda pursued
by the *Gauleitung* in the 1930 election was indistinguishable from
that of late 1929 and early 1930, and the suggestions of the RPL did
not shape the regional activities to any noticeable extent. There
were attacks on the Young Plan in many of the speeches given in
August and September, but these were incidental. Anti-Young
propaganda had been much more prominent in Nazi agitation in the

province in the first half of 1930.[105]

The results of the Reichstag election in Westphalia, although they demonstrated significant growth in support for Nazism, fell well short of the 18.3 per cent achieved by the NSDAP nationally. In Westphalia-South the party acquired 13.9 per cent of the valid votes, and in Westphalia-North the return was 12.9 per cent.[106] As was to be the case in all of the elections before 1933, the NSDAP was unable to surmount the formidable barriers represented by class and religion which faced it in the province. The Centre Party dominated those *Landkreise* in which the Catholic population was concentrated, as well as being a complicating factor in the electoral geometry of the many urban areas in which there was also a significant Catholic presence. In the urban centres, especially in the conurbations of the Ruhr, the SPD and the KPD remained a block to Nazi expansion. Overall the class barrier proved a less formidable factor to overcome, for already by 1930 the Nazis were able to record, especially in the less industrialised, medium-sized towns, such as Iserlohn (25.6 per cent), Minden (22.7 per cent), Herford (22.1 per cent), Detmold (22 per cent), and Siegen (19.5 per cent), quite creditable performances. In the major industrial cities the party did less well, though some quite good results were achieved in Hagen (21.8 per cent), Bochum (17.6 per cent), and Bielefeld (17.4 per cent). The highest percentage share of the poll was secured by the NSDAP in the predominantly Protestant *Kreise* of Wittgenstein (32.9 per cent), Halle i./W. (31.2 per cent), Herford (29.6 per cent), and Lübbecke (26.5 per cent), but the number of votes involved was relatively small (see Table 4.2). In comparison with the returns of 1928, the Nazis were able to develop their urban base in Westphalia, and were more strongly supported in the major cities and medium-sized towns rather than in small towns and in rural communities.

Table 4.2: Share of the vote by the NSDAP in Westphalia according to community size in the 1930 Reichstag election

Community size	share of poll (%)
over 100,000	27.6
10,000 to 99,999	31.4
2,000 to 9,999	22.5
under 2,000	18.5

IV

The electoral breakthrough of September 1930 gave a major stimulus to the fortunes of the Nazi Party. In Westphalia the party increased its membership by some 500 per cent within two months of the election.[107] The influx of what veteran Nazis disparagingly described as *Septemberlinge* and *Konjunkturritter*, and the continued growth of the party, which reached a total membership of 36,500 by January 1931, was behind Wagner's decision to divide *Gau* Westphalia into two *Untergaue*, over which he planned to retain full control.[108] The proposed reorganisation, in which the boundaries of the two *Untergaue* were to correspond with those of electoral districts Westphalia-North and Westphalia-South, though passed on to the RL for consideration, was implemented before Munich's attitudes were known. It was on Wagner's authority that the Bielefeld *Bezirksleiter* Homann took over control of *Untergau* Westphalia-North. Wagner's plans came to nought when the RL intervened to assert its authority. Although Strasser agreed with Wagner that the time was right for the division of *Gau* Westphalia, he favoured the Gelsenkirchen *Bezirksleiter* Dr Meyer as *Gauleiter*. The latter was duly appointed by Hitler, provisionally for one year at first, a probationary period in which Meyer was given the chance to prove his worth.[109]

Following a conference at Hamm on 4 January 1931, at which the boundaries of the two Westphalian *Gaue* were defined, Meyer took over a *Gau* beset with problems. *Gau* Westphalia-North was not only suffering from a limited membership, but also from the fact that the small number of Nazi members were unequally distributed within the *Gau*. The membership of 4,256 was organised in 115 *Ortsgruppen*, of which 46 were situated in the Bielefeld region.[110] In the predominantly Catholic areas around Münster, Rheine and Paderborn, the party was hardly visible. The *Gau* organisation was also underdeveloped, and consisted of but five functionaries at the time of Meyer's takeover.[111] Much of Meyer's energy was initially taken up with the development of this small organisational structure, which he was able to expand considerably in the course of 1931. By November the *Gauleitung*, beyond the posts of *Gauleiter* and that of the SA leader, could already boast of 18 functionaries administering 18 departments.[112] Many of these were, however, limited in terms of their experience, for the bulk of the trained personnel of the former *Gau* Westphalia had been retained by

Wagner at the time of the division.[113] To add to all of these problems, a weak financial situation, and a series of internal party squabbles, further exacerbated the difficulties faced by Meyer. His only initial success, which proved an astute move on Meyer's part, was his appointment of Homann to the post of *Gauorganisations-leiter*. Together with this experienced functionary, Meyer was able to put some drive into his *Gau*. Constant membership growth in 1931 and 1932 did allow the *Gauleitung* some scope in overcoming its chronic financial situation. Between September 1930 and January 1933 *Gau* Westphalia-North was able to record an addition of 14,467 new members, the total membership standing at 16,546 by the time of Hitler's appointment to the chancellorship on 31 January 1933. In the same period *Gau* Westphalia-South attracted an additional 20,514 members, giving it a total membership of 34,214.[114] Admittedly these increases were relatively small compared to the growth rates recorded by other *Gaue*, but they did ease the financial strains imposed on the rank and file by an expanding party bureaucracy, as well as the pressures occasioned by the five electoral campaigns which the party was to fight in 1932.

As part of the general organisational expansion of both *Gaue* in 1931, the propaganda departments of the Westphalian Nazi Party were subjected to further development and refinement. The initiative for the construction of a more sophisticated and effective propaganda arm for the party as a whole came from the RPL, which also expanded its personnel in the spring of 1931, and came under a more effective control exercised by Goebbels.[115] One of Goebbels' concerns, to secure better information about the propaganda activities of the NSDAP, as well as that of its political opponents, lay behind his instructions to monitor such activity, and his orders to the *Gauleitungen* in the spring of 1931 that they should send in monthly reports, recording developments in their areas, to the RPL for analysis.[116] In Westphalia these RPL instructions were rapidly transmitted to the *Bezirksleiter* and to the *Ortsgruppenleiter* by the *Gaupropagandaleiter*. In a *Rundschreiben* of the *Gaupropagandaleiter* of Westphalia-South, *Bezirksleiter* were ordered to provide him with monthly activity reports for their areas, with the threat that failure to comply with the instruction would result in the names of their *Bezirke* being forwarded to Munich. Beyond providing detailed information on their own activities, including such items as the number of meetings organised in their areas, the size of audiences attracted to the public meetings, details of propaganda marches undertaken, and the number of pamphlets distributed by the party, *Bezirksleiter* were also asked to give accounts of the propaganda projected by the opposition, and required to forward, with each report, the pamphlets that were distributed by rival parties in their regions. *Bezirksleiter* were also encouraged to suggest specific propaganda actions deemed suitable for their areas. All of this information and material was then passed to the RPL.[117] The reports submitted by the Westphalian *Gaue* from 1931 were remarkably detailed, and reflect the perpetual motion which increasingly characterised Nazi propaganda actions at grassroots level.[118] Instructions by Wagner to the *Ortsgruppen* under his control in November 1931, demanded even more detailed monitoring of the opposition, including requests for information on their organisational arrangements, the names of rival party functionaries, and analysis of opposition press activity. The reports were to be submitted to the *Gauleitung* under the code word '*Nachrichtendienst*'.[119] All the material provided by the *Gaue* was used by the RL in the production of monthly reports, which were sent regularly to the *Gauleitungen* from 1931. These kept the *Gauleiter* and his propaganda staff well informed on new propaganda themes and techniques, which could be exploited at *Gau* level if deemed appropriate in particular regions.[120] The information gathered in this way was also used by the RPL to fashion its monthly publication *Unser Wille und Weg*, which was made available to local Nazi functionaries from April 1931, and provided them with the latest RL attitudes on various important political and economic issues of the day.[121]

The internal party correspondence of the Westphalian *Gauleitungen* in 1931 and 1932 reflects an increasing responsiveness to the demands of the RL and of the RPL, and a growing dependence by the *Gaue* on information and propaganda material furnished by Munich party headquarters. One of Meyer's first efforts on becoming *Gauleiter* was to secure the RPL's agreement to have parts of his *Gau* declared as a *Grosskampfgebiet*. This was to facilitate the Nazi campaign in a forthcoming *Landtag* election in Schaumburg-Lippe, as well as to support the Nazi-initiated plebiscite in Lippe-Detmold, which was designed to remove the Socialist-led government by forcing a new *Landtag* election.[122] The increase in the volume of information and instructions to the *Gaue* by the RL and the RPL, and the transmission of such material downwards to the *Ortsgruppen* level by the *Gauleitungen*, is very noticeable in the course of 1931. In one of his *Gau Rundschreiben* of 1931, Meyer communicated to the *Bezirksleitungen* and *Ortsgruppenleitungen* decisions reached by the *Reichs-Uschla*, which concerned the exclusion of party members, instructions from the RL, which related to the party's propaganda directed at disabled exservicemen, and *Rundschreiben* by the RL which dealt with agrarian, economic, racial and cultural questions. Attention was also drawn to Strasser's orders in the *Völkischer Beobachter* of 17 November 1931, and the RL's *Rundschreiben* of 10 September, which dealt with the *NS-Frauenschaft*. A lengthy section of Meyer's *Rundschreiben* was also devoted to a number of propaganda matters, such as new propaganda literature available from the RPL, instructions from the RPL to the *Ortsgruppen* which ordered them to produce more *Flammenwerfer* (based on enclosed RPL examples) to further local propaganda, and a reminder to *Ortsgruppenleiter* to subscribe regularly to the RPL's *Unser Wille und Weg* publication. The *Rundschreiben* also contained a whole host of other informational items by various *Gau* specialist organisations, and general reminders on all sorts of matter.[123] The *Rundschreiben*, sent out at a time when the party was not facing any particular task, such as preparing for an election campaign, when the flood of instructions from the top usually became a torrent, demonstrates the extent to which the RL, and the RPL and the *Gauleitungen* had secured 'informational and control functions', and the extent to which the *Gauleitungen* were subjected to the flow of orders from party headquarters.[124]

The closer relationship established between the *Gauleitungen* and the central offices of the NSDAP, and the extent of the subordination of the former by the latter, were highlighted in the major election campaigns faced by the party and its propaganda apparatus in the course of 1932. In 1932 the RPL, and the movement as a whole, were faced with four efficiency tests in the shape of two presidential and two Reichstag campaigns, as well as, in the case of Westphalia, a fifth, in the form of the Prussian *Landtag* election in April.[125] At the very beginning of the year, the morale of the Westphalian NSDAP was lifted by a very good performance in the *Kreistag* elections on 10 January in the tiny state of Lippe-Detmold. This was part of the operational area of *Gauleitung* Westphalia-North, which orchestrated the campaign, in which the Nazis secured 30.7 per cent of the vote, a useful increase on the 22.4 per cent which had been given to the Nazi ticket in the Reichstag election of

1930.[126] A more formidable task faced the Westphalian NSDAP in the presidential election set for 13 March. Even before the announcement of Hitler's candidature in the race for the presidency, a campaign strategy to support 'candidate X' had been drawn up by Goebbels. This laid down that an attack on 'the system in force since 1918' was to be the prevailing theme of the Nazi campaign.[127] The formal announcement of Hitler's candidature on 22 February put the RPL into overdrive.[128] In the run-up to election day, the RPL bombarded the *Gauleitungen* with a ceaseless flow of instructions and directives on how to conduct their propaganda, and on which themes they should concentrate. To further the Nazi effort the RPL produced innumerable pamphlets, posters and stickers, the texts of which were sent to the *Gauleitungen* on an almost daily basis.[129] The propaganda literature made available to *Gau* propaganda organisations was voluminous and designed to attract support from a variety of social, interest and age groups.[130] The camps of both of the main candidates projected their man as saviour of all Germans, be they male or female, young or old, working class or middle class, peasant or civil servant, Protestant or Catholic. The same diet was pumped out in increasing volume in both the pro-Hindenburg and in the Nazi press.[131]

In Westphalia the NSDAP was placed in a particularly difficult position. It faced not only a very forceful pro-Hindenburg campaign conducted by the Centre Party, but also a more muted campaign for Hindenburg by the SPD. To add to the difficulties of the Hitler camp, the Nazis had also to contend with an aggressive KPD campaign supporting Thälmann. Both of the important regional Catholic and socialist papers were very active on Hindenburg's behalf.[132] Most vulnerable to Nazi and Communist propaganda was the SPD, which was clearly embarrassed by the position it found itself in, and which was almost apologetic in its support for Hindenburg. The discomfort of the SPD was increased by the Nazi ploy of distributing among the working class, in the last few days before the poll, the SPD's anti-Hindenburg pamphlets of 1925.[133]

The result of the poll on 13 March was a great disappointment for the Nazi movement. Although Hindenburg did not achieve, by a mere 0.4 per cent, the necessary absolute majority to secure his re-election, his vote of 49.6 per cent dwarfed the 30.1 per cent given to Hitler, which made Hindenburg a virtual certainty to win the run-off. In Westphalia the Hitler vote was quite low, with Hindenburg securing an absolute majority in both of the Westphalian electoral districts (see Table 4.3).[134]

In the second round of the presidential election, involving a triangular contest between Hindenburg, Hitler and Thälmann, the optimism that Hitler would win the presidency, which had sustained the Nazi campaign in February and March, was largely absent.[135] It was clear to all but the Nazi diehards, that Hitler had no chance of success. This could not, however, be admitted, and the RPL conducted the second campaign as though miracles were possible. New instructions were issued to the *Gaue* by Goebbels, who again masterminded the Nazi effort, and determined the tactics to be adopted by the party to secure a Hitler victory.[136] Although Goebbels was aware that, given 'the short time available', little could be done to win over Hindenburg's Centre Party and SPD supporters, his hopes were pinned on attracting the bourgeois voters who had backed Hindenburg in the first round. Goebbels' instructions for the second campaign were framed with this in mind. Thus every *Gau* was urged to find out 'which baker, butcher, shopkeeper, publican etc.' had voted for Hindenburg and why. Once such Hindenburg voters had been identified, personal efforts were to be made to win them over. Goebbels also pointed to the need for the party to be more careful in the distribution of propaganda material, since 'it is pointless to press a pamphlet designed for the peasantry into the hands of the worker or *vice versa*.' The female voters were also to be cultivated more assiduously and to be made more thoroughly aware as to what National Socialism had to offer them. Another group singled out by Goebbels for special attention were pensioners. Finally, Goebbels demanded a more effective use of the Nazi press, especially during the Easter period, during which three times the normal edition of Nazi papers was to be printed, in order to compensate for the government ban on electioneering during the holiday period.

Table 4.3: Results of the *Reichspräsidentenwahl* in Westphalia, 13 March 1932

	Duesterberg %	Hindenburg %	Hitler %	Thälmann %	Winter %
Westphalia-North	5.2	60.4	22.1	12.1	0.2
Westphalia-South	4.3	52.7	24.2	18.7	0.1
Reich	6.8	49.6	30.1	13.2	0.3

In Westphalia preparations for the second presidential election were set in motion almost immediately after the first results had been declared. In *Gau* Westphalia-South, Wagner sent out a number of instructions to the *Ortsgruppen*, which were called upon to secure an additional 100,000 votes for Hitler.[137] In his *Rundschreiben*, Wagner placed special emphasis on intensive house-to-house canvassing, on the important role which the *NS-Frauenschaft* could play in winning over the female voter, and on the need to organise meetings to specifically attract Hindenburg supporters. Both the unemployed and the rural voter were also to be singled out for special attention. Wagner's guidelines anticipated in a number of aspects the instructions sent out in Goebbels' *Rundschreiben* of 23 March. The RPL's orders were immediately passed on to the *Ortsgruppen* by the *Gauleitung* of Westphalia-South on 24 March.[138] From Wagner's *Rundschreiben* covering the second round of the presidential election it is clear that he worked as hard as it was possible to implement the RPL's instructions, which were again designed to standardise both the methods to be employed in the campaign, as well as to control the content of propaganda. To ensure the latter, Wagner summarised the main themes contained in the mass of propaganda material passed to the *Gauleitung* with each RPL *Rundschreiben*, and ordered party speakers and *Ortsgruppenleiter* to adhere rigidly to his guidelines.[139] Wagner ordered his subordinates to frame all their speeches around the theme 'Away with the Hindenburg Front to German Freedom under Hitler'. Each speech was initially to deal with the diversity of the 'Hindenburg election-community', and the 'chief characteristics' of those parties which were backing his candidature. The SPD was to be condemned for representing 'Marxism, nationalisation, treason, atheism, and pacifism', and vilified as 'a guarantor of Versailles, and as an enemy of the Churches'. The Centre Party was to be accused of the 'misuse of religion, the abuse of the pulpit and of the confessional', as well as being 'an enemy of the Army', and of 'walking arm in arm with atheists'. The *Staatspartei* was to be summarily dismissed as being little more than 'a representative of Jewish money sacks'. After these preliminaries, Wagner urged all speakers to deal with 'the stature of Hitler and the positive nature of the National Socialist programme'. The opportunity was then to be taken to clarify those points on which the NSDAP had been attacked in the first campaign. Thus speakers were instructed to project the NSDAP's favourable attitude towards the Churches, to point out the anti-inflation policies which the party would pursue when Hitler became president, and to underline the *Volksgemeinschaft* concept for which the party stood. A few further points were then to be made about Nazi attitudes to women, to the sanctity of property, and to the rights of workers to enjoy social security and union representation. In conclusion, a number of aspects of Nazi foreign policy ideas were to be outlined, especially the NSDAP's opposition to reparations, to the Versailles Treaty, and to the Young Plan. This mixture, in the format prescribed by Wagner, was closely observed by Nazi speakers active in *Gau* Westphalia-South.[140]

The insight into the conduct of the campaign for the presidency, provided by the numerous *Rundschreiben* of *Gauleitung* Westphalia-South, suggests that Wagner and his staff had very little room for manoeuvre, and were very much subject to the dictates of the RPL. The degree of independence allowed to the *Gauleitung*, and one can assume that the same applies to *Gau* Westphalia-North, was very limited. In a few areas one can detect the continuation of a degree of freedom in that Wagner and the *Gaupropagandaleiter* could still exercise their judgement in deciding on which of the vast number of texts for leaflets produced by the RPL, and there were some 58 of these sent out during the second presidential campaign alone, were best suited to Westphalian conditions.[141] Only one act of real independence is recorded in Wagner's *Rundschreiben* during the campaign. There is reference to a locally written pamphlet entitled 'Hitler or Marx?', which Wagner had personally approved for use in the region.[142] For the rest, the campaign material used by the party appears to have been provided virtually exclusively by the RPL.[143]

Despite the tremendous effort made by the Westphalian Nazi movement in March and April, the vote for Hitler in the poll on 10 April increased only marginally in both *Gaue* (see Table 4.4). Hindenburg secured an absolute majority in 45 of the 53 urban and rural *Kreise* of Westphalia, with 70 per cent or more of the vote in 18 predominantly Catholic *Kreise*. For the Nazis it was to be the highpoint in their electoral fortunes in Westphalia during 1932 (see Table 4.5).

It was not until after the elevation of Hitler to the chancellorship in January 1933 that the Westphalian NSDAP was able to boost its share of the poll once more in what turned out to be the last so-called 'free' election on 5 March 1933.

Table 4.4: Results of the *Reichspräsidentenwahl* in Westphalia,
10 April 1932[144]

	Hindenburg	Hitler	Thälmann
Westphalia-North	63.9	27.2	8.9
Westphalia-South	57.7	29.0	13.3
Reich	53.0	36.8	10.2

Table 4.5: Results of the Prussian *Landtag* election, 24 April 1932;
and of the Reichstag elections of 31 July and 6 November 1932[145]

	Prussian *Landtag*	Reichstag I	Reichstag II
	%	%	%
Westphalia-North	24.3	25.7	22.3
Westphalia-South	28.9	27.2	24.8
Prussia	36.3		
Reich		37.3	33.1

V

The degree of control exercised by the RPL over the NSDAP's
propaganda activities by the end of the two presidential campaigns
is very striking in comparison with the situation prevalent at the
time of the 1930 Reichstag election. By the spring of 1932 Goebbels
had gone a long way towards achieving his aim of placing a strait-
jacket on the Nazi Party's propaganda organisation. Although the
Gauleitungen were still allowed limited movement to take account
of local conditions, they retained very little of the freedom which
they had enjoyed in the 1920s. The RPL did not relinquish the
power it had secured over the conduct of election campaigns, and in
all of the subsequent elections of 1932 a similar pattern of central
control and direction was in evidence.[146] Nor were the RPL's
activities confined merely to national elections. Already by April
1932, the RPL's sphere of control had widened to embrace the
direction of the important Prussian *Landtag* election.[147]

In Westphalia, the *Gauleitungen* demonstrated a continued
willingness to dance to the RPL's tune during the major campaigns
of the summer and autumn, though some limited resistance to the
party's propaganda control mechanisms did emerge at the local
level. Rumblings of discontent, generated by the administrative and
financial pressures exerted on the *Kreisleiter* and *Ortsgruppenleiter*,
as one election followed another, surfaced as early as the second

presidential campaign. A number of local functionaries began to object to the reduction of their role to the point at which they were little more than recipients of *Gau* and central directives. The loss of freedom, the difficulty of exercising even limited initiative, was felt especially because of the centralisation of party propaganda, coupled with the often unrealistic demands made on the *Ortsgruppen* by the *Gaupropagandaleiter*.[148] These complaints, and growing misgivings as to where the party was heading, grew in volume by the end of the year, by which time the NSDAP had fought, and won, a series of elections, but without seemingly securing any tangible rewards.[149] More significant than the occasional grumbling from below, were the reservations which began to be expressed even at the *Gau* level as to how the party was being led. After the July Reichstag campaign, Wagner questioned the wisdom of following centrally determined political decisions which he viewed as electorally damaging in Westphalia. Most critical were his remarks concerning Goebbels' instruction to party officials on 4 June that they should not comment on the Papen government during the Reichstag election campaign.[150] The 'neutral stance adopted towards the Papen Cabinet' was viewed by Wagner as a real handicap, for it 'gave our opponents the chance to pursue a primitive, psychologically astute and effective propaganda against us'.[151] The order was rescinded by Goebbels a fortnight later, but the damage had been done by then. The passive attitude towards Papen's government, which was faithfully followed by the Westphalian Nazis to mid-June, left them saddled with the *Papenkreuzler* tag attached to them by their socialist opponents.[152] Wagner was also displeased with the way in which the entire election campaign had been handled by Goebbels and the RPL, for he complained that 'our whole propaganda in this campaign has suffered because of its lack of clarity and cohesion'.[153]

Although it is clear from the Westphalian example that fundamental changes had taken place in the way propaganda was formulated and projected by the early 1930s, one must guard against the idea of seeing the RPL in a dominant position in all aspects of Nazi propaganda activity by 1932. The role played by Goebbels and the RPL looms so large in 1932 because it was a year of virtually permanent electoral campaigning, an area of party activity in which the RPL did control and direct affairs. However, at the very time when the RPL, under Goebbels' guidance, centralised the Nazi party's propaganda arm, new avenues were opening up for sections of the party to pursue propaganda which was outside the RPL's direct sphere of influence. For the early 1930s witnessed the often quite rapid growth of a series of Nazi specialist organisations, a development which complicated the issue of the formulation, dissemination and control of propaganda. Although a number of the party's specialist organisations, such as the HJ (Hitler Youth), the NSDStB (National Socialist Student Association), and the *NS-Frauenschaft* (National Socialist Women's League), as well as Nazi 'professional' organisations, such as the NSLB (National Socialist Teachers' League), the BNSDJ (League of National Socialist German Lawyers), and the *NSD Ärztebund* (National Socialist League of German Doctors), were of comparatively little significance before 1933, the leaders and functionaries of these organisations also acquired propaganda functions.[154] The more significant, rapidly expanding specialist organisations, the SA, the NSBO (National Socialist Factory Cell Organisation), and to a lesser extent the ApA (Agrarian Political Apparatus), also had particular axes to grind, and generated propaganda which deviated, at times, from the more bland programmatical statements made by the party at the national level.

A good example of a specialist organisation which pursued propaganda which was out of step with the approach taken by the party hierarchy is that of the Westphalian NSBO. This organisation projected a very strident anti-capitalist propaganda in the early 1930s, at a time when Hitler was doing his best to cultivate friendly relations with the business community.[155] Thus in a fortnightly news-sheet produced by the Wanne-Eickel NSBO, the editorial on forthcoming redundancies, and proposed wage cuts, in the mining industry, condemned such measures as 'exposing the ugly face of capitalism', and as 'an insult to national and socialist thinking Germany'. The editorial went on to denounce the plans since they 'mean that a whole industrial province will be subjected to hunger to further the interests of the big industrialists and their finance-capitalist backers'. The reader was assured that the NSBO and the NSDAP not only strongly opposed the measures, but that such actions would not be tolerated in a Nazi Germany under 'the leadership of the worker [*sic*] Adolf Hitler', since Nazi economic thinking held that 'the economy is not to be used for profiteering, but for sustaining the German *Volk*'.[156] The 'left-wing' slant of the Rhenish-Westphalian Nazi party in the early 1930s, which became even more pronounced in 1932, was strongly criticised by pro-Nazi industrialists of the Ruhr. As emerges from a letter sent by one of their spokesman to the RL, the major complaints were about the 'pure Marxist character' of much of the propaganda of the regional party, with its emphasis on nationalisation, the support it gave to socialist wage theories, and the fact that in the phraseology used by the party the words 'employer and exploiter were synonymous'. Anxiety was also expressed about the attempts of the regional NSDAP to set 'one social group against another', as well as the 'personal defamation' of local industrialists in Nazi pamphlets distributed in the region, which 'echoed Communist publications' in every respect.[157]

Despite the high degree of co-ordination and control exercised by Goebbels and the RPL over Nazi propaganda in the early 1930s, it would be a mistake to view Nazi propaganda as monolithic by 1932. By the time of the 1932 elections the Westphalian *Gauleitungen* did conform to the dictates of the RPL, but in the conduct of everyday propaganda in the province, control was anything but total. The Westphalian Nazi functionaries still retained, in the formulation of propaganda and in the matter of issue viability, some discretion, even if they had lost much of the autonomy which had been the norm in the 1920s.

Notes

1. A representative list of works which stress the importance of Nazi propaganda in explaining the growth and success of Nazism in the endphase of the Weimar Republic would include M. Broszat, *German National Socialism* (Santa Barbara, Cal., 1966); K.D. Bracher, *The German Dictatorship. The Origins, Structure and Consequence of National Socialism* (Harmondsworth, 1973); and W. Ruge, *Deutschland von 1917 bis 1933* (Berlin-East, 1967).

2. A stimulating revisionist approach is suggested by R. Bessel, 'The Rise of the NSDAP and the Myth of Nazi Propaganda', *Wiener Library Bulletin*, 33, 1980, pp. 20–9. The problems surrounding Bessel's arguments are discussed by I. Kershaw, 'Ideology, Propaganda, and the Rise of the Nazi Party', in P.D. Stachura (ed.), *The Nazi Machtergreifung* (London, 1983), pp. 171–8.

3. Thus Zeman devotes but one of his seven main chapters to Nazi propaganda before 1933: Z.A.B. Zeman, *Nazi Propaganda* (Oxford, 2nd ed., 1973); similarly Bramsted, in his evaluation of the career of Goebbels, devotes a mere fraction of his lengthy study to events before 1933: E. Bramsted, *Goebbels and National Socialist Propaganda 1925–1945* (London, 1965).

4. Some basic aspects of the history of the *Reichspropagandaleitung* are touched upon by D. Orlow, *The History of the Nazi Party. Vol. 1. 1919–1933* (Newton Abbot, 1971); cf. W. Horn, *Führerideologie und Parteiorganisation in der NSDAP* (Düsseldorf, 1972).

5. Even in a recent specialist study on Nazi propaganda by Welch, he erroneously

asserts that Goebbels was appointed as head of the *Reichspropagandaleitung* in November 1928: D. Welch (ed.), *Nazi Propaganda. The Power and the Limitations* (London, Totowa, N.J., 1983), p. 3. On the confusion surrounding the date of Goebbels' appointment, see H. Heiber, *Goebbels* (London, 1972), pp. 72–3.

6. U. Kissenkoetter, *Gregor Strasser und die NSDAP* (Stuttgart, 1978), pp. 28–34, 55–60.

7. T. Childers, *The Nazi Voter. The Social Foundations of Fascism in Germany, 1919–1933* (Chapel Hill, London, 1983).

8. Nazi propaganda at the regional level is extensively dealt with by J. Noakes, *The Nazi Party in Lower Saxony 1921–1933* (Oxford, 1971); E. Schön, *Die Entstehung des Nationalsozialismus in Hessen* (Meisenheim am Glan, 1972); G. Pridham, *Hitler's Rise to Power. The Nazi Movement in Bavaria 1923–33* (London, 1973); W. Böhnke, *Die NSDAP im Ruhrgebiet 1920–1933* (Bonn, Bad Godesberg, 1974); R. Hambrecht, *Der Aufstieg der NSDAP in Mittel- und Oberfranken (1925–1933)* (Nuremberg, 1976); and J.H. Grill, *The Nazi Movement in Baden 1920–1945* (Chapel Hill, 1983). At the local level there are studies by E-A. Roloff, *Bürgertum und Nationalsozialismus 1930–1933: Braunschweigs Weg ins Dritte Reich* (Hanover, 1961); W.S. Allen, *The Nazi Seizure of Power: The Experience of a Single German Town 1930–1935* (London, 1966); U. Mayer, *Das Eindringen des Nationalsozialismus in die Stadt Wetzlar* (Wetzlar, 1970); A-G. Politz, 'Die NSDAP im Raum Hildesheim', *Alt-Hildesheim*, 42, 1971; R. Mann, 'Entstehung und Entwicklung der NSDAP in Marburg bis 1933', *Hessisches Jahrbuch für Landesgeschichte*, 22, 1972; and I. Buchloh, *Die nationalsozialistische Machtergreifung in Duisburg: Eine Fallstudie* (Duisburg, 1980).

9. Noakes touches on this aspect: Noakes, *The Nazi Party*, pp. 148–9, 209–19 and 238–41. Cf. Grill, *The Nazi Movement*, pp. 160–1, 206–9 and 235.

10. J. Ciolek-Kümper, *Wahlkampf in Lippe. Die Wahlkampfpropaganda der NSDAP zur Landtagswahl am 15. Januar 1933* (Munich, 1976).

11. Ibid., pp. 81–7.

12. This is reflected in the title of the Nazi account of the campaign by A. Schröder, *'Hitler geht auf die Dörfer . . .' Der Auftakt zur nationalsozialistischen Revolution. Erlebnisse und Bilder von der entscheidenden Januarwahl 1933 in Lippe* (Detmold, 1938).

13. Ciolek-Kümper, *Wahlkampf in Lippe*, p. 127 f.

14. R.F. Hamilton, 'Reply to Commentators', *Central European History*, 17, March 1984, pp. 80–1.

15. Orlow, *History of the Nazi Party*, pp. 59–60, and 71. Cf. Horn, *Führerideologie*, pp. 220–6.

16. 'Rundschreiben. An die Ortsgruppen der National-Sozialistischen Deutschen Arbeiter-Partei', Munich, 20 March 1926, and 'Organisationsplan zur Einrichtung von Propagandazellen der N.S.D.A.P.', Bundesarchiv Koblenz (hereafter BA), Sammlung Schumacher 373. The *Rundschreiben* is wrongly ascribed to Esser by Kissenkoetter, *Gregor Strasser*, p. 33.

17. In the many histories of Nazi *Ortsgruppen* included in a Nazi account on the origin and development of the NSDAP in Westphalia, there is reference to only three as having a propaganda cell or a propaganda organiser by 1926. See F.A. Beck, *Kampf und Sieg. Geschichte der NSDAP im Gau Westfalen-Süd von den Anfängen bis zur Machtübernahme* (Dortmund, 1938), pp. 204, 221 and 394.

18. Ibid., p. 571.

19. 'Gau Ruhr der NSDAP. Mitgliederstand vom 31. Mai 1926', BA, NS1/342.

20. Only the *Ortsgruppen* of Bochum and of Hattingen had developed a horizontal organisational structure by 1926; see Beck, *Kampf und Sieg*, pp. 201 and 221. In 1925 and 1926 'one-man-band' type of organisations were quite common. In Bielefeld, for example, one individual held the posts of *Bezirksleiter, Ortsgruppen-*

leiter, party treasurer, SA leader and party speaker all at the same time; see M. Hiemisch, *Der nationalsozialistische Kampf um Bielefeld. Die Geschichte der N.S.D.A.P. Bielefeld* (Bielefeld, 1933), pp. 7–9.

21. Records covering the *Ortsgruppen* of Gelsenkirchen, Bottrop, Osterfeld, Haltern, Dorsten and Münster note a membership decline of some 30 per cent in 1927: police report, Recklinghausen, 9 January 1928, Staatsarchiv Münster (hereafter StAM), VII-2, Bd. 5.

22. The growth rate of the Westphalian NSDAP in 1930 was quite rapid, rising from circa 3,500 members in January 1930 to around the 36,500 mark by January 1931 (the figures probably include members not paying regular party dues): figures taken from police reports, Bochum, 3 October 1930, StAM, VII-67, Bd. 1, and Bochum, 21 January 1931, StAM, VII-67, Bd. 2.

23. Cf. 'Grundsätzliche Richtlinien für die Neuaufstellung der NSDAP', *Völkischer Beobachter* (hereafter *VB*), 26 February 1925.

24. See J. Nyomarkay, *Charisma and Factionalism in the Nazi Party* (Minneapolis, 1967), pp. 78–9.

25. This is clear from the correspondence between Pfeffer and the RL concerning membership matters contained in the Hoover Institution NSDAP Hauptarchiv Microfilm Collection (hereafter HA), Reel 8, Folder 165. Cf. Bouhler's letter to *Gauleitung* Rhineland-North, 24 October 1925, BA, Sammlung Schumacher 603.

26. Pfeffer's dictatorial leadership style emerges clearly in Pfeffer to Schlange, 14 May 1926, BA, NS1/342.

27. Pfeffer to Hitler, 31 January 1925; the letter is reprinted in Beck, *Kampf und Sieg.*, pp. 589–91. The tone of the letter is one of an equal writing to an equal, rather than that of a subordinate writing to his superior.

28. Ibid., pp. 589–90. Cf. Orlow, *History of the Nazi Party*, pp. 64–5.

29. See Pfeffer's article 'Gemeinnutz geht vor Eigennutz', *NS-Briefe*, 15 December 1925.

30. Homann to Goebbels, 21 July 1925, 17 December 1925 and 27 January 1926, BA, NS1/341.

31. 'Bericht über die Bezirkstagung in Bochum am 3. Oktober 1926', reprinted in Beck, *Kampf und Sieg*, p. 571.

32. The individual function of each of the *Gauleiter* of *Gau* Ruhr is noted in a letter from *Gauleitung* Ruhr to RL, 29 March 1926, BA, Sammlung Schumacher 203.

33. 'Bericht über die Bezirkstagung in Bochum am 3. Oktober 1926', in Beck, *Kampf und Sieg*, p. 572.

34. 'Aufruf', *VB*, 24 March 1926; 'Parteigenossinnen! Parteigenossen!', *VB*, 27 March 1926; 'Für den Volksprotest gegen das gesetzwidrige Redeverbot Adolf Hitlers', an eight-page special edition on 'Warum Adolf Hitler nicht reden darf', *VB*, 30 March 1926.

35. Wagner to *Gauleitung* Ruhr, 7 April 1926, BA, NS1/338 Bd.1.

36. Ibid.

37. Police report, Recklinghausen, 22 May 1926, StAM, Nr. 2076.

38. Homann to *Gauleitung* Ruhr, 20 May 1926, BA, NS1/342.

39. P.Hüttenberger, *Die Gauleiter* (Stuttgart, 1969), p. 38. The increasingly acrimonious relationship between the three *Gauleiter* is also reflected in Goebbels' diary entries for 30 May, 5 and 7 June 1926; see H. Heiber (ed.), *The Early Goebbels Diaries. The Journal of J. Goebbels from 1925–1926* (London, 1962).

40. Hüttenberger, *Die Gauleiter*, pp. 46–8.

41. Kissenkoetter, *Gregor Strasser*, pp. 31–2.

42. A popular pamphlet distributed in *Gau* Ruhr was entitled 'Ist das dein Kampf gegen den Kapitalismus, Marxist?': text reprinted in Beck, *Kampf und Sieg*, pp. 592–3; the original is to be found in HA, 58/1399. A number of pamphlets and texts supplied by the RPL to *Gau* Ruhr for election propaganda in 1928 are contained in

HA, 5/136.

43. See police reports on speeches by Kaufmann, Duisburg, 10 October 1925, StAM, VIII-64, Bd.1; and on Wagner, Recklinghausen, 1 October 1925, StAM, VII-2, Bd.4. Goebbels' views emerge from his 'Lenin or Hitler?' speech, a great favourite of his, frequently given in the Ruhr; it is reprinted in Zeman, *Nazi Propaganda*, pp. 189–211.

44. See police report, Recklinghausen, 21 December 1925, StAM, VII-2, Bd.4; also report by *Landrat*, Beckum, 17 May 1926, StAM, VII-64, Bd.1.

45. Working-class members accounted for 44.3 per cent to 56.8 per cent of the Nazi membership in the *Ortsgruppen* of Barmen, Langerfeld, Mülheim and Mettmann by 1926: M. Kater, *The Nazi Party. A Social Profile of Members and Leaders 1919–1945* (Oxford, 1983), p. 246, table 4.

46. The following files contain numerous reports on Nazi meetings covering the 1925 to 1928 period, BA, NS1/338, Bd.1; StAM, Nr. 2076 and VII-2, Bde.4–5.

47. Beck, *Kampf und Sieg*, passim.

48. See a number of reports submitted to *Gauleitung* Ruhr by the *Bezirksleitungen* of Bielefeld and of Arnsberg for 1926 in BA, NS1/338, Bd.1. Cf. Hiemisch, *Nationalsozialistische Kampf*, passim.

49. Orlow, *History of the Nazi Party*, pp. 78–82.

50. By 1928 the larger *Ortsgruppen* had extensive horizontal organisational structures, as is clear from a report on Hattingen *Ortsgruppe*, dated 26 April 1928, in HA, 5/136.

51. Beck, *Kampf und Sieg*, passim.

52. Wagner in particular had developed into an effective speaker and propaganda specialist. He was invited by Strasser to speak on propaganda aspects at a special conference organised by the RPL during the Nuremberg Party Conference in August 1927: details in HA, 21/390.

53. 'Rundschreiben', 1 September 1927, BA, Sammlung Schumacher 373.

54. *VB*, 14 December 1927.

55. On the changes see 'Lagebericht Nr. 63', 29 January 1928, HA, 70/1529. On Himmler's role in the RPL see Kissenkoetter, *Gregor Strasser*, pp. 35, 55–60.

56. 'Rundschreiben Nr. 76', section 5, 24 April 1928, HA, 5/136.

57. Ibid., section 1.

58. 'An alle Gaue und selbstständigen Ortsgruppen der N.S.D.A.P.',7 May 1928, HA, 3/81–82.

59. See, for example, Himmler's instructions relating to the distribution of pamphlets in 'Anordnungen der Propagandaleitung', *VB*, 8/9 May 1928.

60. For the following see 'Rundschreiben Nr. 76', 'Rundschreiben Nr. 77', and 'Nachtrag zu Rundschreiben Nr. 77', 24 April, 7 and 8 May 1928, A, 5/136.

61. These were entitled 'Ich hasse die soziale Revolution wie die Sünde' (anti-SPD, pro-labour), '2500 Millionen Goldmark' (anti-Dawes Plan), and 'Die Regierung ist gestürzt!' (anti-Marxist); copies in HA, 5/136. For leaflets produced by the RPL for use in the 1928 campaign see HA, 3/81–82.

62. Probably few branches bought their leaflets from Munich. There is positive evidence of one pamphlet which was printed in Munich and distributed in Westphalia in 1928, namely that entitled 'Idiotentraum oder Teufelspakt. Der Dawes-Vertrag'; typewritten text in HA, 3/81–82, and copy of leaflet in HA, 5/136.

63. The well-supported Hattingen *Ortsgruppe* was using locally printed leaflets to support its electoral propaganda; a copy of one of these, entitled 'Tod dem Militarismus' (anti-Marxist, anti-Dawes), is to be found in HA, 5/136.

64. A report on the Nazi campaign in the Recklinghausen area notes that 'the few election meetings held by the NSDAP were poorly attended'; police report, Recklinghausen, 10 July 1928, StAM, VII-2 Bd.5.

65. The primary purpose of Kaufmann's 'Nachtrag zu Rundschreiben Nr. 77' was

to put some momentum into the campaign, HA, 5/136.

66. Hiemisch, *Nationalsozialistische Kampf*, pp. 41–3.

67. Cf. Childers, *The Nazi Voter*, pp. 122–4.

68. The disappointment felt by the party hierarchy is noted in 'Runderlass', Berlin, 13 July 1928, HA, 69/1509.

69. See commentary in *VB*, 31 May 1928. Cf. P. Stachura, 'Der kritische Wendepunkt? Die NSDAP und die Reichstagswahlen vom 20. Mai 1928' (hereafter 'Wendepunkt'), *Vierteljahrshefte für Zeitgeschichte*, 26, 1 (1978), pp. 88–90.

70. Percentages relating to the 1928 election based on data taken from *Statistik des deutschen Reichs* (hereafter StDR), Band 372, II (Berlin, 1930), pp. 35–41.

71. 'Rundschreiben Nr. 79 — Lehren aus dem Wahlkampf', 6 June 1928, HA, 5/136.

72. On the conclusions reached by the RL see Stachura, 'Wendepunkt', pp. 93–9.

73. Hüttenberger, *Die Gauleiter*, pp. 48–9. Cf. Böhnke, *NSDAP im Ruhrgebiet.*, pp. 119–20.

74. 'Rundschreiben — Parteigenossen Gau Ruhr', 8 November 1928, HA, 5/136.

75. Beyond acquiring the *Gauleiter* position, Wagner was also one of the 12 Nazis elected to the Reichstag in May 1928.

76. 'Rundschreiben', 18 August and 11 September 1928, HA, 5/136.

77. On the drastic impact of the economic crisis in Westphalia see the reports by the *Landesarbeitsamt* for 1929, 1930 and 1931 in the Westfälisches Wirtschafts Archiv (Dortmund), file K2/410; the collapse of local government finance is reflected in the reports contained in file K2/743; an insight into the difficulties of regional industry is to be found in files K2/49 and K2/284.

78. For the development of the party see Orlow, *History of the Nazi Party*, pp. 175–84.

79. The growth of the party is mentioned in the reports by the authorities contained in StAM, files VII-2, Bd.6 and VII-64, Bd.2; see also Staatsarchiv Detmold (hereafter StAD), file M1 IP/604.

80. 'Bezirksvertretertagung, Gross-Dortmund', 2 February 1930, StAM, VII-67, Bd.1.

81. Noted in report by the *Regierungspräsident*, Minden, 23 August 1929, StAD, M1 IP/604. Cf. Childers, *The Nazi Voter*, pp. 129–30.

82. Wagner to Strasser, 2 September 1929, BA, NS22/1076.

83. In his report to the RL on 7 November 1930, Wagner claimed a membership strength of 32,186 for *Gau* Westphalia, StAM, VII–67, Bd.1.

84. Police reports, Bochum, 1 and 24 April, and 16 September 1930, StAM, VII–67, Bd.1.

85. K. Klotzbach, *Gegen den Nationalsozialismus. Widerstand und Verfolgung in Dortmund 1930–1945* (Hanover, 1969), pp. 22 and 28 f. Cf. Hiemisch, *Nationalsozialistische Kampf*, pp. 23–6; also Beck, *Kampt und Sieg, passim.*

86. Beck, *Kampf und Sieg*, pp. 76–9.

87. 'Propaganda-Schreiben I. An alle Sektionsführer der OG Dortmund', 18 August 1930; copy in StAM, VII–67 Bd.1.

88. Cf. Stachura, 'Wendepunkt', pp. 92–3.

89. In a secret memorandum to the RL, Wagner claimed that 57.7 per cent of the party membership in the 'inner Ruhr' consisted of 'workers', just over half of these being miners: 'An die RL der NSDAP', 7 November 1930, copy in StAM, VII–67, Bd.1. The regional SPD press was also beginning to express concern about the drift of the working class towards the Nazi Party; see especially *Westfälische Allgemeine Volks-Zeitung*, 2 July 1930.

90. 'Rundschreiben', 8 May 1930, StAM, VII–67, Bd.1.

91. See police report, Recklinghausen, 12 October 1929, StAM, VII–2, Bd.6; also report by the *Regierungspräsident*, Minden, 23 August 1929, StAD, M1 IP/604.

92. For the following see the numerous reports by the authorities covering the 1929–30 period in StAM, file VII–67, Bd.1; also StAD, M1 IP/604.

93. Report by the *Landrat*, Halle i./W., 18 February 1930, StAD, M1 IP/604.

94. See reports in StAD, M1 IP/520, M1 IP/604 and M1 IP/623; also StAM, VII–89, Bd.2.

95. 'Betr. Stellung der NSDAP zum Landvolk und zur Landwirtschaft', *Rundschreiben* of the RL, Munich 3 February 1930; copy in StAM, VII–67, Bd.1.

96. Report by the *Landrat*, Ahaus, 30 August 1930, and police report, Beckum, 26 August 1930, StAM, VII–67, Bd.1.

97. Police report, Bochum, 9 January 1930, StAM, VII–67, Bd.1.

98. Thus in *Bezirk* Dortmund in 1930 the Hamm *Ortsgruppe* thought that its best hope lay in winning over the middle class, and moved the question of the *Mittelstand* into the forefront of its propaganda activity. The Mengede *Ortsgruppe* believed that the *Stahlhelm* members were ripe for conversion, and concentrated its energy in that direction. The Westerfilde *Ortsgruppe* also thought that the patriotic associations, strongly represented in the town, were the ideal target. In the *Ortsgruppen* of Selm, Bork, Olfen and Nordkirchen, where miners dominated the membership, propaganda appealing to the interests of the working class was to be pursued. See 'Arbeitsplan 1930' determined at the 'Bezirksvertretertagung Bezirk Gross-Dortmund', 2 February 1930, copy in StAM, VII–67, Bd.1.

99. Police report, Bielefeld, 16 July 1930, StAD, M1 IP/625.

100. See the analysis of Nazi propaganda in the period April to end of June in 'Lagebericht II', Police President Bielefeld, July 1930; copy in StAD, M1 IP/625.

101. The RPL was divided into two sections in April 1930. The head of Abteilung II was Fritz Reinhardt. *Gauleiter* of Upper Bavaria; see Kissenkoetter, *Gregor Strasser*, p. 55.

102. Ibid., p. 59. Whereas Kissenkoetter minimises Goebbels' role in the organisation of the September election, Childers sees Goebbels as playing a more central role; see Childers, *The Nazi Voter*, pp. 138–9.

103. *Gau* Greater-Berlin was provided with 10 pages of very precise and detailed propaganda instructions in the run-up to the September Reichstag election; see 'Propaganda Rundschreiben Nr. 16', 15 August 1930, HA, 70/1529.

104. Reports on Nazi speeches for the period August to September are to be found in StAM, VII–67, Bd.1; also StAD, M1 IP/605. Cf. Hiemisch, *Nationalsozialistsche Kampf*, pp.57–9. Böhnke overestimates the extent to which *Gau* propaganda had been co-ordinated by the RPL by 1930. The smooth-running apparatus he describes applies to 1932, and not to 1930; see Böhnke, *NSDAP im Ruhrgebiet*, p. 177.

105. The Dortmund *Gautag* of the Westphalian NSDAP on 3–4 May 1930 had been organised around the 'Against the Young-Slavery' theme; see Böhnke, *ibid.*, p. 213.

106. The following percentages are based on data in *StDR*, Band 382, II (Berlin, 1932), pp. 35–41.

107. Official figures published after the 'seizure of power' gave the Westphalian NSDAP a membership strength of 5,779 by 14 September 1930; see *Parteistatistik*, Stand 1 Jan. 1935. Herausgeber, Der Reichsorganisationsleiter der NSDAP, Band I (hereafter *Parteistatistik*), p. 26. According to a report by the *Gauleitung* Westphalia to the RL, dated 7 November 1930, the membership figure given for the *Gau* was 32,186 as by the 31 October 1930; copy of the report in StAM, VII–67, Bd.1. The figures produced by the *Gauleitung* probably included a significant percentage of 'members' not formally enrolled in the party.

108. Police report, Bochum, 21 January 1931, StAM, VII–67, Bd.2.

109. Strasser to Wagner, 24 December 1930; Strasser to Meyer, 24 December 1930, B, NS22/1076.

110. Meyer to Strasser, 5 January 1931, BA, NS22/1075.

111. The *Gauleitung* following Meyer's appointment consisted of a *Gau* manager-treasurer, a party auditor, the chairman of the *Gau-Uschla*, a propaganda leader, and the leader of the Hitler Youth; see A. Schröder, *Mit der Partei vorwärts! Zehn Jahre Gau Westfalen-Nord* (hereafter *Mit der Partei*) (Detmold, 1940), p. 16.

112. 'Gau Rundschreiben Nr. 15', 20 November 1931, StAM, VII–67, Bd.3.

113. Not surprisingly, *Reichsorganisationsleiter* Ley, in his first 'inspection' of *Gau* Westphalia-North, commented on the low standard of the *Gau* organisation; see 'Bericht über den Gautag Westfalen in Münster', January 1932, BA, NS22/1075.

114. *Parteistatistik*, p. 26.

115. Childers, *The Nazi Voter*, pp. 194–5.

116. Orlow, *History of the NSDAP*, pp. 204–05.

117. 'Rundschreiben der Propaganda Abteilung der NSDAP Gauleitung Westfälen-Süd', Bochum, 14 February 1931; copy in StAM, VII–67, Bd.2.

118. See 'Tätigkeitsbericht der Gaupropagandaleitung' of *Gau* Westphalia-North for October 1931 in Schröder, *Mit der Partei*, pp. 56–65.

119. 'Sonderrundschreiben', Bochum, 2 November 1931; copy in StAM, VII–67, Bd.3.

120. The 'Monatsberichte der RPL — Abteilung Nachrichtendienst: Information über den Gegner' are to be found in HA, 14/263, 15/284 and 285, and 89/1849.

121. Childers, *The Nazi Voter*, p. 194.

122. Meyer to Strasser, 5 January 1931, BA, NS22/1075. Cf. Ciolek-Kümper, *Wahlkampf in Lippe*, pp. 35–41.

123. 'Gaurundschreiben Nr. 15', Gelsenkirchen, 20 November 1931; copy in StAM, VII–67, Bd.3.

124. Cf. Orlow, *History of the Nazi Party*, pp. 204–07.

125. For a perceptive review of the RPL's activities in 1932 see Childers, *The Nazi Voter*, pp. 196–203.

126. A. Milatz, 'Das Ende der Parteien im Spiegel der Wahlen 1930 bis 1933', in E. Matthias and R. Morsey (eds.), *Das Ende der Parteien 1933* (Düsseldorf, 1960), p. 759, table.

127. RPL 'Sonderrundschreiben an alle Gaue und Gaupropagandaleitungen', 20 February 1932, HA, 15/287.

128. On the background to Hitler's decision to be a presidential candidate see Orlow, *History of the Nazi Party*, pp. 247–8; cf. J. Goebbels, *My Part in Germany's Fight* (New York, reprint 1979), diary entries from 17 to 22 February 1932, pp. 38–41.

129. The RPL's *Rundschreiben* and typewritten texts relating to the first presidential campaign are in HA, 15/287. Cf. material in HA, 3/81–82 and 58/1399.

130. The same approach was used by the Hindenburg camp: see pro-Hindenburg material in HA, 29/563, 30/564 and 50/1399.

131. Compare, for example, the issues of *Germania* (Catholic, pro-Hindenburg) and of the *VB* in the week before 13 March 1932, especially *Germania*, 13 March 1932, and *VB*, Sondernummer 23.

132. See the issues of *Tremonia* (Catholic), 10 March 1932, and of the *Westfälische Allgemeine Volks-Zeitung* (SPD), 3 March 1932.

133. 'Rundschreiben der RPL', Berlin, 5 March 1932, HA, 15/287.

134. Percentages taken from data in *StDR*, Band 427 (Berlin, 1932), pp. 6–7, 28–31.

135. In Westphalia many *Ortsgruppen* lacked enthusiasm and willingness to put all into the second presidential campaign, as can be seen from the admonitions handed out by Wagner in his 'Rundschreiben Nr. 4' and 'Rundschreiben Nr. 5', Bochum, 24 March and 1 April 1932; copies in StAM, Víí–67, Bd.3.

136. 'An alle Gauleitungen', Reichswahlleitung der NSDAP, Berlin, 23 March

1932, HA, 15/288.

137. For the following see 'Rundschreiben Nr. 3', Bochum, 14 March 1932; copy in StAM, VII–67, Bd.3.

138. 'Rundschreiben Nr. 4', Bochum, 24 March 1932; ibid.

139. For the themes, and the sequence of points to be made in every speech, see Wagner's 'Anordnung für den 2. Wahlgang und die kommende Preussenwahl' (n.d.); ibid.

140. See, for example, reports on Nazi election meetings in Iserlohn on 3 and 7 April 1932. The speech given on 7 April was even entitled 'Über die Hindenburgfront hinweg, mit Adolf Hitler zur Freiheit!'; reports on the speeches in *Iserlohner Kreisanzeiger und Zeitung*, 4 and 8 April 1932.

141. In his 'Rundschreiben Nr. 5' of 1 April, for example, Wagner recommended to *Ortsgruppen* the use of 'a very effective poster' directed at the female voter, 'a very good poster for farmers', and one 'for use in the red corners of our area'; copy of circular in StAM, VII–67, Bd.3.

142. Ibid.

143. Some of the RPL pamphlets and posters used in Westphalia in the presidential elections, and in subsequent campaigns, are reprinted in Beck, *Kampf und Sieg*, pp. 432–3, 437–40; see also Schröder, *Mit der Partei*, pp. 57 and 59.

144. Percentages calculated from data in *StDR*, Band 427 (Berlin, 1932), pp. 7, 28–31.

145. Prussian Landtag results taken from *Iserlohner Kreisanzeiger und Zeitung*, 27 April 1932. The Reichstag results are from Milatz, in Matthias and Morsey (eds.), *Das Ende der Parteien*, p. 782, table.

146. The RPL churned out a flood of *Rundschreiben* and texts for propaganda material for both the July and the November Reichstag elections. The material is contained in HA, 14/263, 15/288 and 289.

147. The *Rundschreiben* and election material for use in the Prussian Landtag election of 24 April are in HA, 15/286.

148. A strong critic of the way propaganda was being handled by 1932 was the *Kreisleiter* of Werne. His letters of complaint to the *Gauleitung* involved objections to his lack of freedom to formulate propaganda to suit his area, to the unrealistic demands made by the *Gauleitung* as to the number of meetings to be organised in his *Kreis*, and to the practice of the *Gauleitung* of sending him unsolicited propaganda material, the cost of which he was forced to meet. See his letters to Meyer, 7 April and 28 June 1932, in BA, NS22/1075.

149. For an account of the pessimistic mood of the Westphalian Nazis by the autumn of 1932 see Schröder, *Mit der Partei*, p. 22. Cf. Horn, *Führerideologie*, pp. 357–8.

150. The instruction was contained in Goebbels' *Rundschreiben* 'Zur vertraulichen Kenntnisnahme an alle Parteistellen', 4 June 1932, HA, 15/289.

151. Wagner to Strasser, 4 August 1932, BA, NS22/1076.

152. The way in which the opponents of the Nazis exploited the NSDAP's seeming toleration of the Papen government can be seen in the SPD's main regional paper, the *Westfälische Allgemeine Volks-Zeitung*, especially the issues of 3, 7 and 14 June 1932. The neutral stance towards Papen was soon dropped by the party; see 'Denkschrift der RPL zur Reichstagswahl 1932', 18 June 1932, HA, 15/289.

153. Wagner to Strasser, 4 August 1932, BA, NS22/1076.

154. Even the comparatively small auxiliary organisations of the Westphalian NSDAP developed their own propaganda sections in the early 1930s, as is clear from the brief accounts of the histories of the *NS-Beamtenschaft*, the NSLB and the *NS-Frauenschaft* in Beck, *Kampf und Sieg*, pp. 166–84, 190–2.

155. Cf. Turner's 'Big Business and the Rise of Hitler', in H.A. Turner, Jr. (ed.), *Nazism and the Third Reich* (New York, 1972), pp. 89–108, here p. 93.

156. *Betriebsarbeiter und Hakenkreuz*, 21 November 1931.
157. Heinrichsbauer to Strasser, 20 September 1932, National Archives, 7/1/11441.

5 RESOURCE MOBILISATION AND LEGAL REVOLUTION: NATIONAL SOCIALIST TACTICS IN FRANCONIA

Michaela W. Richter

I

Until recently, historians and social scientists studying National Socialism have concentrated on two problems: *Who* supported the Nazis? *Why* did they do so? As yet there have been few systematic analyses of questions no less significant for our understanding of the NSDAP's seizure of power: *How* did the Nazis go about recruiting and maintaining support among mass and elite publics? *How* did they manage to profit from a political, economic and social system that defeated both political parties originally far more powerful and movements no less radical.[1]

The more general issue raised by these questions is how do movements in their strategies for mobilising support take advantage of the opportunities presented by the societies in which they operate. This has been the central concern in recent investigations by social scientists of collective violence and of present-day forms of protest in advanced democracies. Such recent work has converged in a common emphasis upon the importance of movement strategies to mobilise 'resources' within a given society. This focus contrasts to previous theoretical insistence that movements be viewed as the products of a society's structure and functions. Because it analyses movement mobilisation as strategic responses to a society's 'opportunities' and 'constraints', the distinctive approach that had dominated the recent social science literature on movements is known as 'resource mobilisation theory'. After a brief account of this theory, I shall seek to apply it to Nazi mobilisation strategies and how these worked in the region of Franconia. In this way, I hope to show the potential value of this social science theory when studying the Nazi movement and its methods for achieving power.[2] The main thrust of this mode of analysis is to shift emphasis away from the 'underlying' causes of discontent, and away from the social groups allegedly drawn to social movements, towards:

the variety of resources that must be mobilized, the linkages of social movements to other groups, the dependence of movements on external support for success, and the tactics used by authorities to control or incorporate movements.[3]

Resource mobilisation theory rests on 'rational choice' models of behaviour. Social movements are studied as organisations, i.e. as collectives of rational decision-makers confronted by a set of strategic problems. These include motivating and activating members and supporters; mobilising or neutralising mass and elite publics; competing against rival movement organisations for public and elite support; utilising all possible resources offered by existing social, economic and political 'opportunity structures'; overcoming different cognitive, institutional, organisational and resource constraints. Both movement activists and ordinary members are treated as rational actors whose willingness to work on behalf of the movement organisation may be guided less by their commitment to the movement's cause than by rational calculations of the costs and benefits (in terms of expenditure of time, material rewards and losses, impact on private or social relationships) entailed by personal participation in the organisation's affairs and activities. Thus even the most fanatic members must at times be persuaded or coerced to do tasks which, in the view of the leadership, need to be done in order to achieve movement goals. According to resource mobilisation theory, therefore, a movement can compete effectively only if it maximises such internal 'resources' as the skill of its leaders, the commitment of its members, the available incentives and coercion to sustain membership activity, its organisational apparatus.

Rational calculation is no less decisive in determining how the 'targets' of movement mobilisation, i.e. friendly and hostile mass and elite publics, respond to the movement organisation's appeals and tactics. Thus the resource mobilisation approach assumes that 'deprivation' or disaffection are not enough to guarantee support for a movement organisation no matter how well it articulates the grievances, demands or expectations of those groups it seeks to attract. A movement organisation often faces competition from rival organisations within a larger movement 'sector' as well as from established parties which, of course, possess the advantage of having access to, or control of, resources vital to the very individuals or groups targeted for mobilisation. These 'targets' are in a position to choose among a variety of other organisations seeking to represent or promote their interests. Hence support for any one organisation hinges on calculations of the benefits and risks entailed by this choice. Crucial in such calculations are the prospects for the movement's success in light of the prevailing institutional arrangements, the established decision-making procedures, and the current power positions of institutional and extra-institutional competitors.[4]

Movement organisations, therefore, must strive to improve their competitive positions *vis-à-vis* their movement and party rivals. Competition forces choice among discrepant strategies. These range from attempts to present a new, or at least different, 'product'; to packaging the old one in more distinctive ways; to improving selling techniques; to offering rewards to those who choose their own product and 'disincentives' to those opting for rival products. Resource mobilisation theorists, however, stress that both the choice and the chances of success of a given mobilisation strategy depend upon a society's overall structure of opportunities. A movement organisation, in other words, must above all understand and respond to the structure of the 'market' within which it competes.[5]

The objective of external resource mobilisation, therefore, is to enhance a movement's competitive position by exploiting or altering a society's 'political opportunity structure'.[6] This is a set of conditions which potentially favour or constrain a movement's emergence, its mobilisation of mass or elite support, as well as its chances of achieving some or all of its goals. Components of a given opportunity structure may comprise any of the characteristics that define a society's political, economic and social systems.[7] Potentially favourable conditions may be conceived as 'external resources' — external, that is to the movement organisation. Like internal resources, they must first be identified and subsequently utilised or 'mobilised' by the movement organisation's leaders. Potentially unfavourable conditions are obstacles that must be overcome, neutralised or even transformed into advantages. Those structural conditions crucial to the success or failure of social movement mobilisation are: 1) the 'openness' or 'closure' of the political system to movement activity and demands; 2) the presence of 'influential' allies and support groups in the society at large; 3) the structure of party conflict and competition.[8]

Taken together these conditions establish the strategic context for movement activities. In other words, favourable as well as unfavourable opportunity structures are best viewed as sets of resources or constraints that present movement organisations with particular strategic challenges, options or possibilities. The contribution of resource mobilisation theory is precisely that it invites us to treat as dynamic the relationship between movements and their political environments. Indeed, it regards the interaction between movements and opportunity structures as a complex system of ongoing negotiations, exchanges, decisions and counter-decisions.

Few cases have provided more striking arguments for emphasising the critical role of internal and external resource mobilisation in explaining successful movement outcomes than that of National Socialism. This has been increasingly recognised by historians. Whereas earlier explanations of Nazism's electoral successes and its seizure of power had stressed the importance of unresolved structural conflicts and the psychological impact of two major economic crises on broad sectors of the German electorate, much of the current work by historians emphasises the centrality of Nazi mobilisation as the critical explanatory variable.

Thus far, however, historical studies convey little of the interaction between the NSDAP's own choice of strategies and the larger 'structure of opportunity and constraint' within which it functioned. One exception is Thomas Childers' book, which examines the NSDAP's electoral strategies and appeals against the background of the activities and orientations of the NSDAP's principal party competitors. In the following section, I shall analyse the relationship between the Republic's structure of opportunities and constraints and the NSDAP's choice of mobilisation strategies. My principal focus will be on the extent to which the Weimar party system influenced the NSDAP's mobilisation strategy, especially in the last phase of its electoral competition. I also examine how after 1928 the NSDAP developed a grassroots mobilisation strategy that successfully exploited the 'opportunities' found within the Weimar party system. In analysing Nazi implementation of their mobilisation strategy at the local level, I shall rely on my earlier study of Nazi voting and mobilisation in Franconia.[9]

II

In analyses of contemporary protest, the system of party competition has emerged as perhaps the most significant component of a
society's political opportunity structure. The dimensions of a party
system which have the greatest impact on a movement's choice of
strategy and its prospects are the following: a) the rules of electoral
competition; b) the underlying cleavages around which party
competition is organised; c) the number of parties competing; d) the
ideological distance and levels of hostility between competing
parties; e) the stability or instability of political alignments as
measured by the amount of change in the support of a given party
from one election to the next.

In democratic societies, party systems affect the goals, tactics and
prospects even of those 'revolutionary' movements which pursue
their objectives outside the existing institutions and legal procedures. But the conditions defining a society's system of party
conflict and competition become most significant when a movement
decides to forgo violent revolution and seeks instead to carry on its
struggle 'legally', i.e. within prevailing procedures and institutions.
Once a movement chooses to become a party and to achieve power
electorally, its strategic options and its chances of success are in
large part determined by the characteristics of the party system
within which it must compete. As the NSDAP was to learn,
however, the appropriate choice of strategy is not necessarily
evident from the obvious structural characteristics of a party
system; often it must be discovered through a process of trial and
error. Finally, for a movement turned party, achieving power
electorally requires a mobilisation strategy that is congruent with a
party system's distinctive features and that maximises all its opportunities while minimising the impact of its constraints. The
NSDAP's meteoric electoral rise after 1928 hinged on its adoption
of precisely such a strategy.

The NSDAP's transformation from a radical movement
committed to overthrowing the Weimar system by violence to that
system's most successful party occurred in three stages, each lasting
about four years. The first phase, which culminated with the unsuccessful *Putsch* of 1923, prompted the Nazis to adopt its 'legal'
strategy for achieving power. The second phase, which began with
the party's participation in the *Land* and Reichstag elections in 1924
and ended with its dismal electoral performance in the Reichstag

election of 1928, forced it to redirect its propaganda and to reshape its mobilisation efforts. The third phase marked the emergence of the NSDAP as Germany's strongest party. In each stage, the party's choice of tactics and its prospects for success were shaped by the character and structural logic of the Weimar party system.

During the first phase, the Nazi movement functioned outside and in opposition to the Weimar party system. Between 1919 and 1923, despite efforts by the NSDAP to acquire a mass following, its principal objective was to overthrow the Republic by force. Widespread opposition to the Republic, especially in Bavaria, provided the NSDAP with considerable elite support but its allies were not willing to risk a direct and violent confrontation with the Republic and those forces politically or legally committed to its defence. From the failure of its attempt to seize power by force, the NSDAP learned that it could never succeed without a stable mass base.

Under the Weimar Republic's system of proportional representation, the 'entry costs' for a new electoral competitor were low enough to make the 'legal strategy' attractive. But having accepted the necessity for building a mass constituency through the electoral process, the NSDAP still had to choose the appropriate 'target' to be mobilised. The NSDAP's strategic problem during the second stage of its transition from revolutionary movement to electoral competitor arose from the fact that it was forced to compete in a party system at once highly 'crystallised' and deeply polarised.[10]

At the time the NSDAP entered the electoral scene, all available 'political space' had already been staked out and pre-empted by a firmly entrenched constellation of socially-based party blocs. Between 1919 and 1933, German political and electoral conflicts were structured around three major party groups: the Marxist, consisting of the SPD and the KPD; the Catholic, consisting of the Centre Party and its Bavarian off-shoot, the BVP; and the Protestant bourgeoisie, comprising the two main liberal parties (the DDP and DVP), the leading conservative party (the DNVP) and a host of smaller special interest and regional parties. These party groupings, which had first emerged in the *Kaiserreich*, reflected the main cleavages in German society and politics: class and confession.

The Weimar Republic's party system was 'crystallised' insofar as its inherited structure of party competition persisted despite fundamental changes in the constitutional and electoral rules of the game, despite a dramatic expansion of the electorate, despite the momentous economic and political convulsions during the Republic's first years. Even the relative strength of the blocs in terms of their share of the overall vote remained analogous to that prevailing before World War I. The stability of alignments along these lines both preceding and following World War I, suggests that as German voters entered the active electorate, they identified with and formed stable attachments to parties appealing above all to distinct socioeconomic or confessional groups. Voter movements across these alignments did take place, especially in 1919 and in the period of 1930–33. But on the whole, while Weimar voters frequently switched *parties*, they generally did not move outside their respective *party blocs*.[11]

These 'crystallised' electoral alignments produced what was essentially a 'multi-polar' structure of party competition. This system has been blamed by some for having produced the Republic's governmental instability and political immobilism, which alienated so many Weimar voters.[12] The fatal flaw in the Republic's party system, however, was not so much its 'multi-polarity' but rather a pattern of party conflict that Giovanni Sartori calls 'polarised pluralism'. By this he means a competitive situation marked by deep cleavages; virtually unbridgeable ideological distance among the major parties; their inability either to agree on fundamental principles or to arrive at a consensus on basic policy issues; the predominance of centrifugal over centripetal forces to an extent discouraging all parties from occupying the political centre, and pushing them instead toward 'irresponsible opposition'.[13] This condition had its source in social, economic and political conflicts long predating the Republic. These conflicts were exacerbated by the adoption among all Weimar parties of electoral strategies which maximised differences between competing 'poles'. In multi-party systems with 'crystallised' alignment patterns, this is generally the most advantageous strategy for strengthening a party's electoral and political position. In Weimar Germany, however, such polarising strategies only intensified already deep antagonisms.

What were the implications of this crystallised and polarised party system for the electoral strategy of a 'latecomer' party such as the NSDAP? Essentially the party had two choices. It could firmly anchor itself to one or another camp, and become a particularly aggressive advocate of its interests. Alternatively, it could step outside the prevailing structure of conflict, and rally disaffected voters from all camps. In the first phase of its 'legal' strategy, the

NSDAP tried to combine both alternatives. Between 1924 and 1928, it opted for a 'catch-all' strategy aimed at reaching disappointed voters in all three camps. Within this overall strategy, the party at first tilted more towards Protestant middle-class voters, as was the case during the 1924 *Land* and Reichstag elections.[14] With the adoption of the 'urban strategy' in 1925, the NSDAP's emphasis shifted towards converting working-class supporters of the Marxist parties.[15]

Although Nazi propaganda between 1924 and 1928 was sensitive to the concrete interests of the various groups to which it appealed, its principal emphasis was on the party's anti-Semitic, anti-party, anti-parliamentarian, anti-capitalist, anti-Marxist, only vaguely socialist but decidedly nationalist positions. Using appeals which were 'left' on social and economic issues, and 'right' on those essentially political and 'national', the NSDAP sought to achieve two goals simultaneously: to transcend existing sociopolitical alignments, and to introduce a new type of cleavage in the Weimar party system. This 'new' division was meant to isolate the parties and voters who supported or at least tolerated the Republic. Against them the Nazis wished to create a common front of disappointed members of all socioeconomic and confessional groups who fundamentally opposed the 'Weimar system'.

The 'catch-all' strategy was a plausible response by a 'latecomer' party seeking to differentiate itself from all its established competitors. In Weimar Germany's 'crystallised' and 'polarised' party system, however, the Nazis' attempt to mobilise voters from all social and partisan backgrounds only blurred its image. The failures of that strategy became all too evident in the Reichstag election of 1928. After four years of intensive organisational and propaganda work, the party was left further away from power than ever. It had failed dismally in its attempt to detach working-class voters from their Marxist party affiliations. It had not added to its support among the *Mittelstand* voters who had backed the party in 1924, despite persisting economic hardships for this sector of the Weimar electorate.[16] It had failed to break down the structural barriers of the Weimar party system.

The inability of the NSDAP to capture the disaffected voters in all camps (the underlying objective of its 'urban' and 'catch-all' strategies), had brought the NSDAP once again to a critical turning point.[17] Short of abandoning the 'legal' path altogether, the NSDAP's remaining strategic alternative was to concentrate all its resources, all its organisational and propaganda efforts on the conquest of the *Lager* least likely to resist a determined assault. From this strategic perspective, the most promising target was clearly the Protestant bourgeois camp. In the first place, while the NSDAP had not done particularly well among Protestant bourgeois voters nationally, in areas where the local organisation ignored the 'urban strategy', as in Protestant Franconia, the NSDAP managed to expand its support.[18] More importantly, within the Protestant bourgeois camp were strategic 'opportunities' not found in the other two *Lager*. The most important of these were: first, the absence of cohesive, defensive organisations which had made penetration of the Catholic and Marxist camps so difficult; second, the fragmentation of the Protestant bourgeois camp into electorally weak, narrowly-based, sectarian splinter parties; third, the volatility of Protestant bourgeois voting patterns as manifested by frequent changes of parties within that *Lager*; fourth, the absence of any profound ideological and programmatic 'distance' among the NSDAP and other Protestant bourgeois parties. Together, they would greatly facilitate the task of mobilising Protestant bourgeois voters.

Within months of the 1928 election, therefore, the NSDAP's leadership redirected its propaganda and organisational efforts toward the electoral conquest of the Protestant bourgeois camp. The first step it took in this direction was to alter its propaganda approach. Abandoning the 'social revolutionary' commitments which it had emphasised during the 'urban strategy', the party once again restored to full prominence those elements of its 25-point programme which reflected traditional middle-class concerns. Henceforth, party propagandists addressed themselves more forcefully and systematically to the grievances and demands of various middle-class groups in a vocabulary meaningful to them. Subsequently, the party also established or incorporated a number of specialised departments to bring middle-class grievances to the party's attention and to aid it in formulating proposals attractive to middle-class voters. These departments (of which the *Agrarpolitischer Apparat* was the most successful) also provided local organisation with information, appropriate propaganda materials, and with specialised speakers.

As a second step, the party initiated a series of important organisational reforms. Their objective was to maximise the effectiveness of the party's drive for members and voters by establishing centralised control over every aspect of the party's organisational and propaganda resources and activities.[19] Of even greater importance than the reorganisation of the party's administrative and propaganda machinery were the changes in its electoral tactics. The Nazi leadership was well aware of the fact that its latest strategy could bring the party into power 'legally' only if the entire Protestant bourgeois vote were consolidated. To create just such a cohesive *Bürgerblock* had been the dream of every Protestant bourgeois party both during the *Kaiserreich* and the Republic. Yet none had ever managed to overcome the serious divisions among the competing parties or their electoral supporters.

For the Nazis to succeed where other Protestant bourgeois parties had failed, the party would have to meet two strategic goals. The first was to convince Protestant middle-class voters that the NSDAP was the most attractive party for them. But as long as this electorate had other options, the NSDAP could not be certain of gaining absolute control over it. Consequently, the party's second strategic goal was to remove for Protestant bourgeois voters the element of choice altogether. This electorate, in other words, had to be convinced that its very survival depended on bringing the NSDAP to power. Having failed to achieve power first by force and then by 'legal' methods, the Nazis' leaders after 1928 were determined not to be thwarted again.

To achieve both these strategic objectives, therefore, the party after 1928 adopted two sets of tactics. The first consisted of electoral and propaganda tactics that were primarily 'persuasive' in nature; their point was to 'package' and present the 'party product' in a way irresistible to 'consumer voters'. Such essentially 'legal' techniques of mass persuasion were meant to transform the NSDAP into the dominant force within the Protestant bourgeois camp. Unconvinced that persuasion alone would bring them to power as speedily as they desired, however, the party's leaders also opted for 'coercive' tactics as an integral part of its new mobilisation strategy. This second type of tactics encompassed extra-, semi- or illegal methods ranging from overt and indirect forms of violence directed at individuals or specific groups to public activities and behaviour designed to undermine the routine functioning of existing institutions and procedures. By creating political chaos and uncertainty on the one hand, and an atmosphere of personal fear on the other, these coercive tactics aimed to force still reluctant Protestant bourgeois voters to back the Nazis. A second purpose underlying the use of coercion was to cow the weaker and more timid partisans of the Catholic and Marxist parties into supporting the Nazis. The following section examines just how the Nazis used both persuasion and coercion to eliminate its rivals within the Protestant bourgeois camp and to challenge the hold both the Catholic and Marxist parties traditionally exercised over their own supporters.

III

In its efforts to acquire an electoral monopoly within the Protestant bourgeois camp, the NSDAP relied predominantly (but not exclusively) on 'persuasion'. In Franconia as elsewhere in Germany, its grassroots tactics aimed to 'sell' the party as the only one within this camp both genuinely committed to the interests of all middle-class voters and capable of winning power. As of 1928, it was no easy task to convince Protestant bourgeois voters to experiment with yet another party claiming to defend their interests.

By the time the NSDAP began to pursue the Protestant bourgeois vote in earnest, the Franconian electorate had been profoundly shaken by a prolonged economic crisis. Throughout the 1920s, Franconia's agriculture had been in a severe state of depression. The dismal state of agriculture caused hardships for the shopkeepers and artisans in rural areas whose principal clientele were farmers. Franconia's industries, most of which were engaged in small-scale manufacturing and handicrafts, were equally depressed. Lacking the necessary funds to modernise and to meet stiff international competition, most firms were working at only a fraction of total capacity. Unemployment rose, straining the finances of Franconia's rural and urban communities. Many of these were forced to cut back services, civil service salaries and positions.[20]

Franconia's grim economic situation offered the NSDAP a golden opportunity by providing it with an aggrieved electorate desperate for drastic and radical solutions to their problems. But this crisis also had consequences which could potentially impede the mobilisation of Protestant bourgeois voters. First, years of economic hardship had produced a sharp rise in voter hostility toward all parties claiming to represent their interests. By 1928, the rural population in particular had come to view elections as meaningless because parties only 'made speeches and excuses'. In some Middle Franconian communities, popular resentment of the main parties resulted in boycotts of party meetings, the organisation of counter-meetings, and in calls for a boycott of the 1928 *Land* and Reichstag elections.[21] Although the Nazis certainly shared this aversion to political parties, as an electoral contender they would nonetheless have to overcome widespread voter apathy or suspicion within the Protestant bourgeois camp to yet another middle-class party.

A second effect of the economic crisis of the mid-1920s was that it heightened antagonisms within the middle-class electorate. In their anxiety and anger, middle-class groups often blamed each other for their own economic plight. Thus Franconia's farmers viewed civil servants as parasites whose jobs in the rural counties (*Bezirksamt*) should be eliminated. Civil servants, in turn, complained that by doing the state's dirty job, they earned the hatred of the local populace but not a sufficient income.[22] *Handwerker* in Franconia's small towns were accused by their farmer customers of being overpriced, while *Handwerker* felt farmers were depriving them of work by doing their own slaughtering and baking. Both felt that shopkeepers paid them too little for their goods and services, while overcharging their customers. Shopkeepers, in turn, resented competition from consumer co-operatives and department stores. So intense had these antagonisms become that many of the co-operative efforts traditional in rural communities had ceased.[23] For the Nazis (as for Protestant bourgeois parties in general) mutual resentments within the middle-class electorate made its mobili-sation potentially difficult since any programme or position which might please one middle-class group was bound to alienate another.

To overcome the obstacles of voter hostility and internal fragmentation, as well as its own electoral weakness, the NSDAP had to differentiate itself sharply from its competitors within the Protestant bourgeois camp. By 1928, middle-class voters generally perceived their own parties as indifferent to the plight of the *Mittelstand*; as perfunctory in their contact with voters once elections were over; as divisive and forever squabbling; as far too weak and timid to protect their voters against the 'threat' of the more cohesive Marxist and Catholic camps. Against these percep-tions, the NSDAP strove to project an image as the only party really concerned about and active on behalf the interests of this electorate; as a visible, dynamic, aggressive competitor bound to succeed where the other middle-class parties had failed; as unified, powerful and implacable in its dealing with the Protestant *Mittelstand*'s Marxist and Catholic opponents. How did the NSDAP manage to create such a favourable image in Franconia?

By far the most important tactics for making itself attractive to middle-class voters were those designed to demonstrate the NSDAP's active commitment to their interests. Without any distinctive economic ideas and programmes of their own, Nazi propagandists sought to distinguish the NSDAP from its competitors by contrasting their party's readiness to do something about the economic problems facing middle-class voters with the inactivity and empty rhetoric of all the other parties claiming to defend middle-class interests. Thus to project an image of concern to Franconia's farmers, Nazi councillors in communal and district councils (*Bezirks-* and *Kreistage*), pushed legislation prohibiting all forced sales; reducing local taxes; and requiring the take-over of farmers' debts by the district council to prevent forced farm auctions.[24] Similarly, to show its commitment to the region's shopkeepers, merchants, artisans and civil servants, local Nazi councillors pressed for bills imposing higher taxes on department stores, chain stores and consumer co-ops; reducing taxes for small businesses, shopkeepers, and artisans; giving public contracts to smaller businesses and shops rather than to co-ops; demanding that councillors forgo their own salaries in order to save those of lower civil servants.[25] But unlike all the other Protestant bourgeois parties, the Nazis went beyond mere verbal and legislative support of middle-class groups. To dramatise its solidarity with farmers, for example, Nazi activists frequently organised or participated in actions with local farmers aimed at impeding or physically preventing forced auctions from taking place.[26] In Franconia's towns, a favourite tactic for winning approval from small businessmen was to organise boycotts against department stores and consumer co-operatives. For example, prior to the opening of a new department store in the Upper Franconian city of Bayreuth, the NSDAP organised a week-long campaign (*Grosskampfwoche*) against it.[27]

For the most part, these endeavours on behalf of middle-class groups were symbolic gestures. For the Nazis, concrete results were less important than the appearance of commitment. Indeed, most measures pushed by Nazis in local councils, were designed to be rejected by the other parties. Had these measures been passed, they would have proven liabilities for the Nazis. As it was, they could use rejections of their proposals as evidence that the Protestant bourgeois parties did not really care for their constituents or to argue that the SPD and BVP actively opposed the interests of the *Mittelstand*. Most importantly, through such symbolic legislative acts and public activities, the NSDAP projected a concern that had enormous impact on voters who felt betrayed and deserted by their own parties.

In persuading Protestant bourgeois voters to desert their own parties, Nazi propagandists sought to present the NSDAP as a 'super interest party', more committed to middle-class interests than any of its Protestant bourgeois rivals. The Nazis realised, however, that attempts to reach and unify this electorate with coherent programmes equally attractive to all its competing sectors had traditionally failed. Consequently their own tactics aimed not to transcend but to exploit the divisions and antagonisms within the Protestant bourgeoisie. The party's campaign appeals, therefore, were highly differentiated, focusing on the grievances and interests of distinctive occupational groups within the larger middle-class electorate. Thus many of its public meetings were addressed to carefully circumscribed middle-class audiences: civil servants, teachers, artisans, shopkeepers, farmers, rentiers, white-collar workers. In these specialised meetings, each group was made to feel that its interest was central to the party's concerns. The speakers used by the Nazis on such occasions came from the same occupational background as their audience; thus their promotion of the NSDAP's programme seemed plausible. Such specialised audiences also enabled the Nazis to make promises to each group without challenge.[28]

The NSDAP, however, took care to phrase its appeals in terms that combined interests and principles. Nazi propagandists were especially adept at making their audiences feel that their demands were both justified and in the interest of the entire national community. Furthermore, the fact that the Nazis shifted to more concrete economic proposals after 1928 did not mean that they moderated any of their extremist views and rhetoric or abandoned any of their more abstract core propaganda themes. Instead, they strove to get their audiences to recognise the larger cause of their own immediate, everyday problems. Thus the Nazis linked the salary cuts of civil servants, or the high taxes of farmers and shopkeepers, to the huge sums Germany had to pay for reparations. Similarly, it always connected its attacks on banks, department stores and the middle class's economic devastation to the machinations of Jewish capitalism or to the Jewish-Bolshevik conspiracy to destroy German society and its true foundation, the *Mittelstand*.

To convert its image as an attractive, committed middle-class party into electoral support, however, the NSDAP had to be perceived by middle-class voters as a potential 'winner'. By 1928, many supporters of the Protestant bourgeois parties had come to feel that their votes were 'wasted' because of the number of competitors within this camp and their congruent electoral weakness.[29] The NSDAP's own electoral performance in the May 1928 Reichstag election was not likely to encourage voters who wanted their vote to be a 'sound investment'. Consequently, the party had to convince voters that it had the resources, the energy, the drive, the capacity for achieving power. Toward this end, party strategists devised a carefully planned set of tactics.

The objective of these tactics was both to make every voter in the Protestant bourgeois camp aware of its existence and positions and to maintain the party's visibility and pressure at all times. Locally, the techniques used by the Nazis involved agitational activities at both the mass and individual level. In Franconia, the NSDAP's principal techniques of 'mass persuasion' were the tactic of 'perpetual campaigning'; periodic propaganda saturations of selected areas; incessant public meetings during and between elections; a massive and a constant flow of propaganda materials in the form of party newspapers, stickers, flyleafs, posters, handbills or emblems; weekend propaganda trips into rural areas; organising and participating in communal festivals, public ceremonies and holiday festivities; and presenting various forms of public entertainment such as SA marches and concerts, dances, film and slideshows and theatre performances. To reach individuals personally the Nazis relied on such tactics as door-to-door canvassing, direct mailing, discussion evenings in local bars and restaurants, personal visits by Nazi activists, and providing practical assistance for needy individuals whom public authorities were unable or unwilling to help.[30]

Many of these mobilisation tactics had the additional objective of conveying to Protestant bourgeois voters an image of dynamism, strength, unity, determination. This was the purpose of the Nazis' saturation campaigns and the strategy of perpetual campaigning; of SA marches, demonstrations, military exercises; of the flood of propaganda materials unleashed at the grassroots; of the party's drive to penetrate even the most remote area or the tiniest of villages. The NSDAP's incessant activities and propaganda barrages enabled it to drown out rival political messages, to overwhelm Protestant bourgeois voters with its omnipresence, to convince them that the party was more likely to succeed than any of the other competitors in this camp. The Nazis also challenged the bourgeois parties more directly with scathing attacks on their weakness, ineffectiveness, divisiveness and readiness to compromise with the Republic and the Marxists.[31] But it was the NSDAP's own organisational and propaganda skills in creating the image of an invincible, irresistible, powerful political machine that was to be its best and most convincing advertisement.

IV

The NSDAP, however, went considerably beyond legitimate activities to achieve its electoral goals. The party's post-1928 mobilisation strategy combined to an equal degree persuasive and coercive tactics. Hans Schemm, perhaps the most skilled and dynamic of Franconia's Nazi leaders, captured the essence of the NSDAP's new propaganda approach when he referred to it as combining *'Geistigkeit und Armgewalt'*.[32] This duality essentially reflected the view Nazi propagandists and strategists had of voters as 'enemies' to be 'assaulted' and 'conquered'. Consequently, even their 'persuasive' tactics had a 'coercive' quality. In outlining tactics to their cadre, for example, Nazi leaders and propagandists consistently employed military imagery. The *Reichspropagandaleitung* memo of 4 July 1932, describes the effect to be achieved by the party's co-ordinated saturation campaigns as a 'unified assault' on the 'system and its parties'.[33] Reinhold Muchow's pamphlet on how to organise and maintain a local party cell, 'Guerrilla war: Experiences and advice for the daily battle' (*Kleinkrieg: Erfahrungen und Ratschläge des Tageskampfs*), exemplifies the Nazis' conception of grassroots mobilisation as a military operation.[34] Nor did the coercive character of Nazi electioneering go unnoticed by contemporaries. Especially prior to and during elections, the bi-monthly reports to Munich from Franconia described the region as being 'assaulted', 'besieged', or 'bombarded' by waves of meetings and masses of propaganda.[35]

Nazi coercion, however, was not limited to symbolism and

imagery. On the contrary, such blatant forms of coercion as vicious verbal attacks, violence, open threats on life and property, and general intimidation were all integrated into Nazi mobilisation strategy. The principal purpose of these coercive methods was to convert a potential into an actual revolutionary situation. For the NSDAP, the advantage of this strategy was twofold. First, it would create such extreme and chaotic conditions as to push into support of the NSDAP those Protestant bourgeois voters not 'persuaded' by the Nazis' legal tactics. In other words, these reluctant middle-class voters were forced to choose between Nazism and continued upheavals or even the putative triumph of Bolshevism. Secondly, such an extreme revolutionary situation might stimulate defections from weaker and more timid Catholic and Marxist partisans uncertain that their own parties could withstand the Nazi onslaught enough to protect their supporters.

What presented the Nazis with a potential revolutionary situation was the condition of 'polarised pluralism'. This characteristic feature of the Weimar party system can be likened to a potential revolutionary situation as defined by Charles Tilly: 'when a government becomes the object of effective, competing, mutually exclusive claims of two or more distinct polities.'[36] The condition of 'polarised pluralism' had resulted from unresolved conflicts among the principal party blocs on the one hand, and from the mode of voter mobilisation adopted by all the Weimar parties, on the other. Generally speaking, Weimar parties pursued mobilisation strategies which aimed both to create strong 'boundaries' around their constituencies and to develop a 'siege mentality' (*Lagermentalität*) among their own supporters by treating electoral competition as zero-sum conflicts between 'friends and foes'. The point of this strategy of 'negative integration' was less to mobilise hitherto untapped sources of support than to ensure the absolute loyalty and solidity of a party's traditional electoral base.

To turn the high level of conflict inherent in Weimar party politics into an actual revolutionary situation, the NSDAP adopted grassroots tactics designed to: 1) intensify polarisation to the point of civil war; 2) undermine the will and the capacity of governmental authorities to respond to the Nazi challenge; 3) destroy popular confidence in the integrity of governmental authorities and their capacity to maintain 'law and order' or to protect the life, security, property of individual citizens. All three conditions are generally vital to the success of any revolutionary movement. The success of the NSDAP's 'revolution-making' strategy of mobilisation hinged above all on the party's ability to exploit at the grassroots level the extreme antagonism between the major party camps as well as on its adoption of tactics characteristic of the more lethal forms of '*Klein-krieg*' or guerrilla warfare.[37]

In Franconia, all parties resorted to electoral strategies which heightened antagonisms among the competing party blocs. The Catholic Centre's right-wing offshoot in Bavaria, the Bavarian People's Party (BVP), persistently attacked Protestant bourgeois parties for aiming to destroy Bavaria's separate identity and for perpetuating religious conflicts. It reminded its voters of the unbridgeable chasm between Catholicism and Protestantism on the one hand and Catholicism and Marxism on the other.[38] It identified the DNVP as the party of 'Prussian Junkers'; the liberal parties as the representatives of '*Grosshandel*', '*Judentum*' and '*Frei-maurer*'.[39] The SPD was depicted as the party of international Jew-ry, as atheistic and anti-clerical, as determined to expropriate the property of Bavaria's peasants.[40]

Franconia's Protestant bourgeois parties, in turn, accused the BVP of maintaining a 'party tyranny' aimed at the 'ruthless exploi-tation' of Protestant Franconia and of favouring the SPD at the expense of the 'patriotic' NSDAP.[41] They vilified the SPD for its radicalism, for representing Jewish Bolshevism, for trying to destroy the region's *Mittelstand* by its support for department stores and consumer co-ops. The SPD response was to accuse these parties and the BVP of sympathising with the Nazis, of wanting to overthrow the Republic, and destroy the few gains the working class had made under the Republic.[42]

Party-political divisions governed all aspects of people's associa-tional life. Thus in Franconia's small towns one would frequently find socialist, Catholic and 'bürgerliche' glee clubs, sports clubs, hiking and bicycle clubs, veterans' associations, sewing and reading circles. Political orientations even influenced charity so that many a town in the region supported three politically-based Red Cross associations.[43] Even in small communities, this segmentation of all associational life minimised contacts across party lines and thus reinforced the mutual antagonism separating the major camps.[44]

In Franconia as elsewhere in Germany, the National Socialists took full advantage of this embattled political milieu. The NSDAP's mobilisation strategy, unlike that of the other Weimar parties, went considerably beyond converting existing tensions into useful propaganda slogans. Its principal endeavour was to so intensify the level of conflict among the major party camps as to create an atmosphere of civil war. The tactics they used toward this end combined vicious verbal attacks and considerable physical violence directed above all at the Marxist and Catholic parties and their supporters. These were depicted as such a threat to middle-class interests that extreme steps had to be taken to safeguard Protestant bourgeois voters. The NSDAP offered itself as the only party within the Protestant bourgeois bloc willing and able to confront the grave danger posed by the Catholic and Marxist camps.

In their verbal attacks, Nazi speakers vilified the SPD and the BVP in the crudest possible terms. The SPD was represented as an evil, satanic, anti-Christian, Jewish-backed force which aimed to destroy German society and culture as well as the economic existence of the *Mittelstand*. The BVP and the Centre Party were described as political whores for their willingness to co-operate with the SPD at the national level. Nazi propagandists labelled BVP politicians as black Jews and dismissed them, like the Socialists, as criminals, scoundrels, pigs, curs and vermin who deserved to hang from the next lamp post. Indeed, Nazi speakers made it clear to their audience that they had every intention of doing just that once they came to power. Even the Catholic clergy did not escape the Nazis' scurrilous attacks. Catholic priests were accused of worrying more about the people's wallet than about their souls and of using their office to sell the corrupt politics of the BVP; there were even calls for the elimination of this 'black breed'.[45]

To heighten anti-SPD and anti-BVP feelings among Protestant bourgeois voters, Nazi speakers also made every effort to lump the SPD and BVP together. Thus they increasingly spoke of a Red-Black conspiracy against the Protestant middle class, of a Red-Black murder front, of Red-Black thiefs. In demonstrations through Catholic and working-class areas, the SA had a marching refrain that accused the BVP of having helped the SPD to betray Germany: 'Who betrayed the fatherland? The Social Democrats! Who was there with them? The Bavarian People's Party.' ('Wer hat das Vaterland verraten? Die Sozialdemokraten! Wer war auch dabei? Die Bayrische Volkspartei!')[46] The point was, of course, to simplify the lines of conflict as being essentially a choice between the 'black' supported 'Bolshevik' menace and the National Socialist *Volksgemeinschaft*. In this struggle, Nazi speakers insisted, there could be no neutrality. Whoever did not join or support the NSDAP must be a Bolshevik and should expect to be treated as such once the Nazis came to power.[47]

The NSDAP did not confine itself to verbal assaults. Beginning with the communal elections of 1929, the NSDAP unleashed systematic, massive violence against the supporters of the BVP and SPD. Disruptions of SPD and BVP meetings, preventing such meetings from being held altogether, provocative marches through Catholic and socialist areas, communities and neighbourhoods were all occasions for increasingly nasty and lethal brawls and battles. To these were added literally thousands of fights between individual supporters of the NSDAP, the Marxist parties and the BVP. Nor was this violence limited to larger cities. On the contrary, the Nazis quite deliberately made physical clashes a daily occurrence in every Franconian community. The scale and pervasiveness of violence and terrorism had three purposes: first, to convince middle-class voters that Marxism and 'political Catholicism' constituted a real, physical threat which only the Nazis were capable of meeting; second, to make it so difficult and costly for the BVP and the Marxist parties to meet publicly as to force their followers to conclude that these parties had ceased to be a real match for the Nazis; third, to create a civil war psychosis among the supporters in all camps.

Such an atmosphere, the Nazis calculated, would help them either by provoking supporters of the left and Catholic parties into actions that would prompt Protestant bourgeois voters to close ranks behind the NSDAP, or else enable the NSDAP to present itself as the only party capable of restoring 'law and order'. With the help of the SA, the NSDAP was able to achieve all the objectives. Throughout 1931 and 1932, the region was described as close to civil war. In every community the atmosphere was filled with implacable hostility and pervasive violence. Despite valiant efforts by the BVP and SPD to counter the Nazis, they found it increasingly difficult to meet publicly with their supporters. Finally, popular anxieties and fear were exacerbated by perpetual rumours of *coups*.[48]

In addition to creating civil war-like conditions at the local level, the NSDAP's grassroots activities, both violent and non-violent, had two further purposes. The first was to undermine the capacity and will of local authorities to respond to the Nazi challenge. The second was to destroy public confidence in governmental authority. To achieve the first objective, the Nazis used several tactics.

Knowing that the Bavarian government required every Nazi meeting to be reported by local gendarmes, the NSDAP sought to overwhelm the resources of local governments and the local police through its perpetual campaigning and its pervasive use of violence. Furthermore, Nazi speakers would use these meetings to wear down the police, ridiculing the policeman's assignment, encouraging him to join them, or threatening him with reprisals once the Nazis came to power. Regional reports to the Munich government attest to the success of these tactics. They persistently point to the physical and psychological exhaustion of the gendarmes assigned to control the Nazis as well as to police conversions to the NSDAP.[49]

To intimidate other local officials and civil servants, the NSDAP used overt threats of widespread dismissals or reprisals as well as 'rumours'. Thus local Nazis were reputed to have drawn up 'blacklists' with the names of all those who opposed the NSDAP. So successful were these tactics that when the heads of Middle Franconia's rural districts were asked if they had heard such rumours or threats, 20 admitted that they had but did not report them because of possible risks to their lives or positions.[50] Still another tactic was to make authorities look ridiculous. Thus SA and Nazi members sought to circumvent the *Uniformverbot* of 1930, by appearing in full formation dressed in white shirts, or even wearing no shirt at all. To ridicule the prohibition of inflammatory speeches, Nazi propagandists announced talks with deliberately absurd titles.[51] Finally, the SA and Nazi party members would openly defy local authorities in their attempt to enforce prohibitions restricting them. By 1931, the party had so demoralised Franconia's local police and authorities that the Munich government was frequently forced to admonish Franconian officials for failing to enforce directives against the Nazis.[52]

The NSDAP's evident success in undermining the capacity of local governments to respond to its challenge also served the party's other important objective, namely to weaken public confidence in local authorities and institutions. The Nazis deepened this public disillusionment by 'politicising' local government; by making it difficult for local government to function; by reducing popular respect for individual officials through character assassination, lies, or linking local government officials to scandals and corruption.[53] No less important were those tactics designed to heighten the sense of vulnerability and insecurity among individual citizens.

Anonymous and open threats against individuals, actual acts of terrorism and attacks on property, rumours of job losses, fear of Nazi-organised boycotts of stores and small businesses were frequently cited by local authorities as the principal reasons for Nazi support.[54]

After 1928, this combination of highly sophisticated techniques of mass persuasion with all-out coercion helped the NSDAP to achieve the first of its strategic objectives, the conquest and consolidation of the Protestant bourgeois vote. That these tactics worked so well, however, was due above all to the party's effectiveness in mobilising both the external 'resources' or opportunities in the Weimar party system and those internal to the party. Conditions in the Protestant bourgeois camp provided not only the Nazis but other bourgeois parties with potentially favourable external 'opportunities'. But unlike its bourgeois rival parties, the NSDAP understood how to turn these into an electoral advantage. The absence of a strong defensive party and a high degree of fragmentation provided the NSDAP with easy access to Protestant bourgeois voters and a virtual monopoly over the flow of information reaching them. But the NSDAP also made sure to fill the organisational vacuum left by the underorganised *Honoratiorenparteien*, or splinter parties, with its own extensive organisation and its aggressive propaganda activities. It also utilised this camp's fragmentation by playing off group against group, and by countering it with an image of strength, unity and determination. Finally, the party profited from the fact that many of its positions were part of the ideological 'mainstream' of the Protestant bourgeois camp so that there was little 'distance' between it and most of its rivals. To derive maximum advantage from this opportunity, however, the NSDAP actively recruited local bourgeois politicians, officials and 'opinion leaders' as members and speakers. This was critical for giving the party the respectability and legitimacy it needed to sway the generally cautious voters of Franconia's rural communities and small towns.

Once the NSDAP had begun, after 1928, to exploit the structure of party conflict in Weimar Germany, the Nazis could take advantage of yet another 'opportunity'. In the first stage of its electoral participation, the extreme antagonism among the three major party blocs had undermined the NSDAP's 'catch-all' strategy. For its 'revolution-making' strategy, however, Weimar Germany's crystallised and polarised party politics was ideal. The NSDAP's competitors within the Protestant bourgeois camp had done much to create and maintain their supporters' resentments toward the more cohesive and powerful Marxist and Catholic parties. But beyond highly combative rhetoric, they had done little to counteract these parties. By contrast, the Nazis used the antagonism Protestant bourgeois voters felt towards these powerful competitors to launch a frontal assault on them. Their ruthless exploitation of the intense conflicts which defined Weimar party politics brought the NSDAP the desired electoral gains within the Protestant bourgeois camp.

No less important for the party's post-1928 electoral surges was the effectiveness of its 'internal resource mobilisation'. When the NSDAP's leadership moved towards the rapid expansion and centralisation of the party's organisation and activities, they were careful to devise ways for preventing the expanding party bureaucracy from weakening the drive and enthusiasm of grassroots activists. By making the SA a central part of its mobilisation strategy, the party not only retained the loyalty of its most radical activists but could marshal their fanaticism and energy for its ambitious and extensive electoral and propaganda schemes. By requiring local branches to keep the national organisation regularly informed of their organisational and propaganda efforts the party discouraged any laxity among its grassroots leaders and members. Forcing local branches to be financially self-sufficient and also to provide the national party with badly needed funds, had the effect of pushing local leaders and members into an endless stream of activities designed both to spread the party's message and to generate additional 'resources' (e.g. members or funds) for the party. Such activism served yet another purpose, namely to create a strong bond among new members and thus to intensify their commitment to the party. The NSDAP, in other words, used activism both as a 'resource' for mobilising potentially passive members and as a means to acquire additional capacities needed for effective mass mobilisation.

The NSDAP had adopted the 'legal' path to power with great reluctance. Unlike its major foe and rival, the SPD, however, the NSDAP refused to be tamed or moderated by its entry into competitive party politics. Thus whereas the SPD has been described as 'a *revolutionary* but not a *revolution-making* party', the NSDAP was the reverse, a revolution-making but not necessarily revolutionary party. As opposed to the SPD, Nazi strategists treated electoral participation not as an alternative to revolution but as the pursuit of revolution by other means. In the process, the NSDAP demonstrated that turning a radical movement into an effective electoral competitor does not invariably moderate a movement's goals or behaviour.

After 1928, the NSDAP succeeded in mobilising the 'opportunities' of the Weimar party system in a way that enabled it to achieve power without having to abandon its radicalism. It should be stressed, however, that the 'legal' transfer of power was not the result of an electoral majority. Indeed, even in the second phase, when the NSDAP used every possible legal and illegal method, it fell short of achieving this objective. Certainly, its 'revolution-making' strategy only partially succeeded in persuading or coercing Catholic and Marxist voters to jump on its 'bandwagon'. Despite considerable defections, enough remained faithful to their parties to prevent the NSDAP from achieving the electoral majority needed for a strictly 'legal' seizure of power. In the final analysis, it was the NSDAP's 'influential allies' that made possible its victory. In a sense, therefore, the real makers of the Nazi revolution were Weimar Germany's conservative economic, social and political elites who had hoped to use this radical movement turned party for their own objectives. That many of the party's elite supporters instead fell victim to the revolution they helped to succeed is one of history's fitting ironies.

Notes

1. Two notable exceptions are the recent study by Thomas Childers, *The Nazi Voter: The Social Foundations of Fascism in Germany, 1919–1933* (Chapel Hill and London, 1983), and Jutta Ciolek-Kümper's *Wahlkampf in Lippe* (München, 1976).
2. The major works in the development of resource mobilisation theory have been: John D. McCarthy and Mayer N. Zald, 'Resource Mobilization and Social Movements: A Partial Theory', *American Journal of Sociology*, 82, May 1977, pp. 1212–41; Charles Tilly, *From Mobilization to Revolution* (Englewood Cliffs, N.J., 1978), Mancur Olson, Jr., *The Logic of Collective Action* (New York, 1968), W.A. Gamson, *The Strategy of Protest* (Homewood, Ill., 1968); James Q. Wilson, 'The Strategy of Protest: Problems of Negro Civic Action', *Journal of Conflict Resolution*, 5, 1961, pp. 291–303; Anthony Oberschall, *Social Conflict and Social Movements* (Englewood Cliffs, N.J., 1973). An excellent review of resource mobilisation theory can be found in Sidney Tarrow, *Struggling to Reform: Social Movements and Policy Change During Cycles of Protest*, Western Societies Program, Occasional Paper No. 15, 1984, Center for International Studies, Cornell University.
3. McCarthy and Zald, 'Resource Mobilization', p. 1213.
4. See especially Craig Jenkins, 'Dancing Among the Elephants: Thinking Small in a Restrictive Polity', Paper presented at the Conference on Social Movements and

Policy Outcomes, Cornell University, May 6–8, 1983. John W. Foley and H.R. Steedly, Jr., 'The Strategy of Social Protest: A Comment on a Growth Industry', *American Journal of Sociology*, 55, May 1980, pp. 1426–7.

5. The treatment of social movement organisations as part of 'movement sectors' forced to compete in a political 'market' is most developed by McCarthy and Zald, 'Resource Mobilization'.

6. The concept of opportunity structure was first developed by Peter K. Eisinger in his article 'The Conditions of Protest in American Cities', *American Political Science Review*, 67, March 1973, pp. 11–28.

7. For a comprehensive breakdown see especially Roberta Garner and Mayer N. Zald, 'Social Movement Sectors and Systemic Constraints: Toward a Structural Analysis of Social Movements', Working Paper No. 238, Center for Research on Social Organization, University of Michigan, Ann Arbor, Michigan, July 1981.

8. These conditions are stressed in particular by Peter Eisinger, 'Conditions of Protest', Frances Fox Piven and Richard A. Cloward, *Poor People's Movements: How They Succeed, How They Fail* (New York, 1979); Dorothy Nelkin and Michael Pollack, *The Atom Besieged: Extraparliamentary Dissent in France and Germany* (Cambridge, Mass., 1981).

9. Michaela W. Richter, 'The National Socialist Electoral Breakthrough Opportunities and Constraints in the Weimar Party System', Ph.D. Dissertation, City University of New York, 1982.

10. For the concept of a crystallised party system see Juan Linz, 'Some Notes Toward the Comparative Study of Fascism in Sociological Historical Perspective', in Walter Laqueur (ed.), *Fascism: A Reader's Guide* (Berkeley, Cal., 1972), p. 5.

11. The stability of the Weimar electoral alignments has been stressed especially by W. Phillips Shively, 'Party Identification, Party Choice, and Voting Stability: The Weimar Case', *American Political Science Review*, 63, 1969, pp. 1203–25.

12. This argument has been made especially forcefully by F.A. Hermens, *Democracy and Anarchy* (Notre Dame, 1941); also by Maurice Duverger, *Political Parties* (New York, 1954).

13. Giovanni Sartori, *Parties and Party Systems: A Framework for Analysis* (New York, 1976). See especially pp. 130–45 for his discussion of the major characteristics of polarised pluralism.

14. See especially Childers, *Nazi Voter*, pp. 64–87.

15. For Hitler and most of the party's Southern leadership, efforts to attract working-class voters were never understood as excluding the mobilisation of middle-class voters. Indeed, in areas where a predominantly urban focus made little sense, such as Bavaria, the party line was largely ignored. For detailed discussions of Nazi strategy between 1925 and 1928 see especially Dietrich Orlow, *The History of the Nazi Party, 1919–1933*, 2 vols. (Pittsburgh, 1969), I, pp. 76–127; Peter Stachura, *Gregor Strasser and the Rise of Nazism* (London, 1983).

16. For the causes and effects of this crisis, see Thomas Childers, 'Inflation, Stabilization, and Political Realignment in Germany', in Gerald Feldman, Carl-Ludwig Holtferich, Gerhard R. Ritter and Peter Christian Witt (eds.), *Die Deutsche Inflation: Eine Zwischenbilanz* (Berlin, 1982).

17. An especially good analysis of the 1928 Reichstag election as a turning point for the NSDAP's electoral strategy is provided by Peter Stachura, 'Der kritische Wendepunkt? Die NSDAP und die Reichstagwahlen vom 20, Mai 1928', *Vierteljahreshefte für Zeitgeschichte*, 26, 1978, pp. 66–99.

18. In Franconia, the party's share of the vote in the 1928 Reichstag election was 8.1 per cent compared to its national average of 2.6 per cent.

19. For a detailed analysis of the party's reorganisation after 1928, see especially Thomas W. Arafa, Jr., *The Development and Character of the Nazi Political Machine, 1928–1930, and the NSDAP Electoral Breakthrough*, Ph.D. Dissertation,

Louisiana State University, 1976.

20. For Middle Franconia, see especially *Halbmonatsberichte/Mittelfranken, Geheimes Staatsarchiv, München* (MA) GSA MA 102153; hereafter HMB/Mfr. GSA MA 102153; for Upper Franconia, see *Halbmonatsberichte/Oberfranken,* hereafter HMB/Ofr. GSA MA 102155/3.

21. HMB/Mfr. GSA MA 102153, 1.19.1928.

22. Antagonisms between farmers and civil servants had become so sharp that one of the bi-weekly reports Franconian Minister-Presidents had to submit to Munich noted a new form of radicalism, *Beamtenhetze.* HMB/Ofr. GSA MA 102155/3, 8.2.1929; HMB/Mfr. GSA MA 102153 8.5.1931; 10.6.1931.

23. Among examples of *gemeinnützige* work that had ceased was road repair, cleaning of drainage moats, repairs on village buildings, including the church, HMB/Mfr. GSA MA 102154, 2.5.1931.

24. HMB/Mfr. GSA MA 102154, 1.19.1932.

25. For examples of these activities see especially *Akten des Staatsminsteriums des Innern,* Neue NSDAP, files 81576–81588; (hereafter MINN) #81584 1.30.1930; HMB/Ofr. GSA MA 102155/3 1.7.1930.

26. HMB/Mfr. GSA MA 102154, 12.18.1931; 10.5.1932.

27. HMB/Ofr. GSA MA 102155/3 11.16.1928.

28. In rural communities where the salaries of civil servants was a thorny issue, the NSDAP promised to reduce civil service salaries and pensions once in power; but in towns with a large proportion of civil servants, such as Ansbach and Bayreuth, party speakers promised salary increases and better retirement conditions. GSA MA 102154, 12.16.1931; 12.18.1931; HMB/Ofr. MA 1092155/3, 2.18.1932.

29. HMB/Mfr. GSA MA 102153, 6.19.1928.

30. Franconia's ministerial reports constantly point to the NSDAP as conducting by far the largest number of meetings, as being the first party to campaign, the last to fade away, that it was active even when all the other parties lay dormant, that it was tireless in its efforts to recruit people even during times when most other parties would not dare to approach voters as, e.g., during the Christmas-New Year period or during the harvest time in the summer. By 1931 the NSDAP was described as the only visible party in Protestant Franconia; the reports also stressed that by this time not even the BVP and SPD as well as their affiliates could match the NSDAP's number of meetings. HMB/Mfr. GSA MA 102155/3 8.4.1931; HMB/Mfr. GSA MA 102153 12.4.1931.

31. One standard speech given had the title: 'Nationalsozialistische Front und bürgerlich-marxistische Zersplitterung. MINN 81582, 12.3.1929; see also MINN 81584, 3.29.1931.

32. Hambrecht, *Aufstieg,* p. 219.

33. Quoted in Childers, *Nazi Voter,* p. 199.

34. *Nationalsozialistische Briefe,* Heft 7, 1929.

35. HMB/Ofr. GSA MA 102155/3 8.18.1930; 102155/4 2.3.1932; 5.2.1932.

36. Charles Tilly, 'Revolutions and Collective Violence', in Fred I. Greenstein and Nelson Polsby (eds.), *Handbook of Political Affairs,* 8 vols. (Reading, Mass., 1975), III, 519.

37. For the objectives and tactics of guerrilla warfare, see E. Ahmad, *Revolutionary Guerrilla Warfare.*

38. HMB/Mfr. GSA MA 102153, 3.4.1928; HMB/Ofr. GSA MA 102155/2, 3.11.1926.

39. HMB/Mfr. GSA MA 102153, 5.20.1929; 6.20.1929.

40. Falk Wieseman, *Die Vorgeschichte der Nationalsozialistischen Machtübernahme* (Berlin, 1975), pp. 111–19.

41. HMB/Mfr. GSA MA 102153, 6.20.1929; 1.7.1930; 11.4.1931; HMB/Ofr. GSA MA 102155/2 4.6.1926.

130 *Resource Mobilisation and Legal Revolution*

42. HMB/Ofr. GSA MA 102155/2 4.18.1925; 10.5.1925; 3.18.1926; 10.4.1927.

43. HMB/Ofr. GSA MA 102155/3 3.3.1931.

44. Indicative of this hostility was the case of two shopkeepers in the Upper Franconian town of Rehau who were excluded from the bourgeois glee club, sports club and veterans' association for having signed two years earlier the petition for the Communist-sponsored armoured cruiser referendum. See *Polizeidirektion Nürnberg-Fürth, Politische Lageberichte der Bezirksämter*, #389 Rehau, 11.14.1928.

45. These comments were taken from a list of 50 proscribed speakers (both Nazi and Communist) and the remarks which led to their prohibition. This list, which covered the most offensive of the speeches held between April and August 1932, was to help Franconia's local authorities in banning speakers and topics the Bavarian government considered unacceptable. *Stadtarchiv Nürnberg, Bestand LRA Schwabach*, #8958.

46. Hambrecht, *Aufstieg*, p. 207.

47. MINN 81585, 6.17.1932.

48. Letter of the BVP's leader in Upper Franconia to the Bavarian Ministry of Interior of 4.16.1932, MINN 81587; HMB/Mfr. GSA MA 102153, 9.19.1929; 6.20.1930; MA 102154, 2.5. 1931; 2.19.1931; *Polizeidirektion Nürnberg-Fürth*, letter to the Bavarian Ministry of Interior, 2.18.1932; 18.8.1932; MINN 71718.

49. See for example HMB/Ofr. GSA 17.3.1931; 18.5.1931; HMB/Mfr. 102154 5.5.1931.

50. HMB/Mfr. 102154, 4.5.1932; 4.18.1932.

51. One such title was 'The cow is laughing — a dairy-political exchange' (Es lacht die Kuh — eine milchwirtschaftliche-politische Auseinandersetzung.) Hambrecht, *Aufstieg*, pp. 152, 207.

52. Letter from the Ministry of Interior to the regional governments and police authorities of 7 December 1931; GSA MA 100399.

53. *Polizeidirektion Nürnberg-Fürth, Politische Lageberichte* 151/II/29.

54. HMB/Ofr. 4.18.1932; 5.2.1932.

6 VIOLENCE AS PROPAGANDA: THE ROLE OF THE STORM TROOPERS IN THE RISE OF NATIONAL SOCIALISM

Richard Bessel

There can be little doubt that violence played an important role in the rise of the Nazi movement. The Nazi press proudly reported the violent confrontations between Hitler's supporters and their political opponents; Nazi leaders made a point of presenting themselves as tough characters who — in contrast to the men leading other political parties — were not afraid to back up words with deeds; and the Nazi movement attracted hundreds of thousands of young men into an organisation — the *Sturmab-teilungen* ('storm sections', or SA) — whose primary task lay in providing the muscle for the violent propaganda campaigns of the NSDAP. The public face of National Socialism during the 'struggle for power' was openly aggressive, and representatives of the Nazi movement made a point of asserting their willingness to engage in violence. Here at last, so the impression was cultivated, was a nationalist political movement prepared to take its message on to Germany's streets.

Examples of violent and aggressive posturing abound in the literature which emanated from the Nazi movement and in the speeches of Nazi leaders during their campaign to seize power. 'Struggle' was indeed the key word used to describe the Nazis' assault on German politics. Military metaphors permeated the Nazis' accounts of their own activities. Thus Hitler's much-publicised airborne propaganda tours during 1932 were described as a 'combat flight' (*Kampfflug*);[1] and the competition for the votes of the German electorate often was viewed in terms of war.[2] The activities of the storm troopers were described in particularly aggressive language, of 'offensives' and the 'annihilating assaults of our armies' upon the enemies of National Socialism.[3] Goebbels, in his account of the struggle for power on the streets of Berlin, portrayed the brown-shirted defenders of the Nazi faith in the following terms:

131

The SA man wants to fight, and he also has a right to be led into battle. Without a fighting tendency the SA is absurd and pointless.[4]

And the official Nazi historian of the Berlin SA described the spirit of Nazi politics succinctly when he wrote that the 'battling brownshirts of Berlin-Brandenburg' wrote their history 'not with the pen but with the fist'.[5]

The violent image which the Nazi movement wanted to present to its supporters and to the public at large was expressed clearly in the following description of a confrontation near the small Schleswig-Holstein town of Eutin in March 1929, when 'reds' threw stones and bottles at a van full of SA men after a Nazi rally:

As the vehicle was leaving the village it suddenly was pelted with stones and bottles. It halted immediately, in order to catch the perpetrators. These fell into a house. The SA now faced . . . the decisive question: Should we here and now, without any hesitation — and contrary to the principles of bourgeois law — set an example of how we apply the law of action? . . . After a short time the SA decided to follow its own revolutionary law, not bourgeois conscience, and administer the appropriate response to the cowardly ambush. The door was broken open, the windows were smashed in; in the meantime the attackers had hidden away in the house. They were taken out and beaten. In the process some of the furniture ended up in pieces. Then the SA men went on their way home.

The SA now had set out on a path for which it had been prepared spiritually long before. Even though this had not taken place in the face of great danger, it was clear now once and for all the storm troopers would never quit the field [*niemals das Feld räumen würden*], even if more difficult situations should arise.[6]

A key element of the image projected by the NSDAP was that it — alone of all the political parties — was prepared to abandon respectable bourgeois behaviour in the struggle against the 'reds' and 'would never quit the field'. Nazi spokesmen made a point of depicting their movement as the one nationalist political force whose supporters had the guts to stand their ground and fight.

Of course, Nazi violence was not just a matter of a talk. From the very beginning of the movement in the Munich beer halls of the early 1920s violent confrontation had been a staple of Nazi politics. And during the early 1930s the explosive growth of the Nazi movement was paralleled by a staggering increase in the number of politically motivated confrontations on Germany's streets. In the process, scores were killed and hundreds seriously injured. The Nazis themselves registered a growing number of 'martyrs' to the cause — rising from five in 1928 to nine in 1929, 15 in 1930, 42 in 1931 and 70 during the first eight months of 1932.[7] During the ten days preceding the July 1932 Reichstag elections, when political activity reached a feverish pitch, the Prussian Interior Minister recorded 317 'political excesses' on Prussian territory in which 24 people lost their lives and 285 were injured.[8] Even during the later months of 1932, when the political violence had ebbed somewhat from the summertime peak, the Prussian Interior Ministry continued to record hundreds of 'political excesses' monthly. In most instances either Nazis or Communists were identified as the 'aggressors', each in roughly 40 per cent of the cases; members of Social Democratic organisations, the *Reichsbanner* or the Iron Front, generally figured as 'aggressors' in fewer than 10 per cent of the confrontations.[9] With the Nazi propaganda machine staging thousands of political demonstrations and rallies — any one of which could provide the spark for a confrontation — and as the Nazis sought to challenge the grip of the 'Marxist' parties (the SPD and KPD) in working-class districts, virtually every German city and town came to be treated to a regular diet of political violence.

Although the lion's share of this violence involved the Nazis and the parties of the Left, it did not stop there. Among their targets the Nazis included Jews and Jewish businesses, Poles living in the eastern Prussian provinces, representatives of the Catholic Centre Party (for example, in Upper Silesia), and, on occasion, even supporters of the German National People's Party, with whom Hitler had formed the short-lived 'Harzburg Front' in the autumn of 1931 and with whom he was to form a coalition government in January 1933.[10] And the violence was not limited to urban areas. The countryside too was affected. Indeed, once the Nazi movement had grown to mass proportions and come to dominate politics in the Protestant countryside, the tactics of the storm troopers often were more effective on the land (where they met with relatively little opposition and where the SA easily could outnumber left-wing opponents and police) than in the cities. And as the number of violent political confrontations escalated, the police too became involved in countless brawls sparked by rallies, marches and demonstrations. Thus during the final years of the Weimar Republic political activity increasingly came to involve violence or at least the threat of violence. Violent incidents became so widespread that virtually no corner of Germany had been spared by the time Hitler arrived in the Reich Chancellory.

Nazi politics during the 'period of struggle' can be characterised with much justification as the politics of aggression and violence. Yet it is one thing to note that violence was of importance to the rise of the Hitler movement; it is another to determine what role the violent aspects of Nazi politics played in mobilising support. It is the purpose of this article to suggest what was the contribution of the politics of violence to the Nazi rise. To what extent did political violence, as practised by the Nazi storm troopers, actually succeed in mobilising the masses?

In approaching this question, it is necessary to be aware not just of the widespread nature of Nazi violence during the final Weimar years but also of its limits. To begin with, violence did not bring Hitler to power, at least not directly. Hitler was not carried into the Reich Chancellory on a wave of revolutionary violence created by the SA but was, in the apt and oft-quoted phrase of Alan Bullock, 'jobbed into office by a backstairs intrigue'.[11] Some SA leaders may have fantasised about a violent seizure of power, particularly during late 1932 when it appeared that the 'legal' road to power was blocked by the inability of the NSDAP to continue attracting ever larger proportions of the German vote and the apparent unwillingness of President von Hindenburg to place Hitler at the head of a government armed with emergency powers. Thus the leadership of the Silesian SA — perhaps the most radical in Germany — spoke in December 1932 of marching towards the 'Third Reich' via the 'bloody path' since the road via the ballot box had been blocked; reviewing a specially-trained SA unit (which was intended to become a match for the *Schutzpolizei* in 'technical ability') in the Upper Silesian border town of Ratibor on 27 December 1932, Edmund Heines stressed 'that the SA must be kept ready to fight and fit to march, because it must be reckoned that the SA will march, if not already in January then in the spring at the latest'.[12] Of course such talk was absurd, for the Nazi brown shirts would have been no match for the police and the army in a violent struggle for state power. Indeed, Hitler had been forced to realise precisely this as a result of his ill-fated *coup* attempt in Munich in 1923, and for that reason had committed himself subsequently to achieving power via 'legality'.

What is more, despite the concern about it at the time and the attention paid to it by historians since, Nazi violence before 1933 was peculiarly limited in scope. True, the list of Nazi 'martyrs' numbered well over one hundred and those injured in violent political confrontations numbered in the tens of thousands by the time Hitler was given the keys to the Reich Chancellory. Yet when one considers, for example, the thousands who died in the political violence and terror which led to the collapse of Turkish parliamentary democracy in 1980 or the level of politically-motivated violence in Northern Ireland since 1969, the troubles on the streets of Weimar Germany seem rather mild by comparison. For all their violent rhetoric, the storm troopers did not engage in frontal attacks against the power of the state; these Nazi activists may have been fanatics, as Hitler was so fond of boasting, but they were not so fanatical as to attack police stations and army barracks.[13] Indeed, it appears that the German police were fairly successful in keeping a ceiling on the level of political violence, and the concern which was felt within the SA not to be caught with firearms betrayed a considerable respect for the forces of law and order. On the whole, the violence in which SA members were involved usually took place within fairly clear limits and in situations where the rules of the game generally were understood. The violence of the Nazi brown shirts did not comprise an uncompromising organised assault on state power, but rather consisted of a vast number of often chance encounters with opponents in which creating an impression of toughness and avoiding a loss of face took on paramount importance.

It follows from this that Nazi violence functioned less as part of a strategy aimed directly at seizing power than as propaganda. Nazi politics before 1933 were propaganda; the purpose of the NSDAP was not to formulate policy but to disseminate propaganda.[14] The policy of the party was to put Hitler into power, and the adoption of tactics of 'legality' meant that the sole function of the Nazi movement was to win as many converts as possible to the cause. Loud-mouthed SA leaders might talk about how they were going to seize power through direct action once the route via the ballot box seemed a dead end, but the truth of the matter was that the politics of violence as practised by the Nazi storm troopers was essentially propaganda.

Nevertheless, the contribution of political violence to the rise of the Nazi movement was contradictory, and the reception of the Nazis' aggressive posturing was far from clear cut. Few episodes in the history of the Nazi movement before 1933 better illustrate the contradictory nature of this violence than the Potempa murder — the brutal killing of a Polish Communist sympathiser in an Upper Silesian border village on 10 August 1932 by a drunken band of SA and SS men.[15] The Potempa murder, which was only one of an alarming number of acts of political terror committed by Nazis in the days after the July 1932 Reichstag elections,[16] became a national sensation due to a combination of circumstances: the crime itself — the sadistic murder of a defenceless young man in his home in the middle of the night and in front of his mother — was particularly disgusting; the trial which resulted was the first test of new anti-terrorist legislation brought in by the Reich government to curb the alarming spiral of political violence; the Silesian SA leader, Edmund Heines (who was to meet his inglorious end in the purge of 30 June 1934), behaved in an extremely disruptive manner during the court proceedings; and — most importantly — Hitler felt compelled to issue a message of public support for the convicted murderers. Once death sentences were passed on five members of the murder party, Hitler sent the condemned men a telegram, which was reprinted not only in the Nazi press but also in newspapers opposed to National Socialism:

> My comrades! Considering this incredible blood-judgment I regard myself bound to you in unlimited loyalty. From this moment onwards your freedom is a question of our honour, the struggle against a government under which this was possible is our duty.[17]

The leader of Germany's largest political party, the man who was insisting that he be allowed to form the next government and become Reich Chancellor, had found it necessary to voice public support for a group of drunken murderers. Alan Bullock, in his classic biography of Hitler, summed up the position well when he wrote:

> There is no doubt that Hitler's action shocked German public opinion, for the justice of the sentence scarcely admitted dispute.

Yet this was the price which Hitler had to pay if he meant to keep his movement together and preserve his authority.[18]

It is apparent that the extreme violence of some Nazi followers during the immediate aftermath of the July 1932 elections had negative effects upon the ability of the NSDAP to retain support among the electorate. Thus for example in East Prussia, where some of the worst of the terror had taken place and where the downturn in votes for the NSDAP in November 1932 was particularly steep, the *Gau* propaganda chief saw a close connection between the two developments: 'The acts of terror, which were executed systematically in the entire province, have . . . repelled the population from us.'[19] And in January 1933, shortly before Hitler became Chancellor, the Stettin Nazi Party leadership explicitly distanced itself from a bomb attack by Nazis on the offices of the city's SPD newspaper the previous summer, noting that the culprits no longer were in the NSDAP, suggesting that the attack may have been the work of a 'Marxist' provocateur in brown uniform and categorically rejecting acts of terror.[20] Yet, as the Potempa episode and particularly Hitler's remarkable reaction to it suggests, there also was a 'positive' effect of violence in attracting and keeping support. Had this not been the case, there would have been no reason for Hitler so to go out on a limb, leaving himself open to criticism and ridicule by his political opponents, in order to 'keep his movement together'. While violent excesses no doubt frightened off some of the Nazis' supporters, there were many others who either accepted or actively approved of such behaviour on the part of the brown shirts.

There is, indeed, evidence that Nazi violence generated support for the movement in some circles. Ian Kershaw has noted that the violent campaigns against the Left in 1933, particularly those against the Communists, helped bring popularity to the new regime and its leaders.[21] And the fact that millions of people cast their votes for a party which bathed itself in such violent rhetoric and gloried confrontation, that hundreds of thousands of young men joined the SA — an organisation whose functions largely revolved around violent confrontations — indicates that such activity must have had its attractions. The Nazis themselves certainly did not hesitate to give the maximum publicity to the violent confrontations in which their supporters got involved, and few of the millions of Germans who cast their votes for Hitler in 1932 could have been unaware that the Nazi movement took pride in a violent and aggressive style of politics.

But what was the appeal of this violence for the millions of good German citizens who lent their passive support to the NSDAP? Some clues may be gathered from a look at the nature of those confrontations and the role of the storm troopers in them. The first point to note in this regard is that the main thrust of Nazi violence was directed against the Left: Communists, Social Democrats, the trade unions. The struggle against the Jews and other minorities was of secondary importance in the drive for political power, and the major outbreaks of Nazi anti-Semitic violence — during August 1932 and in the spring of 1933 — took place in the wake of large-scale campaigns against the Left.

A second, related point is that there were important differences between the storm troopers' confrontations with the Communists and their struggles with Social Democrats. As has been noted above, Communists were as likely as Nazis to be the 'aggressors' in political confrontations; even when allowance is made for the anti-Communist bias of the police forces which kept records of this violence, it is apparent that the Communists were both willing and able to give as good as they got. Indeed, during the early 1930s the Communists embraced violence as part of their public image, as a necessary response to the challenge posed by the growing Nazi movement. Thus Eve Rosenhaft, in her brilliant discussion of political violence and the KPD in Berlin, describes the *'prima facie* common sense in the explicit and implicit arguments of the [Communist] streetfighters . . . that the toughness of the SA, which attracted some young men nearly as often as it threatened others, had to be met by an equally visible toughness on the part of the Communists'.[22] Such a response was virtually dictated by the rough proletarian culture of the urban environments in which the KPD operated with most success. The Social Democrats, on the other hand, figured much more frequently as the *targets* of Nazi violence. Their many party offices, trade union headquarters, newspapers and frequent attempts to stage public rallies offered tempting and, as the Nazi movement (and the SA) grew, increasingly easy targets for the storm troopers. What is more, the Social Democratic movement generally found it difficult to embrace the politics of violence. The SPD was a party which fundamentally supported democratic and parliamentary government and placed its faith in the rule of law. This helped explain the decision after von Papen's

'Prussian coup' of July 1932 by the deposed Prussian SPD ministers to resist their removal from office by recourse to the courts,[23] and also was revealed in Social Democratic responses to Nazi terror tactics.[24] Although its supporters in the republican protection squads, the *Reichsbanner*, often gave good account of themselves on Germany's streets, the ethos of the Social Democratic movement was not a violent one.

Although the Nazi violence against the Left was both aggressive in nature and directed particularly against Social Democratic targets, the impression given by the Nazi press was quite different. This discrepancy offers interesting insight into the function and appeal of violence as propaganda in the Nazi attempts to mobilise mass support before 1933. In the Nazi press confrontations with Communists were given prominence and of course the storm troopers invariably were portrayed as innocent victims of unwarranted attacks who honourably and resolutely stood their ground. A few examples should suffice. Describing an incident in Upper Silesia in January 1932 in which an SA man was killed, the *Völkischer Beobachter* reported the following under the heading 'Red Murder in Silesia':

> Party Comrade Schramm, who lives in Krappitz at present, wanted to visit his parents in Zülz. In Zülz he met *Truppführer* Steinhardt from his [SA-]*Sturm* and the town police officer Paczulla, whom he knew. Together with these two he went to the SA-barracks, Neustädterstrasse. In the Neustädterstrasse, roughly 100 metres from the SA-barracks, all three — that is, two SA men and a police officer in uniform — were attacked at 7 p.m. by 30 Communists, all of whom were armed with truncheons and knives. During this attack Schramm received a terrible blow to the back of the head from a truncheon, which was fatal. . . . Zülz, a small Upper Silesian town of 2500 inhabitants, has altogether two police officers, one of whom was on holiday. The other police officer, who was attacked as well, could do nothing against the Communists.[25]

The components of the story are revealing: innocent Nazis vastly outnumbered and attacked by a band of Communist savages; the suggestion that the victim held good family values (he was in Zülz to visit his parents!); and the impression that only the Nazi movement could prevent the red mob from taking over, since the police obviously were incapable on their own of preserving order. Another example is the reporting of one of the more serious incidents which took place in the run-up to the July 1932 Reichstag elections, the shootings in Greifswald on 18 July in which three SA men were killed.

> The march past of the [SA-] Standarte 19 in Greifswald went completely peacefully. The SA [then] was divided [into smaller groups] to eat in various inns. After almost all the SA men already were in the municipal hall, suddenly bricks were thrown from the building of the Cooperative Society (*Konsumverein*) at the SA marching by. The SA men defended themselves. The police appeared. They cleared the square, but attacked primarily the SA men. Then shots were fired from the building of the Co-operative Society, whereby two SA men were wounded . . . After calm was re-established more or less, the inspection of the SA continued. As the SA from [the nearby villages of] Dereskow and Pansow were returning home, at about 10 p.m. they were attacked and fired upon by Communists in the Loitzerstrasse. Roughly 70 shots were fired.
>
> In the process SA-Mann Ulrich Masse was seriously wounded, shot in the lungs. He collapsed and was then so worked over by the red mob with an iron crowbar that his own comrades no longer could recognise him in the clinic. He died . . . [26]

That something approaching 800 SA men had converged for a march on this small university town (which had a strong SPD and KPD presence), that during the midday meal break some groups of storm troopers had gone off to smash windows and doors in a working-class housing estate, and that the SA men fired upon as they returned to nearby villages responded by trying to storm the buildings from whence the shots had come causing more shots to be fired — such details were left out of the Nazi accounts. These accounts, predictably, stressed the bestiality of the 'red murder unity front'[27] and the alleged unfairness of the police; the Nazis were portrayed as innocent victims. In other instances even the most outrageous acts of Nazi violence were described in such terms. Thus unprovoked attacks on opponents during the Silesian and East Prussian terror campaigns of early August 1932 were reported in the *Völkischer Beobachter* under the heading: 'Self-Defence against the Marxist Blood Rabble-Rousers'.[28] And even the Potempa murder was explained away with the observation that along the Upper Silesian border 'the struggle between National Socialism and Communism is generally simultaneously a struggle between conscious Germandom and Polish insurgents — as the Potempa case has demonstrated'.[29]

Of course the Left and, when the supporters of the Centre Party were the objects of the Nazis' attentions, the Catholic press reported political confrontations in similar terms, with their followers presented as innocent victims of Nazi attacks. In this respect the manner in which the Nazi movement made propaganda out of political violence was not terribly exceptional. What merits critical attention, however, is the relationship of the reporting of an allegedly *defensive* struggle by steadfast Nazis against the 'red mob' to what in fact was an *offensive* struggle against the Left, and the degree to which this propaganda succeeded. For an important aspect of the Nazis' success in mobilising the masses appears to have been their ability to convince millions of people that they indeed were defending German civilisation against the 'Marxist' onslaught, that their violent struggle was essentially defensive in nature. This helps explain a fundamental paradox of the role of violence in generating support for the Hitler movement: that it comprised an important element of a political strategy that proved stunningly successful in mobilising those social strata — in particular middle-class groups — which one would not normally expect to endorse an outspokenly and aggressively violent political movement. The reason why violent, aggressive Nazi politics proved an attraction to so many Germans in the early 1930s was that the Nazis essentially were able to have it both ways: they could appeal *both* to roughness *and* respectability. It has been noted many times that the Nazis' propaganda during the struggle for power enabled them to appear as all things to all men. Usually such observations are made with reference to the Nazis' programmatic statements, whereby different groups were fed different and often quite contradictory diets of propaganda.[30] But Nazi propaganda was contradictory in terms not merely of what was *said* but also of what was *done*. Not just the policy statements but also the *style* of Nazi politics offered a successful mix of contradictory messages.

Through the storm troopers' activities the Nazi movement both demonstrated a readiness to challenge the Left on the streets and held out the promise of a restoration of order. Indeed, once political violence became a major component of life in Weimar Germany it could appear that the only route back to public order lay in the SA finally being allowed to wipe out the Marxist 'plague'; and in this way the mounting violence of the final Weimar years helped condition acceptance of the brutal suppression of the Left in 1933. People who were increasingly concerned about 'law and order' also often held violent antipathy towards the 'Marxists', and the Nazis were able simultaneously to profit from both sets of prejudice. For young men concerned to prove their toughness, involvement in the Nazi movement offered a way to involve themselves in politics on what might appear to be their own terms; for more elderly, more respectable members of the community, the fact that the Nazi movement was able to harness the energies of the young in a crusade against the Left considerably enhanced its appeal. Because outside the working-class ghetto the Left was perceived widely as a threat to order, the aggressive politics of the Nazis could be regarded as essentially defensive. In this way, the frame of reference within which this violence was reported in the Nazi press and in the speeches of Nazi luminaries paralleled the prejudices of a large proportion of the German electorate.[31] Thus violence itself could prove an important propaganda card with regard to both the respectable bourgeois and the young man out to demonstrate his toughness.

Another way in which the violence fit in well with the contradictory nature of Nazi politics was how it reinforced the anti-elite character of the movement. Although Hitler finally was able to get his hands on the levers of power by striking deals with men of power and influence in Berlin, one of the most important attractions of the Hitler movement was its anti-elite character. This can be seen in a number of areas. In rural communities, for example, the rise of the Nazis often consisted of a revolt of the smaller, family farmers against the political hegemony of the (Conservative) large land-owners, as the spectacular victories of the NSDAP in the elections of the Prussian agricultural chambers (*Landwirtschaftskammer*) in late 1931 clearly demonstrated.[32] The extremely positive response to the Nazi message among many smaller industrialists (as opposed to the 'captains of industry', who tended to be cooler towards the Hitler movement) points in the same direction.[33] And, of course, the oft-noted appeal of the NSDAP and the SA to the young can be seen within this framework. Not only the verbal hostility which Nazi spokesmen displayed towards established elites but also activities such as the violent disruption of attempts to auction farm properties after their owners had failed to pay debts and back taxes[34] reinforced the image of the Nazi movement as a crusade against established authority and the old elites which had had their way for so long.

That said, it also is important to recognise that one reason why violence occupied a significant place in the Nazi propaganda onslaught was that, in a sense, it was harmless. This is not to deny that being an active member of the Social Democratic *Reichsbanner*, the Communist 'Fighting League against Fascism' or the SA could be dangerous, or to assert that the street fighting which engulfed Germany during the final Weimar years was harmless child's play. However, this violence did not threaten state power; it never really reached such proportions that the police were unable to keep public order and the army was compelled to intervene; and it never really threatened the social or economic order. Indeed, for all the huffing and puffing of SA leaders, the violence in which the storm troopers so frequently were engaged was not directly relevant to the struggle for state power: as observed above, whatever the more wild-eyed SA leaders may have thought, there never was any chance that the brown shirts would carry Hitler to power by a violent attack upon the state. The fact that SA violence never posed this sort of fundamental threat to the political order could make it more acceptable to people who never would have engaged in violent politics themselves and who were desperately concerned about the maintenance of 'order'.

What this discussion suggests is that Nazi propaganda needs to be seen as more than the sum total of rallies and printed materials. Indeed, such aspects of Nazi propaganda may have been more important for the party's activists than for the German public; their main function may have been to provide the finances needed to keep the Nazi movement afloat and to give a growing army of political activists something purposeful to do.[35] But, as Ian Kershaw has noted, this is not to say that Nazi propaganda — in the wider sense — was unsuccessful: 'What the Nazis achieved above all was the creation of an image: that of a vigorous, dedicated and youthful party of force, drive and *élan*. The image, rather than any specific point of the Party programme, was often the attraction.'[36] In the construction of this image, violence played a key part. This is not to assert that the attraction of violent politics as practised by the Nazis was totally irrational, the consequences of people being swept off their feet by the intrusion of 'fanaticism' into German political discourse. The appeal of this violence could be disturbingly rational — for onlookers who were pleased to see the 'reds' being challenged, and beaten, on their own terms (even if these onlookers were unwilling to do the dirty work themselves), and for Nazi activists to whom the SA gave purpose and direction to otherwise not terribly exciting lives. But the fact that this violence comprised an important element of the Nazis' appeal helped set the NSDAP apart from most other political parties (particularly from the bourgeois parties from which the Nazis managed to draw so much of their electoral support). The Nazis were able to project an image that brought dividends at the ballot box, and one of the reasons for this success was that their propaganda involved more than pamphlets, newspapers, rallies and speeches: it also included the actions of thousands of political activists organised in the SA, actions which themselves were an expression of Nazi ideology, of the 'struggle' which was the cornerstone of the Nazi 'world view'.

Finally, it should be noted that Nazi political violence was an expression of *male* politics, as indeed was National Socialism generally. As is well known, women comprised only a small proportion of the Nazi Party membership before 1933.[37] Indeed, the participation of women was greater in just about every other major party on the Weimar political landscape. Although millions of women lent the NSDAP their passive support at elections,[38] they tended to shy away from active involvement. As Michael Kater has noted, 'it was in the final analysis a male party'.[39] But the success of National Socialism lay not simply in creating a 'male party', but in purveying male politics in general. Toughness, readiness to stand one's ground and 'never quit the field', the ability to fight for a cause and risk physical danger were values associated with manliness, and part of the success of the Nazi movement (including, perhaps, its ability to attract women's votes) was due to its ability to represent such male cultural values in the political arena. It was this mobilisation of commonly accepted values which helped the NSDAP draw mass support from across class, confessional and geographical divides to an extent never before achieved in Germany. The mobilisation of the masses which helped bring Hitler to power was not merely, or even necessarily primarily, the consequence of the Nazi Party's propaganda in the conventional sense. It was much more a reflection of the success of the Nazi movement in co-opting mainstream social and cultural values, giving them a partisan political focus, and exploiting them to construct an image which attracted a large proportion of the German electorate. In a society where politics were seen largely as a male preserve, where toughness was highly regarded, where aggressiveness was accepted so long as it did not appear aimed at destroying the social order, political violence proved an important component of a horribly successful campaign to mobilise the masses.

Notes

1. Thus the *Völkischer Beobachter*, 19 July 1932, p. 1.
2. Thus, for example, in December 1931 the Nazis described their task in Upper Silesia as conducting a 'two-front war . . . against the Poles on the one hand and against the Marxists and the Centre Party on the other'. See *Völkischer Beobachter*, 2 Dec. 1931, p. 2.
3. *Der SA-Mann*, 17 Sept. 1932, p. 1.
4. Joseph Goebbels, *Kampf um Berlin*, 9th edn. (Munich, 1936), p. 30.
5. Julek Karl von Engelbrechten, *Eine braune Armee entsteht. Die Geschichte der Berlin-Brandenburger SA* (Munich, 1937), p. 9.
6. Quoted in Lawrence D. Stokes, *Kleinstadt und Nationalsozialismus. Ausgewählte Dokumente zur Geschichte von Eutin 1918–1945* (Neumünster, 1984), pp. 75–6.
7. *Halbmast. Ein Heldenbuch der SA und SS* (Munich, 1932).
8. Institut für Zeitgeschichte (Munich), Microfilm MA 198/5, from Zentrales Staatsarchiv, Dienststelle Merseburg, Rep. 77, tit. 4043, Nr. 126, Der Minister des Innern, Berlin, 23 Nov. 1932.
9. Ibid.: reports from the Prussian Interior Ministry dated 22 Nov. 1932, 23 Nov. 1932, 7 Dec. 1932, 13 Feb. 1933, 12 March 1933.
10. See Richard Bessel, *Political Violence and the Rise of Nazism. The Storm Troopers in Eastern Germany 1925–1934* (New Haven and London, 1984), pp. 78–80.
11. Alan Bullock, *Hitler. A Study in Tryanny* (Harmondsworth, 1962), p. 253.
12. Archiwum Panstwowe w Wroclawiu, Rejencja Opolska I/1806, ff. 1043–4: Der Polizeipräsident, Landespolizeistelle, an den Regierungspräsidenten, Oppeln, 3 Jan. 1933, ibid., ff. 1037–8: Der komm. Polizeipräsident, Landespolizeistelle, an den Regierungspräsidenten, Oppeln, 2 Dec. 1932.
13. See Bessel, *Political Violence*, Chapter VI.
14. For a good illustration of this in the sphere of economic policy, see Henry Ashby Turner Jr., *German Big Business and the Rise of Hitler* (New York and Oxford, 1985), esp. pp. 60–71, 181–91.
15. For accounts of the Potempa murder and its ramifications, see Paul Kluke, 'Der Fall Potempa', *Vierteljahreshefte für Zeitgeschichte*, v (1957), pp. 279–97; Richard Bessel, 'The Potempa Murder', *Central European History*, x, 1977, pp. 241–54.
16. For accounts of the terror campaigns which followed the July elections in East Prussia and Silesia, see Bessel, *Political Violence*, pp. 87–92.
17. *Völkischer Beobachter*, 24 Aug. 1932, p. 1. The *Berliner Tageblatt* printed the text of Hitler's telegram under the heading, 'Hitler Covers for the Convicted Murderers'. See *Berliner Tageblatt*, 23 Aug. 1932. The death sentences were commuted barely two weeks later.
18. Bullock, *Hitler*, pp. 243–4.

19. Geheimes Staatsarchiv, Berlin-Dahlem, Rep. 240/B.7.d.: 'Stimmungsbericht der Gau-Propaganda Ostpreussen über die Wahlen vom 6. November 1932', Königsberg, 10 Nov. 1932.

20. *Völkischer Beobachter*, 9 Jan. 1933, p. 2.

21. Ian Kershaw, *Der Hitler-Mythos. Volksmeinung und Propaganda im Dritten Reich* (Stuttgart, 1980), pp. 48–9.

22. Eve Rosenhaft, *Beating the Fascists? The German Communists and Political Violence 1929–1933* (Cambridge, 1983), pp. 208–9.

23. See Hagen Schulze, *Otto Braun oder Preussens demokratische Sendung. Eine Biographie* (Frankfurt/Main, Berlin and Vienna, 1977), pp. 745–62.

24. A good example of this is the SPD's reaction to the first major instance of SA terror in eastern Germany: a planned attack on a Social Democratic assembly in the Silesian town of Schweidnitz. The local SPD called for tougher police action, trials were held which resulted in prison terms for 15 SA men, and the Social Democratic *Oberpräsident* in Breslau used the incident to justify ordering the dissolution of a number of NSDAP and SA groups in and around Schweidnitz. See Bessel, *Political Violence*, pp. 83–5.

25. *Völkischer Beobachter*, 26 Jan. 1932, p. 1.

26. *Völkischer Beobachter*, 20 July 1932, p. 2.

27. This phase was used in the account in the Nazi newspaper in Stettin, referring to the fact that both Social Democratic and Communist supporters had been involved. See *Pommerische Zeitung*, 19 July 1932.

28. *Völkischer Beobachter*, 2 Aug. 1932, p. 1.

29. *Völkischer Beobachter*, 24 Sept. 1932, 'Erstes Beiblatt'.

30. For Nazi 'policy' statements aimed at industrialists, see Turner, *German Big Business*, pp. 60–71, 181–91.

31. Of course the same might be said of the ways in which the Communists and Social Democrats depicted violent confrontations in the newspapers. The difference, however, was that the left-wing parties never were able to extend their support significantly beyond the working class, and thus the perceptions and prejudices which the Left built upon proved of more limited propaganda value than were the prejudices of the Nazis, who registered considerable success in attracting support from different social groups. For the best discussion of where the Nazis received their support before 1933, see Thomas Childers, *The Nazi Voter. The Social Foundations of Fascism in Germany, 1919–1933* (Chapel Hill and London, 1983).

32. See Dieter Gessner, *Agrarverbände in der Weimarer Republik. Wirtschaftliche und soziale Voraussetzungen agrarkonservativer Politik vor 1933* (Düsseldorf, 1976), pp. 248–9; Richard Bessel, 'Eastern Germany as a Structural Problem in the Weimar Republic', *Social History*, iii (1978).

33. See Turner, *German Big Business*, pp. 191–203.

34. Bessel, *Political Violence*, p. 81.

35. For this argument, see Richard Bessel, 'The Rise of the NSDAP and the Myth of Nazi Propaganda', *Wiener Library Bulletin*, 33 (1980) (= New Series, nos. 51/52), pp. 20–9. See also Turner, *German Big Business*, pp. 117–20. For criticism of my views, see Ian Kershaw, 'Ideology, Propaganda and the Nazi Party', in Peter D. Stachura (ed.), *The Nazi Machtergreifung* (London, 1983), pp. 162–81.

36. Ibid., p. 173.

37. See Michael H. Kater, 'Frauen in der NS-Bewegung', *Vierteljahreshefte für Zeitgeschichte*, xxxi (1983), pp. 204–5.

38. See Helen Boak, 'Women in Weimar Germany: The "Frauenfrage" and the Female Vote', in Richard Bessel and E.J. Feuchtwanger (eds.), *Social Change and Political Development in Weimar Germany* (London, 1981), pp. 155–73.

39. Kater, 'Frauen in der NS-Bewegung', p. 209.

7 THE NAZI PHYSICIANS' LEAGUE OF 1929. CAUSES AND CONSEQUENCES

Michael H. Kater

During the National Socialist party rally of 1929 in Nuremberg, several veteran Nazi physicians gathered together on August 3 to found the *Nationalsozialistischer Deutscher Ärztebund* (NSÄB) or Nazi Physicians' League. No action was taken at the time, but several months later it was specified that the new union should constitute a 'combat organisation' for the goals of the Nazi movement. Among its stated aims were assistance of Hitler's party in all matters affecting population and health policy, and the introduction of the newly emerging doctrines of race science into all future planning on behalf of the German *Volksgemeinschaft*.[1]

In the narrower context of the development of the medical profession in Germany since World War I the physicians' league was the result of a heightened politicisation of doctors because of very specific dislocations affecting their everyday work. Yet in a much wider sense this novel professional association must be viewed as a symptom of certain developments in the history of the Nazi Party in the latter half of the 1920s: the increasing interaction between Hitler's movement and occupational strata typically belonging to the upper layer of German society. In February 1926 the Nazi Students' League (NSDStB) had been formed, in October 1928 the Nazi Lawyers' League, and in April 1929 a Nazi Teachers' League came into being.[2] By early 1930, Weimar administrators were noting the growth of Hitler's following among the traditional professions, 'civil servants, physicians, jurists, and all manner of academics'.[3] Even before the onslaught of the Great Depression in 1929–30, which accelerated this process, the Nazis were gaining an ever firmer foothold in the German upper bourgeoisie.[4]

I

In the more specific terms of the medical profession with which this essay will be concerned, the Nazi Physicians' League was brought about by a postwar 'crisis of medicine' that had German doctors worried in city, small town and country alike. This crisis possessed socioeconomic, medico-ethical and, ultimately, political dimensions that have largely gone unnoticed in the post-1945 literature on the Weimar period, even though they are well documented in contemporary records. It would appear that such neglect has been the consequence of an undue preoccupation of modern historiography with the political history of the republic. Indeed, it is only in comparatively recent times that social historians have turned to an examination of individual strata of Weimar society and, imbedded within them, of particular occupations, of cohorts defined by gender or generational experiences, and also of interest groups.[5]

The socioeconomic aspects of the German 'crisis of medicine' may be partially traced to the immediate pre-World War I phase when somehow a larger number of medical students was admitted to the universities than could be phased into society as mature professionals in the decades to follow. After 1918, with scores of military physicians returning from the fronts, the former equilibrium between the number of sick people to be tended and the number of doctors to perform medical service was disturbed to the extent that there were not enough patients to go around to guarantee *all* the doctors the minimum standard of living they had anticipated. This problem was complicated further by the broadening of the state-anchored sickness insurance system (*Krankenkassenversicherung*): the mandatory inclusion of relatively affluent patients in the scheme meant that privately doctors could no longer charge them higher fees. In collaboration with the Weimar governmental bureaucracy and sometimes at the acquiescence of the already established resident panel doctors, the socialist-controlled sickness insurance funds established a patients-per-doctor quota and, in conjunction with this, panel practice closure for younger physicians and incoming medical graduates.[6] Throughout the 'Golden Twenties' the number of youthful applicants for an insurance panel practice on the waiting lists grew alarmingly, until by 1929 there were nearly 4,000 of them. They could ill afford to practise privately because their access to the few remaining wealthy non-insured patients was severely limited.[7]

Indubitably, most of these inadmissible *Jungärzte*, who in 1929 constituted almost 10 per cent of all the doctors in the Reich, were suffering financial hardship and, under the pall of an uncertain economic future, they harboured resentment against their established, older peers. Their opportunities for intermittent survival were limited; some worked in hospitals as voluntary or assistant doctors, often training for a specialty, but invariably on humiliating pecuniary conditions. Others eked out a meagre living as 'private doctors' after all, and others again would deputise for resident panel doctors away on vacation or sick leave. Few were fortunate enough to be offered what was considered to be an acceptable salaried position, such as in a well-to-do private clinic, and fewer still could travel the arduous route of an aspiring medicine professor at one of the nation's universities.[8] In 1927, at the apex of republican stability, a cynical observer noted that junior physicians awaiting panel certification had to be either independently wealthy, run up huge debts, or simply go hungry.[9]

As disconcerting as this situation was, it did not mean that all the established practitioners were thriving. It is true that in their earnings the most successful among them, up to 8 per cent of the total, consistently exceeded the average for the profession, and many of those lived not only affluently but liked to flaunt their wealth.[10] Nonetheless, for the profession as a whole the postwar inflation came as a shock; many practitioners lost their savings, and some were hurting because patients paid them so late as to make the remittance worthless. Relatively speaking, physicians are said to have suffered more than comparable professional groups, such as lawyers or some higher civil servants, at that time.[11]

Although in the period of economic normalisation between 1924 and 1929 the physicians were doing palpably better, they were still behind professionals in other fields, and there was an unusually high proportion of near-paupers in their ranks.[12] Thus doctors of all ages continued to request financial assistance from the *Hartmannbund*, the physicians' economic lobby, and certain doctors still would lower themselves to perform degrading physical work.[13] In 1927, country doctors were starting to get restless because of a threatening infrastructural imbalance between the city and the village that tended increasingly to impose undue economic burdens on the rural dwellers, especially in East Elbia. This latter problem was to become hugely compounded during the Depression.[14]

Throughout the period medico-ethical issues were closely tied to the economic ones by an acrimonious inter-generational conflict in the ranks of the medical profession. In 1926, those unfortunate doctors who had for years been excluded from panel practice had organised themselves under the leadership of the Cologne

University lecturer, Dr Fritz Lejeune. Their lobby, the *Reichsnotgemeinschaft deutscher Ärzte*, or Reich Physicians' Emergency League, stood in opposition to the sickness insurance funds as well as the Hartmannbund, as both were held responsible for the panel closures, even if Lejeune was eventually allowed to join the Hartmannbund's hierarchy.[15] But before this actually came to pass, the tremendous friction between older and younger colleagues erupted in the pages of the professional journals, during the summer of 1929, when Lejeune referred to an 'irrefutable cleavage between the "haves" and the "have-nots"'. Backing him, excluded doctors were charging their established peers with heartlessness, only to be told in turn that in the last few years *Gymnasium* leavers had consistently been warned not to take up medical studies.[16] As the Depression was making inroads, it was thought likely that because of their mounting 'spiritual and material destitution' young doctors would soon succumb to political radicalisation of one sort or another.[17]

The tension between young and old served to highlight other inadequacies in the medical profession, which, so it seemed, was losing some of its time-honoured moral standards. If scores of younger physicians were not allowed to benefit from the public health care delivery system at all, others, on the established side, were exploiting the lump-sum payment scheme, based upon as large a patient clientele as possible, to the fullest. A few so-called *Kassenlöwen*, 'fund lions', were amassing fortunes by treating in bulk a maximum number of patients in a minimum time-span. In so doing, they were exposing themselves to charges of mechanising the art of medicine, of turning it into a dehumanised business, so that in the end the classic physician would be replaced by what the agnostic critic Dr Erwin Liek liked to call the 'medical technician'.[18]

According to Liek and his many naturopathically inclined followers, the implications of this were grave, for the Hippocratic ideal itself appeared in jeopardy: that the patient be treated holistically, as a total organism. The fact that more and more patients were avoiding their doctors in favour of the ubiquitous quacks was interpreted by them as a sign of medico-professional deficiency. Those patients who decided to stay with their family physicians would seek to exploit the dubious benefits of blanket health insurance coverage by falsely claiming sick-leaves, sick-pay and free medications. The credibility gap between doctors and patients was compounded, so the critics charged, by the patients' tendency to let themselves be pampered for each and every ailment, allowing effeminisation to take root. This dangerous trend could only be reversed after the application of racial-eugenic principles to the science of healing, acknowledging medicine in its true role as a valuable tool of nature's own selection. Hence a reform of the medical art as presently taught in the universities was a key demand: there should be less scientific theory at the expense of pragmatic courses, and general medicine should once again receive precedence over the specialties. Only if all those conditions were met could the future health of the *Volk* be safeguarded and the 'crisis' in the medical profession itself be resolved.[19]

Ultimately, there was agreement that these solutions would have to be cast into a strong political mould in order to meet with any measure of success. At least this was the consensus among the more militant members of the Hartmannbund and of Lejeune's Emergency League, for by 1929 the conviction was growing among them that the German physician's traditional mien as a *medicus neuter*, an unpolitical creature, was about to do irreversible harm to the profession as a whole.

II

In restrospect it is clear that the reputation of the doctors as 'unpolitical' constituted a myth that was in need of exposure throughout the 1920s just as much as it still is today. Indeed, certain West German historians of medicine like Hans Schadewaldt have perpetuated it in a self-satisfying manner. By downplaying the political aspects of the German medical establishment they have been able to render more credible their version of the total victimisation of German physicians at the hands of the Nazi rulers, thus exculpating the corps of the doctors from all crimes against humanity. Politically naive professionals, so they want their readers to believe, could hardly be charged with complicity in calculated anti-Semitism, acts of medical perversion, and finally, the Holocaust.[20]

If by 1929 German doctors of medicine were, politically, not exactly polarised, the fact of the matter is that a small but virulent fringe existed on the Left, while the great majority of practitioners sympathised strongly with the nationalist Right, and a few were active on behalf of the German National People's Party

(Deutschnationale Volkspartei — DNVP) if not the growing NSDAP.

German doctors to the left of centre were the last to deny that the practice of medicine was predicated on politics and invariably had political consequences. Julius Moses, one of the most sincere physicians of the Weimar era and a prominent Social Democratic deputy, even went so far as to claim that doctors would fall victim to 'tragic self-deception' if they negated these connections.[21] On the extreme left were the Communist doctors whose political effectiveness came to be hampered by the fact that they were completely beholden to the German Communist Party (KPD) line, which implied demonstrable allegiance to the Soviet Union. Conforming with the KPD's platform, they stood for the total and compulsory adoption of communised health care, to be enforced in authoritarian fashion by the KPD's medical cadres. In such a regimen, all German doctors would have lost their highly prized professional freedom; reduced to the status of bureaucratic helots and irrespective of merit, they would have received equal salaries. Nevertheless, realising these goals for the sheer utopia that they were, Communist physicians put in selfless service for workers and paupers alike, sometimes as resident practitioners like Karl Gelbke in Leipzig, but also as local health officers like Friedrich Wolf in Remscheid. Excelling both as doctor and politician in this camp was Georg Benjamin, who served as KPD deputy in the Reichstag and wrote poignantly on issues of public health care and social work.[22]

Social Democratic physicians were both more numerous and more credible than the doctors of the KPD. In part this was because they enjoyed a genuine humanistic tradition that harked back to the prewar activities of universally respected figures like proletarian doctor Ignaz Zadek, whose charisma persisted through the entire twenties. The pioneering social hygienics scholar Alfred Grotjahn had received his decisive political impulses in the late nineteenth century, and Moses himself acknowledged as the forefather of a social-oriented medicine none other than Rudolf Virchow.[23]

Physicians associated with the SPD actively worked for the expansion of the existing state-sponsored sickness insurance system and often influenced its planning and bureaucracy. Like their Communist brethren, they were more interested in communal welfare than in the doctors' professional advancement, especially as this had lately manifested itself in the interest-lobbying of the politically right-wing Hartmannbund. Typically, they entered the public health networks in the large cities such as Berlin and Frankfurt, where they founded and administered free health-care services, homes for unwed mothers, as well as sex education and alcoholic rehabilitation centres. In 1923–4 they were instrumental in the creation of autonomous mobile medicare dispensaries (*Ambulatorien*) to offset the Hartmannbund-backed physicians who were withholding their skills in protest against the restrictive economic contracts offered them by the insurance funds. With their high proportion of Jews, these socialist physicians again resembled their Communist colleagues, but unlike those, they took seriously the mandate of the Weimar constitution to provide a comprehensive system of social — including medical — insurance for the entire citizenry of the republic, whose original political aims they shared and whose early pillar of strength, the SPD, they supported enthusiastically.[24]

If in 1927 the SPD-organised physician members of the Hartmannbund felt obliged to secede from that lobby's ranks, this more than anything was a comment on the increasing politicisation of the German doctors, those in the Leipzig union not excluded. Indeed, the SPD physicians left because they could no longer tolerate the anti-insurance system stance by leaders of the Hartmannbund, a system that was of course controlled by the Social Democrats.[25]

After World War I, in contradiction of the official stereotype of the 'unpolitical physician', the German doctors, who sociologically were a part of the educated upper bourgeoisie, typically leaned in the direction of the nationalist parties, in particular the DNVP. In domestic policy, this party observed monarchist-restorationist goals, while in foreign policy it was squarely revisionist, clamouring for the renunciation of the Treaty of Versailles and all subsequent 'fulfilment' measures *à la* Gustav Stresemann. This party was unreservedly anti-republican, anti-parliamentarian, anti-democratic, and it countenanced more than a smattering of anti-Semitism. As a staunch defender of the principles of private property and free enterprise, it was in constant readiness to strike against all forms of Marxism.[26]

Most German physicians subscribed to this platform. After having fully developed their tendency toward authoritarianism during the Wilhelmine era, they believed in the protection of their professional and social privileges through adherence to nationalist organisations.[27] After 1918, basic notions of self-interest would naturally impel them to reject Social Democrats and the republic they had erected, and the most consistent and committed ones among them would actually join the DNVP.[28]

Some doctors of medicine, characteristically teachers with a great influence on youth, had gone on record in the Great War's aftermath as uncompromising foes of the winds of change, as defenders of the old order, if need be, to the point of death. Ferdinand Sauerbruch, then in Munich and self-admittedly an 'unpolitical person', nonetheless deplored the fall of the monarchy in 1918 to such a degree that he became embroiled in the turmoil surrounding the suppression of the Soviet Bavarian Republic on the nationalist side in early 1919, risking his life by a hair's breadth.[29] Several medicine professors, among them Adolf Schmidt and the anatomists Semon and Adolphi, committed suicide over the fall of the Kaiser's Reich.[30] Berlin pathologist Otto Lubarsch, an anti-Semitic Jew who lived to hail the inauguration of Hitler as chancellor, had been a co-founder of the pre-1914 Pangermanic League. For a brief spell, the events of November 1918 rendered him physically incapable of working; later he would refer to the Western Powers merely as the 'enemy alliance states'.[31] In the early 1930s Lubarsch cited with approval the example of his Rostock colleague Ernst Schwalbe who had fought with the March 1920 Kapp insurrectionists high on horseback, only to be felled by a bullet.[32]

Schadewaldt's assertion that the Hartmannbund itself had consistently striven for 'political neutrality' is a gross exaggeration. If at all, this held true only in the most narrow sense, that of formal party-political participation.[33] As Georg Kuhns, the erstwhile executive secretary of the organisation, has seen fit to admit, the league's foundation in 1900/01 even as primarily an economic lobby had strong political overtones, for since the 1890s the regionally based insurance funds (*Ortskrankenkassen*) were, almost without exception, ruled by the SPD. On the other hand, the relationship between the Hartmannbund and the various levels of government in the Reich was not really defined in political terms; whereas Hartmann's followers remained suspicious of the originally Bismarckian, and forever after state-sponsored, social insurance schemes for the lower classes, they had no difficulty identifying with all the other political goals of the Wilhelmine monarchy, which caused them to be very loyal subjects, by and large.[34] They demonstrated their patriotism when they rushed to the colours to fight for the fatherland in 1914.[35]

The political acumen of the Hartmannbund's programme was sharpened considerably when in 1918–19 the triangular relationship between insurance funds, government and physicians' lobby changed into a bilateral one, to the extent that the former two were now merged together under single-minded Social Democratic control. From now on, every economic struggle waged by the lobby for higher lump-sum professional payments became, at the same time, a fight against the champions of the republican regime, against 'the blessings of parliamentarism', as Kuhns remarked sarcastically in 1925.[36]

Hence it was only natural that the Hartmannbund, slowly but inexorably, should drift into the DNVP's sphere of influence, which happened to be the only bourgeois party committed to the outright destruction of Weimar. The linkage was further sanctioned when in December 1924 Carl Haedenkamp, a former imperial submarine medic who had joined the Hartmannbund as its new executive secretary in 1922, was elected a Reichstag DNVP deputy, not by popular ballot which could have jeopardised electoral success, but on the guaranteed (direct-mandate) blanket roster of the Reich.[37] Conveniently, a new Hartmannbund office was set up for him in Berlin so that he could be close to the political action, and looking back, the Nazi rulers later credited him with having taken up the cudgel against everything that was obnoxious to the organised doctors, namely Marxism, 'the socialisation attempts in health insurance, the autonomous medicinal operations of the local insurance funds, the goal of a socialisation of doctors, not to forget the Socialist spokesmen'. In retrospect, the Nazis acknowledged as a clever move that Haedenkamp had waged parallel battles in the Berlin parliament.[38]

As early as the middle twenties, a small group of committed National Socialist physicians was also thriving, and growing stronger daily. It is significant that some of them, like Friedrich Bartels and Wilhelm Klein, had gained their formative political experience on the extreme *völkisch* fringe of the DNVP.[39] A collective profile of these men shows them to have been born, typically, in the 1880–1900 range, to have eagerly embraced World War I and often *Freikorps* service thereafter, and to have been prone to participation in illegal secret-society dealings that frequently led them directly to their Nazi contacts. These men had an obsession with everything that was identifiable, for rightists, with the decrepit republican value system: Marxism, parliamentary democracy and Jews. Not a few of them may have been influenced by the novel race-scientific creed, as it was being propounded by writers like Alfred Ploetz, Eugen Fischer and Fritz Lenz, and actually taught by Lenz (since 1923) at Munich University. Some became local or regional functionaries of the Nazi Party administration that was being developed; like clergy, they had built-in leadership qualities and were deemed eminently suited for the spreading of ideas.[40]

It needs emphasising, however, that on the whole these Nazi physicians of the first hour were motivated for Hitler by nationalistic and ideological factors, and not by socio-economics. Most of them were professionally well entrenched, and there is no evidence that the indigent or the obstructed *Jungärzte* among them would have looked to the pre-1929 NSDAP as a panacea for their specific problems, even though individual examples to the contrary cannot be discounted.[41]

III

On 3 August 1929, the founders of the Nazi Physicians' League set out to organise all physician members of the NSDAP, in order to harness their resources for the future of the Hitler movement. Between 30 and 50 doctors attending the party rally were readily coopted for the NSÄB.[42] They were convened by a few established senior physicians, chief among them the gynaecological surgeon Ludwig Liebl, who assumed the headship, the tuberculosis specialist Kurt Klare, and the Munich general practitioner Gerhard Wagner.

To a greater or lesser extent, these founders fitted the mould of early Nazi doctors. Dr Liebl was born in 1874 as the son of a Lower Bavarian county judge and had been practising medicine in Ingolstadt since 1909. One of the mainstays of Ingolstadt society, this World War I veteran moved from the liberal DDP to the proto-Nazi *Völkischer Block* and visited Hitler in Landsberg prison in 1924. Having joined the newly constituted NSDAP in May 1925, he continued to lend his social and financial prestige to the Nazi movement. Hitler repeatedly stayed at his house, but there is no record to show that their personal relationship had anything to do with Liebl's initiative at the 1929 Nuremberg party rally, nor do we know which particular grievances activated Liebl, political or medicinal.[43]

There is more evidence in this regard for the second among the founders of 3 August, Dr Kurt Klare. Born in 1885 in Bielefeld, he had become a doctor in 1912. Perhaps because he himself fell victim to tuberculosis (and on account of it was prevented from serving in the Great War), he dedicated his professional life to the fight against that disease. In May 1918 he was appointed Chief Physician of the medicinal spa for tubercular children, Scheidegg, in the Bavarian Allgäu. A Nazi Party member by March 1927, he had been fully engrossed in the study of racial hygienics (eugenics) since the war and attempted to link his search for a TB cure to the new dogma. In letters to colleagues and friends from the late twenties to the time of the Nazi takeover, at which point he decided to publish them, he laid down a set of rulings on 'German medicine' that could pass as a Nazi model for those years.[44] In more ways than one, they could be made to look as alternatives to the manifestations of the medical crisis currently deplored by many. Tuberculosis, which gnawed at the very marrow of the German people's backbone, could best be contained with open-air exercise, disciplined diet and self-control, rather than costly medication and protracted hospitalisation. Jewish physicians, allegedly in cahoots with morally inferior Communists, Klare regarded as swindlers, for they would advertise medicines and cures for TB that turned out to be expensive and fraudulent. There were far too many Jews in the medical faculties, said Klare, and, to make matters worse, the teaching by medicine professors was devoid of practical meaning. Nature with its healing powers had to be trusted more than books and science, for it would facilitate the 'selection of the worthy and the liquidation of the inferior' — twin goals that were seen as important projections into the future. For the present, it was only the false sense of humanitarianism that Jewish-dominated Germans had inherited from the liberal era, which prevented the full implementation of nature's selection processes. Throughout his harangues, Klare stressed the importance of instinct over reason, of the heart over the brain, and of German subjectivity over universal objectivity. His tenets implicitly served as the intellectual underpinnings for the new Physicians' League, and Klare easily assumed the mantle of the NSÄB's ideologue-in-chief.[45]

Gerhard Wagner, the third co-founder, was born 1888 in Upper Silesia. He served as army medic at the front throughout the war and then became a Freikorps member. On the staff of *Freikorps Oberland*, which earned the (later legendary) victory against the Poles at the Upper Silesian Annaberg site in early 1921, he did not return to the practice of medicine until 1924, meaning that for the better part of three years he remained involved with illegal, anti-republican schemers. When he arrived at Nuremberg from Munich in 1929, he was a card-carrying Nazi member.[46]

While nothing is known about a fourth founding father of the NSÄB, Dr Theo Lang of Munich, no doubt because he had little to contribute and soon fell into oblivion, the information on Leonardo Conti, one of the secondary movers at the Nuremberg backroom meeting, is both more plentiful and more interesting. The 29-year-old son of a Swiss postal official and his Hanoverian wife who was an anti-Semite and early follower of Hitler, Conti already had an impressive personal history of Judaeophobia from his Gymnasium days, of altercations with postwar Marxists, and of stints in a Berlin-based Freikorps. As a right-radical student leader, he had imported his anti-Semitism into Berlin University, and the Kapp Putsch found him on the side of the insurrectionists. In 1923, still a student, he stood in the ranks of *Organisation Consul*, the notorious murder squad, and from there he entered the SA. Since 1924, he had been a general practitioner in Greater Berlin, with little time for his patients, for he became involved in the organisation of the Storm Troopers (SA) medical network. With such expertise to his credit, he had been put in charge of first-aid services at the party rally in 1929. Conti's formal NSDAP membership dated from 1927.[47]

The Nazi Physicians' League lay virtually dormant for a year, for the problems of the day were not yet severe enough to propel it into action. In Munich, for instance, by July 1930, out of approximately a thousand doctors eligible for membership, only 23 had joined the organisation.[48] Interest in the union resumed in the fall of 1930, however, when the depression was taking hold of German society and, as a partial consequence of this, the Nazis gained their spectacular Reichstag victory in the September elections. It was then that the union's statutes were reviewed and finalised.[49] To spotlight it, a national convention was called in Nuremberg in early December: over 300 doctors attended, listening to papers on race or social insurance, but also to an address by party Organisation Chief Gregor Strasser, who admonished these academics to become active on behalf of the NSDAP.[50]

The next months were spent putting the NSÄB's institutional

network into place, always with a view to current recruitment needs. With NSÄB Central in Munich under Liebl and his executive secretary Dr Bernhard Hörmann, important branches were established in Württemberg (under Dr Eugen Stähle), Hamburg (Dr Wilhelm Holzmann), and Halle-Merseburg (Dr Erhardt Hamann).[51] By 1932 the NSÄB was firmly anchored in Westphalia (Dr Franz Vonnegut) and Mecklenburg (Dr Kurt Blome), with local subsidiaries in the larger cities, such as Wiesbaden and Kassel, becoming more common.[52] The second national convention in Leipzig in December 1931 already had augmented German doctors' interest in the League, and for the third Reich gathering in Brunswick, in September of 1932, as many as 1,000 came, to listen, once again, to Strasser.[53] Helped along by regional and local conferences, the NSÄB reached a national membership of just over 3,000 by the end of January 1933.[54]

As gratifying as these developments must have been to the strategic planners of the Nazi Party proper, they did not take place without a hitch. There were several leadership changes and an actual leadership crisis at the end of 1932, which threatened to disrupt the union. Secretary Hörmann was replaced by the Munich general practitioner Dr Hans Deuschl in March of 1931, and at the annual meeting of December the entire caucus was changed around. One of the new office-holders at that time was Leonardo Conti, who had been building the NSÄB chapter in Berlin since January 1931.[55] As a member of the SA, Conti had made further strides by leaking vital information regarding the first revolt of SA Captain Walter Stennes in 1930 to Goebbels, thus ingratiating himself with the SA's rival, the SS. He joined the Black Shirts in December of that year at the comparably high rank of *Obersturmbannführer* (Major). Hardly ever venturing out of Berlin, Conti built his NSÄB dependency into the strongest and most viable of all regional branches; in this he was assisted by Dr Kurt Strauss, a spokesman for the Berlin *Jungärzte*.[56] Because the ambitious Conti had irrepressible leadership aspirations of his own, he attacked the Munich duumvirate of Deuschl and Liebl in the summer of 1932, accusing it of slackness and demanding the resignation of the secretary, if not that of Dr Liebl himself. Thereupon a NSÄB honour court was convened, which almost evicted Conti from the Nazi league, but the doctor's large Berlin following and his SS connections saved him.[57] When later in the year the ailing Liebl proved too weak to continue the league's leadership, it was not

Conti who was chosen to succeed him, but Gerhard Wagner, another Bavarian-based physician, who enjoyed the special protection of Rudolf Hess and the SA.[58]

IV

The Nazi Physicians' League initially had difficulty finding its *raison d'être* for lack of an attractive cause and a distinctive target group. In claiming that it was merely a party-political combat organisation, and *not* an economic lobby,[59] it was at first puzzling to all those potential converts from the Hartmannbund who had been told by their Leipzig functionaries that it was economics that mattered and not politics. But except for size and historical background, both lobbies really were not so very different from each other, especially since they pandered to the same clientele. They were rivals rather than adversaries. It is important to remember that structurally and programmatically, the Hartmannbund was sufficiently pre-fascist and the NSÄB was enough restorationist that large parts of both were interchangeable, and significantly, in 1930–31 there was nary a Nazi physician who was not at the same time in the ranks of the Leipzig league.[60]

In the ensuing power play, the NSÄB's problem was that it had to gain on the Hartmannbund, while the Leipzig league knew that it could ill afford to lose its time-honoured priority position. In their relationship together, both lobbies were rather like NSDAP and DNVP on a larger scale. Usually quarrelling, they were resigned to the necessity of temporary alliances, though each sought to outmanoeuvre the other in the end.[61] As it turned out in the course of the Depression, the Hartmannbund's economic and political agenda appeared less and less satisfactory to many of its members, while the NSÄB seemed to embrace, in a forthright manner, political objectives that would ultimately wreak economic change. As time was to tell, that proved to be the Nazi league's principal highway to success.

One area of potential recruitment, largely ignored by the Hartmannbund, seemed particularly convenient for the Nazi Physicians' League. To seize upon the question of the profession's youth, its unemployment and economic adversities, might entail promising possibilities, especially since the generational gap between the young and the old physicians was widening dangerously every month.[62] However, the Nazi doctors were slow to recognise this opportunity, for in the generational conflict, certain of them were naturally aligned with the camp of the *beati possidentes*. It was their representatives who had founded the Nazi league: well-endowed, mature men who did not share in the problems of the *Jungärzte*, either those struggling in private practice or the wretched assistant physicians in the hospitals. They tended to agree with many Hartmannbund mandarins that the young were merely impatient and greedy, trying to dislodge older doctors from their deserved berths.[63] Some were even saying that the unprivileged junior doctors were unduly influenced by materialistic Jews in their midst.[64] Until the end of 1932, NSÄB functionaries often argued in a fashion that seemed to favour the rights of established panel physicians, urging curbs on hasty fund admittances, to be coupled with tight closure in the universities.[65]

But on the other hand, the NSÄB's doors were slowly being opened to the *Jungärzte*. In September 1930 Liebl had made a point of advertising low membership fees, so as not to discourage the poor junior incumbents.[66] Concomitantly, the Nazi league had started to publish as one of its goals the need to find openings for all the 'National Socialist recruits' to the profession.[67] Instantly, Fritz Lejeune and his Emergency League of Junior Doctors responded. Notwithstanding his formal association with the Hartmannbund, Lejeune was known to favour the Nazis and to counsel his fledglings to maintain close contact with the NSÄB.[68]

It may be assumed that one of the reasons why Conti staged his futile palace revolt in late summer of 1932 was the fact that he, as a younger doctor and in league with Berlin *Jungarzt* functionary Strauss, wanted to pursue the *Jungärzte* issue for the NSÄB much more energetically. He could see its propagandistic value as a political power tool for the entire Nazi movement. When Conti himself proceeded to talk about Jewish competitors in the profession, this made a lot of sense from his Berlin vantage point, for the capital was known to host the highest number of Jewish doctors in the Reich.[69] By 1931–2, of the thousands of German physicians on the dreadful waiting lists, a sizeable proportion possessed World War I veteran status.[70] In the face of the reported Jewish competition, and with Hartmannbund measures such as job registers and special emergency levies sadly failing them, their capacity for empathy with tough-talking Nazi functionaries like Conti, who called out solutions for the severe depression facing the nation at the

time, became larger with each passing day.[71] By this time the NSÄB
had its own job register well in place,[72] and the Nazi Party itself by
now had firmly established its reputation as a protest movement of
and for the young.[73]

Hence without actually having invested in the *Jungärzte* issue as
vigorously and as early as they could have done, the NSÄB leaders
eventually were able to profit from a situation in which young
German professionals were quickly becoming disillusioned with the
traditional mores of the bourgeois parties and their agencies. In the
Nazi Physicians' League of the early thirties, a Saxon panel doctor
who later became a victim of Third Reich terror recalls, those young
colleagues proliferated 'who hitherto had not been able to found
their own practice'. He surmises that many of the ones he knew
coveted his own establishment: a large, comfortable flat, a throng of
dedicated patients, and an influential staff position at the local
hospital.[74] In the clinics also, many a subordinate assistant doctor
appears to have cast his lot for the NSÄB, but usually in secret, so as
not to be dismissed from his post.[75]

Anti-Semitism, readily conjured up by Conti on behalf of the
neophyte doctors, was also used as a drawing card for the
entrenched physicians. Within the German medical establishment,
anti-Jewish sentiments had been widespread since the early 1880s
and were reinforced considerably after World War I.[76] During the
Weimar Republic anti-Semitic propagandists from the medical
camp like Professor Martin Staemmler of Chemnitz incited racial
hatred further by publishing various diatribes against their Jewish
colleagues.[77] It was true that Jewish physicians were overrepresented in the Reich by a ratio of about ten to one, and that in
some states like Prussia and some of the large cities like Berlin,
Frankfurt and Hamburg, the degree of overrepresentation was even
higher.[78] But it was also irrefutable that the Jewish population in the
Reich had been declining in the twenties and that because of this,
the German-Jewish physician ratio was changing as well.[79]

In regard to anti-Semitism, the Nazi Physicians' League's chances
materialised towards the end of the Weimar Republic, when the
'Jewish problem' among German doctors again became a broader
issue because of the ramifications of the economic depression.
Those chances lay in the potential for publicly upstaging the
Hartmannbund. For in spite of its inherent nationalism and its
proximity to the DNVP, the Leipzig union was at pains not to
display a racist bias, as, indeed, many of its members were Jewish

and Jews had always been prominent in its leadership echelons.[80] With the onset of the Depression, the Nazis found it auspicious to use anti-Semitic arguments against various social and professional groups in the lower and the upper middle class.[81] Against this wider background, the NSÄB after 1929 began to concentrate attacks on Jewish doctors in the profession as a whole and, to embarrass the Hartmannbund, in the ranks of the medicinal functionaries. It shrewdly calculated that a significant number of German physicians, already ill at ease over Jews on the one hand and the Leipzig league's waning credibility on the other, would lend a sympathetic ear, eventually becoming loyal converts.

While the NSÄB officially protested against 'the massive penetration of doctors' circles by Jews', individual members of the league took action on their own.[82] Some tried to prevent their 'Aryan' patients from visiting a Jewish colleague.[83] Others either strove to have Jewish physicians dislodged from local hospital positions or to keep them from starting a practice.[84] A minority of Nazi doctors also became physically abusive to Jewish patients, as did the Frankfurt physician who in 1930 in a public clinic 'goaded a seriously injured Jewish patient to stand and, in doing so, to fracture both his leg bones'.[85]

But since the opportunities for physical outrage to be vented against Jews in general and Jewish doctors in particular remained limited and, moreover, since even very few NSÄB members were willing to go to such extremes, anti-Semitic polemics through the printed or the spoken word became the usual weapon. The effectiveness of such polemical campaigns was not lost on the Hartmannbund leaders. Hence Kurt Klare, the tuberculosis specialist, conducted an extensive paper campaign against Jewish Professor Friedrich Franz Friedmann, who had invented a TB medication that had become quite popular in certain circles. Because the Nazi doctors themselves had to concede that the Friedmann cure, while not a wonder drug, was no better and no worse than other, 'Aryan' medicines, it was clear to impartial observers that the Nazis wanted it smeared merely because a Jewish physician with ties to the Prussian SPD government had made his name with it.[86]

Yet another preferred method of anti-Jewish assault was in the wider framework of cultural politics. In the final analysis, accusations of this nature could easily be linked to the new *völkisch* pseudo-science of racial hygienics, which by its very definition was aimed at the Jews. Racial hygienics was 'a branch of medicine', declared Staemmler before Saxon NSÄB members in September 1931 at Dresden.[87] That the Jewish element figured negatively in any attempt to purify the 'Nordic' race, an attempt in which the true German physician would have to play a dedicated role, was hammered into an increasing number of doctors attending NSÄB conferences in 1931 and 1932. Jews were held responsible for the deplorable decline of morals in Germany, especially during the current period of socio-economic hardship, because they reportedly advocated sexual licence. That in turn would cause disease and misery for the German race. In analogy to the problem posed by the Negro population in South Africa, the allegedly high rate of Jewish fecundity in Germany and all of Europe was denounced and an encompassing 'eugenic' solution recommended for the future.[88] These were no idle threats, for such ideas were to provide the blueprint for the *medically* informed pieces of anti-Semitic legislation as implemented by Hitler in autumn 1935, counselled, as they were, by NSÄB founder and Judeophobic activist Dr Gerhard Wagner.[89]

In the capital, with its inordinately high proportion of Jewish doctors, Leonardo Conti pursued the issue like no other functionary of the Nazi Doctors' League. Charging that the local physicians' chambers were dominated almost totally by Jews, he insinuated that the Hartmannbund itself was at the mercy of Mosaic colleagues. Using his own tabloid, Conti hurled invective against Jews not only in the city's hospitals and private practices, but also in the socialist-controlled insurance network. The Hartmannbund was reviled specifically for not being able to forestall the operations of the fund insurance's *Ambulatorien*, but also for such trifles as being susceptible to the influence of Jewish sexologist Dr Magnus Hirschfeld. Exploiting the Jewish presence in Berlin to the fullest, Conti's overall tactic was to present the NS-Ärztebund, in matters of professional politics, as the only realistic alternative to the Hartmannbund.[90]

In late summer of 1931 Conti's machinations were aided, on a national scale, by a NSÄB provocation that managed to expose, like no other incident before, the growing inertia of the Hartmannbund in the face of ever more daring political activism from the extreme right. Blaming the Leipzig league for lax political commitment in matters of concern to the medical profession, Hans Deuschl of NSÄB headquarters published an article in the Nazi press in which

Dr Alfons Stauder, the Hartmannbund's president, was characterised as a corrupt, self-serving freemason, surreptitiously backed by Jews.[91] These charges were reiterated by Deuschl and Liebl in September when it was held that they had a right to protest the leadership of German physicians, in so far as it was 'in the hands of freemasons or Jews'.[92] Recognising this challenge for what it was, namely a reckless attempt by the Nazis to rob them of their credibility, the Leipzig functionaries contemplated legal action. To postulate that Stauder was the lackey of Jews was, according to the Hartmannbund's legal advisors, an indictable offence and, along with the other insults, certainly a matter for the courts. Nevertheless, 'The point is not merely to obtain punishment of the slanderer, but also to communicate through such a verdict to the general public that these open attacks constitute sheer treachery. Yet this effect will not be reached if the judgment is handed down only a year from now.'[93]

For a while the Leipzig doctors contemplated the expulsion of Deuschl and Liebl from the Hartmannbund (which would have deprived these physicians of their panel practice privileges). But instead of pursuing this line of action further, the Leipzig league decided merely on internal censorship proceedings, which the Nazis effectively countered by claiming political motives rather than the desire to libel the private persona of Dr Stauder.[94] In October of 1932, a full year later, Stauder as much as conceded that no matter what the outcome of the drawn-out internal trial might be, the Nazis had accomplished their premeditated goal, namely 'to advertise the National Socialist movement among the doctors'. In November, the Nazi doctors were again writing with impunity that the Hartmannbund was 'marching arm in arm with Jews'.[95] Nothing more came of the affair until the Nazi takeover in January 1933, when it was hushed up, but to all intents and purposes the NSÄB, with its brazen strategy, had demonstrated a strong presence and chalked up a moral victory in the mind of many a German physician.

V

In the last 18 months or so before Hitler's debut as chancellor, the relationship between the Hartmannbund and the Nazi Physicians' League developed into a mid-size power struggle, the reverberations of which were being felt as much in public life as in intraprofessional dealings.[96] The aim of the maverick NSÄB remained unchanged: to facilitate the crossover from the larger, traditional league to the much smaller upstart by demonstrating greater awareness of professional and public concerns and by expending infinitely more energy in its promotional work. In keeping with Nazi propaganda directives in those final months of the republic, the object of Hitler's doctors was not necessarily to do more, but to give the appearance of doing more than the principal rival. Since the Leipzig league still enjoyed its monopoly as a clearing house for all panel practitioners, making resignation from its ranks an economic folly for most,[97] the NSÄB leaders could hope for nothing more than parallel membership in both organisations. Yet, as time was to prove, having one's stooges in the Hartmannbund later served admirably for the Nazi *Gleichschaltung* of that institution after 1933.[98] Presaging this, Nazi functionary Dr Deuschl exclaimed to a cheering crowd, at an extraordinary meeting of the Leipzig league on 1 November 1931, that for the present, the Nazi physicians had no stakes in toppling the Hartmannbund from its entrenched position, but that this would surely happen as soon as the swastika flag was mounted on the Brandenburg gate. While it took courage to speak such words in the lion's den, it also showed the high degree of self-confidence possessed by the Nazi strategists in those days.[99]

In its everyday polemics against the Hartmannbund, the NSÄB observed a few simple but effective rules of polemics, designed to impress the growing minority of German physicians who were ever more doubting the Leipzig league's integrity. One inviting target for the Nazis were the insurance funds themselves, whose SPD hierarchy was berated for financial waste and corruption during difficult economic times. Knowing that the Hartmannbund was anything but a friend of the funds, the best the Nazi physicians could do in this area was to accuse it of complicity or weakness in its dealings with the fund officials. In the way this message was put across, it sounded convincing to many Nazi sympathisers.[100]

Another tactic was to link the Hartmannbund's professional lobbying with Weimar politics, and notably to charge collusion with the Brüning administration. This was particularly effective after the Leipzig league had acquiesced in specific emergency legislation by the Berlin government in an attempt to approach a solution to acute problems like the *Jungarzt* impasse.[101] The Hartmannbund did not wish to annoy the 'Weimar system', charged the Nazi doctors, for it adhered to a similar philosophy of governance. In order to remain a corporate *persona grata* with the powers that be, said the NSÄB, the Leipzig league had taken a neutral stand in the contentious Young Plan issue. It had been impotent when faced with stinging emergency decrees because of the apolitical character of its upper echelons, while the NSÄB men were quite the opposite. Political animals *par excellence*, they were 'National Socialists first, and doctors second'. Because of its proximity to the Weimar regime which regulated the funds, the Leipzig league, the NSÄB physicians claimed, had damaged its reliability as interest broker for the German doctors and was well on the way to surrendering its priority position to the NS-Ärztebund.[102]

To challenge the Hartmannbund in the realm of political decision-making, and, in accordance with prescribed Nazi strategy, to force a political takeover by, formally, legal means, Nazi doctors were encouraged to run in elections at all levels of the government. To act as the chief co-ordinator in this strategy became one of the NSÄB's major functions, especially after autumn 1930. Its leaders exhorted their members to advance the cause of the Hitler movement during office hours and on social occasions, but also by declaring a willingness to assume political responsibilities to help topple the moribund Weimar system.[103] Soon socialist physicians were complaining that Nazi doctors endeavoured to put pressure on their patients, especially the workers, handing them propaganda leaflets during office visits and urging them to attend Nazi rallies.[104]

But as it turned out, in the political arena Nazi doctors were less in evidence, possibly because not enough of them would volunteer for public office. After the September 1930 general elections no physician was among the 107 Nazi deputies, even though it is not known how many of them had stepped forward to serve in the first place.[105] This situation improved somewhat when in the July 1932 Reichstag elections there were four successful physicians in the 230-strong Nazi contingent.[106] At the local and regional levels, Nazi success was also less than spectacular. Only very salient pioneers of the movement entered municipal councils, as did Dr Wolfgang Saalfeldt in Eutin in early 1931, or Dr Wilhelm Holzmann in Hamburg in the same year.[107] Even at the state level in mid 1932, no more than eight Nazi physicians, all followers of the NSÄB, had made it into *Länder* parliaments, although a fairly prominent colleague was among them, the Rostock hygienicist Professor Hans Reiter who represented Hitler's party in the Mecklenburg assembly.[108]

More conspicuous were those Nazi physicians who decided to aid the Hitler movement in some party slot, possibly because many of those chores could be done after office hours and hence professional work and income would suffer only minimally.[109] Some doctors remained in the NSÄB hierarchy, devoting themselves to the institutional development of that organisation.[110] Others branched out, discovering potential for leadership in the NSDAP at lower and, more typically, intermediate levels, but never at the highest ones. Hence Dr M. Senfftleben was party chapter leader in Freyhan, a small village in East Elbia, and the general practitioner Dr Naunin was district leader in Marienwerder, in the Polish Corridor.[111] Gynaecologist Saalfeldt was made local NSDAP chief of Eutin and regional leader for the whole province surrounding Lübeck, as well as a district functionary of the NSÄB.[112] One physician, Gera regional Nazi leader Dr Engelstädter, who served from September 1931 to the end of the republic, became something of a local legend. Credited with considerable oratorical gifts, he is reported to have advanced the cause of Nazism immeasurably in his native Thuringia, wooing the masses, haranguing the Communists, and supplying much-needed publicity to the influential press.[113]

If Engelstädter appears to have done more than his fair share for Adolf Hitler's party, the same must be said about the many NSÄB members who resolved to join the growing Storm Troopers as staff physicians. To the extent that during the Depression brawls between SA men and KPD activists were increasing in town and country, casualties in the Nazi camp were on the rise, making the services of skilled SA physicians a dire necessity.[114] Doubtless because the NSÄB provided a co-ordinating network, the creation of physician staff positions for local and regional SA formations was facilitated from early 1931 on. Hence Kurt Blome became *SA-Gausturmarzt* in Mecklenburg, attracting others in his tracks, and even the busy Saalfeldt donned the uniform of an *SA-Gauarzt* in his native Holstein. In Wiesbaden, Nazi physician Dr Althen founded SA motor battalions and trained his own SA medics.[115] In order to uphold as respectable an image as possible, the SA doctors geared themselves to the medical practices observed in the Reichswehr, and by 1932 the SA supreme command had seen to it that all physicians enjoyed the equivalent of an officer's rank.[116]

In Berlin, where circumstances warranted it, NSÄB deputy Conti had managed over time to set up a relatively elaborate SA medicinal base. This was not easy, for in the capital thousands of party and SA cronies had to be cared for, the intensity of street fights was unusually high, and rival party organisations, such as Elsbeth Zander's Nazi Women's League, tried to interfere with their own, rather more amateurish efforts.[117] Nonetheless, in April of 1931 Conti, who had some experience in these matters,[118] had organised SA and SS emergency stations in the Baerwaldstrasse, with 13 beds and support devices under the supervision of Dr Doepner. Even though this foundation relied mainly on private donations, it flourished to the point where by October 1932 a convalescence centre and staff pharmacy had been added to the initial skeletal operation.[119]

Other doctors, more or less firmly associated with the Nazi Physicians' League, chose to assist the Hitler movement from the sidelines rather than from centre stage. Using the alias of 'Kurt van Emsen', the well-known physician Dr Strünckmann published a book that polemicised against Jews and hailed the imminent coming of Hitler.[120] Certain of the doctors may have had reason to shield their vulnerable positions during months when some state governments ruled it illegal for civil servants to belong to a radical party.[121] Police physicians fell under these ordinances, as did medicine professors, in as much as they were considered civil servants.[122] Thus very few medical scholars dared to reveal themselves by showing their support for the NSÄB and National Socialism too openly. One who did so, albeit carefully, was the Würzburg forensic pathologist Professor Herwart Fischer. Born in 1885, a Great War and Freikorps veteran and an early member of the DNVP, he joined the Nazi Party in September 1930. Thereafter he became one of the very few academics on the Würzburg faculty, and certainly the only medical scholar, to put himself at the disposal of the Nazi movement. He excelled by proffering his hospitality to visiting Nazi dignitaries like Ernst Graf zu Reventlow and Hitler himself, whom his wife once welcomed publicly with flowers.[123] *NSÄB-Gauobmann* Fischer is said by a post-World War II colleague to have enjoyed quite a reputation in his field and the commensurate respect of his peers,[124] but the movement for which he risked his career later unseated him. In 1935, this father of four children was sentenced to 18 months in prison for having sexually molested his laboratory assistant. He also lost his party posts as well as his university chair.[125]

In November 1932, Fischer may have guarded himself by not becoming a signatory to a resolution entitled 'German University

Teachers for Adolf Hitler', published in the *Völkischer Beobachter* on the 5th, one day before that crucial Reichstag election. Only 56 academics had endorsed the document, less than a third of those who had been expected to do so, had it not been for the prevalent 'fear of economic disadvantage', specifically the danger of losing one's 'life position'.[126] Still, among these academics, there were several medical men, such as the surgeon Willy Usadel, brother of an exposed NSDAP functionary in East Prussia and then a mere lecturer in Berlin. Usadel was a party comrade since 1931, and he evidently accepted a political gamble, which eventually he won in May 1934 when at Tübingen was appointed full professor over the heads of two much better qualified candidates.[127]

Another signatory was the above-mentioned Professor Reiter, who probably could afford to be intrepid, for as a Nazi deputy in the Schwerin Landtag he represented an officially Nazi state.[128] Be this as it may, Reiter performed sacrifices for the Nazi movement by initiating a private series of bursaries for needy Nazi students, whom he pledged to support with a fund of more than 10,000 marks per year — a welcome bonus at the height of the Depression in 1932.[129]

Ultimately, the National Socialist Physicians' League assisted the Nazi Party leaders in their bid to appeal to as many members of the German educated classes as possible. For Nazi doctors would talk to other potential converts from those classes, whether they were job-related like pharmacists and dentists, or beholden to similar notions of professional elitism like lawyers or higher civil servants. It also enabled the party to monitor closely the movement's progress among putative proselytes such as disaffected country doctors in East Prussia.[130] It aided in concentrating on possible cadre prospects, identifying and establishing contact with prolific university teachers such as Professor Johann Daniel Achelis, the Heidelberg physiologist, who would later be recruited as an official in the ministry of education.[131] It provided moral support to scores of young assistant doctors in university clinics and public hospitals, who dared not yet profess their Hitler allegiance for fear of recriminations, and to a whole phalanx of medical students who were more openly committed, all of them waiting for that important day that would unlock their future.[132]

The well-publicised existence of the doctors' league, after all the lampooning and lambasting, encouraged medical personnel, closed groups and individuals alike, to bring their growing sympathies for

Hitler and his movement more out into the open and allow themselves more readily to be inducted into various party formations. Similar to comparable Nazi professional leagues — the lawyers' union or the student league — the NSÄB acted as a catalyst in the ongoing process of social and organisational bonding between the Nazi Party and upper bourgeoisie. Thus it was no accident that within a few weeks of Hitler's assumption of power, several medical societies in Germany publicly subscribed to concepts of race-eugenic regulation that heretofore had been a spiritual preserve of the Nazi Party and its doctors' league.[133] Elated, pillars of the medical establishment like Frankfurt surgeon Professor Victor Schmieden became first-time voters for Hitler, while still priding themselves on never having joined any political party in their lives.[134] In 1931–2, clearly, the Nazi movement membership curve for doctors and medical students was on the upswing, also.[135] By January 1933, when virtually every tenth medical professional was locked into Hitler's ranks in one capacity or another, the NSÄB had succeeded with its original aim: to prove its value as a social recruiting mechanism for purposes of the Third Reich, and to prove, indeed, that academics, medical professionals, could be useful to Fascism, as much as they could benefit from it in turn.[136] The tribute paid by the early Nazi doctors now was a matter of record, and the time had come to collect the rewards.

Notes

1. I am grateful to the Social Sciences and Humanities Research Council of Canada, Ottawa, for funding the research for this study. Professors Charles Roland and William Seidelman, Faculty of Health Sciences, McMaster University, kindly helped me out with medical information. Quotation is from statute, 'Nationalsozialistischer Deutscher Ärztebund e.V.', Munich, 1930, Bundesarchiv Koblenz (=BA), Schumacher/213. Also see Dr Lang, 'Der Nationalsozialistische Deutsche Ärztebund', in *Nationalsozialistische Monatshefte*, 1, 1930, pp. 38–9; Wilhelm Ackermann, 'Der ärztliche Nachwuchs zwischen Weltkrieg und nationalsozialistischer Erhebung', MD Dissertation, Cologne, 1940, p. 73.

2. Michael H. Kater, 'Der NS-Studentenbund von 1926 bis 1929: Randgruppe zwischen Hitler und Strasser', in *Vierteljahrshefte für Zeitgeschichte*, 22, 1974, pp. 148–90; Rainer Bölling, *Volksschullehrer und Politik: Der Deutsche Lehrerverein 1918–1933* (Göttingen, 1978), p. 125; Hans Volz, *Daten der Geschichte der NSDAP*, 9th edition (Berlin and Leipzig, 1939), pp. 25–7. It should be noted that in this article I shall be concerned with physicians (*Human-Ärzte*) only, not with veterinarians (*Tierärzte*) or dentists (*Zahnärzte*), who were also allowed to join the NSÄB but, based on their lower professional status, were hardly influential in policy-making.

3. Ministerialrat Zimmermann's remarks as pertaining to Oldenburg. See doc. 63, April 28–29, 1930, in Klaus Schaap (ed.), *Oldenburgs Weg ins 'Dritte Reich': Quellen*

zur Regionalgeschichte Nordwest-Niedersachsens (Oldenburg, 1983), p. 74. For an example of Nazi initiative in those circles see doc. 94, Hamburg, 20 July, 1929, in Werner Jochmann (ed.), *Nationalsozialismus und Revolution: Ursprung und Geschichte der NSDAP in Hamburg 1922–1933: Dokumente* (Frankfurt am Main, 1963), p. 283.

4. For the general phenomenon and its background, see Dietrich Orlow, *The History of the Nazi Party: 1919–1933* (Pittsburgh, 1969), pp. 128–238; Thomas Childers, *The Nazi Voter: The Social Foundations of Fascism in Germany, 1919–1933* (Chapel Hill and London, 1983), pp. 119–91; Michael H. Kater, *The Nazi Party: A Social Profile of Members and Leaders, 1919–1945* (Cambridge, Mass., 1983), pp. 62–71; Michael H. Kater, 'Sozialer Wandel in der NSDAP im Zuge der national-sozialistischen Machtergreifung', in Wolfgang Schieder (ed.), *Faschismus als soziale Bewegung: Deutschland und Italien im Vergleich*, 2nd edition (Göttingen, 1983), pp. 27–36.

5. A typical example of 'political' history is the (still very useful) work by S. William Halperin, *Germany Tried Democracy: A Political History of the Reich from 1918 to 1933* (New York, 1965; first published 1946). More recent is Karl Dietrich Erdmann, *Die Weimarer Republik* (=*Gebhardt Handbuch der deutschen Geschichte*, 9th edition, XIX) (Munich, 1980). It is indicative of the relative backwardness of Weimar social history that the pioneering work of Hans Speier on the lower employees, written *before* 1945, could only be published in the late 1970s, after prompting by members of the Bielefeld School: *Die Angestellten vor dem Nationalsozialismus: Ein Beitrag zum Verständnis der deutschen Sozialstruktur 1918–1933* (Göttingen, 1977) (see p. 10). There were early exceptions, of course, such as Ludwig Preller, *Sozialpolitik in der Weimarer Republik* (Stuttgart, 1949); and Felix Raabe, *Die Bündische Jugend: Ein Beitrag zur Geschichte der Weimarer Republik* (Stuttgart, 1961). It must be noted, however, that the historiography of academic professions in the republic such as physicians and lawyers is presently just at the beginning stage. On this, see the pioneering article by Konrad H. Jarausch, 'The Crisis of German Professions 1918–33', in *Journal of Contemporary History*, 20, 1985, pp. 379–98.

6. Georg Kuhns, *Fünfundzwanzig Jahre Verband der Ärzte Deutschlands (Hartmannbund)* (Leipzig, 1925), pp. 72, 141, 148–55; Michael H. Kater, *Studentenschaft und Rechtsradikalismus in Deutschland 1918–1933: Eine sozialgeschichtliche Studie zur Bildungskrise in der Weimarer Republik* (Hamburg, 1975), p. 70; Otto Baumgarten, *Die Not der akademischen Berufe nach dem Friedensschluss* (Tübingen, 1919), p. 24; *Burschenschartliche Blätter* (August/September 1925), p. 245; Preller, *Sozialpolitik*, p. 234; Ackermann, 'Der ärztliche. . .', pp. 12–15; *Wirtschaftstaschenbuch für wissenschaftliche Assistenten*, ed. Julius Hadrich (Leipzig, 1925), pp. 297–302, 507–8; Martha Eva Frochownik, *Die wirtschaftliche Lage der geistigen Arbeiter Deutschlands: Erhebungen der Deutschen Gesellschaft zur Bekämpfung der Arbeitslosigkeit* (Berlin, 1925), pp. 33–4; Anton Graf, *Die Stellung des Arztes im Staate* (Munich, 1935), p. 77.

7. See: Ackermann, 'Das ärztliche. . .', pp. 19, 27; *Ärztliche Mitteilungen*, 30 (1929), p. 544; J. Diehl, 'Aussichten der akademischen Berufe', in *Academia* 15, April 1929, p. 328.

8. B. Noltenius, 'Die Aussichten des ärztlichen Berufes', in *Die Schwarzburg*, May 1927, p. 130; Kurt Opitz (ed.), *Bestallungsordnung für Ärzte und Prüfungsordnung für Zahnärzte*, 4th edition (Berlin, 1936), pp. 5–6, 35–7; *Gewerkschafts-Zeitung*, 34, 1924, p. 47; Graf, *Die Stellung*, pp. 33, 38; Rudolf Neubert, *Mein Arztleben: Erinnerungen* (Rudolstadt, 1974), pp. 33, 37, 46, 50; Ferdinand Fried, *Das Ende des Kapitalismus* (Jena, 1931), p. 107; Otto Oertel, 'Der Arzt (Voraussetzungen, Studium und Berufskreis)', in Hans Sikorski (ed.), *Wohin: Ein Ratgeber zur Berufswahl des Abiturienten*, 2nd edition (Berlin, 1930), p. 89;

Rudolf Nissen, *Helle Blätter — dunkle Blätter: Erinnerungen eines Chirurgen* (Stuttgart, 1969), pp. 57, 62–3.

9. Noltenius, 'Die Aussichten. . .', p. 131.

10. Baumgarten, *Die Not*, p. 22; Hans Tobis, 'Das Mittelstandsproblem der Nachkriegszeit und seine statistische Erfassung', Ph.D. Dissertation, Frankfurt am Main, 1930, pp. 83–4; Theodor Geiger, *Die soziale Schichtung des deutschen Volkes: Soziographischer Versuch auf statistischer Grundlage* (Stuttgart, 1967),pp. 43–4; Martin Kaehler, 'Die Berufsaussichten der Mediziner', in *Die Schwarzburg*, February 1932, p. 56.

11. Cf. n. 6 and the following: Baumgarten, *Die Not*, pp. 22, 24; *Die Schwarzburg*, February/March 1921, p. 11; Adolf Günther, 'Die Folgen des Krieges für Einkommen und Lebenshaltung der mittleren Volksschichten Deutschlands', in Rudolf Meerwarth *et al.*, *Die Einwirkung des Krieges auf Bevölkerungsbewegung, Einkommen und Lebenshaltung in Deutschland* (Stuttgart, 1932), p. 252: Noltenius, 'Die Aussichten. . .', p. 132; Siegmund Hadda, 'Als Arzt am Jüdischen Krankenhaus zu Breslau 1906–1943', in *Jahrbuch der Schlesischen Friedrich-Wilhelms-Universität zu Breslau*, 17 (1972), p. 214; Hans Schadewaldt, *75 Jahre Hartmannbund: Ein Kapitel deutscher Sozialpolitik* (Bonn-Bad Godesberg, 1975), p. 103.

12. Doctors' earnings and living standards are documented in: *Ärztliche Mitteilungen*, 31, 1930, p. 224; Carl Haedenkamp, 'Die Vorschläge der Ärzte für eine Reform der Krankenversicherung', ibid., 32, 1931, p. 688; Erwin Liek, 'Die Aufgaben der Künftigen deutschen Ärzte', in *Ärztliche Rundschau*, 41, 1931, p. 30; Heinrich Kluge, 'Die wirtschaftliche Lage der Ärzte im Deutschen Reich', in *Deutsches Ärzteblatt*, 66, 1936, p. 1207. Also see: Prochownik, *Die wirstschaftliche Lage*, p. 18; *Ärztliche Mitteilungen*, 30, 1929, p. 190; ibid., 31, 1930, p. 635.

13. *Ärztliche Mitteilungen*, 31, 1930, p. 635; Erwin Liek, *Der Arzt und seine Sendung: Gedanken eines Ketzers*, 4th edition (Munich, 1927), p. 165.

14. See Childers, *Nazi Voter*, pp. 145–6; *Ärztliche Mitteilungen*, 31, 1930, pp. 157–8, 548–50, 1083; ibid., 32, 1931, p. 1005; Haedenkamp, 'Die Vorschläge . . .', p. 687.

15. Ackermann, 'Der ärztliche . . .', passim.

16. Quotation Lejeune's and Niedermayer's report, 'Die Tagung der Reichsnotgemeinschaft deutscher Ärzte in Goslar, 22–24. Juni 1929', in *Ärztliche Mitteilungen*, 30, 1929, p. 605. Also see Fritz Damann, 'Der *Numerus Clausus* und die "Kollegialitat"', ibid., pp. 760–61; Ph. Schoppe, '*Numerus Clausus* und "Kollegialitat"', ibid., pp. 833–4.

17. Quotation *Ärztliche Mitteilungen*, 31, 1930, p. 1039. Also see C. Förster, 'Numerus Clausus', ibid., pp. 99–100; *Münchener Medizinische Wochenschrift*, 77, 1930, p. 1218.

18. Liek saw the problem in terms of *Mediziner* versus *Arzt*. Erwin Liek, *Gedanken eines Arztes: Aus 30 Jahren Praxis*, 3rd edition (Berlin, 1942), p. 204; idem, *Arzt*, pp. 91, 161–2. Also see: Vollmann, 'Der deutsche Arzt in dreifacher Krise? Die wirtschaftliche, berufsethische und allgemeine Vertrauenskrise der deutschen Ärzteschaft', in *Ärztliches Vereinsblatt*, 58, 1929, pp. 675–6; *Ärztliches Vereinsblatt*, 58, 1929, p. 485; Carl Jacobs, *Arzttum in Not: Betrachtungen über die Krise im Ärztestand* (Leipzig, 1929), p. 23; Otto Lubarsch, *Ein bewegtes Gelehrtenleben: Erinnerungen und Erlebnisse: Kämpfe und Gedanken* (Berlin, 1931), p. 423.

19. Vollmann, 'Der deutsche Arzt. . .', pp. 675–8; Liek, *Gedanken*, pp. 103, 204; Liek, *Arzt*, pp. 54, 68, 77–94, 114, 122, 124, 144–7, 161–2: *Ärztliches Vereinsblatt*, 58, 1929, pp. 485–6; Jacobs, *Arzttum in Not*, pp. 23, 26, 62, 101–9; Lubarsch *Ein bewegtes* p. 423. Regarding the quacks, see *Journal of the American Medical Association*, 100, 1933, p. 351.

20. This is the tenor of Schadewaldt's post-1945 apology, *75 Jahre Hartmannbund:*

Ein Kapitel deutscher Sozialpolitik (Bonn-Bad Godesberg, 1975). See his repeated use of the term *medicus neuter*, e.g. pp. 47, 75. Cf. the sharp contradiction recently implied in Walte Wuttke-Groneberg, *Medizin im Nationalsozialismus: Ein Arbeitsbuch* (Tübingen, 1980).

21. Quotation Julius Moses, 'Arzt und Politik', in *Die Medizinische Welt*, 4, 1930, p. 1116. Also see Martin Gumpert, Hölle im Paradies: Selbstdarstellung eines Ärztes (Stockholm, 1939), p. 210; Ernst Luther and Burchard Thaler (eds.), *Das hippokratische Ethos: Untersuchungen zu Ethos und Praxis in der deutschen Ärzteschaft* (Halle, 1967), p. 103.

22. Kurt Kühn, 'Zu Problemen der ärztlichen Spitzenverbände und Reichsärztekammer sowie der medizinischen Intelligenz im Hitlerfaschismus (1933–1945)', in K. Kühn (ed.), *Ärzte an der Seite der Arbeiterklasse: Beiträge zur Geschichte des Bündnisses der deutschen Arbeiterklasse mit der medizinischen Intelligenz* (Berlin [East], 1973), p. 62; Kurt Steude, 'Prof. Dr. med. Karl Gelbke — ein Leben als Arzt und Kommunist', in Kühn, p. 193; H. Schwartze, 'Zur Geschichte des Arbeiter-Samariter-Bundes', in Kühn, *Ärzte an der Seite*, pp. 42, 48–9; Irina Winter 'Ärzte und Abeiterklasse in der Weimarer Republic', in Kühn, *Ärzte an der Seite*, pp. 31–3; Georg Kubik, 'Friedrich Wolf als Arzt und Kommunist in der Weimarer Republik', in *Wissenschaftliche Beiträge der Martin-Luther-Universität Halle-Wittenberg*, 1, 1967, pp. 79, 83; Siegfried Parlow, 'Über einige Aspekte der politisch-ideologischen Haltung deutscher Ärzte in der November-Revolution 1918 bis zum Eisenacher Ärztetag im September 1919 unter besonderer Berücksichtigung der medizinischen Fachpresse', ibid., pp. 58, 62. Some of Benjamin's contemporary writings have been reissued by I. Winter (ed.), *Georg Benjamin: Arzt und Kommunist* (Berlin [East], 1962).

23. Parlow, 'Über einige Aspekte. . .' p. 53; Winter, 'Ärzte', p. 28; Gerhard Baader, 'Politisch motivierte Emigration deutscher Ärzte', in *Berichte zur Wissenschaftsgeschichte*, 7, 1984, p. 68; Alfred Grotjahn, *Erlebtes und Erstrebtes: Erinnerungen eines sozialistischen Arztes* (Berlin, 1932), p. 52; obituary Grotjahn in *Gewerkschafts-Zeitung*, 41, 1931, pp. 590–91; Moses, 'Artz und Politik' pp. 1116–17.

24. Richard N. Hunt, *German Social Democracy 1918–1933* (Chicago, 1970). p. 31; Luther and Thaler, *Das Hippokratische Ethos*, p. 60; Käte Frankenthal, *Der dreifache Fluch: Jüdin, Intellektuelle, Sozialistin: Lebenserinnerungen einer Ärztin in Deutschland und im Exil*, Kathleen M. Pearle and Stephan Leibfried (eds.) (Frankfurt am Main and New York, 1981), pp. 93–152; Baader, 'Politisch motivierte . . .', pp. 68–71; Atina Grossmann, '"Satisfaction is Domestic Happiness": Mass Working-Class Sex Reform Organizations in the Weimar Republic', in Michael N. Dobkowski and Isidor Wallimann (eds.), *Towards the Holocaust: The Social and Economic Collapse of the Weimar Republic* (Westport and London, 1983), pp. 271–2.

25. Schadewaldt, *75 Jahre Hartmannbund*, p. 126.

26. On the nature of the early DNVP, see Lewis Hertzman, *DNVP: Right-Wing Opposition in the Weimar Republic, 1918–1924* (Lincoln, 1963); Childers, *Nazi Voter*, pp. 40–41, 161–2. For examples of moderate and left-of-centre bourgeois physicians, see Ferdinand Hoff, *Erlebnis und Besinnung: Erinnerungen eines Arztes*, 4th edition (Frankfurt am Main and Berlin, 1972), p. 298; Emil Abderhalden, *Drei Vorträge zu politischen Tagesfragen* (Halle, 1919), especially pp. 14, 16, 22. Cf. Oswald Bumke, *Erinnerungen und Betrachtungen: Der Weg eines deutschen Psychiaters* (Munich, 1952), pp. 80–84.

27. For the historical background and development of this trend beyond 1918 see Michael H. Kater, 'Professionalisation and Socialisation of Physicians in Wilhelmine and Weimar Germany', in *Journal of Contemporary History*, 20 1985, pp. 677–701.

28. See Gumpert, *Hölle im Paradies*, p. 210; Albert Niedermeyer, *Wahn, Wissenschaft und Wahrheit: Lebenserinnerungen eines Arztes* (Innsbruck, 1956), p.

106; Frankenthal *Der Dreifache Fluch*, p. 97; Ariane Hesse, 'Ärztliche Vereine und Standesorganisationen in Freiburg i. Br.: Entwicklung und Struktur' (Freiburg, 1978), pp. 130–1; and the testimony in Monika Richarz (ed.), *Jüdisches Leben in Deutschland: Selbstzeugnisse zur Sozialgeschichte 1918–1945* (Stuttgart, 1982), p. 203. Also see Margret Boveri, *Verzweigungen: Eine Autobiographie*, Uwe Johnson (ed.) (Munich, 1982), pp. 97, 136.

29. Ferdinand Sauerbruch, *Das war mein Leben: Roman-Biographie*, 2nd edition (Munich, 1979), pp. 116–32; quotation p. 195. Also see Parlow, 'Über einige Aspekte . . .', pp. 54–5. For an able qualification of both Sauerbruch's political attitudes in that period as well as the historiographical value of his memoirs see Fridolf Kudlien and Christian Andree, 'Sauerbruch und der Nationalsozialismus', in *Medizinhistorisches Journal*, 15, 1980, pp. 201–22, especially pp. 203, 207.

30, Parlow, 'Über einige Aspekte . . .', p. 51.

31. Quotation Lubarsch, *Ein bewegtes*, p. 365. Also see Parlow, 'Über einige Aspekte . . .', pp. 51, 54; Michael H. Kater, 'Everyday Anti-Semitism in Prewar Nazi Germany: The Popular Bases', in *Yad Vashem Studies*, 16, 1984, p. 140, n. 30.

32. Lubarsch, *Ein bewegtes*, p. 349. For a better perspective on this than Lubarsch's own see Parlow, 'Über einige Aspekte. . .', p. 56; Bruno Gebhard, *Im Strom und Gegenstrom 1919–1937* (Wiesbaden, 1976), p. 13. For additional examples of Kappist sympathisers among medicine professors see Hoff, *Erlebnis und Besinnung*, pp. 223–4.

33. Schadewaldt, *75 Jahre Hartmannbund*, p. 117.

34. Kuhns, *Fünfundzwanzig*, pp. 17–50, 64, 67, 256, 276–7, 280, 282, 287–8, is mildly critical of the Wilhelmine government on pp. 294, 342, 356 of his book. Also see the qualifying remarks in Fridolf Kudlien, *Ärzte im Nationalsozialismus* (Cologne, 1985), pp. 23–4.

35. Kater, 'Professionalization and Socialization of Physicians', p. 684; Parlow, 'Über einige Aspekte. . .' p. 50.

36. Quotation Kuhns, *Fünfundzwanzig*, p. 352. Also see pp. 343–4, 347, 357.

37. For the third republican legislative session (6 January 1925–31 March 1928). In 1923, Haedenkamp, born 1889, also became the influential editor of the Hartmannbund's official monthly, *Ärztliche Mitteilungen*. See: Cuno Horkenbach (ed.), *Das Deutsche Reich von 1918 bis Heute* (Berlin, 1930), p. 452; *Deutsches Ärzteblatt*, 69, 1939, p. 158. Also see the West German physicians' functionary Hermann Kater (ed.), *Politiker und Ärzte: 600 Kurzbiographien und Portraits*, 3rd edition (Hameln, 1968), pp. 133–4, who in characteristic fashion (see text at n. 20) has dwelt only on Haedenkamp's pre-1933 and post-1945 vita, without mentioning his important Third Reich career.

38. *Deutsches Ärzteblatt*, 69, 1939, p. 158; quotation Bewer to Voss, Leipzig, 28 June 1933, Unterlagen der Kassenärztlichen Vereinigung Deutschlands Berlin, facsimile copies at York University Archives (=UK), 196/1.

39. *Das Deutsche Führerlexikon 1934/35* (Berlin, n.d.), pp. 42, 236; 'Begründung des Antrages des Reichsamtsleiters, S.A. San. Brig. Führers Pg. Dr. Friedrich Bartels auf Durchführung eines Verfahrens durch das Oberste Parteigericht der N.S.D.A.P. zur Wiederherstellung und Wahrung seiner Ehre', Munich Harlaching, 18 August 1939, Berlin Document Centre (=BDC), OPG Bartels.

40. Examples Stähle: *Führerlexikon*, p. 469; Lommel: Adalbert Gimbel (ed.), *So Kämpften Wir! Schilderungen aus der Kampfzeit der NSDAP. im Gau Hessen-Nassau* (Frankfurt am Main, 1941), pp. 61–2; Blumm: Rainer Hambrecht, *Der Aufstieg der NSDAP in Mittel - und Oberfranken (1925–1933)* (Nuremberg, 1976), pp. 104, 184, also see p. 311; and Johnpeter Horst Grill, *The Nazi Party in Baden, 1920–1945* (Chapel Hill, 1983), p. 111.

41. For a discussion of these pre-1929 Nazi doctors, their collective make-up and motives, see Michael H. Kater, 'Hitler's Early Doctors: Nazi Physicians in Pre-

Depression Germany', in *Journal of Modern History* (forthcoming).

42. In its report of 6 August 1929, the *Völkischer Beobachter* put the number of first-time attending members at 50, but Leonardo Conti, an influential participant, later pared this down to 30. See his 'Entwicklung und Grundsätze des NSD-Ärztebundes', in *Mitteilungsblatt der Arbeitsgemeinschaft Gross-Berlin des National-sozialistischen Deutschen Äztebundes* (=*MAG*), p. Berlin (February 1931), p. 1 (BA, NSD 53/2).

43. BDC, Reichsärztekammer Liebl; BDC, NSDAP Zentralkartei Liebl; Geoffrey Pridham, *Hitler's Rise to Power: The Nazi Movement in Bavaria, 1923–1933* (London, 1973), pp. 110–13.

44. This was Klare's intention. Klare was disappointed when his booklet (see n. 45) did not receive the official party blessing he had anticipated. See Klare to Hinkel, Scheidegg, 18 March 1939, BDC, PK Klare.

45. For Klare's vita, see BDC, NSDAP Zentralkartei Klare; summary of personal and professional details, n.d., BDC, PK Klare. Klare's personal statements are contained in his book *Briefe von Gestern für Morgen: Gedanken eines Arztes zur Zeitenwende* (Stuttgart and Leipzig, 1934), especially pp. 22, 26, 34, 40–41, 44–5, 50, 53–4, 57, 64, 75, 111–16, 132–6, 142–3, 146. Quotation p. 122. Also see Klare to Strasser, Scheidegg, 2 July, 1931, BA, NS 18/5018.

46. *Ziel und Weg*, 8, 1938, pp. 420–21. Also see Georg Lilienthal, 'Der National-sozialistische Deutsche Ärztebund (1929 bis 1943/1945): Wege zur Gleichschaltung und Führung der deutschen Ärzteschaft', in Kudlien, *Ärzte*, p. 108.

47. Protocol Conti, Berlin, 19 March 1934, BDC, OPG Ketterer; vita Conti, Berlin-Wilmersdorf, 11 November 1936, Archiv 'Verschüttete Alternativen in der Gesundheitspolitik', Universität Bremen (Nachlass Conti. I am indebted to Frau Elfriede Conti and Professor Stephan Leibfried, Bremen, for granting me access to this document); BDC, SS Files Conti; *Führerlexikon*, p. 86; *Völkischer Beobachter*, 24 April 1939. On Leonardo's mother Nanna, see Ilse Szagunn, 'Frau Nanna Conti zum 60. Geburtstag', in *Die Ärztin*, 17, 1941, 154.

48. 'Vormerkung', Munich, 16 July 1930, Bayerisches Hauptstaatsarchiv München (=BHSAM), Sonderabgabe I/1868. The number of eligible Munich doctors has been estimated according to the names in *Münchner Stadtadressbuch 1933*, 83rd edition, as of mid-October 1932, III, pp. 52–66. This contains 1,181 *Human-Ärzte*, of whom up to 200 must be discounted as Jewish.

49. See Lilienthal, 'Der Nationalsozialistische. . .', pp. 105–6.

50. Conti, p. 1 (as in n. 42). According to this author, the NSÄB convened in Nuremberg and not in Leipzig, as some authors hold, e.g. Lilienthal, 'Der National-sozialistische. . .', p. 105; Albert Zapp, 'Untersuchungen zum Nationalsozialis-tischen Deutschen Ärztebund (NSÄB)', MD Dissertation, Kiel, 1979, p. 21. Nuremberg as the venue is verified in *Führerlexikon*, p.169; [Eugen Stähle], *Geschichte des Nationalsozialistischen Deutschen Ärztebundes e.V. Gau Württemberg-Hohenzollern* [Stuttgart, 1940], p. 4.

51. *Ziel und Weg*, 8, 1938, pp. 545–6; Hermann Okrass, *Das Ende einer Parole: 'Hamburg bleibt rot'*, 2nd edition (Hamburg, 1935), p. 184; *Führerlexikon*, p. 169; Stähle, *Geschichte*, p. 4. Also see Lilienthal, 'Der Nationalsozialistische. . .', p. 109. Other branches were set up in Pomerania (Dr Robert Spanuth) and Lübeck (Dr Wolfgang Saalfeldt): *Führerlexikon*, p. 465; Lawrence D. Stokes (ed.), *Kleinstadt und Nationalsozialismus: Ausgewählte Dokumente zur Geschichte von Eutin 1918–1945* (Neumünster, 1984), pp. 345, 781. Now also see Stokes' article, 'Professionals and National Socialism: The Case Histories of a Small-Town Lawyer and Physician, 1918–1945', in *German Studies Review*, 8, 1985, pp. 449–80.

52. *Führerlexikon*, pp. 236, 509; Zapp, 'Untersuchungen . . .', p. 21; *Ziel und Weg*, 7, 1937, p. 543; Althen to 'Deutsche Volksgenossen', [Wiesbaden], 9 October 1934, Hessisches Hauptstaatsarchiv Wiesbaden (=HHSAW), 483/3159; 'SA-Sanitäter-Fragebogen' Kurt Blome, BDC, SA Files Blome; Kurt Blome, *Arzt im*

Kampf: Erlebnisse und Gedanken (Leipzig, 1942), p. 250; Wilhelm Frenz, 'Der Aufstieg des Nationalsozialismus in Kassel 1922 bis 1933', in Eike Hennig (ed.), *Hessen unterm Hakenkreuz: Studien zur Durchsetzung der NSDAP in Hessen* (Frankfurt am Main, 1983), p. 86.

53. *Völkischer Beobachter*, 9 December 1931 and 20 September 1932; Blome, *Arzt im Kampf* p. 249; Stähle, *Geschichte*, p. 6; Lilienthal, 'Der Nationalsozialistische . . .', p. 109. For an objective contemporary criticism of the 1932 conference proceedings, see Professor Richard Koch's penetrating article in *Frankfurter Zeitung*, 6 October 1932.

54. 2,786 regular members and 344 *Sympathisanten* (i.e. employed Jungärzte, see text at n. 75, above). Lilienthal, 'Der Nationalsozialistische . . .', p. 109. For regional gatherings in Saxony (1931), Württemberg (1931–2), Hanover-Brunswick (1932) and Cologne-Aachen (1932), see *Der Freiheitskampf*, Dresden, 9 September 1931; Stähle *Geschichte*, p. 5; *Ziel und Weg*, 2, November 1932, pp. 20–24. Cf. Klare to Dr D. [Scheidegg], 25 May 1931, in Klare, *Briefe von Gestern*, p. 22. At the end of 1932, the Greater Munich locale counted 18 general practitioners, 17 specialists, 17 dentists and 1 pharmacist among its members. See NSÄB membership list for Munich and suburbs, as of 11 November 1932, BHSAM, Sonderabgabe I/1868.

55. Lilienthal, 'Der Nationalsozialistische . . .', p. 108; Ackermann, 'Der ärztliche . . .', p. 73. On Deuschl, see *Führerlexikon*, p. 94.

56. Vita Conti (as in n. 47): Heinz Höhne, *Der Orden unter dem Totenkopf: Die Geschichte der SS* (Gütersloh 1967), pp. 64–6; SS Files Conti, BDC. The vita of Strauss, born 1901, is in *Führerlexikon*, p. 480.

57. 'Disziplinarhof-Entscheid in der Streitsache Dr. Deusch-Dr. Conti', Brunswick, 17 September 1932; Conti to Strasser, Berlin, 25 September 1932; Conti to Rienhardt, Berlin, 26 September 1932; Dr Härtl to Liebl, Berlin-Steglitz, 30 September 1932, BDC, PK Conti.

58. See: *Ziel und Weg*, 2, November 1932, p.2; Blome, *Arzt im Kampf*, p. 263; Pridham, *Hitler's Rise*, p. 113.

59. As in n. 1.

60. The Nazis later claimed that Hartmannbund membership had been one of the prerequisites for joining the NSÄB (Ackermann, 'Der ärztliche . . .' p. 74) — hardly surprising in view of the monopoly status of the Hartmannbund for panel doctors.

61. For the party analogy, see Childers, *Nazi Voter*, e.g. pp. 132–4, 206–7.

62. Carl Haedenkamp, 'Arzttum in Not', in *Ärztliche Mitteilungen*, 31, 1930, p. 40; idem, 'Zur Organisation des ärztlichen Standes', ibid., p. 553; 'Die Not der Jungärzte', ibid., p. 613.

63. Cf. the unsympathetic views by two Nazi-associated physicians: Erwin Liek, 'Die Aufgaben der künftigen deutschen Ärzte', in *Ärztliche Rundschau*, 41, 1931, p. 15; Graf, *Die Stellung*, pp. 78, 111–12.

64 Klare to Liek, [Scheidegg], 1 December 1930, in Klare, *Briefe von Gestern*, p. 146; and the comment about *Jungärzteliste I* (November 1931) in doc. 193, in Wuttke-Groneberg, *Medizin*, p. 340.

65. See the cutting remarks of H. Dettmer in *Ziel und Weg*, 1, 1931, pp. 12–13; and of H. Deuschl (made at the Hanover meeting, July 1932), ibid., 2 (November 1932), pp. 21–2. Also see Ackermann, 'Der ärztliche . . .', p. 101; Zapp, 'Untersuchungen . . .', p. 75.

66. Dr Liebl, 'Sehr geehrter Herr Kollege und Parteigenosse!', Ingolstadt, 1 September 1930, BA, Schumacher/213.

67. 'Nationalsozialitischer Deutscher Ärztebund e.V.', statutes, Munich, [1930], BA, Schumacher/213.

68. Ackermann, 'Der ärztliche. . .', p. 139.

69. See text above near n. 56; and Conti, 'Verraten und verkauft? Streiflichter aus dem Berliner Standesleben', in *MAG*, Berlin (September 1931), pp. 1–3 (BA, NSD 53/2). Also see text after n. 89.

178   *The Nazi Physicians' League*

70. See Ackermann, 'Der ärztliche. . .', p. 29.

71. For Hartmannbund measures, see *Wirtschaftstaschenbuch*, p. 209; Schadewaldt, *75 Jahre Hartmannbund*, p. 102; Ackermann, 'Der ärztliche. . .', pp. 16, 59.

72. *Ziel und Weg*, 1, 1931, p. 30; ibid., 2, March 1932, pp. 35–6, June 1932, pp. 28–9.

73. On the NSDAP and Weimar youth, see Michael H. Kater, 'Generationskonflikt als Entwicklungsfaktor in der NS-Bewegung vor 1933', in *Geschichte und Gesellschaft*, 11, 1985, pp. 217–43.

74. Niedermeyer, *Wahn*, p. 268.

75. See the telling comment in the NSÄB membership application of Dr Karl Brandt (later to become one of Hitler's personal physicians), date of application: 24 February 1932, BA, R 18/3810. To protect these people further, the NSÄB had created the membership category of 'sympathisers' for them. See Lilienthal, 'Der Nationalsozialistische. . .' p. 107. Cf. Werner Forssmann, *Selbstversuch: Erinnerungen eines Chirurgen* (Düsseldorf, 1972), p. 147; Hanns Schwarz's testimony in Günther Albrecht and Wolfgang Hartwig (eds.), *Ärzte: Erinnerungen, Erlebnisse, Bekenntnisse*, 3rd edition (Berlin [East], 1973), p. 58.

76. Kater, 'Professionalisation and Socialisation of Physicians', pp. 689–94.

77. See Martin Staemmler, 'Das Judentum in der Medizin', in *Handbuch der Judenfrage: Die wichtigsten Tatsachen zur Beurteilung des jüdischen Volkes*, 38th edition (Leipzig, 1935), pp. 402–14; Werner F. Kümmel, 'Die Ausschaltung rassisch und politisch missliebiger Ärzte', in Kudlien, *Ärzte*, p. 61.

78. See Esra Bennathan, 'Die demographische und wirtschaftliche Struktur der Juden', in Werner E. Mosse (ed.), *Entscheidungsjahr 1932: Zur Judenfrage in der Endphase der Weimarer Republik*, 2nd edition (Tübingen, 1966), p. 111; Hans Wolfram Gerhard, 'Die wirtschaftlich argumentierende Judenfeindschaft', in Karl Thieme (ed.), *Judenfeindschaft: Darstellung und Analysen* (Frankfurt am Main and Hamburg, 1963), p. 110; Kümmel, 'Die Ausschaltung' p. 62.

79. Kater, *Studentenschaft*, pp. 148–9; Kümmel, *'Die Ausschaltung . . .'*, p. 62.

80. For the pre-World War I period, see Kuhns, *Fünfundzwanzig*, pp. 88–91, 127, 129–30, 144–5.

81. Childers, *Nazi Voter*, pp. 149–52, 214, 218, 231, 246, 258, 267; Kater, 'Everyday Anti-Semitism', pp. 136–8.

82. Quotation Hierl, Organisations-Abteilung II, 'Richtlinien für den National-sozialistischen Deutschen Ärztebund' [summer 1930], BA, Schumacher/213.

83. Siegfried Ostrowski, 'Vom Schicksal jüdischer Ärzte im Dritten Reich: Ein Augenzeugenbericht aus den Jahren 1933–1939', in *Bulletin des Leo Baeck Instituts*, 6, 1963, pp. 317–8.

84. See the examples in Donald L. Niewyk, *Socialist, Anti-Semite, and Jew: German Social Democracy Confronts the Problem of Anti-Semitism, 1918–1933* (Baton Rouge, 1971), pp. 157–8; and Stähle, pp. 6–7.

85. As reported in Niewyk, *Socialist, Anti-Semite, and Jew*, p. 130.

86. See Kurt Klare's incessant polemics in: *Deutsches Tuberkulose-Blatt*, 6, 1932, pp. 11–13, 43–4, 58–9, 76–8, 111–12, 144–6, 158–60, 182. Also see Klare to Dr Kröner, Scheidegg, 28 March 1931; von Kun to Friedmann, Berlin, 22 July 1932, UK, 203. During the Third Reich, the Friedmann medication was not only not used, but its very mention was suppressed. See *Wegweiser durch die ärztliche Berufskunde und das Arztrecht: Ein Hand- und Nachschlagebuch bei der täglichen Praxis*, Trembur and Paech (eds.) (Leipzig, 1937), pp. 272–8; 'Die Bekämpfung der Tuberkulose', in *Der Arzt des öffentlichen Gesundheitsdienstes 1941*, 2nd edition (reprinted Leipzig, 1942), pp. 372–7. From the point of view of state-of-the-art medicine, of course, a tuberculosis 'cure' did not then exist, just as it does not exist today.

87. 'Die Mission des deutschen Arztes: 3. Gautagung des nationalsozialistischen

Ärztebundes in Dresden', in *Der Freiheitskampf*, Dresden, 9 September 1931.

88. 'Tagesordnung für die 3. Reichstagung des NSD. - Ärztebundes in Braunschweig 15. mit 19. September 1932', in *Ziel und Weg*, 2, June 1932, p. 2; Martin Staemmler, 'Wie kann der Arzt jetzt rassenhygienisch wirken? Vortrag gehalten bei der Gautagung des Nationalsozialistischen Deutschen Ärztebundes in Plauen', ibid., pp. 11–16; Walter Gross, 'Braunschweig: Bericht und Sinndeutung', ibid., 2, November 1932, pp. 4–6; Hermann Boehm, 'Rassenhygiene und National-sozialismus: Vortrag, gehalten bei der 3. Reichstagung des NSDÄB. in Braunschweig', ibid., pp. 11–17; 'Gautagungen des Nationalsozialistischen Deutschen Ärztebundes', ibid., pp. 20–24.

89. Karl A. Schleunes, *The Twisted Road to Auschwitz: Nazi Policy Toward German Jews 1933–1939* (Urbana, 1970), pp. 119, 123–4, 127, 133, 135; Uwe Dietrich Adam, *Judenpolitik im Dritten Reich* (Königstein and Düsseldorf, 1979), pp. 99, 106, 126, 135.

90. See the available issues of *MAG*, for February and September 1931, in BA, NSD 53/2; and doc. 193 (=*MAG*, November 1931), in Wuttke-Groneberg, p. 340. Conti (as in n. 69), p. 2, claimed that in 1927 he had been responsible for preventing the induction of Hirschfeld into the Hartmannbund. *MAG*, Berlin, September 1931, p. 2.

91. 'Deutsche Ärzte, wacht auf!', in *Völkischer Beobachter*, 12 August 1931. The reference in this article to 'the Galician Berlin daily' is an allusion to the Jewish-owned Berlin (Mosse) press.

92. Hans Deuschl (underwritten by Ludwig Liebl), 'An die deutschen Ärzte! Eine Erwiderung an den Hartmannbund', in *Ziel und Weg*, 1, September 1931, pp. 18–21, quotation p. 20.

93. Bewer to Stauder, [Leipzig], 20 August 1931, UK, 117; and other relevant documents contained in that voluminous file. Also see Carl Haedenkamp, 'Parteipolitische Angriffe auf den Hartmannbund', in *Ärztliche Mitteilungen*, 32, 1931, pp. 691–2.

94. Deuschl to Jänicke, Munich, 7 September 1932, UK, 117. Also see Zapp, pp. 82–3.

95. Stauder to Schneider, [Nuremberg], 26 October 1932, UK, 117; 'Achtung, Herr Haedenkamp, das geht Sie an!', in *Völkischer Beobachter*, 5 November 1932.

96. Hence Zapp, 'Untersuchungen. . .', p. 83, misses the point as he speaks of 'peaceful co-existence' between the two organisations in the last phase of their relationship before January 1933.

97. For the monopolist character of the Hartmannbund, see corr. regarding case of Dr Felix Boenheim (Berlin, 1930–32), UK, 164; *Gewerkschafts-Zeitung*, 41, 1931, p. 91; Zapp, 'Untersuchungen. . .', p. 81.

98. See the first chapter of my book, *Doctors under Hitler: Professional Crisis of Medicine in the Third Reich*, forthcoming.

99. As quoted in Ackermann, 'Der ärztliche. . .', p. 102: Schadewaldt, *75 Jahre Hartmannbund*, pp. 125–6; Zapp, 'Untersuchungen. . .', pp. 80–81.

100. *Völkischer Beobachter*, 12 August 1931: *Ziel und Weg*, 1, September 1931, p. 23; ibid., 2, June 1932, pp. 22–5: Ackermann, 'Der ärztliche. . .', p. 106; Conti (as in n. 69), p. 3;' *Der Freiheitskampf*, Dresden, 9 September 1931.

101. Details on these attempts are in Michael H. Kater, 'Physicians in Crisis at the End of the Weimar Republic', in Peter D. Stachura (ed.), *Unemployment and the Great Depression in Weimar Germany* (London, 1986), pp. 49-76.

102. Quotation Deuschl (as in n. 92), p. 18. Also see *Ziel und Weg*, 1, September 1931, pp. 19–25; *Der Freiheitskampf*, Dresden, 9 September 1931.

103. H. Dettmer in *Ziel und Weg*, 1, September 1931, p. 11; Deuschl's appeal ibid. (June 1932), p. 1.

104. 'Nationalsozialistische Ärzte als Provokateure', in *Der Kassenarzt*, 8,

December 1931, p. 2.

105. See Horkenbach, pp. 475–89, for a complete listing of all successful candidates' occupations. In Hesse-Darmstadt, the Nazi Dr med. Reinhold Daum of Oppenheim finished third behind the successful candidates, Ludwig Münchmeyer and Friedrich Ringshausen. See ibid., p. 488; *Die Ergebnisse der Reichstagswahlen im Volksstaat Hessen vom 14. September 1930* (Darmstadt, 1930), p. 2.

106. Zapp, 'Untersuchungen. . .', p. 26.

107. Doc. I/23C (January and April 1931), in Stokes, *Kleinstadt und Nationalsozialismus*, pp. 144–5: *Ziel und Weg*, 8, 1938, p. 545. Also see the case of the police physician mentioned in n. 121 below.

108. *Ziel und Weg.* 2, June 1932, p. 28; *Deutsches Ärzteblatt*, 71, 1941, p. 89.

109. On this important aspect, see Blome, p. 257.

110. See text above at n. 51.

111. Scheerschmidt to Reichsgeschäftsstelle der NSDP München, Neuvorwerk, 12 September 1931, BDC, NSLB Scheerschmidt; Naunin to Gauleitung Königsberg, Marienwerder, [June 1930], Staatliches Archivlager Göttingen, Gauarchiv Ostpreussen, Stiftung Preussischer Kulturbesitz, microfilms Niedersächsisches Staatsarchiv Bückeburg (=SAG), SF 6819, GA/34.

112. Doc. I/34A (20 March 1932), in Stokes, *Kleinstadt und Nationalsozialismus*, pp. 287–8; n. 51 above.

113. Karl Heinz Albrecht, *Zehn Jahre Kampf um Gera: Eine Geschichte der NSDAP im Thüringer Osten*, [Gera, 1933], pp. 63–4, 74, 78, 84.

114. All the more so because politically non-aligned physicians often chose not to become involved, even in emergencies. See the example in Gimbel, p. 40. On the scarcity itself see Blome, *Artz im Kampf*, p. 237.

115. Blome, *Artz im Kampf*, pp. 237–8, 243–6; Stokes, pp. 152, 347; Althen to Worthmann, Wiesbaden, 9 November 1934, HHSAW, 483/3159.

116. Blome, *Artz im Kampf*, p. 243: Gruppenarzt Berlin-Brandenburg Doepner, 'Arbeitsbilder aus dem Sanitätsdienst der Gruppe Berlin-Brandenburg', in *Der SA-Mann*, Munich, 29 October 1932.

117. On the Zander-Conti struggle, see Conti to Goebbels, Berlin, 3 June 1931; N.S.D.A.P., Gau Gross-Berlin, Frauenschaft, circular 4, Berlin, 7 October 1931, BA, Schumacher/230. For background see Michael H. Kater, 'Frauen in der NS-Bewegung', in *Vierteljahrshefte für Zeitgeschichte*, 31, 1983, pp. 213–6.

118. See text at n. 47 above.

119. *MAG*, Berlin, September 1931; Doepner (as in n. 116).

120. Kurt van Emsen [=Dr. med. Strünckmann], *Adolf Hitler und die Kommenden* (Leipzig, 1932). On a similar note, published on the threshold of the Third Reich was [Professor Dr. med] Philalethes Kuhn, *Die Führerfrage der Deutschen* (Stuttgart, 1933).

121. See Rudolf Morsey, 'Staatsfeinde im öffentlichen Dienst', in Klaus König *et al*. (eds.), *Öffentlicher Dienst: Festschrift für Carl Hermann Ule zum 70. Geburtstag am 26. Februar 1977* (Cologne, 1977), pp. 111–33.

122. Cf. example of the dismissed Prussian police staff physician in Reinhard Neubert, 'Beamtentum und Nationalsozialismus', in *Deutsches Recht*, 1, September/October 1931, p. 77.

123. BDC, NSDAP Zentralkartei Fischer; 'Personalakte F. 214', BDC, PK Fischer; Linde to Graf [zu Reventlow], Würzburg, 25 November 1932, Archiv der ehem. Reichsstudentenführung und des NSDStB in der Universitätsbibliothek Würzburg (=AR), IV–1 * 45; Joseph Pascher, 'Das Dritte Reich, erlebt an drei Universitäten', in Helmut Kuhn *et al.*, *Die deutschen Universitäten im Dritten Reich: Acht Beiträge* (Munich, 1966), p. 49.

124. Pascher, 'Das Dritte Reich. . .', p. 49. Also see *Wer ist's?*, 10th edition, Herrmann A. L. Degener (ed.) (Berlin, 1935), p. 410.

125. Subsequently Fischer's wife divorced him. See Boepple to Ritter von Epp, Munich, 14 January 1935;'Personalakte F. 214'; Mitgliedschaftsamt to Schneider, Munich, 18 August 1938, BDC, PK Fischer; BDC, NSDAP Zentralkartei Fischer.

126. The entire scheme had been entrusted to the organised Nazi students by Goebbels and Hess, mainly to countermand DNVP assertions of strength. Quotations Blümel to Hess, 3 November 1932, National Archives Washington (=NA), microfilm T–81/244, frame number 5030936. The projections are mentioned in Blümel to Conti, 7 November 1932, AR, phi 351. Also see other docs. in this collection; as well as Anselm Faust, 'Professoren für die NSDAP: Zum politischen Verhalten der Hochschullehrer 1932/33', in Manfred Heinemann (ed.), *Erziehung und Schulung im Dritten Reich* (Stuttgart, 1980), II, pp. 39–40.

127. *Der Führer*, 6 November 1932: Michael H. Kater, 'Medizinische Fakultäten und Medizinstudenten: Eine Skizze', in Kudlien, *Ärzte*, p. 90. Altogether, there were about a dozen lecturers and professors of medicine among the signatories. Kudlien, *Ärzte*, p. 34.

128. Since 13 July 1932. See Cuno Horkenbach (ed.), *Das Deutsche Reich von 1918 bis Heute* (Berlin, 1932), p. 242. Also see *Der Führer*, 6 November 1932.

129. Corr. Reiter-Reichsjugendführung, March 1932, AR, II * 15. Regarding Nazi appeals to students of medicine on economic grounds in 1932, see flyer, Nationalsozialistischer Deutscher Studentenbund, Hochschulgruppe Rostock, 'Zufall oder bewusste Gewissenlosigkeit?', [1932], AR, II * 128.

130. See Kiefert to Paltinat, Tilsit, 29 December 1930; Kiefert to Gauleitung Königsberg, Tilsit, 9 January 1931, SAG, SF 6818, GA/33.

131. Schulz to Feickert, Berlin, 29 April 1932, NA, microfilm T-81/259, frame number 5051126; *Wer ist's?*, p. 4.

132. See Hoff, *Erlebnis*, p. 315; Theodor Brugsch, *Arzt seit fünf Jahrzehnten*, 2nd edition (Berlin [East], 1958), p. 275.

133. Wilhelm Hagen, *Auftrag und Wirklichkeit: Sozialarzt im 20. Jahrhundert* (Munich-Gräfelfing, 1978), p. 129; Georg Lilienthal, 'Rassenhygiene im Dritten Reich: Krise und Wende', in *Medizinhistorisches Journal*, 14, 1979, p. 120.

134. Schmieden made a point of having this recorded in the annals of the *Führerlexikon*, p. 426.

135. Although this cannot be proved here with any scientific accuracy, the available sources point to that conclusion. See the general remark of Blome, *Artz im Kampf*, p. 242, and the case histories of Zeiss: *Führerlexikon*, p. 542; Focke: Focke to Conti, Rostock, 8 July 1943, BA, R 18/3810; Fleischmann: BDC, NSDAP Zentralkartei Fleischmann; Kötschau: BDC, NSDAP Zentralkartei Kötschau; Mennecke: Alice Platen-Hallermund, *Die Tötung Geisteskranker in Deutschland* (Frankfurt am Main, 1948), p. 92; Mrugowski: 'Lebenslauf' Mrugowksi, Halle, 25 June 1934, BDC, SS files Mrugowski. Also see tables 5–7 in Kater, *Studentenschaft*, pp. 212–3; and cf. table 3 in Kater, 'Sozialer Wandel', p. 30. Cf. the interesting parallel example of university psychologists in Mitchell G. Ash and Ulfried Geuter, 'NSDAP-Mitgliedschaft und Universitätskarriere in der Psychologie', in Carl Friedrich Graumann (ed.), *Psychologie im Nationalsozialismus* (Berlin, 1985), p. 266.

136. See the figures in Lilienthal, 'Der Nationalsozialistische Deutsche Ärztebund', p. 109; Volker Schallwig, 'Paracelsus' Bedeutung in der Medizin des Nationalsozialismus', MD Dissertation, Kiel, 1974, p. 10; and, for *Ärzte* (census of 1933), in *Berufszählung: Die berufliche und soziale Gliederung des Deutschen Volkes: Textliche Darstellungen und Ergebnisse* (=*Statistik des Deutschen Reichs: Volks-, Berufs- und Betriebszählung vom 16. Juni 1933*, vol. 458) (Berlin, 1937), p. 49.

8 SPEAKING THE RIGHT LANGUAGE: THE NAZI PARTY AND THE CIVIL SERVICE VOTE IN THE WEIMAR REPUBLIC

Jane Caplan

Before 1933, the publicly professed attitude of the NSDAP towards Germany's civil service was marked by an ambivalence which called into question the party's commitment to the institution and its sympathy for the interests of civil servants. On the one hand, a negative image of the civil service was deployed by the Nazi Party in its relentless campaign against the Weimar Republic: this civil service was an institution corrupted by political favouritism, cravenly submissive to Germany's degradation in the republic, permeated by aliens and a danger to Germany's survival. Though scarcely attractive to civil servants, this could draw upon the unpopularity of the civil service in Weimar Germany — its association with the widely disliked republic, the apparent security of the tenured civil servant in the economic devastation of the mid-1920s and early 1930s. But on the other hand, the $1\frac{1}{2}$ million-strong civil service was itself a reservoir of potential support for the NSDAP, especially in its drive for electoral power after 1928. It was worthwhile for the party to exploit the political and economic disaffection of civil servants with a state that appeared careless of their interests, and to present itself as champion of a traditional pillar of German society. *This* civil service was depicted as the victim of republican mismanagement, its members forced to shoulder the unpopular republic, to see their once honourable profession degraded by the allegedly preferential admission of Jews and socialists, to knuckle down under inadequate salaries, diminished pensions and insecure tenure rights. Simply by shifting the optic of judgement, then, the negative representation of the civil service as a whole could be turned into a statement about its sufferings under the Weimar governments. The maligned object could become the anguished subject, and be herded into the voting booths along with the other victims of the 'November criminals'.

Adept though the Nazi Party was in having it both ways, it was obliged to devote considerable efforts to resolve or at least assuage the contradictions in its position, and to fend off repeated allegations that it was '*beamtenfeindlich*' — hostile to civil servants. The way in which this was attempted, culminating in the party's major propaganda offensive in 1932, is the subject of this essay, but it is first worth noting how very profoundly rooted was the negative imagery of the civil service in National Socialist ideology. At issue was not the civil service as it actually existed in the 1920s, but the civil service as the embodiment of a state whose power to ward off racial disaster was always uncertain to Hitler, the extreme anti-Semite. Purporting to explain how in recent times the Jews had managed to evade the natural watchfulness of the German people and to pass themselves off as Germans, he alleged in *Mein Kampf* that the state was incapable of recognising that, whatever the guise, 'he is always the same Jew':

> That so obvious a fact is not recognised by the average head-clerk in a German government department, or by an officer in the police administration, is also a self-evident and natural fact; since it would be difficult to find another class of people who are so lacking in instincts and intelligence as the civil servants employed by our modern German State authorities.[1]

This was the same Hitler of the later *Table Talk*, which is peppered with deeply contemptuous asides about bureaucrats and jurists.[2] The lesson depended upon the contrast drawn between the instinctively alert and self-protective *Volk* and the state that can be duped and deceived into betraying the interests of the race. Unlike the more common contrast between the 'good' civil service of the empire and the 'bad' civil service of the republic, this imagery is timeless and beyond history — hence its reappearance in the 'Third Reich' itself. It subsisted in a fantasy world of nameless powers, and expressed that profound disbelief in the defensive capacity of the ordered polity which was fundamental to Hitler's ideology, and became so prominent in the policies of the later 1930s.[3] Although this extreme note of savage odium for the state and its officials was more latent than prominent before 1933, it powered the visible antagonism between the Nazi Party as *Kampfbund* and the bureaucracy as a rule-bound system, epitomised in the contrast between the street-fighting SA man and the pen-pushing clerk, between will and paragraph.[4]

In its less disguised forms, the Nazi approach to the civil service, whether as a source of supporters or as an institution in German public life, fell into two main thematic types. These could be labelled the ethical and the material, respectively. The material approach concentrated on the economic interests of civil servants — pay, tenure and the like — and became the dominant note in Nazi propaganda by the early 1930s. The ethical approach drew upon the traditional imagery of the German civil service as a homogeneous *Stand* (estate) bound together by a code of service and sharing a common prestige. The language that this view of the civil service evoked from conservatives was generally hyperbolic, and the Nazi version was no exception:

> The civil servant is the custodian of the welfare of the state and the people; he is the Guardian in the Platonic sense. The people's honour is sacred to him. He serves it with a passionate heart, and brings to it every sacrifice. Any derogation of this precious possession strikes him more heavily than if it were his own property. 'I serve' is his motto . . . Genuine and truthful in his whole outlook, abjuring weakness, hostile to the counterfeit, German, not fashionable, in short Existence not Appearance.[5]

Before 1933, this ethical approach belonged with the repeated Nazi call for the 'restoration' (*Wiederherstellung*) of the civil service, a demand which summoned the image of a corrupted and damaged institution and promised to refound it in a pristine purity. In the words of a 1932 pamphlet addressed to civil servants, 'The NSDAP will not rest until this civil service [i.e. the Prussian service of Frederick the Great] is restored in its old purity and independence.'[6] The contrast between the abasement of the civil service in the republic and the eminence it had once enjoyed was a common theme of Nazi discourse; to quote *Mein Kampf* again:

> The most outstanding trait in the civil service and the whole body of the civil administration [in the empire] was its independence of the vicissitudes of government, the political mentality of which could exercise no influence on the attitude of German State officials. Since the Revolution this situation has completely changed. Efficiency and capability have been replaced by the test of party-adherence; and independence of character and initiative

are no longer appreciated as positive qualities in a public official. They rather tell against him.[7]

The frequency of this vocabulary of restoration suggests that it was seen as an effective means of recruiting the interest and support of civil servants, and yet it was not without its defects as a propaganda vehicle. For one thing, exposing and deploring the contrast between the traditional civil service and its Weimar counterpart was a commonplace of all conservative political propaganda in the 1920s. There was nothing distinctively National Socialist about it — Hitler's statement could as easily have tripped from the pen of a DNVP or DVP politician. If the NSDAP wanted to achieve a conspicuous political profile, this simple contrast between past and present was inadequate; moreover, the implication that National Socialism was primarily about restoring the past rather than creating the future in a new mould was out of keeping with the party's own revolutionary aspirations. Even though a certain amount of tightrope walking between vocabularies of revolution and of restoration might be prudent in addressing civil servants, the latter did not entirely dominate, as we shall see. A second problem with this approach was that a disparaging comparison of Weimar civil servants with their predecessors slighted the officials along with the republic, suggesting that they were as worthless as the state they served. Not only was this highly negative image unlikely to appeal to civil servants, but, as opponents of the Nazis were not slow to point out, it suggested a strenuous future purge of the civil service if it fell into Nazi hands — and later the actual experience of Nazi rule in Thuringia and Oldenburg was seized on as proof.[8] The party's own language of purification and restoration encouraged this belief, and in fact the party's 1924 civil service programme listed those categories of officials whose dismissal was demanded: unqualified party appointees, Jews and 'other aliens'.[9] This was preceded by a commitment to 'the maintenance of the professional civil service with its constitutionally guaranteed rights, in particular freedom of political opinion and freedom of expression for civil servants'. This was another profession that critics begged leave to doubt, though in the context of an unsettled debate about the constitutional limits to civil servants' freedom of political action it exploited a controversial issue.[10]

A good deal of effort thus had to be devoted by party spokesmen to straightening out the contradictions in its programme. These were often denied as merely the effect of malicious lies spread by opponents — a form of self-defence that was felt necessary by the NSDAP across the board, and not solely in relation to civil servants. Early in 1923, for example, Hitler was already trying to assure a large audience in Munich that, contrary to hostile reports, the Nazi Party did not reject the civil service as such, or attack civil service pension rights as such, but only those political appointees who enjoyed the status and rights of civil servants.[11] The drawing of such distinctions was a repeated theme in Nazi public discourse, and was aimed partly at countering alleged misrepresentations or at correcting the damaging effects of some speaker or other's injudicious remarks. But it was also part of a technique of disaggregation in Nazi political propaganda: the identification of specific social and occupational groups in the population, who could then be addressed with a propaganda tailored for their ears alone. This was not an exclusively Nazi technique — Thomas Childers has shown how prevalent in Weimar was the practice of targeting occupational groups with political messages[12] — but it was developed with greater cynicism and sophistication by the NSDAP than by any other party. The civil service presented the party with a double field of disaggregation. Institutionally, it was to be severed not only from the existing republican state, but also from a past which represented tradition and restoration alone. Secondly, within the civil service distinctions were made between the various categories of non-Germans and the 'true' civil servant, and between the elite civil servant complicit in the degradation of the German state, and the ordinary civil servants who were the victims of this situation. Between them, these approaches anchored a new concept of the civil service: no longer a *Stand* representing state sovereignty, but a truly German body, representing the *Volksgemeinschaft*.

It was in this way that the Nazi presentation of the civil service did not simply repeat the generic concept of the institution inherited from the conservative, *staatserhaltende* discourse of the empire. Although the ethical imagery never vanished from propaganda, its unification of civil servants in an abstract ideal was crossed by an alternative imagery which sought to expose the different interests and affiliations of its members, and to suggest how the institution might be reconvened as a genuinely national creation. Thus the first programmatic statement on the civil service published in the *Völkischer Beobachter* in July 1923 was permeated by a sense of the distinction between a 'good' and a 'bad' civil service, but this was not aligned along an axis of historical time. Rather, the positive image presented a civil service genuinely dedicated to the Nazi ideal of the state as an institution designed to safeguard the creative labour of the citizenry and to protect it from exploitation. This state was contrasted with, on the one hand, a state that was the servant of high finance, and on the other the elective institution ascribed to social democratic theory, portrayed here as a gateway to corruption. The writer (himself a civil servant) called for a merit system of appointment and promotion, based on an improved system of training and education, and the guarantee of a decent standard of pay and pensions. He argued finally that 'The whole professional status of the civil servant must be extracted from the atmosphere of scapegoatism for a bureaucratic elite [*eine geheimrätliche Bureaukratie*]'.[13] Ten years later, in a similar vein, the party's civil service department warned civil servants against the threat that they were about to become 'the tools of a privileged upper class in the oppression of the German people'.[14]

These forms of argument were consistent with National Socialist populism, with the stance against *Bonzen*, elites, cliques of insiders. In political discourse they were the equivalent to the party's economic anti-capitalism, and contributed to that reformulation of the relationships between class and nation which eventually led the NSDAP to pivot its propaganda on the *Mittelstand*. This was not simply a cynically opportunist electoral manoeuvre, but recognised that this group offered a viable political space between languages of class and of elite. The capacity to do this was also not simply the result of clever strategic choices, but reflected the changes in German social structure and political discourse which had dispersed the reality of the *Stand* without establishing an effective political response. It was in this sense that the *Mittelstand* was available for a peculiarly ideological appeal — not so much as a genuinely pre-industrial 'survival', but as a social group long excluded from the polarities of German political argument.[15]

The civil service had not been exempted from this interplay of social change and political stagnation. Against the traditional concept of its internal homogeneity stood the increasing differentiation of the civil service in practice from the 1880s. It then began to grow at a much faster rate than total employment in Germany, and progressively lost its character as the embodiment of the state's sovereignty, as it took on tasks and working attributes which were shared with other elements of the workforce. By the end of the 1920s, less than half of Germany's $1\frac{1}{2}$ million civil servants were occupied in the administration proper, while most of the rest (44 per cent)were employed in the public utilities.[16] This suggests that civil servants could no longer look into the mirror of 'the state' and see their clear reflection, but that they might have to struggle to define a new identity. This identity would have to take account of the fact that debates about the cost of sustaining the civil service had begun in Germany before 1914, while civil servants' associations had simultaneously begun to take an active interest in the material conditions of their work. War and revolution had then brought about a radicalisation process similar to that experienced by employees and by wage labour.[17] By 1918 the majority of civil servants were members of organisations affiliated to the umbrella *Deutscher Beamtenbund* (DBB), its leaders committed both to the republic and to the protection of their members' economic interests. The fact that this took the form of a constitutional guarantee of civil servants' 'vested rights' (*wohlerworbene Rechte*) was due not so much to the tenacity of tradition as to a peculiar alliance of defensive reformism and social progressivism. The Ebert government, desperate to anchor the security of the republic in November 1918 and to resist pressure leftwards, extended to civil servants a guarantee of their status which then had to be formalised in the Weimar constitution.[18] This ensured the survival of the peculiar status of civil service employment as an aspect of public law, quite distinct from the contract law that covered other forms of labour. There is no need to go into details here, but the effect of this even before 1918 was that *Beamte* (civil servants proper) enjoyed a series of customary or vested rights which were not contractual but *ex gratia*: they included rights of tenure, salary, pensions and dependents' allowances after death. For the mass of lower and middle officials, this amounted to the provision of a level of security to which they would never have been able to aspire outside state employment. It was thus not surprising that a priority for civil service associations in 1918–19 was to ensure the protection of these rights, and indeed the constitutional guarantee gave them a legal validation more secure than anything hitherto. This achievement was of course partly a victory for tradition and continuity and played its part in saddling the republic with a pre-revolutionary inheritance. But it can also be seen as an aspect of the social state prefigured in other articles of the constitution (notably in the fifth section, on economic life), and partially realised in the labour legislation of the 1920s.[19] One part of this was the extension of labour law into wage bargaining, unemployment insurance and the like — measures which sought to improve the predictability and security of working-class life, and which can be seen as the substitution of legal regulation for revolutionary action in the sphere of labour/capital relations.

The protection of the employment status of civil servants can be seen as part of this project of enhanced social regulation. In the literature of SPD, civil servants' vested rights were often rebaptised as 'social gains', and presented as a prototype of the rights which all workers should ultimately enjoy. The state, in other words, could be seen as a model employer, setting the standards which would then be met through the entire economy. In this context, the constitutional guarantee of vested rights can be seen as somewhat Janus-faced, turning one side towards the traditions of the paternalist state of the past, and the other towards a new collectivism.

However, just as the labour gains of the 1920s proved a stumbling-block to the state in the crisis of 1929, so the constitutional guarantee of 1919 had become an embarrassment to the state in the fiscal emergency of 1923. The massive budget-cutting that accompanied the stabilisation of the currency included the slashing of state expenditure on personnel. Under special legislation which effectively abrogated the guarantee of tenure, about 25 per cent of all state employees lost their jobs, the civil servants among them being propelled into a limbo designated 'suspension' (*Wartestand*). At this point, the DBB retreated to a sectional defence of its members' interests, severing connections with other workers, and successfully protecting civil servants' jobs by shifting the burden of reductions to non-*Beamte* public employees.[20] This marked the definitive end of the radical moment after 1918, already signalled in the disaffiliation of the radical wing of the civil service movement from the DBB in 1922. However, although the DBB had defended its members in 1923–4, the shock of the assault upon tenure persisted, while some tens of thousands of *Wartestandsbeamten* nursed deep grievances against the republic. Moreover, in the 1920s the government began to consider schemes for a radical reform of civil service law, with the aim of restricting the fully privileged status of *Beamte* to an elite of leading officials, while consigning the rest to an inferior and less protected position. For in the civil service the republic had inherited not simply a fifth column of corporatised conservatives, but an expensive and unwieldy bureaucracy, staffed to levels far beyond postwar Germany's capacity to fund it, yet now also protected by the full authority of the constitution. As it turned out, this legislation was never adopted, though rumours of its existence kept civil servants on their toes about their rights. When economic crisis hit again in 1929, it was not staffing but salaries that were cut. Although the depth of the cuts was not unjustifiable, given the extent of the Depression, they were to prove profoundly disturbing to civil servants because of the summary form in which they were imposed. They also raised the spectre of a total deprivation of rights and security.[21]

The existence of these currents of civil service policy seems to have made the development of coherent positions on the left extremely difficult, especially in combination with the left's inherited ambivalence about the status of the petty bourgeoisie. Whereas it had been a radical demand during the revolution to call for the abolition of the special legal status of civil servants and their assimilation into ordinary labour law, within a few years the situation was less clear, for the risk was now that civil servants might lose such rights as they had. The SPD's 1924 civil service programme resorted to impenetrably contradictory language in its demand for the 'retention of the public-law status of civil servants in the framework of German labour law in general'.[22] A few years later, an SPD pamphlet addressed to civil servants contained contributions arguing, ingenuously but confusingly, both for and against the maintenance of the special legal status.[23] The KPD suffered similar embarrassments in trying to reconcile the class distinction it drew between upper and lower civil servants with its commitment to a civil service law that made no distinction between the ranks that might be disadvantageous to the latter.[24] The right-wing parties — DNVP and DVP — had fewer qualms in simply taking over the language of *Stand*, in a deliberate evocation of a recent and more satisfying past.

The context of debate about the civil service in the 1920s was thus framed by arguments about its legal status and material rights. The markers in this debate were the 1923 personnel reductions, the 1927 salary law, and the 1930–31 salary cuts imposed by Brüning, i.e. the critical moments for tenure and salary rights. Just as tenure could raise the question of differential treatment for different ranks in the civil service, so the reform of the salary system involved decisions about differentials, a merit structure, and rationalisation. The DBB was committed not only to higher absolute salaries, but also to a more equitable distribution of total funds between the various ranks and grades. It had thus approved the 1920 salary law, which considerably narrowed differentials and in general eroded the hierarchical privileges built into the prewar system; and it campaigned against the creeping desertion of this law in the salary adjustments adopted during and after the inflation. The terms in which it did this are instructive as an index of its attempt to generate a new language to represent the interests of civil servants free of the traditionalism of *Stand*, but also capable of defending the claim to special status. In a major statement in response to a finance ministry report on salary policy, the DBB offered a reading of recent German history to found its specific demands. It depicted Germany as a society in which real class differences were being progressively narrowed by economic developments, and in which therefore real needs were converging:

> The transition from the authoritarian state to the people's state is a result and a reinforcement of this process. The people's state is committed to a concept of community. It confers on all the same rights and duties. It summons the entire people to consider and decide important questions. It demands an inner sense of commitment and a deep attachment to the whole. It acknowledges no partitions within the people, it aims to mitigate and to reduce distances and differences.[25]

The memorandum went on to offer a vision of social integrity in opposition to the cloven images of left and right, the 'authoritarian' and the 'class' states, and advanced this in the name not of the Republic as such but of history and the people. The Republic was represented as little more than the automatic expression at the political level of a long-term and profound process of social transformation, the effect of Germany's industrialisation. The chief consequence in this context was this secular process of social convergence within the population: 'The various strata are . . . converging in their claims, their needs and their styles of life.' For the DBB, this was a welcome development, and not something to be rejected (as the ministry and conservatives did) as an unfortunate side-effect of the war and inflation which was eroding the privileged status of the upper ranks of civil servants. The DBB criticised that view as reminiscent of 'the time of the authoritarian state, with its divisions into estates and classes', and asserted

> that such principles should be officially recognised and ratified, that the values of class struggle should be thus encouraged in the civil service, must be deplored by anyone with a modicum of political acumen.[26]

Finally, the DBB summarised its position by arguing that 'the division of civil servants into three sharply distinct strata [i.e. by means of very pronounced differentials between the grades] contradicts the principle of the national community [*Volksgemeinschaft*] and leads to the formation of classes in the civil service'.

The language of this analysis was emblematic of the attempt to find new formulations, tucked between the two traditional vocabularies of class and authority (*Obrigkeit*), which could express the mix of sectional and public interests that the DBB claimed to represent. The democratic credentials of the DBB notwithstanding, its tactical choices after 1923 — to co-operate with the government as a corporatist partner, and in dissociation from the trade union movement — helped to open a political space that was then occupied by the Nazi Party after 1930 as it shifted its attention to the civil service vote. The term *Volksgemeinschaft* is important here. In the 1920s, it was not specifically associated with National Socialism but was in common usage and was especially favoured by the Centre party — not surprisingly, considering the claim of the Centre to represent a social totality unmarked by the scars of class. The NSDAP thus took over the usage of a term which simultaneously depoliticised the public sphere, while also providing a site of identification for public officials distinct from the internal homogeneity of *Stand*. The latter word seems hardly to have been used by the Nazis in their civil service propaganda in the early 1930s, except in occasional references to civil servants as one *Berufsstand* (profession) among others. Far more prominent was a form of political address which attacked both the elitism associated with the Right, and the class consciousness cultivated on the Left — both being presented as inimical to the shared interests of the real nation.

This became clear after 1930, when the NSDAP's wavering support of civil servants' material interests solidified into an aggressive attack on those groups and politicians most closely identified with the Brüning salary reduction policy.[27] Between December 1930 and December 1932, a series of presidential emergency orders reduced civil service salaries and pensions by cumulative cuts of between 19 and 23 per cent. On top of that, public officials had been assessed for a *Reichshilfe* or national levy of 2.5 per cent for six months from July 1930, and the intricate system for calculating pensionable service was revised in such a way as to limit the state's heavy obligations there.[28] The NSDAP turned to the opportunities this offered for the organisation of disaffection, though initially without overwhelming enthusiasm. Clearly in response to mounting local pressures, the party's Organization Department authorised in April 1931 the appointment of officials to monitor civil service questions at *Gau* and *Kreis* level. At the end of 1931, a fortnightly paper, the *Nationalsozialistische Beamten-Zeitung*, began to appear, and in April 1932 Strasser and Sprenger, the party's national spokesmen for civil service matters, announced the formation of local *Beamtenarbeitsgemeinschaften*, intended for sympathisers who were deterred from actually joining the NSDAP because of the disciplinary and informal consequences. Finally, in May 1932 a civil service department was established in the party's central organisation. Meanwhile coverage of civil service issues had been stepped up in the party press and other publications, and Nazi deputies savaged the government and the other political parties in the Reichstag for their handling of the civil service pay cuts.[29] The Centre party was a special target of this propaganda offensive. In 1927, its Reichstag fraction had split, visibly and rancorously, over the salary reform of that year, which had conceded relatively large pay increases. The fact that a number of Centre party deputies voted against the law or abstained was to figure prominently in the NSDAP's later attacks. By 1931, government ministers were voicing fears of major defections to the NSDAP from the Centre, especially among the uniformed branches.[30] By the same date, there was evidence that the DBB was being infiltrated by Nazi sympathisers. In other words, these leaky vessels were draining into the party which most resembled them, and which — as in other policy areas — could claim that its own record was untarnished by earlier mistakes or failures.

Had it not been for the coincidence of the enforced salary cuts and the five-election year of 1932, it is unlikely that the NSDAP would have devoted the kind of attention it did to tapping the votes of civil servants. The party's previous record had been sufficiently equivocal, and its reluctance to organise civil servants sufficiently marked, that it is clear that the Nazi leadership had little intrinsic interest in or concern for the problems of civil servants. Yet the opportunity offered in 1932 was finally too enticing to resist. Civil servants were demoralised and fearful; shackled to a state that many of them had never fully accepted, they seemed about to go down with it. In this situation, the crisis-related protest voting of 1924, which had already brought the NSDAP visible increments of civil servant voters, was about to be repeated.[31]

A scrutiny of the propaganda leaflets generated in the *Reichs-organisationsleitung* (ROL) in 1932 offers a chance to assess the issues that the NSDAP felt most liable to attract civil servants' votes, and those it felt as it were comfortable in espousing. The four campaigns for which long runs of propaganda survive in the records of the NSDAP party archive produced some 131 propaganda leaflets, their texts drafted in the *Reichspropagandaleitung* (RPL) and circulated to the *Gaue* for national use throughout Germany.[32] Of these, 22 were addressed to civil servants, or about one in six: this was the highest proportion for any single occupational group. This may perhaps be partly attributed to the exceptional clarity of the occupational boundaries defining civil servants, and to its sheer numerical size — up to $1\frac{1}{2}$ million Germans would recognise themselves as the target of this propaganda. Yet it must also be the case that the NSDAP propaganda leadership saw civil servants as a worthwhile target, as voters vulnerable to the NSDAP because of their grievances against the Brüning government, their desertion by their professed friends, and their commitment to some version of the national interest at a time of obvious crisis. This tactic of fishing in the reservoir most richly stocked with potential prey was typical of the NSDAP's electoral opportunism, of course, and fulfilled Hitler's old declaration that his aim was to outvote rather than outshoot his opponents and thus gain the seal of the constitution for his victory. At the same time, the party's strategy revealed an astute assessment of the campaign tactics of its opponents, and a delib-erate selection of the grounds on which to fight. Thus, for example, the Prussian Landtag campaign was fought on the slogans 'Prussia must be Prussian again/We are the last of the Prussians/Smash Severing and his party'.[33] The instructions for the first round of the presidential election in February 1932 have a distinctly contem-porary ring:

The consistent and endlessly repeated phrase is: Adolf Hitler is not just our candidate, Adolf Hitler is the next president. We will win, because we want to win. The whole party's belief in victory must be raised to the level of blind faith.[34]

However, the speed at which Hitler's presidential campaign was organised (he only belatedly decided to run) may have left too little time for a clear group-directed propaganda campaign, and most of this early RPL material was issue- rather than voter-oriented. The analysis of the results of the first round of the election (in which Hindenburg easily outdistanced Hitler) argued for a different strategy in future, and is worth quoting at length:

The relatively large total of votes that Generalfeldmarschall Hindenburg was able to attract on 13 March is certainly to be attributed to the typical mentality of particular bourgeois circles. It is a question here of the German *Spiessbürger* in particular, won by sentimentality and fear of the unknown; of women, whose votes were likewise obtained by an appeal to the tear ducts and through their fear of war; and of pensioners and civil servants, lured by references to inflation, reduced pensions and National Socialist hostility to the civil service . . . It was from these motives, and not out of approval of the existing system, that these bourgeois circles gave their votes to Reich President Hindenburg.

Starting from the consideration that, given the extremely tight time-limit left us by the government, it is hopeless to win any considerable number of votes from the Centre and SPD, we must make every effort to break into the bourgeois elements in the Hindenburg front. Even in the short time that remains to us, we can still win these people . . .[35]

It was no doubt in response to this analysis that by late March the RPL had shifted its propaganda strategy, producing copy aimed at the specific voter groups identified in it. Thus whereas the first presidential campaign had resulted in only a single leaflet (out of a total of 50) aimed at civil servants, the instructions issued by the RPL for the second round on 10 April included copy for nine (out of a total of 56). The Prussian Landtag elections on 24 April generated ten such leaflets (out of 47). In both these campaigns, civil servants were accorded more attention than any other occupation or social group (compare for example the three leaflets addressed to peasants in the second round of the presidential election). Five of the Prussian Landtag leaflets shared their copy with the presidential material, the wording slightly amended to make them appropriate for this later campaign. Both sets of propaganda gave great prominence to defending the NSDAP against other parties' allegations of its hostility to the civil service. Thus one of the presidential campaign leaflets bore the title 'Is Hitler an enemy of the civil service?', and defended the party by making the usual discrimination between its attacks on party appointees (*Parteibuchbeamte*) and its commitment to the trained civil servant (*Berufsbeamte*). The same leaflet also enumerated 'four facts' about National Socialism: Hitler's father had been a civil servant; Frick (a leading Reichstag spokesman and the NSDAP interior minister in Thuringia in 1930) was a civil servant; Klagges, a minister in Braunschweig, was also; ten Nazi Reichstag deputies were too.[36] A similarly defensive leaflet from the Landtag campaign was headed 'The National Socialists want to deprive civil servants of their rights', and went on:

> LIES! One more stupid and contemptible than the next!
> *Who* took away the civil servant's *freedom of expression*!
> *Who* has *cut his salary* with ever *new emergency orders*!
> *Who* has taken away from him every *security for the future* by an *irresponsible financial policy*!
> THE SOCIAL DEMOCRATS AND THE CENTRE!
> They're the ones making policy in Prussia!
> *These parties* have no right to act as accusers!
> *They are the accused!*[37]

Clearly, the NSDAP had decided that attack was the best form of defence: it caught the Centre in particular on its weakest point, and left the Nazis free to claim whatever they wanted as their own objective — in this case 'a healthy, solid and incorruptible civil service . . . decently paid, and able on retirement or illness to enjoy the evening of their lives in security'.

The presidential campaign material clearly embodied the lessons of March, and was appropriately in tune with the mentality of the 'bourgeois circles', at least as this was understood by the Nazis. The leaflet quoted above ('Is Hitler an enemy . . .') was one of only two leaflets in the entire run of 22 which took a predominantly 'ethical' rather than 'material' approach, appealing to the traditions of the civil service and the value of the profession. (The other exception was the sole leaflet addressed to civil servants in the first round of the presidential election, which was a wordy and obscure defence of the professional civil service; its obvious defects may have led to the reconsideration of strategy in later propaganda.)[38] By contrast, the Prussian Landtag material was aimed at lower civil servants, at least according to the internal evidence of its content. This included repeated references to the SPD and to the Allgemeiner Deutscher Beamtenbund, the most radical of the civil service associations and affiliated to the ADGB. It also strenuously and persistently attacked the emergency orders, urged as a Nazi policy the adoption of minimum and maximum salaries, and combined criticisms of political appointees with allegations about the extent of corruption in the civil service — the latter vastly exaggerated.

Reviewing the material overall, a clear profile of issues and positions emerges. Firstly, as already noted, there are virtually no appeals to the civil service as a corps or estate; indeed, that vocabulary is nowhere in evidence, but is eclipsed by a much more pragmatic and practical attention to material issues, even if couched in terms appealing to a sense of professional pride. This is true both of the critique of existing policy and of the promises about future Nazi programmes, which are largely concerned with job stability and financial security — obvious themes for a depression audience, of course. The critique of 'outsiders' (*Aussenseiter*) in the civil service is directed almost exclusively at political appointees, while racial attacks are conspicuously missing. In the series of Landtag election leaflets, and even in some of those chosen for the second round of the presidential elections, the political opponents attacked by name are mainly the Centre, the SPD and the Allgemeiner Deutscher Beamtenbund, suggesting that the NSDAP saw itself largely in competition for votes with these radical and democratic groups.

The themes in this propaganda intended for mass distribution contrast to some extent with the approach taken at the time in the party press and in longer political pamphlets. Here there is a greater emphasis on the quality of the profession as such — thus one article (by Heinrich Müller) on the imminent elections of 31 July 1932 could be titled 'In Duty and Conscience',[39] while another could declare that 'It is an unchangeable fact that state and state civil service present an indissoluble whole'.[40] In these appeals, a more elitist and ethical tone can be detected. The difference may be explicable by the likelihood of different readerships for the different material. Leaflets would presumably be intended for fairly indiscriminate saturation use, while the party press was more likely to be read by civil servants with an existing interest in the NSDAP. As so frequently, the party appears willing to say whatever it thought its audience was willing to hear.

Although it is, of course, impossible to demonstrate conclusively that the NSDAP reaped direct rewards from its assiduous courting of the civil service, the evidence we have on both voting and party membership does suggest a detectable upswing after 1930 and a more marked increase in 1932. Childers' figures for 1930 and 1932 demonstrate an affinity between the NSDAP and the civil service vote, though given the nature of the evidence this cannot wholly confirm the view that there was an absolute rise in the popularity of the party among civil servants.[41] Kater's investigations of party membership led him to conclude that it was not until 1932 that civil servants of any rank were over-represented in the NSDAP by comparison with their numbers in the population.[42] These findings differ somewhat from the party's own statistical survey, published in 1935, which showed a slight over-representation of civil servants in both 1930 and 1932.[43] The quality of the party's survey is not wholly reliable, however, and the same point may be made about its claim that the *Nationalsozialistiche Beamten-Zeitung* had 80,000 subscribers before 1933, and that by 1933 there were 120,000 'sympathisers' attached to the NSDAP through its local organisations.[44] Nevertheless, the party's decision to organise 'sympathisers' did take account of an important fact in this context — the existence in some areas, notably Prussia, of legal bans on civil service membership of the 'anti-constitutional' parties, the NSDAP and KPD. This, along with informal pressure against support for the party, must have deterred some civil servants from joining. And although not everyone in the party sympathised with this problem — a speaker in Bavaria in 1932 taunted anyone too scared to join with the comment 'he'd better stay away from the party: the movement's better off without members like that'[45] — the lifting of the Prussian ban in July 1932 did coincide with the membership increase detected by Kater. It is likely, then, that the NSDAP was more popular among civil servants than the membership evidence suggests. In any event, the accumulation of evidence we now have about membership and voting might well be supplemented in future by comparative investigations of the structure of support for other parties, and of the relationship in any one group between membership and voting behaviour.

The burden of this evidence thus tends to support the now increasingly documented conclusion that by 1932 the NSDAP had become a relatively broad-based protest party — to use Childers' words, 'a catch-all party of protest'.[46] Although it was most durably located on a lower-middle-class base, the old petty bourgeoisie of town and country, it had managed to reach beyond this and make inroads into a much wider range of social and occupational groups. By disaggregating the electorate and tailoring its propaganda to specific groups, the NSDAP convened their electoral strength upon itself, creating a massive, though in all likelihood fugitive, alliance of repugnance against the crisis-torn republic. Civil servants, unprotected against the real effects of the crisis by fine words and fair phrases recalling a tradition of dedication and sacrifice, listened instead to the catalogue of their woes and the litany of their fears provided for them by the propagandists of National Socialism.

Notes

My thanks for helpful comments on an earlier draft of this essay are due to the members of the Columbia Social History Seminar, and to my colleagues in the German Women's History Group.

1. Adolf Hitler, *Mein Kampf* (London, 1939), p. 262.
2. See for examples *Hitler's Table Talk 1941–44*, 2nd edn. (London, 1973), pp. 103–6, 373–7.
3. The relationship of fantasy and realism in Hitler's ideas is discussed in Tim Mason, 'Intention and Explanation: A Current Controversy about the Interpretation of National Socialism', in Gerhard Hirschfeld and Lothar Kettenacker (eds.), *Der 'Führerstaat': Mythos und Realität. Studien zur Struktur und Politik des Dritten Reiches* (Stuttgart, 1981), pp. 23–42.
4. A contrast which was reflected in the relatively low recruitment of civil servants into the SA; see Richard Bessel, *Political Violence and the Rise of Nazism. The Storm Troopers in Eastern Germany 1925–1934* (New Haven and London, 1984), pp. 36–7.
5. [Heinrich] Müller, *Beamtentum und Nationalsozialismus* (Munich, 1931), pp. 36–7. For a typical conservative counterpart, see Hans Gerber, 'Vom Begriff und Wesen des Beamtentums', *Archiv des öffentlichen Rechts*, N.F. XVIII (1930).
6. NSDAP Reichsorganisationsleitung (ed.), *Quo Vadis Deutsches Berufsbeamtentum?* (Frankfurt, 1932), p. 9.
7. Hitler, *Mein Kampf*, pp. 236–7.
8. See in particular *Der Nationalsozialismus — eine Gefahr für das Berufsbeamtentum* (Berlin, 1932), a publication of the Allgemeiner Deutscher Beamtenbund. For a discussion of the effect of Nazi rule on the civil service vote, see Klaus Schaap, *Die Endphase der Weimarer Republik im Freistaat Oldenburg 1928–1933* (Düsseldorf, 1978), pp. 224–42.
9. The programme can be found in the *Völkischer Beobachter*, 8 July 1926, and in

200   *Speaking the Right Language*

Quo Vadis, pp. 23–4.

10. For the problem of compatibility between constitutional guarantees of free speech and subsequent restrictions on civil servants, see Hermannjosef Schmahl, *Disziplinarrecht und politische Betätigung der Beamten in der Weimarer Republik* (Berlin, 1977).

11. See the report of this meeting in the *Bayerische Staatszeitung*, 9 February 1923.

12. See Thomas Childers, *The Nazi Voter. The Social Foundations of Fascism in Germany, 1919–1933* (Chapel Hill and London, 1983). Appendix III reproduces examples of such propaganda.

13. *Völkischer Beobachter*, 8–9 July 1923, p. 2: 'Der Beamte im nat.-soz. Staate' (15 col. ins.).

14. *Quo Vadis*, p. 14.

15. The debate about this has persisted from the 1920s (and earlier) to the present. Classic sources include E. Lederer and J. Marschak, 'Der neue Mittelstand', in *Grundriss der Sozialökonomik* (Tübingen, 1926), pp. 120–41; Theodor Geiger, 'Panik im Mittelstand', *Die Arbeit*, 7, 1930, pp. 637–53. For recent discussions see for example Jürgen Kocka, *Die Angestellten in der deutschen Geschichte 1850–1980* (Göttingen, 1981), chs. 4 and 5; Hans Speier, *Die Angestellten vor dem Nationalsozialismus* (Göttingen, 1977).

16. The best source for the size and composition of the state administration is *Der Personalstand der öffentlichen Verwaltung im Deutschen Reich am 31. März 1928 und am 31. März 1927* (Einzelschriften zur Statistik des Deutschen Reichs), Nr. 18 (Berlin, 1931).

17. In general, see Jürgen Kocka, *Klassengesellschaft im Krieg 1914–1918* (Göttingen, 1973), ch. III especially.

18. The tactics of Ebert and the SPD are discussed in Gabriele Hoffmann, *Sozialdemokratie und Berufsbeamtentum. Zur Frage nach Wandel und Kontinuität im Verhältnis der Sozialdemokratie zum Berufsbeamtentum in der Weimarer Zeit* (Hamburg, 1972), Part I, 2.

19. See Otto Kahn-Freund, *Labour Law and Politics in the Weimar Republic* (Oxford, 1981); also David Abraham, *The Collapse of the Weimar Republic. Political Economy and Crisis* (Princeton, 1981), ch. V especially.

20. The full story is told in Andreas Kunz, 'Stand versus Klasse. Beamtenschaft und Gewerkschaften im Konflikt um den Personalabbau 1923/24', *Geschichte und Gesellschaft* 8, 1982, pp. 55–86. See also his 'Verteilungskampf oder Interessenkonsensus? Einkommensentwicklung und Sozialverhalten von Arbeitnehmergruppen in der Inflationszeit 1914 bis 1924', in Gerald D. Feldman *et al.* (eds.), *Die deutsche Inflation. Eine Zwischenbilanz* (Berlin and New York, 1982), pp. 347–84.

21. See Hans Mommsen, 'Staat und Bürokratie in der Ara Brüning', in Gotthard Jasper (ed.), *Tradition und Reform in der deutschen Politik. Gedenkschrift für Waldemar Besson* (Frankfurt, 1976), pp. 81–137.

22. Quoted in *Deutscher Beamtenbund. Ursprung. Weg. Ziele* (Bad Godesberg, 1968), p. 179.

23. A. Freymuth, E. Falck and H. Wäger, *Sozialdemokratie und Berufsbeamtentum* (Berlin, 1927).

24. The KPD's 1927 civil service programme is reprinted in *Deutscher Beamtenbund*, pp. 181–3.

25. Deutscher Beamtenbund, *Stellungnahme des Deutschen Beamtenbundes zur Denkschrift des Reichsministers der Finanzen über die Besoldung der Reichsbeamten*, 19 March 1925, p. 2.

26. Ibid., p. 7.

27. Before 1930, the most prominent themes in the public statements of NSDAP spokesmen had included the demand for a political and racial purge of the civil service, which was linked to calls for the reinstatement of *Wartestandsbeamten*; and

demands for a salary ceiling and for limits on pensions payable to ministers. In these and similar demands the party aligned itself with lower and middle civil servants against the senior ranks, though as has been suggested a degree of confusion about the party's objectives persisted. See for a survey of Reichstag motions and interpellations Wilhelm Frick, *Die Nationalsozialisten im Reichstag 1924–31* (Munich, 1931); also, for the shift in 1930/31, Michael Kater, *The Nazi Party. A Social Profile of Members and Leaders, 1919–1945* (Cambridge, 1983), pp. 59–61; Jane Caplan, 'The Civil Servant in the Third Reich', D. Phil. Dissertation, Oxford, 1974, pp. 81—8.

28. The fullest discussion is in Mommsen, 'Staat und Bürokratie'; see also Hans Mommsen, 'Die Stellung der Beamtenschaft in Reich, Länder und Gemeinden in der Ära Brüning', *Vierteljahrshefte für Zeitgeschichte*, XX, 1973, pp. 151–65.

29. See for example speeches by Jakob Sprenger, the Reichstag spokesman on civil service matters, in the Reichstag debates of 9 December and 10 December 1930; Reichstag, V. Wahlperiode, *Stenographische Berichte*, vol. 444, at pp. 453–5 and 527–9.

30. Dietrich (finance) and Schätzel (posts) voiced their fears of Nazi infiltration in their departments; see minutes of cabinet meetings of 19 December 1930 (Bundesarchiv (BA) R 43 I/2682) and 13 April 1932 (BA R 43 I/2684).

31. See Childers,*The Nazi Voter*, pp. 97–9, 228–32.

32. The materials are collected in the NSDAP-Hauptarchiv, microfilm reel 15, folders 268–289. They consist of drafts produced in the RPL, together with copies of instructions and analytical circulars which accompanied the distribution of the material to the *Gaue*. The elections covered are the Landtag elections of April (with the Prussian election clearly the most important), the two rounds of presidential voting in March and April, and the Reichstag election in July. There appear to be no comparable materials on file for the November Reichstag election.

33. Hauptarchiv (HA) reel 15, folder 286, RPL instructions 2 April 1932.

34. HA reel 15, folder 287, RPL instructions of 2 May 1932.

35. HA reel 15, folder 288, RPL instructions of 23 March 1932.

36. *Ist Hitler beamtenfeindlich?*, HA reel 15, folder 288.

37. *Die Nationalsozialisten wollen die Beamten entrechten*, HA reel 15, folder 286.

38. *Beamten! Beamtenanwärter!*, HA reel 15, folder 287.

39. *Nationalsozialistische Beamten-Zeitung (NSBZ)*, 20 July 1932, p. 194.

40. *NSBZ*, 20 February 1932, pp. 44–5.

41. Childers, *The Nazi Voter*, pp. 168ff, 240ff.

42. Michael Kater, 'Sozialer Wandel in der NSDAP im Zuge der nationalsozialistischer Machtergreifung', in Wolfgang Schieder (ed.), *Faschismus als soziale Bewegung*, 2nd edn. (Göttingen, 1983), pp. 30, 34; Kater, *The Nazi Party*, pp. 59–61, 68–70.

43. *NSDAP Partei-Statistik* (Berlin 1935), vol. II, pp. 53, 70.

44. For the claimed subscription to the *NSBZ*, see Hermann Neef, *Fünf Jahre nationalsozialistischer Beamteneinheitsorganisation* (Berlin, 1938), p. 20; for the number of sympathisers, E. Mursinsky and J. Brill, *Die Organisation der national-sozialistischen Beamten* (Berlin, 1940), p. 4. For the form by which sympathisers declared their membership of the local organisations, see the copy from the Bavarian political police files, in NSDAP HA reel 89, folder 1867, from which it is clear that this was a deliberate means of circumventing membership bans.

45. See police report of meeting in the Bauerngirgl hall, Munich, 17 January 1932; NSDAP HA reel 89, folder 1867. The speaker was one Blank, a local Nazi civil service spokesman, and other reports of his speeches confirm this impression of contempt for his colleagues.

46. Childers, *The Nazi Voter*, p. 268. For other evidence of the breadth of support for the NSDAP, see Richard Hamilton, *Who Voted for Hitler?* (Princeton, 1982).

9 THE NATIONAL SOCIALIST MOBILISATION OF NEW VOTERS: 1928–1933

Jürgen W. Falter

The Problem

Between 1928 and 1933, the NSDAP vote climbed from 0.8 to more than 17 million. During the same timespan the number of valid votes increased from 30.8 to 39.3 million while the total electorate expanded by approximately 3.5 million. The latter, of course, is a balanced figure representing the numerical difference between newly eligible and deceased voters. The (estimated) gross figure is 6.5 million newly eligible voters, i.e. young men and women coming into voting age after 1928.[1]

The parallel between these three sets of events has led many an observer to postulate a causal link between the increase of valid votes or the influx of new voters on the one hand and the spectacular rise of the NSDAP on the other. Contemporaries such as Theodor Geiger, Hans Neisser, Otto Dix or Hans Jäger, all writing in 1930, but also many postwar analysts such as Samuel Pratt, Alfred Milatz, Alexander Weber or Karl O'Lessker attributed the increase of the Nazi share of the vote in 1930 to a considerable or even preponderant extent to the mobilisation of new or abstaining voters.[2] Another line of reasoning tries to transcend the limits of purely correlative or intuitively won 'knowledge' in offering theoretically-based hypotheses about the attraction of the NSDAP to former non-voters and newly eligible voters. Thus Reinhard Bendix argues that as a result of massification and radicalisation processes triggered by a continuous series of social and economic crises the NSDAP in 1930 profited primarily from increased turnout rates and the influx of young voters.[3]

As the most explicit advocate of a class-theoretical interpretation of the Nazi electoral successes, Seymour Martin Lipset maintains that it was primarily radicalised middle-class voters who in 1930 swelled the ranks of the Nazi electorate. Non-voters, according to Lipset, were too apolitical and too uninformed to realise as early as 1930 the NSDAP as a viable political alternative. Only from July

1932 does Lipset concede a substantial flow of former non-voters to the Hitler movement, as the NSDAP used to be called on the ballot.[4]

Neither Bendix nor Lipset is very explicit about the assumed affinity of former non-voters to the NSDAP. Thus Lipset does not state if in 1932 non-voters joined the Nazi electorate only in disproportionate numbers or if they made up a relative or even an absolute majority of the Nazi gains or what else. Their disagreement, however, is over the role of turnout and of former DNVP voters in the 1930 election.[5] In regard to the later elections their interpretation of voter movements are more or less identical. Furthermore Lipset does not deal explicitly with newly eligible voters as Bendix does.

The same is true for two other interpretations of voter movements to the NSDAP which were developed during the seventies. Neither Walter Dean Burnham in his theory of political confessionalism nor Phillips Shively in his group identification hypothesis is terribly exact in their statements about the voting tendencies of former non-voters. Shively states: '. . . the Nazi party *essentially* was not a party of new and marginal participants' (emphasis added), and Burnham contends that 'the relative extent of Nazi penetration into the party of non-voters — at least before the special conditions of March 1933 — *may have been not much greater* (emphasis added) than among the active voters of bourgeois, conservative, particularist, and interest parties'.[6] Only Theodore Meckstroth discusses the problem in somewhat greater detail, a fact which makes it impossible here to report his extremely differentiated arguments which amount to the expectation that non-voters may well have flocked as early as 1930 in disproportionate numbers to the Hitler movement.[7]

As is the case with the theoretical interpretations sketched out above the empirical evidence on the behaviour of former non-voters and newly eligible voters is mixed. Not quite unexpectedly, the empirical findings and theoretical expectations of most authors tend to coincide. The question of the affinity of former non-voters and newly eligible voters is thus anything but settled despite a newly growing consensus among historians about the manifold social and political sources of the NSDAP constituency.[8] This is especially true for the newly eligible voters who never have been adequately researched for reasons to be spelled out below.

That the problem of the mobilisation of new voters has not yet been definitely solved (and that theoretical expectations and empirical findings are so strongly correlated) has to be mainly explained by inadequacies of data and statistical procedures. Interpretations of net vote changes on the Reich level from one election to the other as practised by Bendix, Milatz or most contemporaries are but the most extreme examples of work particularly prone to ecological fallacies since they do not take into account the very realistic possibility of hidden voter movements.

Simple bivariate correlations, especially when based on very large geographical units or a nonrandom selection of cities, counties or other administrative districts, do not fulfil any strict statistical standards either; they should be discounted as a sound basis of generalisations to the whole Reich.[9] Of course, other parties than the NSDAP could have profited from the increase in turnout and the Nazi Party should have won voters from other parties as well, so that a minimum requirement for any sophisticated empirical study of the problem is multivariate analysis, e.g. multiple regression analysis as practised by Waldmann, Wernette, Levin, Brown or Hänisch.[10]

Even then we are still dealing with aggregate findings which are only valid for a territorial (or any other aggregate) level. To interpret these findings in terms of individual-level relationships always implies the possibility of ecological fallacies, i.e. the mix-up of different levels of analysis. The best but still extremely risky way of inferring individual level relationships such as 'real' voter movements from aggregate level data is the so-called ecological regression analysis as developed by Bernstein and Goodmann.[11] Under some rather restrictive assumptions — the most important of them is non-contextuality — it is then possible to estimate in a rational, i.e. non-intuitive way individual-level voting exchanges between various parties, including the 'party of the non-voters'.[12] Some of the existing studies of the problem indeed refer to ecological regression analysis when discerning the transition probabilities of non-voters to the NSDAP.[13] We will turn to it in the last section of the following chapter.

The Impact of Changing Turnout Rates on the NSDAP Vote

Bivariate Associations Between Turnout and the Nazi Vote

Even from a simple, bivariate point of view there exist at least five different statistical perspectives to study the relationship between turnout figures and the NSDAP share of the vote. Each perspective offers different results and insights. The first is correlating the NSDAP vote with turnout rates at any given election.[14] A positive correlation indicates that the NSDAP vote tends to be high, where turnout rates are above average and tends to be low where turnout rates are below average. A second possibility is correlating turnout rates at the first election of each pair of elections with the NSDAP vote of the second election. The interpretation is similar to the one given above: In case of a positive correlation the NSDAP share of the vote is high in, say, 1930 where turnout was above average in 1928, etc.

A third and fourth way of approaching the problem consists of introducing change variables, i.e. the difference of the NSDAP vote or the turnout rate for any pair of consecutive elections. Thus one could correlate the change of the NSDAP vote between 1928 and 1930 with the percentage of turnout in 1928; a positive correlation then would imply that the NSDAP rise tended to be above average where turnout was high in 1928. The reverse perspective would analyse the relationship between increase or decrease of turnout in consecutive elections and the NSDAP share at any second election. A negative sign would imply that on the average the NSDAP share of the vote was low where turnout increased in a disproportionately high rate.

The fifth and last possibility is the correlation of change variables at both sides, i.e. the percentage difference of the NSDAP vote in each pair of elections and the percentage difference of turnout rates at the same pair of elections. This makes sense only if we relate both the NSDAP vote and turnout figures to the total number of eligible voters at any election under consideration. *If we try to study the relationship between the change in turnout rates and the change in the NSDAP share of the vote as is the case in all analyses where a causal link is postulated between these two sets of events only the last perspective seems to make sense.* We will, however, report the results of the four other possibilities in a note since they are based on a complete and, hopefully, correct data set which takes into account the effect introduced by manifold boundary changes which took place between 1920 and 1933 in Weimar Germany. They thus should be valid for the whole Reich.[15] In the following, however, and in our textual interpretation we will concentrate on the relationships represented by pairs of change variables.

Table 9.1: The percentage change of the NSDAP vote according to turnout percentage change classes

	Classes of turnout change						Regress.		Corr.
	1	2	3	4	5	6	a	b	r
28–30	13	12	14	12	12	13	130.7	−.032	−03
30–32J	10	11	14	15	18	25	142.5	.925	46
32J–32N	−2	−4	−4	−5	−5	−5	−35.2	.286	27
32N–33	8	7	9	12	14	18	51.5	.878	74

	Class widths					
28–30/						
32N–33	−0	0–3	3–6	6–9	9–12	12–100
30–32J	−(−6)–(−3)–(−0)	0–3	3–6	6–100		
32J–32N	−0–(−1.5)–(−3)–(−4.5)–(−6)–(−100					

Cell entries: percentage point change of NSDAP vote $t_2 - t_1$.
Regr. = unstandardised regression coefficients (percentage point change), NSDAP = a + b (percentage change turnout).

To illustrate the correlation coefficients of the change variables reported in the last column of Table 9.1, which are sometimes quite awkward to interpret, we indicate in addition the percentage changes in the dependent variable, i.e. the NSDAP, in ascending classes of change of the independent variable, i.e. turnout. As could be seen already by the correlation coefficient (r) in Table 9.1, there is no clear linear relationship between the increase in turnout and the rise of the NSDAP in 1930. In July 1932 and in March 1933, however, there is a clearly discernible pattern: the stronger the increase in turnout, the stronger — on the average — the increase in the National Socialist vote. In counties with an above average increase of turnout figures the NSDAP tends to rise disproportionately high; in counties with below average increase in voter participation the NSDAP increase is slowed down accordingly.

In both pairs of elections, however, there is an increase of the NSDAP vote even in those few counties of the Reich where turnout fell between the first and the second election. In November 1932, finally, there is again a positive but weak correlation between turnout and the Nazi vote: the stronger turnout figures went down the more votes were lost by the Nazi Party. Even here, however, the NSDAP vote still decreased where turnout rates rose against the nationwide trend. Technically speaking this is an indicator of the all-too-often neglected truism that correlation coefficients cannot substitute for the analysis of scatterplots or percentage distributions as reported in Table 9.1. Substantively speaking this phenomenon should be interpreted as an indicator of an overall swing to and from the NSDAP which cannot be solely explained by turnout changes. Numerically this swing is represented by a, the intercept of the unstandardised regression equation. Thus on the bivariate level, Lipset's position that non-voters swelled the ranks of the NSDAP followers only from July 1932 and not, as assumed by mass theorists, as early as 1930, seems to be corroborated.[16]

The Influence of Social Structure on the Impact of Turnout on the NSDAP Vote

The frequency of non-voting and the change of turnout as well as the development of the Nazi vote depended to a certain degree on the social composition of the geographical units, as can be seen by a cross-tabulation of several social factors with turnout or the NSDAP vote as the dependent variable.[17] This cross-tabulation may be presented in form of a tree analysis (which is not identical statistically with the analysis-of-variance kind of tree analysis developed by Morgan/Sonquist, 1964).[18] In the following we will report the correlation between changes in turnout and the Nazi vote within the segments of such a 'tree' (see Fig. 9.1). To construct the tree we divide the 831 county units of our diachronically stable data set in a first step into two subsets which represent different value ranges of the first independent variable, in our case urbanisation (as measured by the percentage of inhabitants of county units living in towns with more than 5,000 inhabitants). We thus get a first set of two contrasting groups for which we calculate the correlation coefficients for each pair of elections between the percentage of non-voters and the Nazi share of the vote. In step no. 2 we repeat this procedure, now dividing up our two rural vs. urban subgroups into several more subsets according to our next explanatory variable, religious denomination, and again we determine the correlation coefficients for the two variables under consideration within these new subgroups, etc. In our example we thus get 12 subgroups ranging from predominantly urban with a strong Protestant majority and an above average blue-collar population to predominantly rural with a strong Catholic majority and a below average blue-collar population.

We are now able to determine the influence of these interacting structural factors on the relationship between non-voting and the

Figure 9.1. The relationship between the change of turnout and the change of the NSDAP vote, 1928–1933, in counties with differing social composition (Pearson's r × 100)

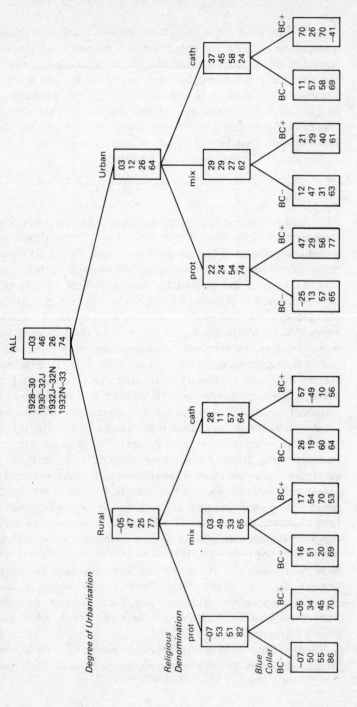

Nazi share of the vote. Before we turn to this we should give some information on the impact of social structure on turnout and the NSDAP vote. Between 1928 and 1933 turnout was constantly lower in the rural parts of Weimar Germany. Furthermore it tended to be lower in the Catholic in comparison to the Protestant parts of the Reich, and in Catholic counties it was low when the percentage of blue-collar workers was high and vice versa. The reverse is true for Protestant counties.

The change in turnout varied from election to election as a function of the social composition of the county units. In 1930 turnout showed an above average increase in the more urbanised regions of the Reich. In July 1932 and March 1933 a disproportionately high increase of turnout could be observed in the predominantly rural counties. There is a particularly marked increase in turnout between November 1932 and March 1933 in the Catholic regions, whether rural or urban. For all regions, Catholic and Protestant, urban and rural alike, it can be demonstrated that in 1933 the increase in turnout was largest when the percentage of blue-collar workers was below average.[19] The strongholds and diasporas of the NSDAP constituency are much better known to a broader public. In 1930 there was not much difference in Nazi voting between urban and rural counties. But already a clear contrast between predominantly Catholic and Protestant regions could be observed. Whether rural or urban in structure, the NSDAP fared much better in the Protestant parts of Germany. This rift even deepened in July 1932 when there was a dramatic difference in the voting behaviour in the different parts of Germany. The NSDAP now became territorially distinctly more Protestant and rural, augmenting its constituency by 23.2 percentage points in the rural Protestant regions as contrasted to only 9.2 percentage points in the rural Catholic parts. In 1933, after Hitler had become Chancellor of the Reich, the Catholic regions showed a slightly above average affinity towards the Nazis. But the NSDAP nevertheless still fared by far best within the rural, Protestant counties with a below average percentage of blue-collar workers.[20]

If we compare the change in turnout with the change of the NSDAP vote within the different segments of our tree we find no clear pattern of covariation between the two change variables. In some subgroups the direction and magnitude of the two coincide. To get a somewhat clearer impression we report in the following the bivariate correlation coefficients between both change variables within all segments of the tree (see Fig. 9.1). We thus get 21 different correlation coefficients for each pair of elections. Of course, we are not able to offer a complete verbal interpretation of all 84 coefficients. We are, however, in a position to give some comments on the general pattern formed by them.

The overwhelming majority of the coefficients are positive, indicating that in by far the most subgroups an above average increase of turnout in July 1932 and March 1933 tended to be accompanied by an above average increase of the NSDAP vote (and, accordingly, in November 1932 an above average increase in turnout by a disproportionately high decrease of the NSDAP vote). There are, however, some differences between the various segments of our tree, differences not only in size but sometimes even in sign. Thus for July 1932 and March 1933 the relationship between turnout and the percentage increase in Nazi vote is much stronger in rural counties than in the more urbanised parts of Germany. In 1930 the connection between both factors is stronger in Catholic than in Protestant regions, and especially so when the share of blue-collar workers is below the Reich average. Furthermore, there is a negative relationship in 1930 between both variables in urban Protestant counties with a below average percentage of labourers while the correlation is positive in urban Protestant regions with an above average percentage of workers. A similar deviation can be found for the 1932–3 pair of elections in urban Catholic counties: where the number of blue-collar workers is low, the NSDAP share of the vote increases with turnout; where blue-collar workers are overrepresented there is a negative relationship between change of turnout and increase of the National Socialist vote.

In general, Fig. 9.1 demonstrates that under the cover of nationwide swings and correlations regional deviations may be hidden which can largely be attributed to the social and demographic composition of the county units under investigation. They indicate differing mobilisation potentials of former non-voters in favour of National Socialism at different points in time. The differing relationships between the various subgroups of our tree furthermore show that the inference from local or regional configurations to the national level is not only dangerous but in most cases simply unacceptable. On the other hand, for the same reasons the inference from the national level to a specific regional or local context may be invalid as well. Both kinds of analysis are valuable in their own right but cannot substitute for each other!

Controlling for General Mobilisation Effects

Before we turn to a real multivariate analysis of the problem it might be advisable to deal with the possibility sketched out by Shively that mobilisation of new voters tended to be generally higher than average in regions with strong NSDAP vote gains. This assumed covariation, which, in turn, would explain the mainly positive relationships reported above, could be a result of the organisational and propaganda efforts of the Nazis themselves or of anticipated electoral successes of the National Socialists which indiscriminately mobilised partisans and adversaries of the NSDAP alike. To rule out this possibility, it might be advisable to take a look at the correlation between changes in turnout and the vote of the other parties (Table 9.2).

Since we are dealing with variables which were defined on the basis of the total number of eligible voters per county, we are in a position to analyse the assumed effect. Indeed there is some strong indication that Shively might be right: changes of turnout rates and party votes are positively correlated in most cases. There are only three noteworthy exceptions: the change in vote of the splinter parties (OTHER) in July 1932 and March 1933 and the change of the SPD vote in November 1932. Those parties which still were able to win votes, such as the KPD up to November 1932 and the Centre party (combined with its Bavarian branch, the Bavarian Peoples party), could do so in a disproportionately high manner where turnout figures rose above average; parties losing votes experienced a below average decrease in regions where turnout showed an above average rise if correlation coefficients are positive. Where they are negative, the reverse is true, of course. At the same time this analysis demonstrates that the effect of non-voting on the rise of National Socialism may well be studied by means of aggregate data using territorially defined units of analysis.[21]

Controlling for the Effects of other Variables

As we have seen in the preceding section, both in July 1932 and March 1933 changes in turnout and party vote are much more strongly correlated for the NSDAP electorate than for the constituencies of the other parties. Nevertheless, there seems to exist an impact of turnout on the voting results of the other parties as

Table 9.2: The correlation between the change of turnout rates and changes of the other parties

	DNVP	LIB	OTHER	CENTRE	SPD	KPD
28–30	29	13	<u>11</u>	<u>24</u>	39	<u>33</u>
30–32J	08	09	−18	<u>14</u>	09	<u>13</u>
32J–32N	<u>27</u>	14	<u>21</u>	45	−14	<u>39</u>
32N–33	<u>12</u>	00	−21	<u>10</u>	23	04

Cell entries: Pearson's r × 100.
Underlined: Parties with a rise in total vote.

well. In the following section we will therefore enlarge our scope of analysis and include in a multivariate model the change of selected other parties in conjunction with the change in turnout figures. This will be done in two steps. The first offers a cross-tabulation of several variables with the NSDAP vote as the dependent variable. It will again be represented in form of a tree analysis (see Figure 9.2). The second will then proceed to a multiple regression analysis of the 'tree variables'.

In the first step of our 'tree analysis' we divide our 831 county unites into terciles, i.e. classes containing each one third of all cases, according to the change of turnout which took place in the counties at each pair of elections. Our dependent variable is the average percentage point change of the NSDAP vote in each class. We are thus able to reproduce our earlier findings that in 1930 there was no linear relationship between the change in turnout and the increase of the Nazi vote. For the following three pairs of elections we manage to discern the same pattern of relationships as in the correlation analysis: there is a six-point difference in the July 1932 and 1933 increase figures of the NSDAP between the first and third tercile; in November 1932 there is a reverse relationship: where turnout went down most the NSDAP lost more votes than in counties with a smaller decrease of turnout figures.

On the second level we split up the three terciles according to an above or below average change of the DNVP vote. There too is a clearcut relationship with the NSDAP development: where in 1930 and July 1932 the DNVP lost an above average share of the vote, the NSDAP increase in all three terciles proved to be disproportionately high. Accordingly, the Nazi losses were above average in November 1932 in those counties where the DNVP regained a

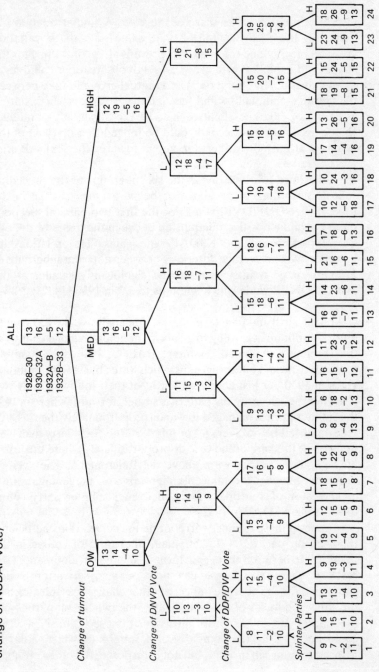

Figure 9.2. A 'Tree Analysis' of the NSDAP gains and losses between 1928 and 1933. (Cell entries: percentage point change of NSDAP vote)

disproportionately large share of the vote. A similar relationship exists for the 1933 election. At the same time the covariation between turnout and the Nazi vote prevails after controlling for the change of the DNVP vote. The first set of observations could serve as an indicator (but not more!) of a mutual give-and-take between the German Nationalists and the National Socialists which started as early as 1930, a possibility denied by Lipset's theory of middle-class extremism. The second could be judged as a first test of the assumed affinity of former non-voters towards the NSDAP *after 1930*.

At the third level we divide the six subgroups of the preceding split-up according to an above or below average change in the Liberal (i.e. DDP/DVP) vote. For the first two pairs of elections there is again a positive relationship between the losses of the two liberal parties and the NSDAP vote gains. This relationship, however, with an average difference between adjacent subgroups of 3.7 percentage points, seems to be significantly smaller as the average DNVP value which amounts to 5.3 in 1930 (1932J: 2.2 vs. 2.3).

At the fourth and final level of this 'tree analysis', the 831 county units are split up according to an above or below average change of the various combined splinter parties, i.e. the manifold particularistic and interest groups which were able to win additional votes in 1930 but lost about four-fifths of their following only two years later. Once more the pattern is straightforward: where in 1930 the splinter parties managed to win disproportionately the NSDAP vote gains fell below average; in July 1932 the Nazi Party managed to increase its share of the vote disproportionately where the losses of the splinter parties were above the Reich mean. The average difference between the adjacent subgroups is 6.7 percentage points, an indicator of a strong affinity of former splinter party voters towards the NSDAP in 1932.

In general these findings corroborate the correlation coefficients reported on pages 204–7. Our main interest is of course in the relationship between changes in turnout and the development of the NSDAP electorate. These can now be analysed after having controlled for the possible impact of other change variables such as the gains and losses of the Nationalists, the two liberal parties and the splinter parties. (For bivariate associations see Table 9.3a). This could be done by the comparison of subgroups which differ in respect to change in turnout, but not in respect to the other variables

Table 9.3a: The relationship between the gains and losses of various parties and the electoral development of the NSDAP[22]

NSDAP	TURN	DNVP	LIB	Other	Centre	SPD	KPD
1928–30	−03	−50	−50	−03	−36	−17	−09
1930–32J	46	−11	−17	−63	−39	−31	−17
1932J–32N	27	−61	−19	−29	−39	−07	−00
1932N–33	74	−11	−01	18	−36	−19	−06

Cell entries: Pearson's r (×100). 831 county units.
Weighted by population per county. All variables change variables: $\%t_2 - \%t_1$.
Percentage base: registered voters.

of the model. We thus have to look for differences between segments no. 1, 9 and 17, 2, 10 and 18, etc., up to segments 8, 16 and 24. (See Figure 9.2.)

We are now able to discern even for 1930 a small but positive association between the increase of turnout and the rise of the NSDAP. In July 1932 this relationship is stronger as could be expected from the correlation coefficients reported earlier. There are, however, some exceptions to the rule where the trend is reversed. In November 1932 figures display the expected negative relationship between the two variables: where the decrease of turnout was above average the NSDAP lost disproportionately many votes. The March 1933 election finally shows a clearcut linear relationship between the development of turnout and the NSDAP vote.

Taken all together the relationship is quite clearcut with only minor flaws or deviations. Since the choice of cutting points is of primary importance in such a variety of tree analysis – it may well be responsible for the deviations from the general trend mentioned — it is advisable to report the results of a multiple regression analysis with the variables which constitute the 'tree' (see Table 9.3b). This kind of analysis which treats the variables as what they are, i.e. as continuous variables (in the 'tree analysis' they were artificially di- or trichotomised), fully corroborates our findings reported in the immediately preceding paragraphs: in 1930 there is indeed a positive but marginal effect of turnout change on the NSDAP increase. By far the most important effects on the development of the Nazi vote between 1928 and 1930 are exerted by the DNVP and the Liberal losses. The electoral change of the 'Others' was deliberately left out of the 1930 prediction equation in order to minimise

Table 9.3b: Multiple regression analysis of the gains and losses of selected parties[23]

Target variable: NSDAP	TURN	DNVP	LIB	OTHER	R^2
		Predictor variables:			
1928–30	.184	−.512	−.487	–	49%
1930–32A	.392	−.492	−.421	−.797	81%
1932A–32B	.469	−.687	−.122	−.094	59%
1932B–33	.758	−.170	−.021	−.061	59%
R^2–Change					
28–30	0.1%	26%	23%	–	
30–32A	21.0%	2%	6%	52%	
32A–32B	7.0%	50%	2%	1%	
32B–33	55.0%	4%	0%	0.3%	

Hierarchical regression analysis of 'tree variables'. 831 county units. 1928–30: OTHER left out of equation in order to minimise multicollinearity. Standardised regression coefficients.

multicollinearity. This seems to be legitimate since the intercorrelation between this variable and the Nazi vote is extremely low while the relationship with the DNVP change is rather strong. The latter may be regarded as an indicator of some voter exchange between the splinter parties and the DNVP after 1928.

As could be read from the July 1932 equation, part of the 1930 DNVP losses seem to have reached the NSDAP via intermediate hosts such as the splinter parties (which indeed were part split-offs of the German Nationalists). In July 1932 the losses of the splinter parties account for at least 60 per cent of the total explained variance of the regression model while the turnout change accounts for maximally 25 per cent. The DNVP losses and the decrease of the Liberals are at that election of minor importance. In November 1932 the DNVP gains are of primary, the decrease of turnout of secondary, importance for the NSDAP losses. In 1933, finally, change in turnout accounts for about 95 per cent of the total explained variance. True, with the exception of 1930, the multivariate analysis confirms the results of the correlation analysis of pages 204–7. These results are remarkably in accordance with the findings of Brown and Hänisch who worked with different data sets and differently specified statistical models.

On an aggregate level neither Lipset nor Bendix could fully be verified. In counties with an above average increase of turnout the

NSDAP gains proved to be only slightly above average in 1930. This finding clearly contradicts Bendix's assumption of non-voting as the most important single source of the Nazi increase. At the same time, however, Lipset's hypothesis that there should be no (or only a negligible) relationship between the losses of the German Nationalists and the NSDAP gains can clearly be refuted: the higher the decline of the DNVP in 1930 the more pronounced the increase of the NSDAP vote. The losses of the two liberal parties are well connected to the NSDAP vote gains, but the relationship is only about the same as that between the DNVP decrease and the NSDAP increase; again Lipset's contention of former voters of the Liberals and the splinter parties being the main source of the NSDAP increase between 1928 and 1930 is not covered by our findings. For the following pairs of elections Lipset's and Bendix's (largely coinciding) assumptions are more or less met by the results of our empirical analysis.

Estimating Individual Vote Switching, 1928–1933

It should be stressed again that the results of our analysis reported so far are only valid on a macro level. They describe relationships between counties and not the behaviour of individual voters. The associations referred to are at best indicators of individual vote switching from, say, the non-voting category to the NSDAP, from the DNVP to certain splinter parties, etc. Under no circumstances should they be interpreted as true switching behaviour since under the disguise of a negative correlation or regression coefficient there may be hidden virtually hundreds of thousands of voters switching in the opposite direction as indicated by the sign. This often neglected fact has led many an historian of elections to give extremely mistaken verbal interpretations of negative correlation or regression coefficients. One noteworthy example is the rather small negative correlation between the percentage of blue-collar workers and the NSDAP vote which is generally read as evidence of the strong if not almost total resistance of workers towards the NSDAP, a misinterpretation which is clearly at variance with the facts.[24]

Statistically the most convincing (but still dangerous) way of inferring individual level relationships from macro data is the computation of transition probabilities between parties by means of ecological regression analysis. If the rather strict statistical assumptions of ecological regression analysis are met by the data this procedure gives very good estimates of the true transition behaviour of the voters. If not, the results may be quite misleading. Unfortunately the historian of elections is not able to test beyond any reasonable doubt if these assumptions are indeed met by his data. Therefore it can always be doubted if the results won by this technique are valid. In conjunction with the macro relationships reported in the preceding chapters, however, they offer sufficient evidence for a test of the hypotheses spelled out in the beginning of this article.[25]

When analysing individual vote switches we must distinguish between two different perspectives which in a contingency table correspond to row or column percentages. They may be expressed in the form of two different questions: (a) How did the non-voters behave in regard to the NSDAP? (b) How large is the share of former non-voters among the NSDAP electorate at a given election? Correlation coefficients mix up the two perspectives; this may serve as an explanation for those many misinterpretations mentioned above.

As Tables 9.4 and 9.5 show, the NSDAP seems to have profited not only in July 1932 and 1933 but already as early as 1930 from rising turnout; indeed, in all three elections former non-voters switched to the NSDAP more frequently than to any other party. It can be seen from the same tables, however, that all other parties were able to profit from the increase in turnout too. On the other hand, only in 1933 did former non-voters represent the largest single source of the NSDAP increase. In 1930 former DNVP voters and switchers from the two liberal parties made up the bulk of the NSDAP gains. In July 1932 former partisans of the various splinter parties accounted for exactly one third of the NSDAP increase, among them probably many former DNVP voters who joined the splinter groups in 1930 or earlier.[26] Switchers from the Liberals and the Nationalists made up for 13 and 10 per cent, respectively, of the NSDAP gains and were clearly outnumbered by former SPD voters who, according to our data, accounted for more than 15 per cent of the 1932J NSDAP increase.

Thus, between 1928 and 1930 the affinity of former non-voters towards the NSDAP in comparison to the total electorate was about average; in July 1932 the tendency of non-voters to join the Nazi electorate was slightly above average and only in 1933 was there a strong disproportionate switch of November 1932 non-voters towards National Socialism.[27] In no pair of elections did voters

Table 9.4: Where did the non-voters go?

	KPD	SPD	Z/BVP	DDP/DVP	DNVP	OTH	NSDAP	NONVOT
1928–30	9	7	6	6	2	8	14	50
1930–32A	8	5	6	2	1	3	19	57
1932A–32B	4	2	1	2	5	2	2	81
1932B–33	2	4	7	1	2	2	42	41

Transition probabilities won by ecological regression analysis with religious denomination and urbanisation as moderator variables. 831 county units. Cases weighted by population figures. Negative estimates smoothed by proportional fitting. Row percentages; basis: eligible voters.

Table 9.5: Where did the NSDAP voters come from?

	KPD	SPD	Z/BVP	DDP/DVP	DNVP	OTH	NSDAP	NONVOT
1930–28	3	14	8	18	22	8	5	24
1932J–30	2	10	4	8	6	18	40	12
1932N–32J	2	4	3	0	0	1	89	1
1933–32N	3	2	1	6	1	2	63	22

Row percentages. Basis: NSDAP voters. Reading example: 24 per cent of the 1930 NSDAP voters had not voted in 1928, 14 per cent had voted SPD, 22 per cent DNVP, etc. Same technical remarks as in Table 9.4.

Table 9.6: Where did the NSDAP voters go?

	KPD	SPD	Z/BVP	DDP/DVP	DNVP	OTH	NSDAP	NONVOT
1930	3	2	4	1	5	0	85	0
1932J	3	5	4	1	3	1	76	6
1932N	2	1	1	1	3	0	92	2

Row percentages. Basis: NSDAP voters. Reading example: 85 per cent of the 1930 NSDAP voters voted NSDAP again in July 1932, 5 per cent voted DNVP, 2 per cent SPD, etc. Same technical remarks as in Table 9.4.

switch to the NSDAP in a one-way stream. The Nazi Party lost regularly voters to the other parties and to non-voters, even if the give and take was asymmetric in essence (see Table 9.6). The November 1932 election is of particular interest for the historian of Weimar elections, because the NSDAP lost over two million voters in that election while turnout went down by about 1.4 million, a parallel which has led many historians to speculate about one-way switches from one camp to other. The results of ecological regression analysis show that during this election the NSDAP indeed lost a disproportionately high number of voters to the non-voting camp. It shows as well, however, that the other parties, the Catholic Centre Party and the Social Democrats ahead, the DNVP and the KPD following, could profit from the NSDAP losses too.

What do these results imply for the theories sketched out above? Are any of them verified while the others have to be dismissed as obsolete? Or does any of them qualify as a 'relative winner'? Neither Bendix nor Lipset seems to be fully corroborated (or rejected) by our data: Bendix is certainly correct in assuming an influx of previous non-voters (and of former DNVP voters) into the Nazi electorate as early as 1930. But this influx of non-voters is anything but the main source of the NSDAP rise from obscurity to national prominence in 1930; only about every fifth of the new NSDAP voters seems to have abstained from voting in 1928. Lipset, on the other hand, is correct in pointing to the role of former liberal voters in the surge of the NSDAP — but they, i.e. mainly switchers from the DVP, were responsible (in the mathematical sense of the word) for only every fifth new NSDAP voter in 1930. He is mistaken in his assumptions concerning the DNVP and the non-voters in regard to the 1928–30 pair of elections.

The splinter parties lost heavily to the NSDAP only in July 1932. And only in 1933 did the non-voters really represent by far the most important source of the Nazi gains. On the later elections, however, there is no serious disagreement between Bendix and Lipset.

If we interpret Burnham's remarks cited above and Shively's notion of no 'unusual support' of the Nazis by previous non-voters as indicating a not stronger than average tendency 'to be Nazis',[28] we have to refer to the transition probabilities of voters of the other parties towards the NSDAP as well. Since we are here concentrating on the role of the non-voters and the newly eligible voters, it may suffice to point out that in 1930 the tendency of previous (1928) non-voters to join the Nazi electorate was less than half of that of the former DNVP voters and only slightly more than half of that of the previous Liberal voters. The same is true in essence for the July 1932 election where former non-voters range only fourth in Nazi affinity after previous splinter party, liberal and DNVP voters. Only in 1933 does the Nazi affinity of former non-voters clearly outrank that of previous voters of other parties. Our results coincide in this respect with Shively's own findings, which were won with different aggregates.[29]

In sum, then, it could be shown that the relationship between non-voting and the NSDAP vote was far more complex than assumed by the four hypotheses sketched out above. The same is true, of course, for the former partisan background of Nazi joiners.[30] Simple theories do not always seem to be fit to explain complex phenomena. The Nazi Party seems to have meant different things at different times to different social and political groups. For some it was a 'catch-all-party of protest' against modernisation and economic hardships;[31] for others it was the last non-Marxist alternative during the economic crisis offering promises instead of Chancellor Brüning's blood, sweat and tears programme; again for others it was the last stronghold against Communism and Socialism; and for some it was the kind of folkish, anti-Semitic party they always had looked for. I seriously doubt if this latter group was of any more prominence within the Nazi electorate of 1930 to 1933 than it was in the decades before within the Weimar or Empire party systems.

The Nazi Affinities of the Newly Eligible Voters

Virtually all contemporaries characterised National Socialism as a movement which distinguished itself from its competitors by the extreme youth of its activists and followers.[32] Its street activities indeed were led by the extremely young SA militia, and the results of the student body elections at German universities showed as early as 1930 the strong affinity of at least the academic part of the youngest age cohorts towards Nazism.[33] Even the party rank and file was considerably younger than the membership of the other parties. With slightly less than 60 per cent of its joiners between 1925 and 1930 being under 30 years, and a mean age of NSDAP joiners between 1925 and 1933 of 31 years, the National Socialist movement was indeed not only in the streets but also organisationally young in appearance and in reality. A good part of its political dynamism may be attributed to this youthful character of the Nazi movement.[34]

But can we really transfer this youthful appearance and organisational composition without further qualifications to the party electorate as a whole as it is so often done in the literature? If in analogy to the party membership about 60 per cent of the Nazi electorate of March 1933 would have been younger than 30 years, this would imply that not only over 10 million NSDAP voters would fall under this category but also that there would have been virtually no young voters of the same age bracket left for the other parties (including, of course, the 'party of the non-voters', where younger people always tend to be heavily overrepresented) since there were only about 12.3 million eligible voters of that age in 1933.[35] Even a somewhat smaller percentage than 60 per cent is highly improbable. Otherwise it would be mathematically impossible to account for the electoral successes of the rather youthful Communist Party and the still existing political ties between the Catholic youths and the Centre Party or its Bavarian branch. When analysing the youth factor at the electoral level one should expect much smaller percentages than those measured in the organisational studies of the SS,[36] the SA or the NSDAP.

Strangely enough the problem has *never* been adequately researched statistically. An overwhelming affinity of young voters towards the NSDAP has simply been taken for granted or 'proved' by plausibility. The only study known to the author dealing with the problem at all statistically is the early, precomputer, analysis of 193 German cities by Samuel Pratt. He correlates the percentage of NSDAP votes with the percentage of votes in different age groups and finds to his own astonishment a clear positive (!) relationship between age and the NSDAP vote: the larger the percentage of young voters the smaller the share of the Nazi vote in July 1932; the larger the percentage of older voters the greater the electoral chances of the NSDAP.[37] The correlation between the Communist share of the vote and the percentage of young voters, on the other hand, is more or less as expected: the younger the electorate, the stronger the Communist Party.

Pratt tries to explain his rather unexpected finding of an inverse relationship between youth and the NSDAP vote by a class-related argument. Earlier he had found a positive relationship between old middle class and the NSDAP vote; and since the self-employed (who constitute the old middle class) tend to be much older than blue-collar or even white-collar workers he was able to offer a plausible theoretical interpretation for his astonishing finding. Unfortunately, however, he was not able to extend his admirable bivariate analysis (which he had to do with the computational tools of the time) in order to control for the effects of such 'disturbing' factors as 'old middle class' or religion.

After Pratt, to our knowledge nobody has ever dealt again with the problem in any greater detail if we do not count those studies which take the answer to our problem as given or simply self-evident. One major reason for this neglect may be the fact that the major publicly available machine-readable data set on Weimar elections, the ICPSR 'German Weimar Republic Data 1919–1933', contains no age variables. One other reason could be that the variability of the age variables is rather restricted since there are simply no geographical units with a very large or very small percentage of newly eligible voters. This restricted range of variability increases the danger of unstable correlations and selection effects (which could well have caused Pratt's counter-intuitive results). What is impossible in case of such restricted variation of the independent variable is ecological regression analysis.[38]

In the following we will present some preliminary results of our attempts at tackling the intricate problem of the newly eligible voters by some new data which is contained in our county data set on the Weimar Republic. This data set includes among its approximately 700 variables a whole series of age variables from the 1925 and 1933 German census. From the 1925 census we obtained the number of male and female young persons between 16 and 18 and between 14 and 16 years of age. These two age cohorts came into voting age (20 years in Weimar Germany) between 1927 and 1929 and between 1929 and 1931, respectively. Together they form the youngest group of voters in 1930. From the 1933 census we collected information on the percentage of people 65 years of age and older.

Furthermore, we constructed from these age variables two additional variables measuring the 'middle-aged' groups and the young voters in 1933. The first is formed by the difference between the total number of registered voters in 1933 minus the old and young (i.e. those who were between 14 and 18 years old in 1925). The second, 'Young 33', is exactly this latter variable, which represents, of course a 'proxy' for some more direct measures to be tested in the future.

Finally, we constructed still another 'youth variable' which is simply defined by the difference in the number of eligible voters at any pair of Reichstag elections after 1928 (with the number of the eligible voters of each second election as the percentage basis). These three variables represent of course the balance between young voters coming into voting age at each election and the deceased voters (plus those moving in and out of a county during the time interval between each pair of elections).

In the first step we present the simple, i.e. bivariate, correlation coefficients for (a) the NSDAP share of the vote, (b) the percentage change of the NSDAP vote on the one hand and the different age indicators on the other (see Table 9.7). There is a rather low but fairly consistent negative relationship between our middle-aged variable and both the Nazi share of the vote and its change in 1930, July 1932 and March 1933. The relationship between the percentage of old voters (65 years and older) and the two NSDAP indicators is even more distinct but positive in sign: the more retired or old people in a county the higher, on the average, the NSDAP share of the vote and the more pronounced the party's increase in 1930, 1932J and 1933.

This latter result corresponds to Pratt's findings referred to earlier in this chapter. For the different youth variables there is no such clearcut picture. Most coefficients are closer to zero than to anything else; they thus indicate that there is no linear bivariate relationship between the two variables under consideration, irrespective of sign. There are, however, some noteworthy exceptions: the higher the percentage of young voters (as defined by the two 1925 census variables and the July 1932 difference variable), the higher on the average the NSDAP increase in 1933 and, perhaps, July 1932. This evidence is anything but overwhelming. Because of the chance of some spurious non-correlations which may be hidden behind close-to-zero relationships it is advisable, however, not to stop the analysis at this point.

A closer look at the intercorrelations between the different age variables and some social factors such as 'urbanisation' or 'religious denomination' prove that the age categories are spread unevenly between counties. Thus 'Youth' and 'Old Age' are positively correlated with 'Catholicism' and negatively with 'urbanisation' while the reverse is true for the middle-aged category. One has to control for the effects of such variables because otherwise it might be them which produce the relationships measured in our correlation analysis.

In the second step the effects of the variable 'percentage of Catholics' are partialled out (see Table 9.8). This procedure which more or less neutralises the impact of a differing religious composition of the counties displays much clearer relationships than the simple bivariate correlation. The positive effect of age is about the

Table 9.7: The relationship between several age variables and the NSDAP vote

NSDAP Share of the vote	Young 33	Middle	Old	14–16	16–18	Y30	Y32	Y33
1930	−09	−12	31	−13	−10	−09	–	–
1932J	01	−28	48	−00	−04	−05	16	–
1932N	02	−28	44	02	−03	−05	15	–
1933	17	−45	57	15	04	−06	25	−05
Percentage change								
1928–30	−07	−16	35	−11	−08	−09		
1930–32J	09	−33	48	11	02	−00	18	–
1932J–32N	07	14	−33	10	07	02	−12	–
1932N–33	35	−41	30	32	16	−02	25	07

Cell entries: Pearson's r ($\times$ 100). 831 county units. Variable definitions: Young 33 = 14–18 years 1925. Middle: Registered voters minus 'Old' minus 'Young 33'. 14–16/16–18: age groups in 1925. Y30/Y32/Y33: Registered voters t_2-t_1/t.

Table 9.8: The relationship between age and NSDAP vote II: Partial Correlation Coefficients

NSDAP Share of the vote	Young 33	Middle	Old	14–16	16–18	Y30	Y32	Y33
1930	10	−18	19	07	05	−08	–	–
1932J	37	−47	41	38	21	−03	35	05
1932N	35	−43	36	36	20	−03	30	06
1933	44	−57	52	44	22	−05	38	06
Percentage change								
1928–30	15	−23	24	11	09	−08	17	−03
1930–32J	42	−49	39	46	25	03	34	09
1932J–32N	−12	20	−23	−10	−08	00	−21	03
1932N–33	28	−42	42	25	09	−04	22	02

Cell entries: partial correlation coefficients (percent Catholic controlled). Same variable definitions, data set, etc., as in Table 9.7.

same as in the bivariate case, while the (negative) coefficients of the 'middle-aged' variable almost double in size. With the religious factor neutralised it is possible to state that the NSDAP had more problems in winning new voters (or in November 1932 keeping the old ones) the more persons between approximately 25 and 65 lived in a county. At the same time there are some rather distinct positive relationships between some of the youth variables and the Nazi vote. The evidence seems to get stronger that there indeed existed the theoretically expected positive relationship between youth and the NSDAP vote.

In order to control as well for the effects of urbanisation and to be able to analyse the separate effects of religious denomination and youth, we have to combine these predictor variables into one multiple regression equation with the percentage change of the NSDAP vote as the dependent variable. To control for multicol-linearity, i.e. unacceptably high intercorrelations of the predictor variables, we have computed for each pair of elections two separate regression equations, one for the more urbanised and the other for the more rural counties of the Reich (definitions similar to those of the preceding section). Since Pratt offers as an explanation of his finding of a negative relationship between young age and the NSDAP vote the impact of the old middle class we have added to our regression equation the percentage of self-employed. As youth indicator we chose the combination of the two 1925 census variables dealt with above, because it does not imply balanced figures. Nevertheless, there may be some 'noise' since the very youngest in 1932 and 1933 are excluded by this procedure. Furthermore it is evident that at least some members of this age cohort (22–26 years in 1933) would have moved to other counties since 1925. In later analyses this 'proxy variable' will have to be replaced by still more direct measures (which will soon be included in our data set).

There seems to have been at least some positive impact of the youth factor on the development of the NSDAP between 1928 and 1933. Thus in the urbanised counties in 1930 and July 1932 'youth' exerted (in our regression model) about the same effect on the NSDAP increase as the self-employed variable (see Table 9.9); if we take into consideration the impact of religion and of old middle class we can state that for the more urbanised counties the NSDAP share of vote in both elections grew faster where the percentage of young voters was high and that it tended to grow more slowly where the (relative) number of young voters was small. In November 1932 the NSDAP lost more voters where the young were underrepre-sented. And in 1933 there is no clear relationship between the youth variable and the NSDAP increase in urban Germany.

In the more rural counties just the opposite of the last statement seems to be true. Here only in 1933 a positive interpretable relationship between the two variables could be discerned by our

Table 9.9: Multiple regression analysis of the NSDAP vote change on youth, religion and old middle class

NSDAP change	Young 33	% Catholic	% Self-employed	R^2
Urban counties				
1928–30	.195	−.520	.218	25%
1930–32J	.223	−.710	.216	45%
1932J–32N	−.101	.290	−.315	20%
1932N–33	−.053	.319	.225	19%
Rural counties				
1928–30	.078	−.636	.005	41%
1930–32J	.004	−.847	.295	65%
1932J–32N	−0.37	.620	−.020	39%
1932N–33	.183	.115	.328	18%

Cell entries: standardised regression coefficients. Same data set and same youth variable as in Tables 9.7 and 9.8.
% Catholic: Number of Catholics/inhabitants.
% Self-employed: number of self employed/total working force.
R^2: Explained variance.

multiple regression analysis. This relationship, however, is higher than between the percentage of Catholics and the Nazi increase.

In sum, there seems to be some statistical evidence for the old assumption of a greater than average affinity of the newly eligible voters towards the NSDAP. But this evidence is still anything but conclusive. The problem certainly needs further elaboration and testing. One should not forget over our rather differentiated findings in regard to the youth factor our perhaps more surprising side-results concerning the old voters who — at least at the aggregate level — display a somewhat stronger effect on the increase of the Hitler movement than the young! In regard to age, a curvilinear relationship seems to predominate with the 25 to 65 years-of-age group at the bottom and the old aged at the top of the distribution while the youngest age group probably ranged somewhere in between these two categories. Again, reality seems to defy simple descriptions and explanations. Not only in regard to non-voting but also to youth it seems to be far more complex than preconceived by contemporaries and theoreticians alike.

228   *National Socialist Mobilisation*

Notes

1. See Hans Striefler, *Deutsche Wahlen in Bildern und Zahlen* (Düsseldorf, 1946), p. 16ff.
2. Samuel Pratt, 'The Social Bases of Nazism and Communism in Urban Germany', M.A. Thesis, Michigan State University, 1948; Alfred Milatz, *Wähler und Wahlen in der Weimarer Republik* (Bonn, 1965); Alexander Weber, 'Die sozialen Merkmale der NSDAP-Wähler', Ph.D. Dissertation, University of Freiburg, 1969; or Karl O'Lessker, 'Who Voted for Hitler? A New Look at the Class Basis of Nazism', *American Journal of Sociology*, 70, 1968/9, pp. 63–9.
3. See Jürgen W. Falter, 'Radicalization of the Middle Classes or Mobilization of the Unpolitical? The Theories of Seymour Martin Lipset and Reinhard Bendix on the Electoral Support of the NSDAP in the Light of Recent Research', *Social Science Information*, 20, 2, pp. 389–430. Bernd Hagtvet, 'The Theory of Mass Society and the Collapse of the Weimar Republic: A Reexamination', in Stein Larsen, Bernd Hagtvet and Jan Myklebust (eds.), *Who Were the Fascists? Social Roots of European Fascism* (Bergen-Oslo-Tromso, 1980), pp. 66–117. Dee Richard Wernette, 'Political Violence and German Elections: 1930 and July, 1932', Ph.D. Dissertation, University of Michigan, 1974; Michaela Richter, 'The National Socialist Electoral Breakthrough. Opportunities and Limits in the Weimar Party System. A Regional Case Study of Franconia', Ph.D. Dissertation, City University of New York, 1982; and David R. Cameron, 'The Mobilization of Nazism: Middle-Class Party or Catch-All Party', paper delivered at the Annual Meeting of the Social Science History Association, 1977.
4. See Falter, 'Radicalization of the Middle Classes or Mobilization of the Unpolitical?'; Dirk Hänisch, *Sozialstrukturelle Bestimmungsgründe des Wahlverhaltens in der Weimarer Republik. Eine Aggregatdatenanalyse der Reichstagwahlen 1924–1933* (Duisburg, 1983), pp. 4ff.; Loren K. Waldman, 'Models of Mass Movements — The Case of the Nazis', Ph.D. Dissertation, University of Chicago, 1973, pp. 18ff.; Mark H. Levine, '"Who Voted for Hitler" Revisited', Ph.D. Dissertation, Bowling Green State University, 1976, pp. 37ff.; and Wernette, 'Political Violence and German Elections'.
5. Falter, 'Radicalization of the Middle Classes or Mobilization of the Unpolitical?'
6. Walter Dean Burnham, 'Political Immunization and Political Confessionalism: The United States and Weimar Germany', *Journal of Interdisciplinary History*, 3, 1972, p. 13; and W. Phillips Shively, 'Party Identification, Party Choice and Voting Stability – The Weimar Case', *American Political Science Review*, 56, 1972, pp. 121–6.
7. Theodore W. Meckstroth, 'Conditions of Partisan Realignments: A Study of Electoral Change', Ph.D. Dissertation, University of Minnesota, 1972.
8. See Falter, 'Radicalization of the Middle Classes or Mobilization of the Unpolitical?'; Falter, 'Die Wähler der NSDAP 1928–1933 — Sozialstruktur und parteipolitische Herkunft', in Wolfgang Michalka (ed.), *Die nationalsozialistische Machtergreifung* (Paderborn, 1984), pp. 47–59; Courtney Brown, 'The Nazi Vote: A National Ecological Study', *American Political Science Review*, 76, 1982, pp. 285–302; Richard F. Hamilton, *Who Voted for Hitler?* (Princeton, 1982); and Thomas Childers, *The Nazi Voter* (Chapel Hill and London), 1983.
9. Pratt, 'The Social Bases of Nazism'; Charles P. Loomis and J. Allen Beegle, 'The Spread of German Nazism in Rural Areas', *American Sociological Review*, 11, 1946, pp. 724–34; Werner Kaltefleiter, *Wirtschaft und Politik in Deutschland*, (Cologne, 1966); Karl Dietrich Bracher, *Die Auflösung der Weimarer Republik*, (Villingen, 1955), pp. 648ff.
10. Waldman, 'Models of Mass Movements'; Levin, 'Who Voted for Hitler?';

Brown, 'The Nazi Vote'; or Dirk Hänisch, 'Sozialstrukturelle Bestimmungsgründe des Wahlverhaltens'.

11. Fritz Bernstein, 'Über eine Methode, die soziologische und bevölkerungsstatistische Gliederung von Abstimmungen bei geheimen Wahlverfahren statistisch zu ermitteln', *Allgemeines Statistisches Archiv*, 22, 1932, pp. 253–56; and Leo A. Goodman, 'Ecological Regression and Behavior of Individuals', *American Sociological Review*, 43, 1953, pp. 557–72.

12. Eugen Würzburger, 'Die "Partei der Nichtwähler"', *Jahrbuch für Nationalökonomie und Statistik*, 33, 1907, pp. 381–9.

13. Meckstroth, 'Conditions of Partisan Realignments'; Shively, 'Party Identification, Party Choice'; Waldman, 'Models of Mass Movements'; Richter, 'The National Socialist Breakthrough'; and Falter, 'Die Wähler der NSDAP 1928–1933'.

14. Loomis/Beegle, 'The Spread of German Nazism in Rural Areas'.

15. See Jürgen W. Falter and Wolf D. Gruner, 'Minor and major flaws of a widely used Data Set — The ICPSR "German Weimar Republic Data 1919–1933" under Scrutiny', *Historical Social Research*, 20, 1981, pp. 4–26.

The Correlation of Turnout and the Nazi Vote

	% Turn.$_{t1}$ vs. %$_{t1}$ NSDAP	% Turn.$_{t1}$ vs. %$_{t2}$ NSDAP	% Turn.$_{t1}$ vs. $\triangle$% NSDAP	$\triangle$% Turn. vs. %$_{t2}$ NSDAP
1928	0	–	–	–
1930	+14	+11	+13	−01
1932J	+37	+04	−05	+45
1932N	+43	+39	−10	+27
1933	+22	+15	−72	+74

831 Kreis units; cases weighted by Kreis population.
Cell entries: Pearson's r × 100.
$\triangle$% NSDAP $\triangle$% Turnout = %t^1 −4 %t^2.

16. We are able to replicate some of these correlation coefficients with another newly established data set containing electoral and some social information on the level of villages, towns and cities. As can be seen from the following table there is not only a remarkable correspondence but near identity between the findings of the two data sets. Unfortunately there is no community level data available for the two 1932 elections. We did, however, compute the correlation coefficients for some change variables for the 1930–33 pair of elections. Here we distinguished some quite remarkable differences between the two liberal parties. Thus in the 1928–30 pair of elections the national liberal DVP seems to account for most of the relationship between the change of the Liberals (DVP+DDP) and the NSDAP vote. Cameron's warning not to mix up the two seems to be fully warranted by these results. In future research one should try to keep the two parties separate. Cameron, 'The Mobilization of Nazism'.

		Turnout	DNVP	LIB	OTHER	DDP	DVP
28–30	county lev.	−03	−50	−50	−03	01	−54
	community 1.	07	−45	−47	−05	−02	−51
30–33	county level	51	−18	09	−64	03	14
	community 1.	53	−18	14	−65	07	15

17. See Jürgen W. Falter, Thomas Lindenberger and Siegfried Schumann, *Wahlen und Abstimmungen in der Weimarer Republik* (Munich, 1986).

18. John A. Sonquist and James N. Morgan, *The Detection of Interaction Effects* (Ann Arbor, 1964).

19. For more details see Falter *et al.*, *Wahlen und Abstimmungen*.

20. Ibid.

21. For a valid argument against the dissenting opinion of Shively, see Waldman, 'Models of Mass Movements', pp. 217ff.

22. See note 16.

23. The corresponding community level multiple regression equations read as following:

		Turnout	DNVP	LIB	R^2	n
1928–30	county level	.184	−.512	−.487	49%	831
	community 1.	.224	−.480	−.463	45%	3957
1930–33	county level	.517	−.181	−.078	29%	831
	community 1.	.528	−.162	−.035	30%	3978

24. See Falter, 'Die Wähler der NSDAP 1928–1933'; and Falter and Reinhard Zintl, 'The Economic Crisis of the 1930's and the Nazi Vote', paper delivered at the Annual Conference of the Midwest Political Science Association, 1985.

25. There is some strong evidence in favour of the assumption that our estimates of individual transition probabilities are indeed unbiased: the near perfect agreement between several estimation models at the county *and community* levels in regard to (a) the transition behaviour of the 1928 nonvoters and (b) the transition behaviour towards the NSDAP in 1930. For further details see Falter and Zintl, 'The Economic Crisis of the 1930's and the Nazi Vote'.

26. Ibid.

27. For almost identical results in regard to nonvoting see Meckstroth, 'Conditions of Partisan Realignments'.

28. Shively, 'Party Identification, Party Choice', p. 1215.

29. For further details of transition probabilities between parties from 1920 to 1933, see Falter and Zintl, 'The Economic Crisis of the 1930's and the Nazi Vote'.

30. Ibid. See also Falter, 'Die Wähler der NSDAP 1928–1933'.

31. Childers, *The Nazi Voter*.

32. For the contemporary analysis, see Herbert R. Knickerbocker, *The German Crisis* (New York, 1932), and Sidney Mellen, 'The German People and the Post-War World', *American Political Science Review*, 37, 1943, pp. 601–25.

33. On the SA, see Conan Fischer, *Stormtroopers. A Social, Economic and Ideological Analysis, 1929–1935* (London, 1983).

34. The age distribution within the party membership is treated in Michael Kater, *The Nazi Party — A Social Profile of Members and Leaders* (Cambridge, Mass., 1983); and J. Paul Madden, 'The Social Composition of the Nazi Party 1919–1930', Ph.D. Dissertation, University of Oklahoma, 1976, p. 261. See Also Hamilton, *Who Voted for Hitler?*, especially chapter 13.

35. See Milatz, *Wähler und Wahlen*, p. 135, and Striefler, *Deutsche Wahlen*, p. 17.

36. Gunnar Charles Boehnert, 'A Sociography of the SS Officer Corps, 1925–1939', Ph.D. Dissertation, University of London.

37. Pratt, 'The Social Bases of Nazism', pp. 206, 218.

38. See Jan-Bernd Lohmöller and Jürgen W. Falter, 'Some Further Aspects of Ecological Regression Analysis. Quality and Quantity', 1986.

Hartmut Bömermann was an invaluable help in doing the numerous computations for this article. Dirk Hänisch was a careful reader of an earlier version of the article;

he gave valuable advice on some interpretations of my findings. The results of the analysis are part of a larger research project on the voters of National Socialism in Germany and Austria sponsored by the Volkswagen Foundation. The community data set which is available through the Cologne Zentralarchiv für empirische Sozialforschung has been sponsored by Deutsche Forschungsgemeinschaft.

10 THE LIMITS OF NATIONAL SOCIALIST MOBILISATION: THE ELECTIONS OF 6 NOVEMBER 1932 AND THE FRAGMENTATION OF THE NAZI CONSTITUENCY

Thomas Childers

I

In the summer of 1927, over a year after the NSDAP had begun to establish a network of propaganda cells all across Germany, a confidential report by the Reich Ministry of the Interior described the National Socialists in the following terms:

> In spite of their very well prepared and thoroughly organised propaganda . . . their successes remain . . . very modest . . . This is a party that isn't going anywhere. Today it is a numerically . . . insignificant radical, revolutionary splinter group that is incapable of exerting any noticeable influence on the great mass of the population or on the course of political developments.[1]

That verdict was resoundingly reinforced by the last pre-depression Reichstag election in May 1928, an election in which the NSDAP had managed to attract a mere 800,000 votes or 2.8 per cent of the national electorate. Just four years later, however, the NSDAP had become the most popular and powerful party in Germany, commanding a socially diverse electoral following that totalled almost 14 million and comprised almost 40 per cent of the voting public.

With the onset and intensification of the Great Depression after 1928, the National Socialists had marched to a series of dramatic electoral triumphs at the local, regional and Reich levels, creating in the process a powerful popular image of a dynamic political movement driving irresistibly toward victory. This rising wave of Nazi electoral successes continued to gather momentum into the spring and summer of 1932, when the NSDAP mounted three impressive national campaigns within six months, while making sizeable gains in a number of important regional contests as well.

232

On 31 July the wave of Nazi victories at last crested, when the NSDAP emerged from the first Reichstag campaign since 1930 as the largest party in Germany.

In the full flush of that triumph, the NSDAP seemed on the very threshold of power, but negotiations for a Hitler chancellorship floundered in mid-August, and within weeks the Reichstag was again dissolved and new elections called for 6 November. In those elections, held less than four months after the NSDAP's greatest political victory, the National Socialists suffered a stunning electoral setback, losing approximately two million votes and seeing their share of the national total tumble by 4 per cent (see Table 10.1). For the first time since the party had begun its startlingly swift and steep ascent in the fall of 1929, the NSDAP had absorbed a potentially serious defeat at the polls, puncturing its aura of invincibility and casting doubt on its promises of an inevitable Nazi seizure of power.[2]

What had gone wrong? What did the November returns suggest about the nature of the NSDAP's popular support and the stability of its diverse social constituency? Had the Nazis reached the limits of their political appeal, or was 6 November merely a temporary setback? Which elements of the Nazi electorate had remained loyal,

Table 10.1: Reichstag elections, 1930–1932

	September 1930	July 1932	November 1932
Turnout	34,961,000 (81.4%)	36,882,000 (83.4%)	35,471,000 (79.9%)
NSDAP	6,383,000 (18.3%)	13,769,000 (37.3%)	11,737,000 (33.1%)
DNVP	2,458,000 (7.0%)	2,177,000 (5.9%)	2,959,000 (8.5%)
DVP	1,578,000 (4.7%)	436,000 (1.2%)	661,000 (1.8%)
DDP	1,322,000 (3.5%)	372,000 (1.0%)	336,000 (1.0%)
Z	5,187,000 (14.8%)	5,782,000 (15.7%)	5,325,000 (15.0%)
SPD	8,578,000 (24.5%)	7,960,000 (21.6%)	7,248,000 (20.4%)
KPD	4,592,000 (13.1%)	5,283,000 (14.3%)	5,980,000 (16.9%)
Other	4,873,000 (14.4%)	1,103,000 (3.0%)	1,225,000 (4.3%)

which had defected, which had simply refused to vote at all, and why? What were the strategic lessons to be drawn from the party's disappointing performance? Was the poor showing in November simply the result of financial and physical exhaustion within both the party's propaganda machine and electoral constituency after almost a full year of intense campaigning, or did the NSDAP's slump have deeper, more portentous causes? What did the November losses suggest about the future electoral prospects of the NSDAP, and, more fundamentally, what did they reveal about the character and appeal of National Socialism as a political phenomenon? These are questions with profound implications for an understanding of the political dynamics of National Socialism, the sources of its success and the limits of its popularity, and it is to this set of issues that this essay is addressed.

Not surprisingly, it was to these very questions that the Nazi high command, but especially the Reich Propaganda Leadership (RPL) headed by Joseph Goebbels, turned in the immediate aftermath of the autumn campaign. To answer them the RPL called on its national network of regional and local propaganda operatives. The National Socialist propaganda apparatus, the extent of which was unparalleled in the Weimar context, was vertically constructed around a system of grassroots political intelligence-gathering that amounted to a crude but, for the period, extraordinarily sophisticated form of political survey research.[3] It was on information generated by this system that the RPL relied for its assessment of the just completed campaign. Each of the NSDAP's local branches (*Ortsgruppen*) was required to submit a detailed report on its propaganda activities during the campaign, providing information on the techniques employed and themes emphasised by the local NSDAP as well as those used by the party's opponents. The reports were to describe what had worked and what had not, to ascertain the sources of the party's support, and to evaluate opinion within the National Socialist membership and in the general public both during and immediately after the election. The party's local propaganda functionaries submitted these reports to their respective *Gau* propaganda leaders, who reviewed them, summarised their views, usually providing particularly relevant quotations, and then dispatched a regional summary on to the Munich headquarters of the RPL. There the *Gau* reports were carefully analysed, and their most important findings were presented in a top secret document, a *Stimmungsbericht*, which was completed in late-November and then circulated only among the very highest leadership of the NSDAP.[4]

When viewed along with the RPL's regular monthly activity report (*Tätigkeitsbericht*) for November, this *Stimmungsbericht* is extremely illuminating, and, remarkably, both documents have almost entirely escaped scholarly attention. Together they constitute an unusually frank post mortem on the party's performance in November, examining the reasons for and the implications of its sudden decline. They are also particularly important since they provide a rare and accurate reflection of the views of the NSDAP's local functionaries charged with the actual conduct of grassroots propaganda operations.[5] These regional and local views, supplemented by the RPL's own highly confidential commentary, offer an extraordinarily revealing glimpse into the NSDAP's internal evaluation of the party's political potential at the close of 1932, an evaluation that was certainly at odds with the NSDAP's confident public posture. Although these reports occasionally attempt to accentuate the positive, they are surprisingly candid and critical documents that vividly reflect serious strains within the NSDAP's membership and electorate as well as fundamental disagreements on strategy and tactics within the leadership. In the process, they also strikingly demonstrate the high degree of cynicism that characterised both the conceptualisation and conduct of Nazi propaganda. Finally, the RPL's assessment of the party's prospects and the startling strategic conclusions drawn from these reports are of critical importance in treating the issues raised above. Thus the RPL *Berichte*, augmented by a number of the regional and local reports on which they were based and by recent statistical analyses of the November returns, constitute the basic points of departure for the following analysis.

II

The major objectives of the National Socialist campaign in the fall of 1932 had been to discredit the Papen regime so thoroughly that it could 'no longer be seen as a bulwark by the wavering middle class'. With the liberal, regional and special interest parties virtually eliminated as serious political competitors, the battle for the middle-class vote, Goebbels was convinced, would be waged between the conservative DNVP and the NSDAP. Much of Nazi propaganda during the campaign was, therefore, directed against 'Papen's reactionary *Herrenklub*' and his supporters in the DNVP. At the same time, the National Socialists had hoped to make a significant breakthrough into the working-class constituency of the SPD, and the party's campaign had sought to portray National Socialism as a dedicated enemy of the Reaction and the only stalwart representative of the German worker.[6]

From the very outset of the campaign, however, there had been disquieting signs that the party's propaganda machine, after months of operating at full throttle, was at last beginning to splutter. Reports from all across the country made clear that the party's regional and local organisations were deeply in debt from recent campaigns and that even party activists were distressed at the prospect of yet another major effort. Goebbels' directives to the *Gau* propaganda leaders throughout the campaign were, therefore, sprinkled with increasingly shrill demands for greater activity and enthusiasm. Implicitly acknowledging a morale problem within both the membership and the party's broader electoral constituency, the RPL's directives during the final weeks of the campaign repeatedly emphasised the need to convince voters that 'public opinion has [recently] undergone a powerful shift' in favour of the NSDAP. After an admittedly slow start, the party campaign was at last gathering 'the old momentum', Goebbels claimed, and

> The circles that only a few weeks ago were beguiled by the flowery speeches of Papen have turned against him. With the beginning of Hitler's [campaign] flight and the deployment of our big speakers, one can see that the people are setting all their hopes on National Socialism . . .. It is, therefore, imperative for our newspapers to nourish this rising mood of victory. Again and again it must be made clear to the broad masses that we will make it, that we must come to power.[7]

Given these repeated, if rather forced, assertions of optimism and the party's ambitious campaign objectives, the election results were particularly discouraging. Although Goebbels and many in the Nazi leadership had anticipated significant losses on 6 November, the results were nonetheless unsettling.[8] Not only had the Nazi vote plummeted but the DNVP had registered significant gains, largely, it was agreed, at the expense of the National Socialists. The Social Democratic vote *had* dropped, just as the Nazis expected, but the

SPD's losses were roughly equalled by Communist gains. Moreover, with turnout dropping for the first time since 1928, the NSDAP's propaganda machine had apparently failed to mobilise many voters who had cast Nazi ballots just four months before.[9]

Turning in a general way to the questions of turnout, organisational fatigue and conservative gains, the RPL report maintained rather philosophically that the public was not merely exhausted by months of political campaigning but disillusioned with the entire system of party politics. Since the electorate had been 'buried by partisan propaganda for years without anyone being able to bring about an improvement in their hard existence, a fundamental mistrust of all parties had developed', which, the report contended, had also had a negative impact on public perceptions of the NSDAP in November. Growing public apathy had been clearly signalled by consistently low attendance at Nazi meetings and rallies throughout the autumn, especially in crucial rural areas, where the campaign had coincided with the potato and turnip harvests in the east and the grape harvest in the west.[10]

In addition to this *Wahlmüdigkeit*, the continued deterioration of the economy, the RPL maintained, meant that the willingness of the public to make financial sacrifices for political causes had contracted sharply, and the ability of the party's local branches to mount their usual propaganda operations had been severely impaired. The RPL also pointed out that the local branches' obligatory contributions to the NSDAP's national treasury 'very often took funds from the *Ortsgruppen* that might have been used in the campaign for well-planned leaflet and newspaper propaganda'. Indeed, because of the party's desperate financial situation,[11] the NSDAP had been forced to downplay its usual large-scale rallies and leaflet campaigns and to concentrate instead on less costly forms of propaganda . . . 'man-to-man' canvassing, the display of flags, stickers, party badges, etc., and the systematic use of '*Sprechchore*' and 'chalk campaigns'.[12]

The 'general impoverishment' of the NSDAP's regional and local formations, which, according to the RPL, had left little 'even for the most essential propaganda', had produced a particularly devastating effect in November, the report maintained, because the NSDAP's 'opponents — especially the SPD and DNVP — waged this campaign with great sums of money'. As evidence, the report noted that the DNVP, which had quite clearly cut deeply into the National Socialist rural constituency in the traditionally conservative east, had been able to organise an effective voter transport service (*Schlepperdienst*) in the countryside and to wage an extensive leaflet and newspaper campaign against the NSDAP. 'From a quantitative point of view', the RPL concluded, 'the DNVP's propaganda — for purely financial reasons — was superior to that of the National Socialists'.[13]

These factors, along with a number of other organisational, tactical and 'technical' propaganda problems, had obviously contributed to the party's poor showing in November and were examined briefly in the RPL's report.[14] For the RPL, however, they were of secondary importance in explaining what was the most serious development of the campaign. Whether in the form of direct crossovers to the DNVP or DVP or in the form of 'no-shows' on election day, the NSDAP had suffered a massive haemorrhage of middle-class electoral support on 6 November, and this sudden and substantial loss of support had extraordinarily important implications for National Socialist strategy. The NSDAP had been unique among the Weimar parties in its systematic efforts to mobilise support in virtually every occupational and demographic group, aggressively attempting to transcend the traditional social, religious and regional cleavages of German political culture. In the process, the party routinely made quite contradictory appeals and promises to the different elements of its surprisingly diverse constituency. This catch-all strategy had proven remarkably successful amid the social and economic traumas of the Great Depression as anti-system sentiment mushroomed and the traditional parties appeared both compromised and discredited.[15] By the autumn of 1932, however, after a year of almost incessant campaigning and intense public scrutiny, the difficulties of sustaining this anti-system, catch-all strategy were becoming increasingly apparent to the NSDAP's propaganda leadership.

'In previous campaigns', the RPL explained with its usual cynicism, 'appeals to the nationalist heart were enough to win the middle-class masses, and the socialist tendencies of the NSDAP could step into the background . . .'[16] During the autumn campaign, however, that strategy had proven impossible. One of the major objectives of each National Socialist campaign in 1932 had been to break into the working-class ranks of the SPD and KPD, and much of the party's propagandistic efforts had been devoted to mobilising a blue-collar constituency.[17] Those efforts were particularly salient in the autumn of 1932, when Nazi attacks on Papen and his 'reactionary cabinet of barons' became so steeped in the language of class warfare that they were often indistinguishable from those of the KPD. Indeed, at one juncture in the campaign, Hitler, acting through his secretary Rudolf Hess, felt compelled to intervene, cautioning against the '*klassenkämpferischen Tendenzen*' in National Socialist propaganda and ordering the RPL to tone down its rhetoric against those forces associated with the traditional right. Such socially divisive tactics, Hess argued, merely played into the hands of Papen and the DNVP by alienating voters from the conservative right, many of whom had cast ballots for the NSDAP in recent elections. Moreover, in Hess's and presumably Hitler's view, losses from the right would not be compensated for by gains from the left. 'A large segment of voters from the right would undoubtedly be swayed by the charge that the NSDAP has gone over to slogans of class conflict' Hess's memorandum contended, while 'those who would be favourably impressed by such slogans would move to and remain where this strategy [of class conflict] is most radical. And Marxism', he concluded, 'will always be the most radical because class struggle is one of the basic tenets of its programme.'[18]

Although Goebbels did attempt to moderate the party's assaults on the traditional right, blasts at the reactionary nature of the Papen government and efforts to mobilise working-class support certainly did not subside. Indeed, those efforts reached a dramatic crescendo during the final week of the campaign, when the Nazis decided to support the Berlin transportation workers' strike, a strike with high national visibility and one also vigorously championed by the Communists. Coming as it did in the very first days of November, the NSDAP's involvement in the Berlin strike was a calculated gamble that would inevitably draw wide public attention to 'Nazi socialism' at a critical stage of the campaign.[19] Yet, in reviewing the impact of the party's pro-labour position and more generally its anti-Papen propaganda, the RPL's post-election report insisted that under the circumstances a clear, firm stand had been unavoidable. In previous campaigns, the report implied, the NSDAP had been able to chart a murky, ambiguous course on such issues, but in the party's battle against the Papen government, the RPL asserted, 'National Socialism found itself forced into an unequivocal stand against the "national" Reaction, rejecting compromises and placing itself — even in the strike question — on the side of the German workers fighting for their rights.'[20]

The Papen government and its supporters in the bourgeois parties certainly sought to make political capital out of the NSDAP's dilemma,[21] and in the aftermath of the election, the RPL was convinced that they had succeeded only too well. In assessing the impact of the strike and related issues, the RPL concluded that the party's aggressive efforts to recruit working-class support had, indeed, alienated significant elements of the middle-class electorate. Reports from the party's grassroots propaganda units indicated that rural voters, in particular — since 1928 the mainstays of the NSDAP's constantly expanding electorate — were shocked by the party's apparent co-operation with the Communists in the Berlin strike, and in many cases even former supporters of the NSDAP had refused to come to the polls as a consequence.[22] Acknowledging this development, the RPL commented with considerable exasperation that 'as a result of the political circumstances in the weeks before the election, a situation developed in which we could not avoid doing things that the middle-class [voter] will never understand . . .' Thus the report bitterly concluded, 'a defection of the bourgeois masses had to follow . . .'[23]

Confronted by the mounting difficulties of maintaining a firm grip on the party's socially heterogeneous electorate and by the incipient but unmistakable erosion of the party's middle-class base, the RPL strongly implied that the moment for hard sociopolitical choices might at last be at hand. Although the report did not advocate discarding the NSDAP's revolutionary catch-all strategy, it did endorse a propaganda more sharply focused on the German working class. The outcome of the election, but especially the NSDAP's obvious loss of support among middle-class voters, had revealed, the RPL maintained, 'that the worker, once converted and embraced by National Socialist organisation, is a thousand times more dependable than the *Bürgertum*, with its nationalist traditions . . .' The report conceded that 'the largely union-organised blue-collar labour force still approaches the NSDAP with a certain mistrust', but the RPL strongly urged that 'careful propaganda activities in working-class circles be continued'.[24]

More specifically, the RPL recommended that the party's courting of established social circles, especially aristocrats or others with prominent ties to the imperial past, should cease immediately, pointing out that 'the conspicuous parading of National Socialist leaders from the old nationalist tradition' produced a particularly chilling effect on working-class opinion. 'In working-class circles', the report continued, 'the complaint surfaces over and over again that too many aristocrats and academics hold leading positions in the NSDAP'. This resentment against National Socialist leaders 'with any sort of connection with the Wilhelmine era' was also shared by many in the party's rank and file, the RPL added. In what was clearly intended as a rebuttal of Hess's earlier memorandum, the RPL report remarked that 'one must keep in mind that the presence of these party comrades alienates at least as many workers as it attracts supporters from the bourgeoisie'. It was, therefore, to be hoped, the RPL argued, 'that in future propaganda tactics, concessions to the *Bürgertum* at the expense of the working class (*Handarbeiterschaft*) will cease'.[25]

This plea for a shift in the social *emphasis* of Nazi propaganda is doubly significant. On the one hand, it clearly indicates a conviction on the part of the Nazi propaganda leadership that the NSDAP had at last reached the limits of its appeal among middle-class voters. Indeed, it constitutes an implicit acknowledgement that even *maintaining* the party's broad-based support within the *Mittelstand* at anything like the levels of the spring and summer 1932 was at best problematic. On the other hand, an intensified effort to cultivate a greater working-class constituency could, as Hess had pointed out, only exacerbate the NSDAP's difficulties within the volatile middle-class electorate, while thrusting it into a more direct and dubiously successful competition with the Social Democrats and Communists.

In fact, by 1932 the NSDAP had already waged a systematic and tenacious campaign to establish a beachhead on the embattled shores of working-class politics, and that campaign had produced at best very mixed results. During the elections of 1930 and 1932, the NSDAP had succeeded in attracting substantial support from workers in handicrafts and small-scale manufacturing, large economic sectors characterised by small shops and a predominantly unorganised labour force. That support, though far greater than traditionally assumed, was highly unstable and in the November elections seems to have dropped precipitously. Moreover, despite their intense and systematic efforts, the Nazis had consistently failed to secure significant support from workers in the major industrial and mining sectors, where the SPD and KPD maintained solid constituencies. More remarkably, the NSDAP had not been particularly successful in mobilising support from the masses of unemployed workers, who on the whole seemed far more inclined to gravitate to the radical left than to the National Socialists.[26]

Although the November returns certainly demonstrated declining support for the NSDAP within the middle-class electorate, there was little to suggest that a major shift in these basic patterns of blue-collar political affiliation was underway. Thus the RPL's intimation that the NSDAP might find significant new reservoirs of support within the blue-collar population resounded with the hollow ring of forced optimism. Indeed, more than a tremor of desperation resonates through its entire assessment of the party's potential working-class appeal. Significantly, the most compelling evidence the RPL could muster on this point was the post-election testimony of the *Gau* propaganda leader of East Prussia, who complained bitterly about middle-class defectors but claimed that 'attitudes within the working class [toward the NSDAP] can be described as very good'. He was forced, however, to admit that 'unfortunately the time before the election was too brief to convince the workers that our socialist slogans . . . were not merely campaign posturing', but he insisted that the party's firm stand in the Berlin strike and the attacks on the NSDAP by the conservative right had made a favourable impression on the working class. It was true, he conceded that the NSDAP had 'not yet succeeded in breaking into the Marxist ranks' but added, in a phrase literally staggering under the weight of its redundant qualifiers, that the party had 'to a certain extent overcome somewhat the mistrust of the working class . . .' ('so haben wir doch bis zu einem gewissen Grade durch unsere politische Haltung das Misstrauen in der Arbeiterschaft zu einem Teil überwunden . . .'). Indeed, 'had the election been held fourteen days later', he gamely if rather unconvincingly added, 'we would have had a powerful surge [of support] from the *Arbeiterschaft*'.[27] In the aftermath of 6 November, the RPL desperately wanted to believe that assertion.

III

If maintaining the NSDAP's catch-all strategy had become increasingly difficult by late 1932, the party's continued failure to seize the reigns of power had an equally negative impact on the party's public appeal in November. Between 1928 and 1932 the National Socialist propaganda apparatus had been remarkably successful in generating a public image of an irresistible political movement marching inexorably towards power. During the spring and summer of 1932, the NSDAP had seemed at last within reach of that goal, and each of the year's many elections had been conducted as if the creation of the 'Third Reich' were imminent. Nazi hopes had been particularly high following the July Reichstag election, but in the highly public negotiations in August, Hitler had steadfastly refused to enter a possible coalition government with the Catholic Zentrum or to join the Papen government as vice-chancellor. Instead, he insisted on an appointment as chancellor of a presidential government armed with emergency powers, a course of action which Reich President Hindenburg found particularly unpalatable. Although Strasser was convinced that the NSDAP had reached its maximum electoral potential and that the time for compromise was at hand, Hitler, backed by Goebbels, refused to budge, and a serious division of opinion concerning the party's strategy options continued well into the autumn campaign.[28]

While this debate within the leadership simmered during the late summer and early autumn, the monthly activity reports flowing in from the NSDAP's regional propaganda operatives left little doubt about the impact of Hitler's decision on the party's grassroots appeal. 'Within the *Mittelstand* generally, within the peasantry [*Bauernstand*], and even among the workers who are our supporters, a very depressed and pessimistic mood prevailed during the month of August,' the propaganda leader of *Gau* Hanover-South-Brunswick reported. 'Everywhere one hears the opinion that we would register significant losses if an election were held in these days and weeks.' With the economic situation continuing to deteriorate, the public expected decisive action from Hitler and the NSDAP, the *Gau-Propagandaleiter* suggested, or the mounting despair and anger that the Nazis had so skillfully tapped might be turned against the party itself. The people 'would rather see an "end with horrors"', he concluded, 'than "horrors without end".'[29]

In its monthly *Tätigkeitsbericht* for August, the RPL soberly acknowledged that Hitler's refusal to enter the cabinet had, indeed, generated considerable division within the party's membership and broader electoral following and predicted serious difficulties for the NSDAP in any upcoming campaign. Although the RPL's report rather lamely asserted that wherever National Socialist leaflets explaining Hitler's position had been widely distributed, the local mood was 'very good', it added ominously that for the most part the prevailing sentiment 'could be expressed with the words: "This time I voted for Hitler and again nothing has happened. Next time I won't vote.'"[30]

A second trend in public opinion was also frequently noted in the regional propaganda reports during the autumn of 1932. In the wake of Hitler's refusal to enter the government, a serious rift appeared to be emerging between the party's hardcore supporters and the NSDAP's broader but more volatile electoral constituency. As the *Gau* propaganda chieftain of Schleswig-Holstein explained it, party 'activists' had enthusiastically welcomed Hitler's refusal to ally the NSDAP with either Papen or the Zentrum, but others, dismissed in his report contemptuously as '*Spiessbürger*', took the view 'that Hitler should have become a member of the government in order to assume the leadership [of the country]'. Given this fundamental difference of opinion, the report continued, 'there could be no united fighting spirit'. Only when the negotiations were at last broken off and the Nazi press renewed its salvos against Papen had the viewpoint of the 'radicals' or 'activists' prevailed. At this juncture, the report less than enthusiastically claimed, 'the masses regained something of their old confidence in victory'.[31]

Even these rather muted attempts to place a positive interpretation of the failed August negotiations and their potential impact on future Nazi electoral performance could hardly conceal the NSDAP's second major strategic dilemma. Although hardcore activists may have been pleased that the NSDAP's uncompromising anti-system purity had been maintained, the electoral message from the party's grassroots propaganda apparatus was both unmistakable and unsettling. That message, recapitulated with unmistakable clarity in the regional propaganda reports both before and during the autumn campaign, was that the party's failure to enter the government after the July 'victory' had produced a profoundly negative effect on sizeable, largely middle-class, and, it was feared, less committed elements of the NSDAP's electoral constituency.

In the aftermath of the November débâcle, regional functionaries in the party's propaganda apparatus saw their warnings grimly confirmed. In what became a typical refrain, the *Gau* propaganda leader of Halle-Merseburg reminded the RPL that before the election he had warned 'that a portion of the public — more specifically, middle-class circles — have not only come to terms with the Papen government but . . . view it as their saviour from economic distress. These are circles that have never inwardly belonged to the NSDAP and now see the opportunity to return to their bourgeois world.' Although the loss of these voters was obviously a serious, indeed potentially devastating, development from an electoral perspective, *Gau* propaganda officials often sought to interpret this massive decline in middle-class support in a positive way. Thus the Halle-Merseburg report characteristically argued that 'perhaps for parliamentary reasons the attempt could be made to win back a portion of these masses, but from an ideological point of view these masses will never constitute a valuable element of our following because they don't understand National Socialism and for the most part can't understand it.' More pertinent to the party's immediate situation, however, the author of the report frankly doubted 'whether it is even possible to bring these circles, who feel comfortable and are completely satisfied with existing conditions, to the polls for the NSDAP.' It was these groups from the established, upper-middle class, the report concluded, who had deserted the party for the DNVP or DVP in November.[32]

Though differing slightly in emphasis, National Socialist propaganda operatives in East Prussia told a similar tale. 'The voters who left us this time are primarily from the circles of the so-called "national *Bürgertum*"', the *Gau* propaganda leader reported. 'The point of view of these predominately older voters was: previously we voted for the Nazis, but now, since they've become so strong and still haven't changed anything, we'll try the DNVP and see whether . . . they can't do something.'[33]

Despite differences in local circumstances, the emerging schism between committed National Socialists and 'fickle' one- or two-time supporters formed a *leitmotif* in the regional reports. A revealing glimpse of the widespread bitterness toward such defectors that permeated these reports is provided by a post-election memorandum drafted by the National Socialist county leader of Heilsberg in East Prussia. With a tone suffused simultaneously with aggression and anxiety, he claimed that

> our political defectors who recognised in time that they did after all belong to the *Herrenclub* or smelled a profit there for their egotistical souls, may wish to help the Reaction shield Jewish liberal capitalism from the deadly thrust that our movement will deliver. We can only be happy to see our ranks cleansed of such white Jews.[34]

Though concurring with his counterparts on the social sources of the party's losses, the *Gau* propaganda leader of Hanover-South-

Brunswick lamented the party's failure to provide adequate indoctrination for the legions of protest voters who had, for a variety of reasons, been attracted to the NSDAP since 1930. 'For the old party comrades who have waited for years to see their most cherished dream [a Nazi *Machtergreifung*] fulfilled, the events of . . . August did not in the least shake their faith in the final victory of the movement.' However, he continued, 'the mass of those [voters] who flocked to us during the past few years were less able to cope with the situation. A mass of voters and party members, driven to us on a wave of emotion and swept along during the movement's unbroken string of victories', were never really integrated into the party and hence were never really committed to National Socialism. These wavering voters had now either defected to the DNVP or had simply refused to cast a ballot in November. 'We have failed to incorporate these people ideologically into National Socialism', his report glumly declared, and now they had been allowed to slip away.[35]

Given this relentless regional testimony, it is hardly surprising that the RPL opened its assessment of the NSDAP's November performance by examining the impact of 'the Führer's historic "no"' on the campaign. With almost startling candour, the RPL report concluded that 'the decline in our votes can in many ways be attributed to the fact that Hitler did not enter the government. Many [voters] quite simply have no understanding of our explanation.' The middle-class voter, in particular, the RPL believed, had been led by 'his neutral press' to believe 'that Hitler had to enter the Papen cabinet on 13 August and', the report stated with undisguised frustration, 'no campaign slogan could disabuse him of that notion.' Indeed, the RPL bluntly admitted that 'when Adolf Hitler allied himself with neither the government nor the Zentrum, opinion within the public and within the party split. From this point onward, opinion was divided, with the middle-class elements going to [the DNVP's] Hugenberg, while the old National Socialists summoned new courage again.'[36]

Disillusioned defectors, however, were only part of the problem for the NSDAP in November. Hundreds of thousands of former Nazi supporters, the RPL was convinced, had registered their disapproval of the party by simply refusing to vote at all. Much of this *Wahlmüdigkeit*, or voter apathy, could undoubtedly be attributed to simple exhaustion after a year of non-stop campaigning. After all, four national elections and regional campaigns in almost every

German state had been held during the course of 1932, and by November funding, enthusiasm and endurance were running low in all the Weimar parties. For the NSDAP, as a party of protest, the problem of growing public indifference was particularly ominous. Maintaining a firm grip on a socially diverse mass constituency held together less by a commitment to National Socialist ideology than by opposition or protest against different aspects of the discredited Weimar 'system' and by vague promises of dramatic 'change' under Nazi regime, would grow increasingly difficult if the party did not actually assume power. The longer the NSDAP was forced to campaign without being able to bring about change, the less convincing its image of irresistible dynamism and power was bound to become and the less appealing its rabid and yet apparently ineffectual anti-system stance would appear. As the year wore on and campaign after campaign was mounted, Nazi propaganda strategists became acutely aware of this problem. Indeed, Goebbels had noted in his diary as early as April, when the NSDAP's political fortunes were still on the rise, that 'we have to come to power in the near future or we will win ourselves to death in these elections'.[37] The party's window of opportunity, as Goebbels realised, was small, and its ability to sustain its protest-oriented appeal over time was tenuous at best.

The results in November seemed to confirm Goebbels' fears. In their post-election reports, *Gau* propaganda leaders were virtually unanimous in stressing that during the campaign the public had turned a deaf ear to any discussion of ideological questions or promises of a rosy future ('*Zunkunftsmusik*') under a National Socialist regime. 'It proved extremely difficult to win the public with tactical campaign slogans', the RPL admitted, '. . . and the constant talk . . . about being on the threshold of the Third Reich' had not only lost its credibility but seemed to have had a negative impact on weary and increasingly sceptical audiences.[38] In a *Tätigkeitsbericht* drawn up a month after the election, regional leaders continued to complain of a lingering mistrust of the party 'among the people to whom we repeatedly said: "In 1932 we will make it for sure".'[39]

Even in areas where the NSDAP had done extremely well in November, local leaders doubted their ability to continue effective mobilisation unless somehow the party attained power — and soon. In one county where the Nazis had captured an astonishing 62 per cent of the vote in November, the *Kreisleiter* warned that 'we cannot risk a new election at the present'. In canvassing local party functionaries (cell and block leaders), he was repeatedly told that 'not only our voters but even party members will no longer go to the polls. Everyone is demanding a positive change now'.[40] Echoing that widespread sentiment, one *Gau* propaganda leader reported that he 'knew of not one but several cases where people say: "When you march, we'll be there, but nobody will get us to the polls again" or "You're just like the others — you only make promises then you don't have the guts to follow through".'[41]

The RPL candidly recognised the party's growing credibility gap, noting that 'during each campaign we conducted this year, the slogan was: "This is the final election and everything depends on it. But no matter what the outcome, we will come to power when it is over".'[42] While many middle-class voters were obviously disappointed that the NSDAP had failed to enter a coalition with either the Zentrum or with Papen, more activist elements of the party were becoming increasingly impatient with Hitler's failure to take dramatic revolutionary action. Indeed, disaffection with the party's policy of 'legality', with its emphasis on electoral campaigning, had grown steadily within the SA and by late summer had become extremely serious.[43]

That mounting disillusionment had been exacerbated by the fact that plans with specific timetables had actually been set for SA 'actions' to be taken after each election to insure the promised Nazi seizure of power. In every instance, however, these operations had to be cancelled, and the result had been growing unrest within the SA. By late summer reports of friction between storm troopers demanding action and local Nazi political leaders had multiplied, and party officials at all levels expressed growing concern that restless SA men were becoming impatient and unruly.[44] The most startling evidence of this increasingly dangerous mood had surfaced in August, when frustrated SA units, severely disappointed by the party's failure to seize power following the 31 July elections, had, on their initiative, unleashed a massive terror campaign all over East Prussia and Silesia. It was during this spasm of SA violence that the infamous Potempa murder was committed, and it was a reflection of Hitler's deep concern about SA loyalty that he felt compelled to issue public praise for the Potempa killers and, by implication, the entire outbreak of SA brutality.[45] In other areas less spectacular but no less disquieting symptoms of SA disaffection were reported. Morale everywhere was low, and even reports of defections to the KPD and other radical formations had begun to circulate.[46]

Looking back at the election, the RPL was convinced that these difficulties with the SA had played a major role in the NSDAP's poor electoral performance. Indeed, criticism of SA behaviour during the campaign occupies the greatest space in the RPL's report and was focused on three central areas of concern. First, though by no means most important, the RPL noted, virtually without comment, the adverse publicity surrounding SA chief Ernst Roehm's private life. During the campaign, several parties, but especially the DNVP, had made highly public charges of homosexuality against Roehm and had distributed leaflets containing compromising private letters and other 'documentation' of what was referred to as Roehm's 'abnormality'. Nazi regional leaders complained that these embarrassing allegations were constantly cropping up in the party's open meetings, rallies and discussion evenings and were, according to one *Gau* propaganda leader, 'greatly disrupting and damaging our propaganda activities'. Although the RPL report did not elaborate on the problem, it concluded tersely that the Roehm issue had 'produced a virtually devastating effect, especially in educated circles'.[47]

Of far greater immediate concern to the RPL and to the Munich Leadership, however, were the disturbing reports, now widespread, of SA refusals to co-operate with local Nazi political leaders in the conduct of the campaign. Indeed, the RPL report noted that 'approximately 60 per cent of the *Gaue* were dissatisfied with the SA's propagandistic assistance during the campaign. Several *Gaue* even attributed a major share of the responsibility for the loss of voters in their region to the SA.'[48]

In Baden for example, where SA strength was estimated at 15,000, *Gau* propaganda officials complained that 'with the exception of perhaps the last two days of the campaign, the SA did not play a significant role'. Unlike previous *Wahlkämpfe*, in which the SA had been instrumental in agitational activities, SA personnel 'had not been made available for the distribution of leaflets, participation in propaganda troops, etc.'. Indeed, 'throughout the campaign', Baden party officials complained, the SA had 'stood at parade rest' (*Gewehr bei Fuss*). Similarly, in *Gau* Magdeburg-Anhalt, Nazi county functionaries reported that SA leaders had simply refused to carry out propaganda directives, telling the *Kreisleiter* to use their own political organisation for campaign activities. In *Gau* Koblenz-Trier, despite good relations between the SA and local political leaders, the diminished enthusiasm of the SA for electoral campaigning had been painfully obvious. 'One cannot remain silent about the meagre effectiveness of our SA in propaganda', *Gau* officials reported. 'One gets the impression that [in previous campaigns] 10 SA men would have generated the same propaganda effect as 100 SA men in this last campaign.' In contrast to previous campaign efforts, the Koblenz officials concluded, it was clear that 'for the SA, propaganda has become less important'.[49]

If some *Gaue* registered their disappointment with this new mood of uncooperative, sullen apathy within the SA, other *Gau* propaganda operatives argued that vulgar, violent, and generally unruly behaviour by SA men had cost the party dearly at the polls in November. Understandably, such complaints were loudest in East Prussia and Silesia, where SA violence had been rampant since August and where relations between local Nazi political leaders and SA units had deteriorated dangerously. *Gau* officials in Lower Silesia, for example, claimed that 'a great segment of the electorate was offended by the rowdy behaviour of the SA, who have become a genuine pestilence in the land following the elections of 31 July'.[50] In the sub-*Gau* Central Silesia, Nazi political functionaries stated that 'if we had more SA men who knew how to behave like decent people on the street', the party's propaganda operations could be conducted efficiently and effectively. 'It has to be made clear to the SS and SA that they are parts of a political movement and as such must co-operate instead of striking out on their own often misguided ways.'[51] In Mecklenburg, the rural population was deeply disturbed by the 'wild' behaviour of the SA, while in urban Rostock, the SA's principal activities were described by local Nazi political leaders as 'pubcrawling, running up debts, and the like'. At the SA leadership school in Parchem, SA leaders provoked particular indignation with the public by behaving 'in every way like mercenaries living off the land (*Landknechte*). They weren't sober a single evening'.[52]

This image of an unruly corps of violent *Landknechte*, reminiscent of the marauding armies of the Thirty Years' War, ran through the regional reports, almost all of which demanded tighter control over and greater political training for the SA. The storm troopers had got out of hand, local leaders were clearly saying, and something had to be done. 'The SA man should not only be a soldier in a military sense but a political soldier as well', the *Gau* propaganda leader of Upper Silesia claimed. He should 'view himself as the representative of the National Socialist *Weltanschauung* and always conduct himself . . . in a manner consistent with this ideology'. The SA, however, 'often creates the impression of mercenaries who have joined the NSDAP out of love of adventure . . . rather than out of ideological conviction'. *Gau* officials in Schleswig-Holstein concurred with that opinion, adding that 'it must openly be stated that the SA man lacks the necessary [political] training'.[53]

Although it is obvious that the RPL had ample reason for wanting to shift the responsibility for the party's November slide to the SA and that its comments must, therefore, be read with some caution, it is equally clear that the NSDAP was, indeed, confronting a very serious internal crisis at the close of 1932. The geographic breadth and organisational depth of the complaints about the SA, especially its increasing disaffection, uncooperative surliness and violence — tendencies richly documented by police reports and other sources — strongly suggest that internal conflict had, indeed, contributed significantly to the party's problems in November. It is indicative of the magnitude of that conflict that at a meeting of the Nazi leadership in Munich on 8 November, SA leaders reportedly responded to charges of undermining the campaign effort by lashing out at Hitler's policy of legality, claiming that it, not the SA, was losing support for the NSDAP. 'The people are no longer satisfied with Hitler's decisions', SA leaders were quoted as saying. 'It doesn't work to keep on talking merely about continuing the parliamentary and propaganda struggle. That will lead the party to ruin, as the last elections have shown. The people', SA leaders maintained, 'urgently demand a revolutionary act'.[54]

IV

As the National Socialist leadership surveyed the political terrain in the aftermath of the November election, it was confronted by three interrelated strategic dilemmas of profound importance for the party's future. The most immediate and potentially explosive of these quandaries centered on the problematic relationship between the revolutionary aspirations of the NSDAP's militant activists and the exigencies of maintaining the party's broader electoral consti- tuency. Specifically, the NSDAP was finding it difficult to satisfy the demands of its increasingly impatient radicals, especially in the SA, without alienating large segments of the party's mass electorate. Already significant elements of the National Socialist constituency, the RPL believed, had been repelled by SA hooliganism, and still Hitler was reluctant to act forcefully against rebellious SA leaders. Until the late summer of 1932, the NSDAP had skilfully steered a very delicate course between what Richard Bessel has aptly described as 'roughness and respectability' in its public appeal.[55] When Hitler failed to attain power in August, however, the party had been blown off that difficult course, and as one *Gau* propaganda leader put it, 'the acts of [SA] terror . . . alienated the public from us . . . frighten[ing] away the fickle *Speissbürger* who had previously voted for us'.[56] By the end of 1932, Nazi policy had not recovered its bearings, and this fundamental dilemma remained unresolved into January of the following year.

Similarly, the party's catch-all electoral strategy had also run to ground in November, and the RPL seemed unable to dislodge it from the shoals of a second major predicament. The limits of Nazi electoral expansion had from the outset been defined by the two most prominent predictors of German political behaviour, class and religion. Despite some gains after 1928, the NSDAP had never significantly penetrated the Catholic constituency of the Zentrum or the organised industrial working-class following of the Marxist parties. Within these broad social parameters, however, the Nazis had managed to mobilise a constituency of unprecedented demographic diversity, attracting support from elements of the affluent *Grossbürgertum*, the unorganised blue-collar labour force, and the lower middle class in both town and countryside.[57]

In pursuing this revolutionary catch-all strategy, the Nazis had two major political assets. Unlike the other Weimar parties, the NSDAP was neither associated with any clearly defined set of economic interests nor had it been saddled with government responsibility in the discredited Weimar state. Thus its unique appeal across the traditional social divides of German politics and its simultaneous insistence that it stood above special interests, that it was, in fact, a genuine people's party, were both refreshingly new in the German party system and carried at least a measure of plausibility to an increasingly angry and disaffected public.

Yet the longer the NSDAP was compelled to compete in free elections, the more likely it was that the inherent conflicts of interest between the different components of its socially diverse constituency would emerge, and the less likely it was that the party could continue its chameleon-like policy of being all things to all people. By the autumn of 1932 it had, in fact, already become apparent that the NSDAP had reached the limits of its middle-class appeal and yet any serious attempt to broaden the party's constituency by more aggressive efforts to mobilise working-class voters ran the very substantial risk of alienating the NSDAP's essential core of middle-class support. Indeed, the impact of the party's radical social rhetoric and, more directly, its support for the Berlin transport strike seemed to have demonstrated precisely that danger to Nazi strategists in November. On the other hand, if the party were now forced to fall back on a more traditional class-based strategy, the NSDAP would be admitting the end of its electoral expansion and would forfeit its cherished claim to be a genuine *Volkspartei*.

Linking these two strategic dilemmas was a third that was, perhaps, the most serious of the problems facing the Nazis as they entered the new year. The NSDAP was above all a successful party of protest. Although the hardcore of its membership and electoral constituency was composed overwhelmingly of elements of the *Kleinbürgertum*, what made the party such an extraordinary political success was its remarkable ability in periods of severe economic and political distress — briefly and incipiently during the inflation and stabilisation crises of 1923–24 and massively after 1928 — to reach well beyond this limited reservoir of lower middle-class support and mobilise crisis-related protest voters from a surprisingly varied array of social and demographic groups. These protest voters, it must be emphasised, were hardly confined to the downwardly mobile or economically marginal but were drawn from virtually all strata of German society. Although socially heterogeneous, this massive collection of protest voters shared at least one trait in common: a profound dissatisfaction with some aspect(s) of the Weimar system. This discontent and anger certainly varied in depth and duration and might be directed against a wide variety of specific social, economic or political features of their 'system', but as Weimar's most relentlessly militant and uncompromised critic, the NSDAP had skilfully mobilised and manipulated that sense of protest in each of the elections of the Depression era. Yet while some might be convinced to cast a protest vote for the NSDAP once, twice, three times or maybe even more, the longer the party campaigned without being able to alter the hated system, the less likely it would be to maintain the credibility of its protest appeal. This problem was particularly dangerous to the NSDAP, since these millions of protest voters were not necessarily committed ideologically to National Socialism. Indeed, most Nazi propaganda strategists assumed that they were not, and in November it appeared that it was to a large extent these volatile, uncommitted protest voters who had either defected or simply stayed at home on election day. The RPL acknowledged this in its report when it concluded that although the party had suffered serious losses in November, 'the results [of the election] proved that the hard core of the party remained unshaken and [had] by no means wavered'.[58] This conclusion, although stated confidently to emphasise the positive, had to be extremely sobering to Nazi strategists. If the party were unable to sustain its mass protest appeal and were once again reduced to the nucleus of its support, as it had been between 1924 and 1928, the NSDAP was doomed to drift inexorably back to the periphery of German political life from which it had sprung at the outset of the Depression.

In the last weeks of 1932 that prospect seemed very real. Regional and local elections in Saxony and Thuringia later in November and early December merely confirmed the outcome of the Reichstag campaign. In both states the NSDAP suffered grievous losses (dropping approximately 40 per cent of its already substantially reduced vote from 6 November) in its Thuringian stronghold. It was becoming increasingly obvious that the results of the last Reichstag election had not been a fluke but marked the onset of an undeniable trend.[59] The volatile National Socialist electoral constituency was fragmenting quickly, and a deep depression settled over the embattled Nazi leadership. Resentment continued unabated in the troubled SA, and tensions within the party's entire organisation soared in early December when Gregor Strasser, convinced that the NSDAP's electoral potential was exhausted and that Hitler's 'all or nothing' strategy was leading the party to ruin, resigned in protest. Only six months after reaching the very threshold of power, the NSDAP was poised on the cusp of electoral decline and internal disintegration.

In evaluating the party's options in this grim situation, the RPL concluded that the cluster of strategic dilemmas facing the NSDAP could not be resolved in the context of a free and competitive party system. After an ascent of unparalleled swiftness, the NSDAP had reached the limits of its electoral potential and now faced almost certain decline. The policy of legality, of mass mobilisation for electoral campaigning, had reached a dead end. Only a National

Socialist seizure of power could ensure the survival of the party as a mass phenomenon. Quoting from a local propaganda functionary whose views it obviously endorsed, the RPL ended its *Stimmungsbericht* with the stunning conclusion that:

> On the basis of numerous contacts with our supporters, we are of the opinion that little can be salvaged by way of propaganda . . . New paths must be taken. Nothing more is to be done with words, placards and leaflets. Now we must act!

Above all else, the RPL frankly asserted, 'it must not come to another election. The results could not be imagined'. It was an astonishing admission for the party's proud propaganda operatives but one that accurately gauged the NSDAP's gloomy electoral prospects. There was still hope, the RPL concluded, 'if Adolf Hitler succeeds in bringing about a political transformation in Germany and appears before the German people as a man of action'.[60]

In January 1933 such a turn of events seemed remote, indeed. None of the fundamental strategic dilemmas that had stymied the NSDAP since the previous autumn had been resolved, and the party's narrow window of opportunity seemed to have been wedged firmly shut. Thus the sudden appointment of Hitler as Chancellor on 30 January, when the party's electoral constituency seemed to be rapidly dissolving, represents a particularly monstrous historical irony. What the NSDAP's propaganda apparatus had failed to achieve at the apex of the party's popular appeal in 1932, Papen and his conservative collaborators managed by engineering the creation of the Hitler cabinet in a woefully misguided palace intrigue.[61] Thus the elections of 6 November 1932, which had marked not only the limits of Nazi electoral mobilisation but had also revealed a potentially important erosion of popular support for the NSDAP, were not to become a major turning point in German history, as they might have been, but constituted instead the last truly free elections of the Weimar era. For Hitler and the NSDAP they were not, as the RPL had feared, the beginning of the end but merely — and tragically — the end of the beginning.

Notes

1. Lagebericht of 15 July 1927, in Bundesarchiv Koblenz (=BA)/R43 I/2696.

2. For the background and conduct of these campaigns see Thomas Childers, *The Nazi Voter. The Social Foundations of Fascism in Germany, 1919–1933* (Chapel Hill and London, 1983), pp. 119–42, 192–211.

3. Remarkably, no study of the Nazi propaganda system exists in the voluminous literature on National Socialism. The basic organisational framework and operating procedures of that system were established during Gregor Strasser's tenure as propaganda chief from mid-September 1926 to January 1928. For the following two and a half years, the NSDAP's propaganda operations were very ably managed by Heinrich Himmler, who served first as Strasser's then as Hitler's deputy. Thereafter, Joseph Goebbels vastly expanded the apparatus and its activities, but the foundations of the Nazi propaganda system – and especially the organisational emphasis on determining and then reporting grassroots opinion – had already been solidly laid when he assumed command in the summer of 1930.

4. The reports of the RPL, whether the regular monthly *Tätigkeitsberichte* or special *Stimmungsberichte*, were composed by the RPL staff in Munich using the same procedures described above and were intended for only five party leaders — Hitler, Goebbels, who, incidentally, did not routinely supervise the drafting of these documents, Strasser, chief of staff Bouhler, and party treasurer Schwarz. One copy was also kept for use by the RPL staff. The *Stimmungsbericht* for the November 1932 elections consists of 14 pages and is found in BA/NS22/1.

5. Since several original *Gau* reports have been preserved, one can check the accuracy of the RPL's summary document against the regional *Berichte*. In addition, a number of local reports from county propaganda operatives, especially in East Prussia, are available, allowing one to follow the reporting process from the grassroots via the *Gau* propaganda leadership to the RPL. At each step in the process in November 1932, the reporting did, in fact, faithfully reproduce the findings presented by lower echelons in the apparatus. A number of those *Gau* reports are located in BA/NS22 and in several regional archives and are cited below.

6. See the RPL's secret communiques to all propaganda units for the fall campaign in the NSDAP Hauptarchiv (=HA), reel 14, folder 263. The quotation is from the RPL circular of 27 October 1932.

7. RPL circular of 25 October 1932, HA/14/263

8. Less than a week before the election Goebbels confided in his diary that the party might lose two million votes. Strasser, he noted, was even more pessimistic. See the diary entries of 4 October and 1 November 1932 in Joseph Goebbels, *Vom Kaiserhof zur Reichskanzlei* (Munich, 1934), pp. 175, 190. For Strasser's gloomy views see Peter D. Stachura, *Gregor Strasser and the Rise of Nazism* (London, 1983), p. 101.

9. See election results in Table 10.1. On the question of turnout and the Nazi vote in 1932 see Theodore Meckstroth, 'Conditions of Partisan Realignments: A Study of Electoral Change', Ph.D. Dissertation, University of Minnesota, 1971, pp. 181–8. See also Jürgen W. Falter's contribution to this volume.

10. Stimmungsbericht der RPL, November 1932, BA/NS22/1.

11. Ibid. On the difficult financial situation of the NSDAP in late 1932 see Dietrich Orlow, *The History of the Nazi Party: 1919–1933*, pp. 287–8; and Henry Ashby Turner, Jr., *German Big Business and the Rise of Hitler* (New York and Oxford, 1985), pp. 292–3.

12. See the RPL's Dendschrift zur Reichstagswahl am 6 November 1932, Niedersächsisches Staatsarchiv Hannover (=NSAH)/Hann. 310 I/E, nr. 23; and the Mitteilungsblätter des Gaues Köln-Aachen, October 1932, in BA/Sammlung Schumacher/203.

13. Stimmungsbericht der RPL, November 1932, BA/NS22/1.

14. Ibid. The report dealt, for example, with the party's leaflet and newspaper propaganda, the effects of local rivalries and scandals within the party's organisation

on propaganda, and the methods and themes employed by the NSDAP's opponents.

15. On the NSDAP's catch-all strategy see Childers, *The Nazi Voter*, pp. 44–6, 262–9.

16. Stimmungsbericht der RPL, November 1932, BA/NS22/1.

17. Nazi efforts to develop a working-class constituency in 1932 are examined in Childers, *The Nazi Voter*, pp. 243–57.

18. Since Hess was virtually never directly involved in the party's propaganda operations, the views expressed in his memorandum are almost certainly Hitler's. See 'Bemerkungen zur Propaganda für den Reichstagswahlkampf' (undated), National Archives (=NA), Series T–81, Reel 1/frames 11427–11432.

19. Goebbels' justification for supporting the strike and his assessment of the public reaction to that decision are found in his diary entry of 2 November and are quite revealing. 'The entire press is railing madly against us,' he wrote. 'They call it Bolshevism, and there's nothing we can do about it. If we had shrunk from this strike . . . then our solid position among the working people would totter.' Goebbels, *Vom Kaiserhof*, p. 191.

20. Stimmungsbericht der RPL, November 1932, BA/NS22/1.

21. For the charges of 'Marxist tendencies' within the NSDAP made by the DNVP and other bourgeois parties during campaigns of 1932, see Childers, *The Nazi Voter*, pp. 207–10. For the negative reaction of business to the very pronounced anti-capitalist rhetoric of Nazi propaganda in late 1932, see Turner, *German Big Business and the Rise of Hitler*, pp. 287–93.

22. See, for example, the reports of the *Kreisleiter* of Sensburg and Stallupönen in East Prussia, 8 November 1932, in the Geheimes Staatsarchiv, Dahlem, (=GStA)/ HA XX/Rep.240/nrs. C74, C75.

23. Stimmungsbericht der RPL, November 1932, BA/NS22/1.

24. Ibid.

25. Ibid.

26. Patterns of working-class electoral behaviour are examined in Childers, *The Nazi Voter*, pp. 102–12, 178–88, 243–57.

27. Stimmungsbericht der RPL, November 1932, BA/NS22/1. Other *Gaue* had also reported that losses had been most severe in middle-class, particularly farming communities, while in working-class areas the NSDAP's vote had fallen but not so dramatically. See, for example, the report of the *Gau* propaganda leader of Hanover-South-Brunswick, 29 November 1932, NSAH/310 I/B3/II.

28. For details on the negotiations see Karl Dietrich Bracher, *Die Auflösung der Weimarer Republik*, 5th edition (Düsseldorf, 1978), pp. 536–41; and Orlow, *The History of the Nazi Party*, pp. 269–72. For Strasser's views and activities in this period see Stachura, *Gregor Strasser and the Rise of Nazism*, pp. 100–4.

29. Report of the *Gau* propaganda leader of Hanover-South-Brunswick, 9 September 1932, NSAH/Hann.310 I/B13.

30. Tätigkeitsbericht der RPL, August 1932, BA/Sammlung Schumacher/382.

31. Quoted in the Stimmungsbericht der RPL, November 1932, BA/NS22/1.

32. Report of the Gau propaganda leader of Halle-Merseburg, November 1932, BA/NS22/1051. The RPL's activity report for November also lamented the loss of many of the party's 'financially strong supporters'. See the Tätigkeitsbericht der RPL, November 1932, in BA/NS22/1.

33. Stimmungsbericht der Gaupropaganda Abteilung Ostpreussen, 10 November 1932, in GStA/ HA XX/ Rep.240/B7.

34. Kreisbefehl of 9 November 1932, Heilsberg, East Prussia, in GStA/HA XX/ Rep.240/C50a-c.

35. Tätigkeitsbericht für den Monat Oktober 1932 bis 6 November 1932, 14 November 1932, *Gau* Hanover-South-Brunswick, NSAH/Hann.310 I/B13.

36. Stimmungsbericht der RPL, November 1932, BA/NS22/1. Goebbels, writing

258 *Limits of National Socialist Mobilisation*

in his diary on 6 November, certainly believed that the failed negotiations with both Hindenburg/Papen and the Zentrum were responsible for the party's slump. 'We have suffered a setback. The reasons: [the negotiations of] 13 August, for which the masses still have little understanding and the unconscionable exploitation of our feelers to the Zentrum by the DNVP's propaganda.' Goebbels, *Vom Kaiserhof*, p. 196.

37. Diary entry of 23 April, Goebbels, *Von Kaiserhof*, p. 87.
38. Stimmungsbericht der RPL, November 1932, BA/NS22/1.
39. Tätigkeitsbericht der RPL, November 1932, BA/NS22/1.
40. Report of the *Kreisleitung* Treuburg in East Prussia to *Gau* propaganda leader, 8 November 1932, GStA/HA XX/Rep.240/C78.
41. Report of the *Gau* propaganda leader of Halle-Merseburg, 9 November 1932, BA/NS22/1051.
42. Stimmungsbericht der RPL, November 1932, BA/NS22/1.
43. Orlow, *The History of the Nazi Party*, pp. 281–2.
44. See Conan Fischer, *Stormtroopers. A Social, Economic and Ideological Analysis, 1929–1935* (London, 1983), pp. 162–3.
45. For details see Richard Bessel, *Political Violence and the Rise of Nazism. The Storm Troopers in Eastern Germany 1925–1934* (New Haven and London, 1984), pp. 86–96.
46. See, for example, the report of the Cologne police authorities on 17 October 1932, which claimed that 'disaffection in the SA has resulted in numerous members crossing over to the KPD'. Hauptstaatsarchiv Düsseldorf, Regierung Aachen, nr.22984. For similar reports from Franconia see Fischer, *Stormtroopers*, p. 162.
47. Stimmungsbericht der RPL, November 1932, BA/NS22/1.
48. Ibid.
49. Ibid.
50. Ibid. For similar observations at the local level, see the reports of the *Kreisleitungen* Allenstein, 8 November 1932, and Rössel, 9 November 1932, in GStA/HA XX/Rep.240/C39 and C73.
51. Tätigkeitsbericht der RPL, November 1932, BA/NS22/1.
52. Stimmungsbericht der RPL, November 1932, BA/NS22/1. See also the report of the Landesinspektion Ost, 9 November 1932, that places much of the blame for SA excesses squarely on the shoulders of Roehm and the top SA leadership. BA/NS22/347.
53. Stimmungsbericht der RPL, November 1932, BA/NS22/1.
54. Report of the Bavarian Staatsministerium, 9 November 1932, in HA/24A/1759.
55. Bessel, *Political Violence and the Rise of Nazism*, pp. 75–83. See also his contribution to this volume.
56. Stimmungsbericht der Gau Propaganda-Abteilung Ostpreussen, 10 November 1932, GStA/HA XX/Rep.240/B7.
57. Childers, *The Nazi Voter*, pp. 262–5.
58. Stimmungsbericht der RPL, November 1932, BA/NS22/1.
59. The lone exception to this trend was the Landtag election held in the Lilliputian state of Lippe, on 15 January 1933. After mobilising all the party's propaganda resources and concentrating them on the campaign in this tiny rural state, the NSDAP was able to win 39.5 per cent of the vote. The party certainly sought to portray the outcome as a great triumph and the beginning of a new upward surge, but it seems unlikely that the NSDAP could have duplicated its campaign in a larger, more diverse state. For details see Jutta Ciolet-Kumper, *Wahlkampf in Lippe: Die Wahlkampfpropaganda der NSDAP zur Landtagswahl am 15. January 1933* (Munich, 1977).
60. Stimmungsbericht der RPL, November 1932, BA/NS22/1.

61. The details of Papen's intrigue are by now well known. See Bracher, *Die Auflösung der Weimarer Republik*, pp. 624–38.

INDEX